Nathaniel Lyon's River
Campaign of 1861

ALSO BY KENNETH E. BURCHETT
AND FROM MCFARLAND

*Massacre at St. Louis: The Road to the Camp Jackson
Affair and Civil War* (2024)

*The Battle of Carthage, Missouri: First Trans-Mississippi
Conflict of the Civil War* (2013)

Nathaniel Lyon's River Campaign of 1861

Securing Missouri for the Union

KENNETH E. BURCHETT

McFarland & Company, Inc., Publishers
Jefferson, North Carolina

ISBN (print) 978-1-4766-9626-3
ISBN (ebook) 978-1-4766-5488-1

LIBRARY OF CONGRESS CATALOGING DATA ARE AVAILABLE

© 2025 Kenneth E. Burchett. All rights reserved

No part of this book may be reproduced or transmitted in any form or by any means, electronic or mechanical, including photocopying or recording, or by any information storage and retrieval system, without permission in writing from the publisher.

Front cover images: Nathaniel Lyon. Commander of federal troops at St. Louis, Lyon engineered a military campaign to keep Missouri in the Union. Photograph by J.A. Scholten, 1861. Courtesy of the Missouri Historical Society St. Louis (P0084-0009). *Background*: Landing of U.S. Volunteers at Jefferson City. Union soldiers disembarked from the riverboat *Iatan* and entered the Missouri state capital at Jefferson City on June 15, 1861, without resistance. Sketch by Orlando C. Richardson, 1861. *Harper's Weekly*, Vol. 5, No. 236, p. 420 (July 6, 1861). Courtesy of the Missouri Historical Society St. Louis (P0084-1255).

Printed in the United States of America

McFarland & Company, Inc., Publishers
Box 611, Jefferson, North Carolina 28640
www.mcfarlandpub.com

In memory of Fran

Table of Contents

Acknowledgments   ix
Preface   1
Introduction   3

Part One—Revolt and Revenge

1. Extraordinary Midnight Session   14
2. Chaos in Saint Louis   23
3. Fear and Distrust   32
4. Calls for Rebellion   40
5. Harney and Price Truce   48
6. Ascent of Lyon   55
7. Planter's House   63
8. This Means War   68

Part Two—Gathering Storm

9. A Plan to Punish the Governor   76
10. Rock Creek   84
11. Riverboats and Gunpowder   91
12. Union Regiments Everywhere   101
13. The Southwest Missouri Column   112
14. Blunder at Boonville   123
15. Skirmish on Rocheport Road   132
16. Occupation of Boonville   142

Table of Contents

Part Three—Forcing Move

17. Muster at Lexington	152
18. Rising Unrest	160
19. Rebels and Federals	167
20. Prelude to Catastrophe	175
21. Cole Camp	183
22. O'Kane's Night Attack	190
23. Into the Spider's Web	198
24. At Wit's End	208
25. The Halfway Ground	214
Chapter Notes	221
Bibliography	247
Index	261

Acknowledgments

I wish to acknowledge the assistance of Kristopher L. Anstine; T. Juliette Arai; Carolyn Atkins; Heather D. Beattie; Christine M. Beauregard; Mike Bieker; Joanne Bloome; Bill Boggess; Troy Branzhaf; Peter F. Brauer; Nancy Brewer; Jeff Bridges; Jennifer Bunselmeyer; Alan Chilton; Alex Choate; Stephanie O. Christensen; Sandy Clark; Amanda Claunch; Kyle Constant; Jonathan Eaker; Jake Ersland; Terry Foster; Jerry Fry; Renee Glass; Aryn Glazier; Michael Glenn; Marcia Goswick; William L. Graves; Michele Hansford; Douglas A. Harding; Irene Harvey; Terre Heydari; Philip Hinderberger; Michael Hoerman; Clyde B. Hood, III; Pam Hunter; Erica Kelly; Keith Kerr; Lauren Leeman; Barbara Leland; David Long; Kaye M. Lundgren; Jim McGhee; Maureen McGrath; Meredith McLemore; William A. McWhorter; Valerie Moore; Beverly Mosman; Daisy Njoku; Doug Para; L. Eileen Parris; Jeff Patrick; Linda R. Pine; Julie Potter; Sara Przybylski; Richard K. Rains, Jr.; Anita Roberts; John Rutherford; Kent Salomon; Daniel C. Schwartz; Donna Schwieder; Jennifer Seaton; Lola Shropshire; Ward W. Slack; Jason D. Stratman; Lynn Sullivan; Ellen Thomasson; Steve Weldon; Deborah Wood; and Jackie Worth.

With apologies to anyone I may have missed, I wish to recognize the special support of the staffs of the many institutions and organizations that contributed to the research, namely Alabama Department of Archives and History, Arkansas Studies Institute, Barton County Library, Butler Center–Little Rock, Butt-Holdsworth Memorial Library, Carthage Press, Carthage Public Library, Christian County Library, Cornell University Library, Dolph Briscoe Center for American History, Drury University Library, Fine Arts Library–Harvard University, Fry's Lyon Foundation, Greene County Archives and Records Center, Hendrix College Library, Jasper County Records Center, Jefferson National Expansion Memorial, Leavenworth County Historical Society, Library Center Springfield–Greene County, Library of Congress, Missouri Department of Natural Resources, Missouri Secretary of State, Missouri State Archives, Missouri State Historical Society–St. Louis, Missouri State Parks, Missouri

State University Duane G. Meyer Library, Museum for Springfield–Greene County, National Archives and Records Administration, National Archives at Kansas City, National Park Service, New York Public Library Manuscripts and Special Collections, Oklahoma Historical Society, Pea Ridge National Military Park, Sarcoxie Public Library, Sedalia Public Library, Southern Memorial Association, Southern Methodist University Degolyer Library, State Historical Society of Missouri–Columbia, Texas Historical Commission, Trails Regional Library–Lexington, U.S. Army Military History Institute, University of Arkansas at Little Rock Archives, University of Arkansas Press, University of California Libraries, University of Central Arkansas, University of Missouri Archives, Virginia Historical Society, W. Dale Clark Main Library, and Wilson's Creek National Battlefield.

Preface

A history of the Civil War would not be complete without including the events in Missouri in the summer of 1861. Missouri was wavering on the brink of secession as storm clouds of civil war gathered on the horizon. The state stood divided. The campaign to settle the question of secession pitted Missouri unionists against Southern sympathizers already inflamed by the slavery issue and the hostile border politics of Kansas statehood.

May 10, 1861, foreshadowed the future of Missouri in the Civil War. On that day, Captain Nathaniel Lyon marched out of the federal arsenal at St. Louis at the head of 7,000 Union Regulars and pro–Union volunteers to break up a Missouri state militia encampment at Camp Jackson on the outskirts of St. Louis, which then amounted to some 700 reputed pro-South sympathizers. Hostilities erupted and several civilians and soldiers died when opposing forces opened fire on each other. The unfolding of subsequent events drove previously undecided Missourians to the Confederate side and turned heretofore loyal Missourians against the central government. Governor Claiborne Fox Jackson received near dictatorial authority from the state legislature to raise a Missouri State Guard force to "protect the State from invaders." There was no preference given at the time to military alignment with either North or South, but everyone generally understood the legislature's action to be retaliation for Lyon's oppressive behavior.

War began in Missouri with the taking of Camp Jackson and advanced beyond reconciliation in Lyon's river campaign to move his army by steamboat up the Missouri River to drive the state government out of Jefferson City and arrest the governor. Armed engagements between Union and Missouri forces took place at Boonville and at Cole Camp more than a month before the Battle of Bull Run, the first major battle of the American Civil War. In less than three months, Lyon secured Missouri for the Union. He held the St. Louis Arsenal and the strategic river city of St. Louis, drove the governor and state legislature out of the state capital at Jefferson City, and ensured the navigability of the Missouri, Ohio, and Upper Mississippi rivers.

When trying to piece together a story about the Civil War, getting the facts right includes recognizing the pitfalls of sectional bias. The old histories and documents often contain prejudices supported by "facts" that are contradicted by the "facts" of the other side. Contemporaneous records challenge even the most candid and impartial historian with the difficulty of evolving the truth unclouded by sensational and personal rancor. Preference for the North or the South still creeps into modern histories of the war, and perhaps no one can be entirely neutral. Nevertheless, every effort has been made here to write a book that anyone may come away from feeling that no point of view went unnoticed.

This book begins as rebellion in Missouri edges the nation into war. The events portrayed come from a lifelong curiosity about the cause of the Civil War and about the people caught up in the tragedy and triumph of it. The character and lifestyles of the people form an important backdrop to the narrative. Descriptions of scenes are in the context of the culture and geography of the time. Place names are those that were in existence in 1861. Illustrations are contemporary with the time of the Civil War where possible. Confederate and Union officer ranks identified are those at the time of the action; photographs taken later may show them in uniforms of a different rank.

Introduction

The likelihood of the United States dividing on the question of states' rights took an ominous turn toward the middle of the 19th century. The long delay of a resolution to the slavery question threatened to dissolve the Union. A growing distaste for slavery throughout the Northern states, and a determination by the Southern states to expand it, factionalized the fragile political harmony that had sustained the precarious balance of the Union for more than six decades. Over a period of seven years, beginning in 1854, the nation unwisely abandoned its long-held posture of an uneasy peace and descended into the hapless abyss of irresoluble conflict. Four things happened to hasten the divisive disputes that led to the American Civil War.

First, the U.S. Congress passed the Kansas-Nebraska Act in 1854, effectively nullifying the Missouri Compromise and erasing three decades of balance between free and slave states by making the path to statehood a popular sovereignty issue controlled by voters.[1] As the frontier of the nation moved into the Great Plains, the first territory in line for statehood under the new doctrine was Kansas. The law gave the right to decide the slavery issue in the territory to the residents of Kansas. A torrent of violence followed. Proslavery and antislavery forces attacked each other, each faction struggling to control the Kansas vote and with it the future of Kansas as a free or slave state. Armed partisans on both sides invaded Kansas, trying to sway the statehood vote. Bloody confrontations erupted all along the Missouri-Kansas border.

A second discordant action of the U.S. government that hastened the country's lamentable march toward war occurred in 1857 when the U.S. Supreme Court found, among other things in a far-reaching opinion, that slaves and their descendants had no rights as citizens. African Americans were, in the judgment of the Court, "beings of an inferior order, and so far inferior that they had no rights which the white man was bound to respect." This decision, which denied St. Louis slave Dred Scott his freedom, pushed judicial reasoning past the edge of humanity. The heavily proslavery court's extrajudicial opinion outraged the North and deepened the shadow over the national conscience.[2]

Third, in the fall of 1859, the abolitionist John Brown left bloody Kansas and took his fight against slavery to Harpers Ferry, Virginia, the heart of plantation slavery in the South. Brown was a prominent national figure, and his relentless and often brutal methods to abolish slavery stirred the emotions of an onlooking nation.[3] Luminaries such as Ralph Waldo Emerson championed him for his simple, artless goodness and his sublime courage, seeing him as a pure idealist who believed in two things: the Golden Rule and the Declaration of Independence.[4] However, the slave revolt Brown intended to start failed. His capture and subsequent execution by Virginia further galvanized the North, still seething with outrage over the *Dred Scott* case two years before.[5]

The fourth and most contentious occurrence of sectional strife came in 1860 with the election of the North's Republican candidate Abraham Lincoln as president. His election heightened the growing discord and further exacerbated the split in public opinion. Secession became the cry of the South. Even before Lincoln's inauguration, the Union had begun to fracture along the borders between free and slave states. A few states refrained from joining either side and reserved for themselves the designation of Border States. One of them was Missouri.[6]

The state of Missouri mirrored the politics of the nation. The rich farmland of the western counties and plantations along the Missouri River in the Boonslick area of Little Dixie belonged to a class of Southerners who settled there. They controlled Missouri politics and the future of slavery in the state. In places like St. Louis, on the other hand, corporate interests sought to balance cooperation with the agrarian slaveholding South and the industrial antislavery North. Talk of limiting slavery in Missouri circulated freely.[7] The feeling on slavery in Missouri was either hard or soft, depending on one's point of view. Boonslick's hard Democrats were heavily proslavery, but they faced growing criticism from the soft Democrats concentrated mostly in St. Louis.

St. Louis was in some ways alien to the outlying regions of the state. The rapidly expanding city threatened the old political power of Little Dixie and the Boonslick leaders who had long controlled the destiny of the state. The most recent wave of new settlers came from Germany. Coming to America to escape political upheaval in their homeland, they were solidly on the side of the Union.

Missouri unwittingly elected a secessionist governor in the election of 1860 in the person of Claiborne Fox Jackson. Jackson was a pro–South Boonslick Democrat but as a matter of political expediency ran on the presidential candidate ticket of Stephen A. Douglas: he feigned support for

Douglas and his platform of popular sovereignty. Missourians adhered to the middle course in the election and the state went for Douglas, sweeping Jackson into the governor's seat in the process. One of Jackson's first orders of business was to call a special legislative session "to place the state in proper attitude of defense" in case Missouri, a slave state, went out of the Union. However, the General Assembly refused to take action that anyone might construe as hostile toward the federal government.[8]

Governor Claiborne Fox Jackson. The proslavery governor of Missouri supported alliance with the South. His failed attempts to prevent occupation of the state by federal forces caused him to abandon Missouri's position of neutrality and engage in open rebellion against the Union. He clashed with President Lincoln over the use of military action to suppress the secession of the Confederate states. Courtesy Missouri Historical Society St. Louis (N21069).

A state convention convened in Missouri to decide the secession question. After several meetings, it ended by rejecting secession in favor of neutrality. The decision of the convention did not satisfy the secessionist-minded, pro–South factions or the increasingly militant Governor Jackson who expected a different outcome. One journalist described the unease in the state: "Missouri might go anywhere at all," he said. "The only safe prediction was that it would produce a great deal of trouble for somebody."[9]

The decision of the state convention to remain in the Union by a decisive vote nevertheless made it clear that the state would defend its policy of armed neutrality by supplying neither weapons nor men to either the Union or the Confederacy if war broke out. Missouri's neutrality policy helped to delay military actions in the West, although many thought the beginning of serious hostilities was only a question of time.[10] The federal government viewed Missouri's position as unwilling to come to the defense of the Union. President Lincoln said it was "treason in effect."[11] Yet Lincoln understood that if Missouri seceded, the job of keeping the Union would be "too large for us."[12]

The nonalignment policy sought to deny any armed transgression across Missouri territory, meaning that Confederate States of the South could not advance on the North and vice versa.[13] Lincoln immediately understood neutrality as a protectionist device that would effectively isolate the Southern states from Union intervention and thus ensure the division of the country. He determined that no state could claim the privilege of denying access to federal troops. The government could go into any state, any time it wanted to. The argument of the pro–South faction in Missouri now switched from secession to defense of the state against invasion by federal troops.

Meanwhile, the South cautioned the Union against federal takeover of states. Jefferson Davis rebuffed authorities and warned against "invasion with military force, the expulsion of the lawful state authorities, and the assumption ... of unlawful powers." He said such actions meant "the election and introduction of persons to offices not vacant, the abandonment of all protection of the unalienable rights of the people, the declaration of martial law without authority for it, and the attempt to emancipate the slaves in violation of every law and constitutional principle."[14] Davis believed it was the duty of the Confederacy to protect states' rights by any means possible, including seizure of federal facilities.

The prime military targets of the seceding states were the United States arsenals kept within the borders of the rebelling states. There was a U.S. Arsenal at St. Louis. Both North and South saw it as critical to the future of Missouri and to the Union. Whoever controlled it would control St. Louis and with it the fate of Missouri to remain in the Union or join the Confederacy. Command of Missouri meant command of traffic up and down the Mississippi and Missouri rivers.[15]

Francis P. Blair, Jr., was a prominent St. Louis antislavery politician, newly elected to the U.S. Congress with connections in the Lincoln cabinet. His brother, Montgomery Blair, was postmaster in Lincoln's administration. The influence of the Blair family, the most powerful Republicans in Missouri, and their connections in Washington helped to persuade Union officials to pay attention to Missouri. Frank Blair saw the danger of a secessionist takeover of St. Louis and lobbied Washington to increase federal military support. The War Department responded cautiously for fear of upsetting the declared neutrality of the state.[16] Acting on his own, Blair secretly organized the German antislavery elements in St. Louis to resist any hostile proslavery movements. Large numbers of German immigrants had come to America to escape the German Revolution of 1848 and had settled in St. Louis. They stood poised to lend their considerable military experience to the cause of abolishing slavery, should it come to that. The Lincoln administration saw the vulnerability of such a military target in a state with secessionists' leanings and sent federal troops to secure it.

A little-known Regular Army captain named Nathaniel Lyon left his post at Fort Riley, Kansas, with a company of U.S. troops to take command of federal property in St. Louis, specifically with orders to guard the St. Louis Arsenal against secessionist takeover. Fresh from the bitter confrontations between slave and free state forces in Kansas, Captain Lyon came to St. Louis already convinced, like many others, that armed conflict between North and South was unavoidable.[17] Lyon understood the military consequences of a pro–South takeover of the St. Louis Arsenal.[18] He shouldered the defense of it amid dissension and growing political tensions.[19] The future of both the state of Missouri and the nation appeared to hinge on the outcome of action in St. Louis.

Soon Lyon met Blair. Together they devised a political and military initiative to thwart a secessionist takeover of the arsenal. Lyon, whose orders were to guard the arsenal, not command it, agitated for command

Nathaniel Lyon. Commander of federal troops at St. Louis, Lyon engineered a military campaign to keep Missouri in the Union. In opposition to the elected state government, his loyalty to the United States drove him to take military action against the Missouri State Militia at Camp Jackson. Photograph by J.A. Scholten, 1861. Courtesy Missouri Historical Society St. Louis (P0084-0009).

that would give him access to the weapons kept at the arsenal and the authority to arm Blair's pro–Union Germans. The commander of the arsenal, General William S. Harney, commander of the U.S. Army Department of the West, denied the request. General Harney opposed arming untrained recruits whose antislavery bias would only fan the flames of discord. In the absence of federal assistance to counter the growing separatist rebellion, paramilitary groups stepped up their organizational activity in the wards of St. Louis. Soon, men on both sides secretly drilled in preparation for military action.

The contest for Missouri took on a new urgency on April 12, 1861. Half a continent away in Charleston Harbor, the South Carolina Militia under Confederate orders attacked the Union garrison at Fort Sumter.[20] The federal garrison refused to retreat, thus giving recently seceded South Carolina the reason it had been looking for to enforce its secession from the Union.[21] After two days of relentless bombardment, the fort surrendered, and the War Between the States descended on the nation. Reaction in Missouri to the Confederate bombardment of Fort Sumter was immediate and divided. Some supported the North, others favored the South, and still others supported neither.[22]

President Lincoln called on the states for volunteers to put down the rebellion. Governor Jackson rebuffed the president in a tersely worded reply: "Not one man will the State of Missouri furnish to carry on any unholy crusade." Lyon and Blair immediately requested authority from Washington to allow them to fill the Missouri quota. Relying heavily on the secret companies of German immigrants organized in St. Louis, they had enough men to meet Lincoln's request and then some. General Harney again objected to arming political recruits. At Blair's urging, Washington relieved Harney of duty and placed Captain Lyon in charge. Volunteers streamed into the Union ranks. Secessionists watched helplessly as hopes of taking the St. Louis Arsenal disappeared. Lincoln authorized an army of 10,000 Missourians. Four-fifths of them were German immigrants determined to fight to preserve the Union.[23]

One of the first acts of armed partisan hostility toward federal authority in Missouri came on the night of April 20, when a band of about 200 renegade secessionists from Jackson County crossed the Missouri River at Sibley, six miles below Independence, and linked up with another group of rebels from Clay County on the north side of the river. They proceeded to the U.S. Arms Depot at Liberty, Missouri, seized the unguarded facility, ransacked it, and made off with a quantity of arms and munitions.[24] The raid meant that the pro–South Missourians planned to resist federal military presence in the state.[25] Union officials expected an attempt on the St. Louis Arsenal, which contained arms in numbers 10 times the number taken from Liberty.

Introduction

On April 26, at the urging of Captain Lyon, a sizable portion of inventory left the St. Louis Arsenal by boat, spirited away into Union hands in Illinois. When the steamboat *Alton* pushed off across the Mississippi River, it carried 20,000 muskets and another 1,000 carbines and revolvers, 110,000 cartridges, and considerable other war material.[26] Union forces secured it from any possible seizure by secessionists, adding yet another setback for the St. Louis secessionists.

Governor Jackson ordered a routine muster of state troops to convene at St. Louis. On May 6, 1861, Missouri state militia troops gathered at Lindell Grove, a wooded valley near the intersection of Olive Street and Grand Avenue, on the outskirts of the city.[27] The encampment bore the name Camp Jackson in the governor's honor.[28] Over the next few days, Captain Lyon concluded that the purpose of the camp was to stage an attack on the arsenal. A number of individuals with avowed secession principles occupied the encampment, and its officers had known contact with Confederate leaders.

The military assembly was constitutionally legal. However, under the prevailing political conditions, Lyon believed it likely to be a ruse for possible armed action against federal troops. He allegedly spied on the encampment dressed as a woman. He discovered that Jackson called up only secessionist-leaning units and appointed known secessionists to command them. Some of the units were drilling with arms furnished by Confederate president Jefferson Davis. Two of the streets at Camp Jackson bore the names of Davis and Beauregard after Confederate leaders. The evidence at the camp was enough to convince Lyon of its threat to Union troops. He decided on military action to break up the camp.

On May 10, four days after the camp opened, armed Union soldiers marched on it in full force. Upwards of seven thousand volunteer and Regular federal troops, mostly Germans, descended on the camp, marching in quick time.[29] Lyon timed the march so that the heads of the different columns left the arsenal and passed through the streets of St. Louis to arrive at their destination almost simultaneously. The total show of force overwhelmed the approximately seven hundred Missouri militia on duty in the camp.[30] Within a matter of minutes, federal troops surrounded the camp and the entire militia force in it. Writing in his native German, John T. Bruegel, a Union soldier in Company F, Third Regiment Missouri Volunteer Infantry, described what happened in his diary: "In the morning of May 10, 1861, we received marching orders. At twelve o'clock noon, we left. In the van was Captain Lyon and the four companies of regulars. In came four regiments of infantry [and] the six cannons, while the home guard regiments brought up the rear. Captain Lyon and Colonel F. Sigel were in command. By two o'clock in the afternoon, the rebel camp was surrounded on all four streets that bordered it. The cannons, in charge of the old German soldiers eager to fire, were loaded and aimed at the camp. After the camp was completely surrounded and no rebel could escape, Captain Lyon sent a messenger to General Frost and demanded an unconditional surrender of the whole camp together with all weapons and war material."[31]

Brigadier General D.M. Frost, commander of Camp Jackson and the architect of Governor Jackson's failed plan to take the arsenal, disavowed any intentions hostile to federal troops at the arsenal. Captain Lyon ignored his entreaties and delivered a peremptory summons for an unconditional surrender. "General Frost feigned bewilderment at such accusations."[32] Being numerically inferior and not prepared to do battle for a cause whose legitimacy was still a question with many of his troops, Frost decided to comply with the demand, and the state militia surrendered to the federal troops. They became Lyon's prisoners.[33] When the prisoners refused to take a loyalty oath to the federal government in exchange for parole, Lyon unwisely ordered the Germans to march the militia prisoners through the streets of St. Louis to the arsenal.[34]

There was a long pause while Union officers lined up the prisoners single file between opposite ranks of federal troops. Bystanders who had followed the federal march pressed closer to the action. By now, several hundred spectators lined the elevated ground around the camp, some of them armed. Secessionists in the crowd began to hurl insults at the German soldiers. When these did not move the Germans to retaliate, dirt clods and stones pelted the ranks. Gunshots rang out. Shots fired from the crowd struck army troops.[35] Young recruits unsure of themselves and fearful of their lives returned fire. A general fusillade followed. When the smoke cleared, 31 people lay dead or dying,[36] among them women and children. About that many more joined a stampede away from the camp back to St. Louis only to die later of their wounds.[37] Another 75 to 100 were hurt but survived.[38] So egregious was the loss of innocent lives that the press labeled the aftermath of the action the "St. Louis massacre."

Lyon's march on the state militia caused more Missourians to resist Union occupation. Had the capture of Camp Jackson not occurred with subsequent loss of life, there was little chance of Missouri joining the Southern cause. The state convention had ruled out secession. Without it, no authority existed for the use of arms within the state. If Lyon had accepted Missouri's desire for neutrality, nothing would have changed. Governor Jackson lacked the number of troops necessary to capture the arsenal, legislative approval to grow the force was stalled at the time and unlikely to be forthcoming, and, as the Camp Jackson business proved, the Union could count on thousands of Missourians to rally to its cause. Civil War historian E.M. Violette wrote, "The capture of Camp Jackson is one of

"Terrible Tragedy at St. Louis." This wood engraving of Camp Jackson appeared in the *New York Illustrated News*, May 25, 1861, page 41. The press called the loss of life the "St. Louis massacre." The artist invented the setting and the scene of the action in this East Coast coverage of the incident. Courtesy Missouri Historical Society St. Louis (P0084-1273).

the most significant events in the history of the Civil War. It was the first really aggressive blow at secession that was struck anywhere within the United States.... Viewed in the light of subsequent events in Missouri, it must be considered, however, as a stupendous blunder."[39]

Lyon believed that sectional strife had no accommodation for neutrality. In other Border States, like Kentucky, for example, wiser leaders avoided the Lyon zest for war. Although Kentucky with its deep Southern roots supplied troops to both North and South in the Civil War, it remained neutral and stayed in the Union.[40] He strongly felt that unaligned states had an obligation to take an active role in defending the Union and should openly commit to that mission. If Missouri was not expressly for the Union, he reasoned, it must be against the Union. Governor Claiborne Jackson and the secessionist State General Assembly would have to suffer the consequences of treason, according to Lyon.

Camp Jackson was not the only rebel enclave in the state. As events unfolded at Lindell's Grove on May 10, eight companies of Missouri militia assembled for drill at St. Joseph under orders of Governor Jackson. Armed with cannon and small arms taken from the Liberty Arsenal, this band of men camped within striking distance of the ordinance stores at Fort Kearney, Kansas. The Union force at Fort Leavenworth stood on alert should the Missouri troops decide to cross the river to threaten the citizens on the right bank. The prospects of armed rebellion loomed large.

Already, Lyon was making plans to widen federal control over Missouri. His action against Governor Jackson had only begun. Meanwhile, General Harney, temporarily relieved of duty in Missouri, had patched up things in Washington, and the St. Louis newspapers announced he was due back in St. Louis at any moment to resume command.[41]

Federal officers restored order at Camp Jackson, and around 6:00 p.m. Lyon marched his prisoners off to the arsenal.[42] Accounts vary as to how many militia soldiers actually became prisoners. Historian John McElroy claimed there were 1,110 enlisted men taken prisoner, along with 50 to 75 officers.[43] General Lyon's official report gave numbers of 50 officers and 639 men.[44] As the march began, Lyon took a cautious path along a route that skirted the middle of St. Louis.

PART ONE

Revolt and Revenge

1

Extraordinary Midnight Session

The procession of troops and prisoners left Camp Jackson, marching down Olive Street toward the arsenal. All along the way, elements of the mob followed, shouting obscenities and hurling insults but keeping a safe distance from the federal column. People were outraged at the sight of the federal invaders parading the state militia in disgrace. Moreover, rumors spread that Lyon had planned all along to capture Camp Jackson and hold militia as prisoners of war.[1]

The column turned south, cutting over to Chouteau Avenue, then east to Broadway, and on to the arsenal. By the time the troops reached the end of Chouteau, Union flags began to appear. The crowds became decidedly friendlier on South Broadway. The residents in this part of the city were mainly Germans sympathetic to the Union volunteers of Lyon's command. St. Louis was like two different cities. Irish Catholics and people of different Southern backgrounds dominated the northern part of the city, while Germans populated a large area in the southern part of the city.[2] Cheers broke out as Lyon's troops herded the prisoners toward the arsenal.

Outbreaks of rioting continued in the city even after the entourage reached the shelter of the arsenal after dusk.[3] Unruly mobs prowled the streets as night fell. Greatly disturbed by the day's events, they particularly directed their scorn at the Republican newspapers, which they blamed for much of the agitation in the city. The atmosphere within St. Louis was one of mayhem and lawlessness that evening. Armed men roamed the streets seeking revenge for the killings. Crowds paraded back and forth, yelling, waving weapons, and now and then firing in the darkness.

A steady rain settled over the city as word circulated during the night that a secessionist mob of about two hundred men had gathered downtown at the Planter's House hotel to hunt down and kill all the Dutch they could get hold of in retaliation for Camp Jackson and the slaughter of innocents in the day's massacre. Everyone wanted to hang Frank Blair.[4]

1. Extraordinary Midnight Session 15

They threatened to plunder and set fire to the whole city.[5] Uriel Wright, a Union man who had fought against secession in the state convention, speaking from the steps of the Planter's House, denounced the Camp Jackson outrage. Addressing a large crowd of agitated men, Wright said, "If unionism means such atrocious deeds as have been witnessed in St. Louis, I am no longer a Union man."[6] The crowd wildly cheered. Parties broke off to destroy the newspaper offices. A mob broke into H.E. Dimick's store on Main Street and seized about 20 guns.[7] Mayor Daniel G. Taylor and Police Chief James McDonough stopped them.[8] Police broke up the raid and placed the Union newspapers' offices and residences of Blair and Union leaders under guard for protection.[9] The agitators went back to listen to more secessionist oratory.[10]

One of the more violent instigators was the avid secessionist Dr. Joseph N. McDowell, who threatened to "kill the Dutch" for the revenge of Camp Jackson.[11] Dr. McDowell was an out and out rebel; an ardent supporter of slavery; and, some said, a pathological revolutionary. He hated immigrants and Catholics and would harangue both at street corners wearing a breastplate of armor. People in the city knew him best perhaps for his art of body snatching, all-night forays into cemeteries to gather specimens for his anatomy classes at McDowell Medical College. The Union later confiscated his college and turned it into a military prison for captured Confederate soldiers. On this night, however, he stirred the rowdy passions of secessionist militants.

Great excitement coursed through the city all night. Restlessness grew among secessionists well into the evening following the massacre. From almost any point along Fourth Street, large crowds gathered in search of the latest news.[12] Lyon's troops stood ready to meet any hostile reprisals that might come their way. In one incident, U.S. troops fired on citizens in self-defense after a provocation by armed St. Louis residents threatened to become a full-scale riot. Anger at Lyon's actions fueled a hatred that many now felt for the Union cause. If these Missourians were not for the South before, they were now. Once predominantly neutral, Union men now became hardened enemies against the government. Previous sentiments toward North and South ripened into convictions very rapidly. Camp Jackson forced a decision for one side or the other.[13] The incident swayed neutral Missourians toward the South and inflamed the opinions of latent secessionists. At the same time, unionists boasted that Camp Jackson was the day that suddenly nipped the treason of secessionist leaders in the bud.[14] It marked the first Union success in the Civil War.[15] In parts of the city, Union supporters celebrated, carrying the United States flag. In other parts, rebels carried the Confederate flag.

The large majority of men who herded the prisoners through St. Louis were German immigrants, or the Dutch, as the locals called them, all of them in Frank Blair's First Regiment U.S. Missouri Volunteers.[16] Excited by the Dutch soldiery, the city erupted into deadly reprisals. A number of German citizens died that evening, killed in cold blood, murdered in a reign of terror that gripped the city and pitted Southern sympathizers against those of Northern persuasion. At least seven more people died as fighting continued late into the night.[17] Over the next few days, an upsurge in reported suicides and drownings of a suspicious nature added to the death toll.

There was already great animosity toward the Germans. There had long existed between native citizens and Germans a feeling of unfriendliness. Songs lampooned them as sauerkraut-eating interlopers, thin and small and a disgrace to Missouri. The German tendency toward military organization increased the dislike between the two classes.[18] One chronicler of the Camp Jackson affair wrongly accused the Germans of firing into the crowd because the crowd mocked the Germans and cheered the prisoners. A good many St. Louis citizens viewed the budding conflict in Missouri as revenge against the Dutch. Although Lyon carried out the raid on Camp Jackson, they held the Dutch accountable. Secessionists regarded Lyon as little more than a pompous tramp of limited military ability. Irish partisans lamented that had Captain Joseph M. Kelly's men only been at Camp Jackson, they would have driven the Hessians from the field. Captain Kelly was in Jefferson City dropping off the last load of Confederate munitions sent there to defend the state capitol.

The prisoner column reached the St. Louis Arsenal at about sundown. Brigadier General Daniel M. Frost and most of the Missouri militia bedded down on pallets of straw and spent the night at the arsenal, jailed as prisoners of Captain Lyon and his Union troops.[19] An offer of army rations went unclaimed. Prisoners kicked over pails of coffee and threw the hardtack and bacon over the wall of the arsenal, then complained that the Yankees tried to starve them.[20] Meanwhile, German artillerymen, who happened to be among the Missouri militia soldiers at Camp Jackson, had dutifully marched off to the arsenal as Lyon's prisoners, but having arrived there, they quietly joined him to serve the Union.[21]

The raid on Camp Jackson captured large quantities of munitions and war materials. When the disarmed Missourians marched out of Camp Jackson, the Third and Fourth Regiments of U.S. Volunteers marched in, along with two companies of Union Regulars.[22] The Regulars, under Captain Thomas Sweeny, took possession of the considerable amount of military stores and personal property left behind, inventoried it, and prepared to transfer it to the arsenal.[23] They recovered Confederate stores stolen from the U.S. Arsenal at Baton Rouge, including three 32-pounder guns, one 10-inch iron mortar, and three mortar beds donated by Jefferson Davis. Heavy plank crates bore the markings, "Tamaroa, care of Greely & Gale, Saint Louis," used to disguise the shipment as marble destined for the bogus business address of unionists.[24] Six brass field pieces, an equal number of six-inch iron cannon, large amounts of rifles, and other tools of war made up a large cache of arms at the camp. Camp booty included a sizable inventory of ammunition: five boxes of canister shot, 96 10-inch and 300 six-inch shells, more than might reasonably be expected at a routine state militia muster of 700 officers and men.[25] It was enough to convince even the most skeptical that the camp was something more than a school of instruction for the state militia, as Governor Jackson had said it would be.[26] They uncovered some 2,500 muskets of late model 58-caliber, half of them still in several chests of arms yet unopened.[27] Contrary to Lyon's earlier intelligence, which branded them as museum pieces, many of the muskets were new and unassembled, suggesting their recent supply to the rebel cause. The loss struck a serious blow to Governor Jackson's plans to arm a force of sufficient strength to take the arsenal, although he denied that such a plan was ever his intent.[28] He lost most of the Confederate-supplied field pieces and muskets, plus 25 kegs of powder and a generous supply of shot and shell. Not only did he lose munitions, equipment, and supplies, the federal troops relieved the militia of 30 to 40 horses, items essential to any military campaign.[29] The camp remained under guard that night. Sweeny's Regulars and the Third and Fourth Volunteers stayed at the camp and spent the night in the tents of the Missouri militia. They cleaned up the camp, burned what was not of value, and prepared to move the rest to the arsenal the next day.[30]

Meanwhile, things moved quickly in Missouri to answer Captain Lyon's march on Camp Jackson. About four o'clock, the news first reached the state capitol at Jefferson City by telegraph while the affair was still in progress.[31] Governor Jackson carried the news to the legislature, which happened to be in session at the time discussing the Military Bill, having adjourned the week before without passing it.[32] For the next two hours, legislators were in disbelief hearing of the capture of Brigadier General Frost's command by federal troops. The news spread like wildfire through the capitol. Captain Nathaniel Lyon, commander of federal troops, had led a detail of German volunteer soldiers against a legally assembled Missouri militia as it drilled on the outskirts of St. Louis, forcing the militia commander to surrender to the federal forces. Righteous indignation quickly turned to open anger as the General Assembly met to decide what to do. The use of deadly force by the Union army constituted an armed invasion of Missouri's sovereign territory as a state, they concluded. It left no doubt of the federal government's total disregard for Missouri's claim of neutrality in the burgeoning conflict between North and South. Previously hesitant to approve a military buildup, within 15 to 20 minutes of hearing the news of Camp Jackson both houses passed the pending Military Bill to reorganize the state militia and give Governor Jackson broad emergency military powers.[33] Lawmakers also authorized the formation of a new military guard to resist the Union presence in the state. Its sole purpose was to protect the people of Missouri from invaders. There was no preference yet given for any military alignment with either North or South, but everyone generally understood the legislature's action to be retaliation for the oppressive behavior of Union Captain Nathaniel Lyon. A strong resolution condemning Lyon and the actions of the federal government passed the House unanimously, notwithstanding the detail that about a third of its members were conspicuously absent. Events moved swiftly from the culmination of disorder toward the clash of arms itself.[34]

The legislature reconvened again at 7:30 p.m. and continued in session until half past nine. They met fully armed, carrying guns of every description. In those days, guns came manufactured to fit the individual. A person was measured for a gun the same as he would be for a suit of

Jefferson City, Missouri. The state capitol building towers over the scene on the hill. A steamboat navigates the Missouri River, while a horse-drawn cart carries a family in the foreground. The alarm bell that alerted the Missouri General Assembly to convene for the extraordinary midnight session is at center. Photograph ca. 1853. Courtesy Missouri Historical Society St. Louis (N45746).

1. Extraordinary Midnight Session 19

clothes, made in length, size, and weight in proportion to the strength and height of the individual.[35] Rifles leaned against desks and chairs, across knees, some lying on the floor. Belts strapped around waists held one to three pistols or Bowie knives fastened to them.[36] They did not yet know the full details of the bloodbath that had followed the capitulation of Camp Jackson, and the lawmakers retired for the night.

Shortly after 11:00 p.m., dispatches arrived confirming the killing of St. Louis citizens. The couriers said German mercenaries had taken the state soldiers from Camp Jackson into St. Louis and paraded them through the streets as their prisoners. Lawmakers learned that large numbers of citizens had died, killed in cold blood, murdered in a reign of terror that pitted northern sympathizers against the peaceful citizens of St. Louis. Such were the stories coming into Jefferson City.

Around midnight, church bells sounded an alarm and the whole town of Jefferson City awoke.[37] Shouts of men summoning the legislature to the capitol broke the night's silence.[38] A rumor circulated that Frank Blair and two regiments of federal troops were on their way to take Jefferson City and capture the governor, state officers, and members of the legislature.[39] Governor Jackson ordered the seizure of a locomotive and sent Minute Men leaders Basil Duke and J. Rock Champion with a company of armed men as fast as possible toward St. Louis to hold the Missouri Pacific Railroad bridges over the Osage and the Gasconade rivers, eight miles below Jefferson City, to prevent federal troops from reaching the capital.[40] They found no enemy anywhere within 40 miles of the capital, but one of the squads took it upon itself to set fire to the Osage Bridge anyway, only to learn later that the warning of a federal invasion was the result of a bogus telegram, was false, and had no merit.[41] Nevertheless, operations began to secure the state treasury from capture and remove 12,000 kegs of powder purchased at St. Louis to a remote place of safety in the countryside.[42] Every man armed himself as best he could with shotguns, rifles, knives, and antiquated swords.[43]

Messengers quickly summoned legislature members back to the capitol to consider the demands and perils of the crisis.[44] A tremendous thunderstorm blew up during the night, heightening the tense drama and excitement of the evening. Vivid and continuous flashes of lightning, followed by deafening thunder and torrential rain, added ominous punctuation to the crisis.[45] The lightning illuminated citizens hurrying through the streets on foot and horse. The members hurried to the capitol and immediately went into secret session.[46] They called it the extraordinary midnight session.[47]

The two houses of the General Assembly did not emerge until half past three.[48] Every jet in the great chandelier of the House of Representatives burned bright.[49] The tall, gaunt Governor Jackson, suffering from a rasping cough that indicated a chronic illness, received a steady stream of visitors famous and strange in his small but elegant executive mansion. In the early morning hours, an act passed detailing the complete authority of the governor to undertake such measures as he saw necessary to repel invasion or put down rebellion.[50]

Governor Jackson received sweeping dictatorial powers.[51] The Missouri legislature, outraged by Lyon's actions, passed legislation to create a new Missouri army and authorized the governor to call for 50,000 volunteers.[52] They authorized Jackson to disband the old Missouri state militia and reform it as the Missouri State Guard. The old informal militia organization was a citizen paramilitary service whose purpose was largely ceremonial. The explicit purpose of the new MSG was to protect the sovereign neutrality of Missouri and repel invasion by outside forces, namely the Union army. It was in essence a preparation for war.[53]

The Military Bill created a fund to equip and arm the army, which it placed at the governor's command, and gave him whatever funding and borrowing authority he needed to assist him in this task, specifically an immediate appropriation of $30,000 and authority to borrow a half million dollars from the banks.[54] They diverted numerous funds from their original uses to the military fund, including the apportionment of the state school money.[55] The Bill also authorized the acquirement of David Ballentine's foundry at Boonville for the manufacture of arms and munitions of war.[56] In a similar move, it authorized the governor to set up an armory in the penitentiary for the manufacture of weaponry.[57] Legislators added an appropriation of $10,000 to secure an alliance with the Indians on the borders of the state. Subsequently, Chief Ross of the Cherokee Nation promised 15,000 armed men to help the secessionist cause.[58]

The Military Bill contained more than 200 sections supplemented by about 50 "Articles of War."[59] Among the articles, lawmakers granted the governor absolute authority and control over St. Louis and conferred on him extraordinary powers to suppress insurrection and defend the state.[60] The Bill outlawed all other militia organizations in Missouri, which included the German Home Guard Union Volunteers. The legislature took another slap at the immigrant population when it declared that English was to be the language of all military commands in Missouri. The law made it illegal to issue a command in any language but English. The Bill instructed officers and men to take an oath to obey only Governor Jackson.[61]

The General Assembly empowered Jackson to name generals to organize their respective divisions of the new Missouri State Guard, and report directly to him. The governor sent word for Sterling Price to come to Jefferson City to be field commander.[62]

1. Extraordinary Midnight Session

Otto C. Lademann. A soldier in Company F of the Third Missouri U.S. Volunteer Infantry, Private Lademann braved violent unrest in St. Louis after the action at Camp Jackson to procure wagons for transport of captured arms to the St. Louis Arsenal. The loss of weapons and equipment hampered the ability of the Missourians to counter federal forces. Photograph 1863. Courtesy Missouri Historical Society St. Louis (N12824).

Back at Camp Jackson, the officers in charge of the garrison decided at about 11:00 p.m. that they should report to Captain Lyon to tell him the camp was secure and ask for instructions for the next day. Colonel Franz Sigel called on a young 20-year-old German named Otto C. Lademann to carry the message across town to the arsenal. Although an ardent Union man, Lademann did not want to be a murdered Dutchman that night and tried to get out of the job. He complained that he had no arms except his 69-caliber musket, which was of a size to invite suspicion as he traveled through the city. Colonel Sigel promptly handed him his own revolver and sent him on his way. It was raining hard now, and Lademann never met a soul until he reached the arsenal. He made his report to Lyon, who, ever the military stickler, expressed astonishment that Sigel sent a non-commissioned man to report to him. Nevertheless, he sent orders to Sigel to procure all the wagons he needed from the city to evacuate the arms and stores at Camp Jackson the next day.[63] Sigel sent the hapless young Lademann back out into the rain to execute the order, not knowing anyone in the city who owned horses and wagons. He made his way to Frenchtown, where nobody but Germans lived. At two in the morning, he came upon a saloon where a group of patriotic Germans were still celebrating the Camp Jackson victory. Upon the promise of a liberal offer of money at federal expense, he returned to camp assured of their help. Shortly after daylight, teams of horses began to arrive, singly, then in pairs, then by the dozens. Before 8:00 a.m., more than enough wagons waited on hand. By 10 o'clock, the whole camp was on wheels and on its way to the arsenal.[64]

As on the previous day with the prisoners, the captured provisions train passed through the streets of St. Louis, east on Market Street to 14th, then south to Chateau Avenue, east to Broadway (Fifth Street), thence south to the arsenal. Angry faces stared sourly as the wagons passed, until the train reached Frenchtown at Broadway and Chateau. The mood of the crowd immediately turned their path into a regular road of triumph for a mile and a half. Everyone in the neighborhood turned out to cheer and wave flags, and anything else at hand. The reception was in stark contrast to that just a few blocks away, where out of curiosity, a motley crowd had gathered at a street corner to see the sight.[65] Two female slaves stood there smiling with delight. A young woman known to be deeply pro–South said excitedly, stretching out her arm and waving her finger, "We'll whip you yet." Quick as a wink, the two slave girls, pointing to the loaded wagons, gleefully cried out, "They've got all your tents."[66] On Pine Street near Fifth stood a building where secessionist Minute Men went to assemble and where for some time a rebel flag had flown from one of its windows. When Camp Jackson fell, Union authorities ordered the emblem of secession taken down, and down it came, never hoisted in St. Louis again.[67]

Such was the harsh reality of the polarized communities of St. Louis in the spring of 1861. The wagons reached the arsenal about noon.[68] The train of recovered munitions notwithstanding, a pessimistic Lyon complained that other arms he believed secretly hidden around the city posed a threat to his army.[69]

2

Chaos in Saint Louis

The militia prisoners arose around 7:00 a.m., ate a breakfast of hardtack biscuits and a cup of water, and sat back to wait out the day. Imprisonment was a degrading experience. Paraded as captives through the city and then confined at the arsenal, most felt they had done nothing wrong. The press characterized them as secessionist partisans when in reality many of the officers and men at the encampment were loyal Union men. Many of them had been at similar encampments in previous years. Their old volunteer companies had organized years before and carried arms received from the state separate from any connections to rebel involvement in Camp Jackson.[1] A large number of the soldiers were from the best families in St. Louis.[2]

St. Louis awoke to a grim scene. Police found several German civilians and soldiers dead, victims of the violence that had swept across the city the night before.[3] They found a dead German on Market Street near 15th; one on Clark Avenue and 10th, near Turner Hall; one on Franklin Avenue and Seventh; one shot in the breast on Chestnut and Sixth; and one badly beaten at Ninth and Market. Attacked under the darkness of night, no one ever discovered the guilty assailants.[4] The bloodshed threatened to intensify as the excitement of the previous day reverberated across town.[5] Hundreds of restless residents congregated along Fourth Street, all in search of the latest news.[6]

Brigadier General Frost sent a note to the wards of the city, entreating his friends and the friends of the state militia to abstain from any further demonstrations. Riotous proceedings threatened to arouse the populace in the lower wards with disastrous results. Already, many prominent citizens were feeling the consequences of strife. Judge Aylett Hawes Buckner stabbed Dr. George B. Sanderson, a proslavery sympathizer, in a saloon confrontation. After an intense argument over Camp Jackson, Sanderson attacked Buckner with a cane, and Buckner fatally stabbed him with a pocketknife.[7]

Brigadier General William Harney arrived back in St. Louis the day after Camp Jackson, having completed his business in Washington, to resume command of Union forces from Captain Lyon.[8] The Lincoln administration had reluctantly agreed to allow him to resume command of the Department of the West. He had lost his command, and his absence had hastened Lyon's movement on Camp Jackson. After an earnest display of loyalty to the U.S., Lincoln restored Harney's command and returned him to St. Louis. He arrived in the city only to reap the whirlwind of Lyon's impetuous actions.[9] He found a city in pandemonium, gripped with fear and seething with anger.[10] Chaos greeted him throughout the city.

He set about trying to reconcile the parties and bring order to the situation resulting from Lyon's actions and the unmeasured response of the state legislature. Harney visited Blair and Lyon at the arsenal. He informed them that he intended to disband the Home Guard. Blair pointed out that the Guard served at the pleasure of the president.[11] Lyon showed no remorse and no desire to compromise with state officials. Anywhere there was a secessionist disturbance, he sent troops to quell it. General Harney found matters very much under the influence of the Blairs—Montgomery and Frank—and in full support of Lyon's actions.[12] Meanwhile, the Missouri legislature was in the process of organizing a military force to resist federal presence in the state.

Immediately upon returning to St. Louis, General Harney issued a proclamation to the people of St. Louis and the state of Missouri.[13] It went out to all the wards of the city where Camp Jackson and the riots burned fresh in everyone's mind.[14] Harney's proclamation took the form of a leaflet widely posted throughout the city and sent across the state. Of typical 19th-century advertisement design, large block letters announced the proclamation, addressed in slightly smaller type to its intended audience of Missourians. The type diminished progressively in size until the last paragraph, in fine print, apologized to the pro–South contingent that Harney had no authority to relocate the Home Guards who figured prominently in the Camp Jackson killings. However, if martial law were necessary, he promised to use only Regular Army troops. He deeply regretted the deplorable conditions that existed in the city. In a conciliatory gesture to Governor Jackson, he pledged to respect the authority of the public officers of the state and city, a clear swipe at Lyon's high-handed approach. Harney committed to preserve the public peace and offered a more compromising attitude than Lyon did.[15] Instead of using force against the Missouri government, as Lyon and Blair did, Harney sought a path of reconciliation.[16]

Brigadier General Frost wasted no time in exercising his family connections. Mrs. Harney was the aunt of Frost's wife. Writing to Harney to complain, Frost vociferously protested Lyon's capture of Camp Jackson and the

PROCLAMATION

Military Department of the West,
ST. LOUIS, MAY 12th, 1861.

TO THE PEOPLE
OF THE
STATE OF MISSOURI
AND
CITY OF SAINT LOUIS.

I have just returned to this Post, and have assumed the Military Command of this Department. No one can more deeply regret the deplorable state of things existing here than myself. The past cannot be recalled. I can only deal with the present and the future.

I most anxiously desire to discharge the delicate and onerous duties devolved upon me, so as to preserve the public peace. I shall carefully abstain from the exercise of any unnecessary powers, and from all interference with the proper functions of the public officers of the State and City. I therefore call upon the public authorities and the people to aid me in preserving the public peace.

The Military force stationed in this Department by the Authority of the Government, and now under my command, will only be used in the last resort to preserve the peace. I trust I may be spared the necessity of resorting to martial law, but the public peace MUST BE PRESERVED, and the lives and property of the people protected. Upon a careful review of my instructions, I find I have no authority to change the location of the "Home Guards."

To avoid all cause of irritation and excitement, if called upon to aid the local authorities in preserving the public peace, I shall, in preference, make use of the Regular Army.

I ask the people to pursue their peaceful avocations, and to observe the laws and orders of their local authorities, and to abstain from the excitements of Public Meetings and heated discussions. My appeal, I trust, may not be in vain, and I pledge the Faith of a Soldier to the earnest discharge of my duty.

WILLIAM S. HARNEY.
Brigadier General, U. S. A. Com'g Dept.

Harney's proclamation of May 12, 1861. This proclamation from the Commander of the Army of the West circulated throughout St. Louis and across the State of Missouri following the tragedy of Camp Jackson. Harney tried to reestablish order following the chaos that gripped the city and divided the state. Courtesy Missouri Historical Society St. Louis (D05125).

subsequent treatment of his militia troops.[17] Frost seized the moment to protest his incarceration at the arsenal. He described what happened in stark detail: "After surrender of arms … whilst thus disarmed and surrounded, a fire was opened upon a portion of it by his [Lyon's] troops, and a number of my men put to death, together with several innocent lookers on—men, women, and children."[18] Frost complained indignantly in his message to Harney that it was a travesty of military justice for his officers and men to suffer embarrassment as prisoners of war with the flag of the Union flying over their heads. He blamed the riots on Lyon's troops, who, he said, opened fire on unarmed men while they were surrounded, putting to death a number of unfortunate Missourians acting in the course of their constitutional duty, not to mention a number of innocent men, women, and children who died from the careless reaction of Lyon's soldiers. Moreover, Frost argued, Missourians should not have to take an oath to a Union army captain to gain their freedom. They had already accepted, after all, the obligation of loyalty that rests upon every citizen, to sustain the Constitution and laws of the United States. He saw no reason to suffer the indignity of swearing to a lesser oath. He asked Harney to intervene and restore their place and property confiscated by Lyon.[19] General Harney forwarded Frost's complaint to the War Department, but by now Harney's own status in Washington was on shaky ground and nothing came of the complaint.[20]

William Selby Harney. Brigadier General Harney commanded the Department of the West. He defied authorities in Washington by refusing to allow Captain Nathaniel Lyon to arm civilian volunteers with weapons from the St. Louis Arsenal. His failed attempt to quell hostilities in Missouri, the Price-Harney agreement, cost him his command. Photograph by Mathew Brady, ca. 1860. National Archives and Records Administration Washington, D.C. (528814).

On the afternoon of May 12, while Lyon steamed over what to do with his prisoners, a restive crowd began to gather outside the arsenal. By Saturday afternoon, agitation in the city resounded with excitement. No one was safe on the streets. A soldier bragged to a friend, "You should have seen them when they was [sic] forced to lay down their arms and surrender. We kept them all night and marched them through the streets."[21]

The prisoners received information that Lyon would release them once they took the oath recanting their actions. Again, as they had at Camp Jackson, they refused to swear allegiance to the federal government because it would be an admission that they had been disloyal. Nevertheless, they compromised and agreed to a parole not to take up arms against the U.S. Eager to return to their homes, the Missourians accepted Lyon's parole.[22] All officers and men took an oath in exchange for their freedom not to fight against the United States during this war, all except one man.[23] Captain Emmet McDonald gained statewide acclaim as the only prisoner out of the Camp Jackson affair who refused Lyon's parole.[24]

Fearing another incident, Lyon put the prisoners aboard a steamer about 5:00 p.m. and released them to go home. The freed Missourians left the arsenal and boarded the steamboat *Isabella* for the short trip upriver, transported around the German neighborhoods rather than marching through them.[25] They disembarked at the levee at the foot of Chestnut Street and made their way into the city. It was the last appearance of the Missouri militia in St. Louis during the war.[26] Most returned home and honored their oaths of allegiance. Some did not and hastened to Jefferson City to join Governor Jackson's new Missouri State Guard force. Others headed straight to the South to join the Confederacy, oath or not.

When everyone else walked out of the arsenal, Captain McDonald, who refused to take Lyon's oath, remained jailed.[27] A few days later, friends obtained a writ of habeas corpus to have him released. Lyon's incarceration of American citizens had no foundation in law. A subsequent court case judged McDonald's incarceration to be illegal. Federal judge Samuel Treat, of the Eastern District of Missouri, ruled that an American citizen has a right to freedom from arbitrary detention even in time of crisis. However, it was a hollow victory for McDonald, whom the government had moved and incarcerated in Illinois.[28] Nevertheless, the judge's opinion underscored the contention of the South and many in the North that the assault on Camp Jackson had no legal standing. The U.S. government did not authorize the action for such a rash act as transpired. In the words of one unionist editor from St. Louis, "Lyon and his staff were irregulars."[29] When Lyon took the militia prisoners, Jefferson Davis asked, "Prisoner of what? There was no war and no warrant for their arrest as offenders against the law. It is left to the usurpers to frame a vocabulary suited to their act."[30] There was little sympathy for Lyon's contention that the innocent victims of Camp Jackson "suffered with the guilty." Angry critics asked, guilty of what?[31]

Lyon did not let up in his quest to build his army. By the time he moved on Camp Jackson, more than 9,000 volunteers and Home Guards had enrolled in the U.S. service. More pro–Union volunteers poured into his army all the time. As fast as a regiment of volunteers formed, the soldiers marched down to the arsenal to join the U.S. service. At the arsenal, they received their muskets, which they loaded, and received cartridges to repel any attack made upon them.

On the afternoon of May 12, Saturday, about the time Lyon released his prisoners, the Fifth Regiment Reserve Corps Volunteers completed mustering another 1,200 German Home Guard reserves from the northern part of the city. The Fifth had remained out of the Camp Jackson march because it was unarmed and not fully formed at the time. They now appeared at the arsenal to enlist into national duty, and to collect arms and instructions for their service. Their presence in the city threatened to erupt in more mob violence.

Shortly after four o'clock, after the new recruits received their weapons, several companies of the Fifth, mostly German officers and soldiers

Attack at Fifth and Walnut, May 12, 1861. United States volunteers returned fire against St. Louis citizens who shot into their ranks as the men marched through the city. Twelve people died, including four soldiers. Sketch by Mat Hastings, *Harper's Weekly*, Vol. 5, No. 231, page 349 (June 1, 1861). Courtesy Missouri Historical Society St. Louis (N34565).

under the command of Lieutenant Colonel Robert White, left the arsenal to return to their quarters at Stifel's Brewery in North St. Louis. They went up Second Street as far as Walnut and turned up Walnut until they passed the Presbyterian Church at the corner of Fifth and Walnut. An anti-Union crowd began to collect along the streets where the troops were marching. The crowd soon took on the tenor of an unruly mob, hurling insults and threats at the soldiers. The now familiar epithets of "blue-bellied Yankees" and "beer-drinking Dutch" rang out.[32] Jeers and hisses that followed them soon turned to brickbats and stones thrown at them.[33]

About half past five o'clock, as the body of troops moved past the columns of the church, the verbal abuse suddenly turned violent. A shot rang out. John Long, a lad of about 19 standing behind the large pillars of the church, in a moment of unrestrained enthusiasm, fired a pistol into the air.[34] Three more shots quickly followed, some from the windows of a house on the street. One soldier fell dead, killed instantly. More lay wounded. Some of the soldiers who had already passed the church and reached Seventh Street wheeled around, leveled their muskets, and wildly fired a volley down the street in the direction of the shots.[35] These were raw recruits who had been given guns only a short time ago. They aimed badly, the balls of their muskets hitting everywhere, including their own ranks and the spectators who lined the pavements.[36] A fusillade of bullets pelted houses from Fifth to Seventh Streets on the north side of Walnut.[37] The shower of bullets shattered the windows along Walnut Street and perforated the doors of private residences, tearing the ceilings and throwing splinters in every direction.[38]

Their wild firing had lethal effects. They killed three of their own men and two unarmed citizens who happened to be passing by, also wounding several people standing on the sidewalk.[39] The windows of the houses filled with people who then emptied onto the street. The soldiers broke ranks and ran. People came out of the houses to pursue them. They pelted stragglers with stones and in one instance, at least one soldier fell, shot dead on the spot.[40]

A huge crowd quickly gathered at the bloody scene. Excitement rose to a fever pitch, threatening to erupt into an even more violent confrontation. The troops hurried to an open square where they organized their ranks. They held their fire and no further outbreak occurred. They marched on to their quarters.

Few doubted now that acts of provocation meant firm and perhaps deadly response from the federal troops. Six people lay dead, four soldiers and two citizens, along with several others, fatally wounded.[41] As a result, of the affair, 12 people died; six more citizens survived their wounds. When Lyon reported the incident to Washington, he put the number of dead at 12, including, in his words, 10 secessionists.[42]

Lyon's plan to capture Governor Jackson was at a standstill. He had planned to take Camp Jackson and in quick succession march on Jefferson City to arrest Jackson and his legislature before they could mass themselves together anywhere or overrun the state while they were in scattered bodies. He was confident he had the support of the president with any additional forces that might be required out of the northwestern states.[43]

Much to the dismay of Montgomery Blair, who had written the orders for both actions—Camp Jackson and Jefferson City—Harney's reappearance without Blair's knowledge put the second order on hold. Blair claimed that even the president did not know his secretary of war had reinstated Harney.[44]

Lyon took the occasion of his report to Washington on the Walnut Street incident to complain about Brigadier General Harney's actions since Harney's return to St. Louis. Lyon wrote, "The authority of General Harney under these circumstances embarrasses, in the most painful manner, the execution of the plans I had contemplated and upon which the safety and welfare of the Government, as I conceive, so much depend, and which must be decided in a very short period."[45] At the same time, he thought it proper to mention to the War Department that the volunteer brigade he had raised had elected him—Lyon—brigadier general of the brigade. He reminded the department that his authority came from the president, and the department might want to accept his election, in essence lobbying Washington for command of the Missouri First Brigade.[46] What he did not mention was that the brigade preferred Blair, but Blair refused in favor of Lyon.[47] Unbeknownst to Lyon, even before hostilities began, Blair had unsuccessfully offered the command to William T. Sherman.[48] Thus, Lyon was the brigade's third choice.[49]

The deadly incident on Walnut Street added to the outrage of the St. Louis citizenry. The collision further embittered the unhappy feeling already existing among the inhabitants.[50] More people died as fighting continued into the night.[51] Several Germans were badly beaten; others disappeared and were never heard from again.[52] Curfews went into effect. City officials ordered all minors to remain indoors for three days and requested citizens to be indoors after nightfall and to avoid gatherings and meetings.[53]

By late Saturday, the nation began to take note of what had happened at Camp Jackson in the collision between the citizens of St. Louis and federal soldiers. Telegraph dispatches carried the news across the country. The fault lay with the mob, the Northern press said. The *New York Times* wrote, in support of Lyon, that reports were untrue to the effect that the troops fired without orders and indiscriminately. The *Times* wrongly determined that the troops were under proper discipline at all times. A coroner's jury found that victims of Camp Jackson came to their deaths from gunshot wounds inflicted by musket balls discharged by U.S. volunteers under Lyon. The *Times* apologized to its readers that an examination of the circumstances of the second collision on Walnut Street at the Presbyterian Church had not yet been finished. Nevertheless, they were sure the tragedy would no doubt prove that as in the first, the mob were the aggressors.[54] The fanned flames of national discontent rose a little higher.

Meanwhile, vigorous currents of electricity coursed through an almost paralyzed Lincoln administration. Camp Jackson was the first blow struck by Union loyalty anywhere within the United States against the front of rebellion.[55] Lincoln had not ordered it, but he owned it. Secessionists saw it as an overt act of federal violence. Washington stood by as St. Louis threatened to come apart. The South watched with growing interest.[56]

3

Fear and Distrust

Sunday came amid the worst panic in the history of St. Louis. Rumors spread that the Germans were going to sack the city. The Germans swore revenge, the rumors said, against those who led the mob against them. Shutters closed, doors bolted in fear of a general riot, and churches did not open for Sunday school and service.[1]

Large numbers of St. Louis's wealthier upper class fled the city, seeking safety away from the violence. Pro-Southerners took the lull in hostilities as an opportunity to leave town, fearing harm at the hands of the pro-Union forces.

Citizens pleaded with Harney to intervene and disarm the Germans. He could not disband them, he said, because Lincoln had ordered them armed and he had no control over them.[2] He informed the panic-stricken residents that the Home Guard regiments were United States volunteers accepted under the call of the president. The government had issued guns to them in due form and he—Harney—could not take them away.[3]

Harney tried to assure the public that there was no further danger and promised peace in St. Louis. He sent detachments of Regular troops to parts of the city to give assurance of protection, carefully avoiding sending any of Lyon's company of Regulars.[4] He restricted all German Home Guard units to the German neighborhoods.[5] He sent one detachment of 250 Regular troops to the center of the trouble, quartering them above Thornton and Pierce's Livery stables under the command of Regular officers Sweeny, Saxton, and Lothrop, all officers known to have been instrumental in stopping the firing at Camp Jackson.[6] To emphasize his intent to keep the peace, he stationed four pieces of artillery there, too, under James Totten.[7] Despite Harney's efforts, and probably because of them, panic continued to feed upon itself, spreading to both the northern and southern parts of the city. At the same time, unrest mounted in the downtown district. Home Guards fired into a crowd on Sixth Street between Pine and Olive Streets.[8]

Harney's statement about the Home Guards added to the imaginary danger when he said, "I have ascertained that I have no control over the Home Guards."[9] People misunderstood his proclamation. They interpreted it to mean that the German volunteers were out of control and Harney was unable to restrain them.[10] Almost immediately, a second exodus took place as another wave of fearful residents left the city. Thousands of citizens fled the city in a panic, in some quarters in anticipation of more bloodshed.[11] Entire streets became vacant.[12] False reports circulated that warned of "wholesale slaughter of women and children in the streets of St. Louis by a brutal and licentious abolition mob armed with U.S. muskets and commanded by German cut-throats."[13]

All manner of appalling stories circulated about the German soldiers. Murder, plunder, house burning, and all the outrages of an uncontrolled army occupied the imaginations of the secessionists with images of the recent massacre still fresh in their minds. Each telling of the story intensified the alarm as the cry spread from house to house. "The Dutch are rising; we shall all be slain in cold blood" was the general refrain.

An eyewitness said, "The city was convulsed with terror. Every available vehicle, including heavy ox wagons, was brought into requisition. Every outgoing railway train was crowded with passengers. Every avenue was thronged with fugitives; every steamer at the levee was laden with families, who, with no definite idea of where they were going, had hastily packed a few articles of clothing to flee from the general and bloody conflict supposed to be impending between the Americans and the Dutch."[14] Men pressed into service any conveyance that could transport a family out of the city at ridiculous prices. Chartered steamboats ferried people to the Illinois shore or to points of shelter up or down the river. The hysteria subsided in a few days and most of the refugees returned to their homes. However, many never came back to St. Louis again, choosing instead to follow the fortunes of the Southern Confederacy.

Meanwhile, people convinced themselves that the Minute Men and their friends intended to raid and destroy the homes of the Germans.[15] Families cowered in fear. One regiment of Union Home Guards, composed principally of Americans and Irishmen who happened to live at the center of town, assembled after dark Sunday night and formed a skirmish line from east to west across the central part of the city. They moved slowly and watchfully southward to determine for themselves what truth was in the reports that the Germans planned to attack the central section. Some distance south of Chouteau Avenue, the American and Irish Home Guards met another long line of Union Home Guards coming north. This detail, made up of Germans, had heard that the Americans were coming down to burn their homes and they were ready to protect their families. The two U.S. units recognized each other and soon realized that each was the victim of alarm by false reports about the other. After some hearty cheering, the lines disbanded and everybody returned to their homes.[16]

A pall of fear and resentment hung over the city. People exchanged stories of the atrocities they had seen at Camp Jackson. Alice Elizabeth Cayton, writing on May 12 to her brother in Washington Territory, summarized what many in St. Louis felt. "On Friday, the 10th about 3 o'clock federals marched out to Lindell Grove, surrounded the camp, that contained 800 [sic] men, about as many more being out on leave in the city. Germans fired into the crowd. I cannot describe the scene to you fully. Imagine to yourself all of those hills surrounding the Grove filled with people, for as soon as it was known the 'Minute Men' had surrendered their arms, it was natural to suppose there would be no fighting; and just as soon as this Company commenced firing, the multitude commenced running, men, women and children were there, some in carriages, buggies on horseback and on foot. Everybody from Aunt Nancy's and our house, with the exception of Mother was out there, Emma and Charlie were there, Dora was there and was knocked down by a man and then run over by a horse and buggy, she was severely bruised but was lucky to have no bones broken. I never was so frightened in all my life before. It was all done so unexpectedly, and so uncalled for. Harry Somers, an engineer you recollect who used to be with Father, lost his daughter, a girl fourteen years old, she was shot in the heart; her funeral took place this morning. The excitement continued Friday night and all day Saturday. During yesterday afternoon, there was another riot on Walnut Street on the part of the Germans, and four of their soldiers were killed, and two citizens making six more on the list. The proceedings of the last three days are enough to make every true American heart swell with indignation against the Germans. I believe in time this place will be entirely cleared of them."

Alice was writing to her brother, a Union soldier.[17]

She felt relieved that her brother was safe on the West Coast. Their father had died recently when his ship, the steamboat *Lexington,* exploded and sank in the Mississippi. She wanted no more violence visited on her family.

The city remained in a heightened state of tension all day Sunday, but the anticipated bloodbath did not occur. Mayor D.G. Taylor ordered all saloons, restaurants, and other public venues closed until further notice and urged people to be off the streets and in their homes by dark.[18]

The mayor's proclamation to close drinking establishments had little observance. People talked and drank themselves into a blind rage. All day there was talk of an attack on Turner Hall. German communities feared more violence.[19] German Home Guard troops were on alert. Somehow, the police kept control of the situation in the city and managed to reduce trouble to only sporadic incidents. In the end, only one fatality marred the Sabbath.

The eminent Civil War historian Bruce Catton summarized the overall significance of the Camp Jackson affair: "Blair and Lyon had won the civil war in St. Louis before it really got started, which was just what they set out to do, but as far as the rest of the state was concerned, they had won nothing; they had simply made more civil war inevitable. The fighting in St. Louis was clear warning that the middle of the road was no path for Missourians. No longer would carefree militiamen lounge picturesquely in a picnic-ground camp.... Now they would fight, and other men would fight against them, and no part of the United States would know greater bitterness or misery."[20] No regional conflict could contain what was about to happen. The Civil War began in Missouri with Camp Jackson on May 10, 1861, and before it ended, it enveloped the entire nation.[21]

Numerous Missouri citizens, heretofore neutral in the conflict, went over to the pro–South side because of Camp Jackson. In places like Carroll County, for instance, where folks had before divided their sympathies about equally between North and South in the secession squabble, people suddenly turned against the Union. The *Carrollton Democrat*, then the only newspaper in Carroll County, had two editors; surprisingly enough, they stood divided in sentiment.[22] One was a Union man, the other strong in his advocacy of Southern rights. In the same edition of the paper, one might find a bitter denunciation of Abe Lincoln, and another article castigating the South Carolina traitors. Everything changed almost overnight. Within days after Camp Jackson, every township in Carroll County had one or more company of troops ready to defend the state against the national government. It went that way all across Missouri.[23]

Calls for rebellion grew wherever word of Camp Jackson spread. The impulse for revolution was particularly high in western Missouri. The Border Ruffian days of Kansas statehood smoldered along the frontier, the politics of the slavery issue divided the state, and hot-blooded young men stood eager to flock to the charm and adventure of the contest. Camp Jackson ignited a wave of state patriotism.

Federal government supporters in St. Louis harbored second thoughts about the federal presence in the state after Camp Jackson. A group of influential pro–Union men, unhappy with Lyon's heavy-handed actions, met in the St. Louis mayor's office the day after the Camp Jackson riots and agreed to send a delegation to Washington to demand Lyon's removal.[24] Led by St. Louis native and U.S. Attorney General Edward Bates, the group met with President Lincoln to urge Lyon's replacement.[25] Hamilton R. Gamble, chairman of the State Convention Committee on Federal Relations that had drafted the resolution against secession for Missouri, argued that the state did not intend to leave the Union. Lyon's tactics, he said, were rash, imprudent, and indiscreet, and dangerously exacerbated an already settled matter.[26] Furthermore, he complained, inexperienced Home Guards, provided at the arsenal with guns and ammunition, fired on citizens and exhibited their utter unfitness to be trusted with arms.[27] The delegation lobbied for Lyon's removal from St. Louis and urged the president to support General Harney's conciliatory policies.[28] Attorney General Bates strongly advocated the same, as did General Winfield Scott, Harney's friend.[29]

Strident voices urged the president to restore the arms of the state militia and restrict the Germans. They called for a court of inquiry to investigate the shooting and hold Lyon responsible.[30] Still others implored Lincoln to hold his ground and put down secession. One citizen wrote, "The time has passed by for timid measures."[31] Every member of the St. Louis Public Safety Committee endorsed Lyon's actions to the president.[32] St. Louis men of weight and influence went to Washington to see Lincoln, either to lobby for Lyon's removal or to endorse his actions. Frank Blair's brother-in-law, F.A. Dick, came away from his meeting with the Lincoln cabinet lamenting the lack of decision in Washington. "The Cabinet is made up of too old men," he said. "It seems to lack vigor, promptitude, and resolution."[33]

Lincoln even received advice to beware of his advisers. Judge Samuel T. Glover, prominent Hannibal citizen, friend of the Mark Twain family, and transplanted St. Louis resident, weighed in on the argument. He wrote to Lincoln to caution him about unsolicited advice: "There is a set of men here [St. Louis] whose special business seems to be to prejudice the leading Republicans with the administration. These gentlemen themselves are enemies of the administration, never support it by word or act, [and] speak of its policy as fanatical, its men as dreamers. They hate the government but seek office under it."[34]

Also meeting with Lincoln were Postmaster General Montgomery Blair and Secretary of War Simon Cameron. Both ably defended Lyon.[35] Blair said those who argued to replace Lyon for alienating the people by the rigor of his movement liked the Union but did not see the necessity of fighting for it. They thought the best way to put down the rebellion, he said, was to make a show of force but not to use it at all.[36]

The rivalry between the factions of radicals and conservatives in their devotion to the government paralyzed each other. Efforts of blind opposition and recrimination repeatedly required the direct intervention of Lincoln and "taxed to the utmost his abounding forbearance."[37] Thus it was that Missouri discord transplanted into the Lincoln cabinet itself at a very early date, Attorney General Bates taking the conservative side and

3. Fear and Distrust

The Lincoln Cabinet. From left, Montgomery Blair, Caleb B. Smith, Salmon P. Chase, President Lincoln, William H. Seward, Simon Cameron, Edward Bates, and Gideon Welles. President Lincoln kept a close eye on events in Missouri but entrusted others with much of the decision-making to keep the state in the Union. *Harper's Weekly*, Vol. 5, No. 237, page 437 (July 13, 1861). Library of Congress Prints and Photographs Division, Washington, D.C. (LC-2003652574).

Montgomery Blair the more radical approach.[38] Unionists in St. Louis had the ear of Montgomery and hence of the president.[39] Accordingly, the local embitterment found adversarial representation in two of its most prominent citizens, which in varying and shifting phases lasted for the duration of the war and gave Lincoln no end of trouble.[40]

U.S. Representative Thaddeus Stevens, a leader of the Radical Republican faction, kept up an ongoing critique of Lincoln's cabinet, which the president deflected with his usual wit. When Lincoln was forming his cabinet, for example, Stevens went to warn him that Simon Cameron was not the man for the War Department post. "You don't mean to say you think Cameron would steal?" Lincoln asked. "No," Stevens replied, "I don't think he would steal a red-hot stove." Lincoln repeated this to Cameron in good humor but Cameron insisted that Stevens must take it back. Stevens went immediately to the White House to inquire of the president, "Mr. Lincoln, why did you tell Cameron what I said to you?" "I thought it was a good joke and didn't think it would make him mad," replied Lincoln. "Well," said Stevens, "he is very mad and made me promise to retract. I will now do so. I believe I told you he would not steal a red-hot stove. I now take that back."[41]

Things had reached a point in the president's mind that the wishes of the local citizenry carried little weight in light of the mounting calamity facing the nation. Censuring Lyon after Camp Jackson seemed unwise to Lincoln when the Northern press gave Lyon great popular applause. Moreover, Lincoln had already reinstated Harney to his previous command and sent him back to St. Louis. Lyon stayed in St. Louis while Harney struggled to restore order. General Scott and Secretary Bates were losing their conservative sway on Lincoln.[42]

To the surprise and disgust of many, General Harney sided with Lyon. He could not overlook Governor Jackson's warlike actions that brought on the confrontation at Camp Jackson.[43] He thought that the taking of Camp Jackson was justifiable.[44] As it turned out, behind the scenes, Harney completely approved of Lyon's actions against the camp, or so he said.[45] While he regretted the loss of life in the aftermath, he felt Lyon took the correct steps. His was a thin line to walk between the irate citizens of Missouri and the anxious Lincoln administration in Washington. It was at this point that Harney probably suspected his days as commander of the Department of the West were numbered. Washington was giving him a second chance, but the political climate was not in his favor.

Nevertheless, on May 14, he issued another proclamation, this time in the form of a letter addressed to the people of Missouri in a further attempt to explain the indiscretion of Camp Jackson and calm the situation.[46] He clearly outlined to the public everything that pointed to an uprising and secession at the camp.[47] The camp contained a body of men notoriously organized in the interest of the secessionists, he said. In addition to arms furnished by the South, men openly wore the dress and badge distinguishing the army of the Southern Confederacy.[48] "It cannot be difficult for anyone to arrive at a correct conclusion as to the character and ultimate purpose of that encampment," he wrote. "No Government in the world would be entitled to respect that would tolerate for a moment such openly treasonable preparations."[49] He condemned the actions of the Missouri General Assembly and pronounced the Military Bill an indirect act of secession.[50] If Harney did not comprehend the political situation, he understood the likely intent of military preparation.[51] He pointed out that Governor Jackson's Military Bill was, in his opinion, equivalent to a secession ordinance.[52] Nevertheless, he vowed to protect all citizens of Missouri. Harney published his proclamation and sent a copy to General Scott at the War Department.[53]

Command of Union forces frustrated Lincoln from the earliest days of the conflict. The debacle in St. Louis was an ominous beginning, which had started with the replacement of General Harney with Lyon. After Frank Blair's arrangement to have General Harney recalled to Washington and replaced with Captain Lyon, the War Department recognized Lyon's fanatical tendencies. Realizing they had placed a mere captain of dubious judgment in command of the entire Department of the West, they sought to alleviate the political mess by rescinding Lyon's appointment and temporarily putting Colonel Edmund Alexander in charge. Alexander, a 60-year-old career army officer stationed in Nebraska, temporarily took over the Department of the West and held titular command until the reinstatement of General Harney and his return to St. Louis.

Washington's political machinations had no obvious effect on Lyon or his plans.

4

Calls for Rebellion

While General Harney worked to quell unrest in St. Louis, secessionist activity in the state surged. In Washington County, for example, the Confederate flag flew over the courthouse at Potosi, and anyone professing Union sentiments soon found themselves rudely driven from their homes and escorted from town. Frequently, people from Potosi arriving at St. Louis complained of outrages against citizens chased out of town because of their loyalty to the federal government.[1] Scores of fugitives, mostly from that vicinity, arrived with stories of insult, indignity, and disgrace. Several came in with their heads shaved.[2]

Word of the unrest at Potosi reached Captain Lyon on May 14, as Harney's proclamation circulated. Lyon had no patience for General Harney's peacekeeping measures and sent an expedition of federal troops to Potosi to apprehend the offending parties.[3] Potosi was on the St. Louis and Iron Mountain Railroad, about 70 miles southwest of St. Louis. The rebels there had control of the lead mines that dotted the region.[4] He ordered a military expedition to check secessionist movement and protect unionists.[5] Thus, he commenced the first active campaign of operations against rural Missouri secessionists.[6]

To put down the Washington County rebellion at Potosi, Lyon dispatched two companies of 150 men of the Fifth Missouri U.S. Volunteers under the command of Captain Nelson Cole. The Fifth Regiment was new, having completed its organization May 11, after the capture of Camp Jackson. The deadly shootout affair on Walnut Street, which included elements of the Fifth, was still fresh in the minds of its soldiers; they welcomed the order to go to Potosi.[7]

Captain Cole's detachment left St. Louis by special train at 10:00 p.m. on the evening of May 14, reached Potosi at three the next morning, and immediately surrounded the town.[8] Moving stealthily in the dark, details of Union sentinels took up stations outside the homes of each resident reputed to be among the prominent secessionist leaders. Local unionists had identified them as those who drove the Union loyalists from town

4. Calls for Rebellion

and threatened others with death if they did not support the Confederacy.[9]

At a prearranged signal, as day broke and citizens began to stir, the rebel ringleaders found themselves prisoners. Shortly after daylight, guards marched about 150 citizens to the courthouse. Most of them turned out to be innocent citizens recognized by Union men, and they went home. Captain Cole arrested 56 men and confined them to the courthouse. Forty-seven of the secessionist captives took an oath of allegiance to the government and accepted parole. Nine refused and wound up prisoners of war at the St. Louis Arsenal.[10]

It turned out to be something of a toothless rebellion. Cole's soldiers diligently searched all the homes of the arrested men but found no arms of any kind.[11] Nevertheless, before returning to St. Louis, Captain Cole visited two smelting furnaces accused of furnishing lead to the Confederacy. His men seized a quantity of lead and other manufactured military supplies stored at the depot and along the Iron Mountain Railroad.[12]

Nelson D. Cole. At the beginning of the rebellion in Missouri, Captain Cole led a detachment of the Fifth Missouri U.S. Volunteer Infantry to Potosi, Missouri, to break up a secessionist stronghold. He took a number of prisoners and confiscated a cache of war material. He later commanded the 2nd Missouri Volunteer Artillery (Union). Photograph 1865. Courtesy Missouri Historical Society St. Louis (P0084-0114).

The Union troops started back to St. Louis around noon. They made another stop at Desoto to break up another secessionist meeting. Desoto was a growing town of about 250 people situated in the lead mining region that lay within a two-mile radius of the town. Located on the St. Louis and Iron Mountain Railroad about 42 miles from St. Louis, it had an easy access connection to the city.[13]

The *St. Louis Democrat* described the Desoto encounter. "Here, where there was to be a grand secession 'love feast' or flag raising, they found a company of secession cavalry drilling for the occasion, which took to their heels as soon as they got a sight of the United States troops." The meeting quickly dispersed when the federal troops appeared. A detachment of 40 of Captain Cole's Federals chased about 50 men on horseback into the woods where most of them dismounted and escaped on foot into the brush.[14] The soldiers took charge of the abandoned horses and turned to the matter of the rebel flag. The *St. Louis Democrat* continued, "The next move was to capture the rebel flag, which was known to be in the town. Cole detailed a guard of six men. The guard surrounded the house supposed to contain the flag. After searching in vain for some time, it was observed that the lady of the house [was] sitting in rather an uneasy position, and she was very politely asked to rise. She hesitated but then rose slowly, and low the blood red stripe of the rebel ensign appeared below the lady's hoops."[15]

Despite its name, the *St. Louis Democrat* was a strongly Republican newspaper. Nowhere in St. Louis was the division of loyalties more evident than in the press, which contributed to the division of the citizenry. There were some 50 periodical newspapers in St. Louis to go with 11 dailies, large and small. The *Democrat* and the *Republican* were the two most confusing to strangers because the *Democrat* was the organ of the Republicans and the *Republican* was the organ of the Democrats. As the conflict broadened, some newspapers issued evening editions, prompting one reader to say, "They issue these evening papers to contradict the lies that they tell in the morning."[16]

The Confederate flag at Desoto was a large banner, intended to fly atop the pole of equally impressive height that secessionists had prepared for the occasion. The soldiers confiscated the rebel flag and hoisted the Stars and Stripes. It would be the first rebel flag taken in the war.[17] Cole left 30 men of Company A to guard the U.S. flag, take charge of the captured horses, and protect the town from any more disgruntled secessionists.[18] The remainder of the soldiers boarded the train and proceeded on toward St. Louis.

They stopped off briefly at Victoria to arrest an unruly protester who insisted on loudly hurrahing for Jeff Davis.[19] Surrounded by a half dozen bayonets and marched onto the train, the man ended up as another arsenal prisoner. By 6:30 p.m., Captain Cole's detachment and his prisoners were back at the arsenal.[20]

Potosi would be the first of many alarms sounded by unionists to call out federal troops against their South-leaning neighbors. For example, Lyon sent another detachment of troops to fortify Bird's Point, a critical point in defending the West, as it lay on the Missouri side of the Mississippi River where the Mississippi and Ohio rivers meet, directly across the river from the Union depot at Cairo, Illinois.[21]

Partisan writers applauded Lyon's autocratic actions. Union

supporter Robert R. Howison wrote, "He established a military despotism in the city [St. Louis], and pushed his armed bands into the country, arresting men whom he suspected of strong sympathy with the South, seizing the State munitions wherever he could find them, and making no secret of his purpose to subject the Governor and the Legislature to the control of the bayonet."[22]

Meanwhile at Jefferson City, the Missouri General Assembly adjourned on May 15, having completed its business to gear up the state for war.[23]

The experiences at Potosi and Desoto played out across the state. Missouri towns and counties became islands of divided sentiments. Some proudly flew the Union Stars and Stripes, while others next door displayed only the state flag, a sign of loyalty to the South. With Union troops on the prowl, only the most ardent secessionist displayed the Confederate flag. Division appeared in odd but predictable ways. For instance, a minister dared to preach in support of the Union on the topic of "The Duty of Obedience to Established Government," much to the consternation of the half of his congregation that was secessionists. He closed his service with "My Country 'Tis of Thee," at which time secessionists did not even bother to open their hymn books.[24] It was common likewise for organizations like the Chamber of Commerce to split into two bodies.[25]

Washington watched as a wary balance of power seesawed between secessionists and unionists across the state. A St. Louis resident writing to Lincoln advised, "The affair of Camp Jackson was unfortunate in some things. The killing of the people was sad enough. In other aspects, it was glorious—broke the spirit of treason here, and has stricken a terror to the end of the state. The little brush at Potosi & De Soto has had the same effect. A panic has seized the conspirators—many of them have fled.... But the moment anything favorable turns up for them if not put down now they will agitate again."[26]

The riots in St. Louis marked the opening scenes of revolution in Missouri. As a direct result of the military action at Camp Jackson, Governor Jackson received dictatorial powers from the legislature. Lawmakers authorized the formation of the Missouri State Guard to resist the Union presence in the state, and gave Jackson the necessary funding and borrowing authority to assist him in this task.[27] From that point forward, the school fund went into the military operations.[28] The *New York Times* announced that the public schools of St. Louis would close henceforth in consequence of an act of the Missouri legislature.[29]

Governor Jackson moved swiftly. He began by calling for a volunteer force of 50,000 men to organize the new Missouri State Guard. The MSG's task was to defend the state against all hostile action from the federal government. News of the massacre at St. Louis had spread rapidly across the state, persuading countless moderate Missourians to side with Jackson and answer his call for troops. The War Department in Washington watched with concern. Missouri's population exceeded a million people. Potential recruits spread over a large territory of some 68,000 square miles. Even a trifling percentage of enlistees would yield a formidable force. There were 236,402 men capable of bearing arms in Missouri.[30] Half or even a third would create a sizable army.[31] Nevertheless, the call for 50,000 troops was a tall order. At the time of the proclamation, there was no military organization of any kind in the state. There had not been a serious militia muster in Missouri for 12 or 15 years because there was no law to require it. Moreover, the state was without arms or ammunition.[32] Howison concluded, "Very few states, either North or South, were in a more defenseless and unprepared condition, as far as public measures of war were concerned."[33]

The MSG formed into nine military districts across the state. These corresponded to the congressional political districts. Jackson, commander in chief of the new army, appointed a brigadier general to each district who was responsible for raising a division of armed troops.[34]

The Military Act legislation provided for nine districts, but the state effectively had only eight. The St. Louis division never formally organized for obvious reasons; Union troops were in total control of it.[35]

A call went out statewide for volunteers to fulfill the mission of the Guard to defend the state against all hostile action from the federal government. Anyone inclined toward insurrection against the Union now had the plausible excuse of authority in the governor and an immediate way to organize under one of the designated military districts. Men between the ages of 18 and 45 could join the MSG. The call was for volunteers, but division commanders could draft individuals if they did not volunteer.[36] Local home guards—different from the German Home Guard—could also form in their respective counties and towns, but only men and boys not of age to serve in the Missouri State Guard could enroll in the home guard units. Boys as young as 14 signed up for the local guard.[37]

The organization of the MSG troops followed the pattern of the federal model. Local organizers recruited companies and placed them in regiments. A regiment was composed of ten companies, each company with 64 to 82 privates, augmented by units of cavalry and artillery. The regiments formed into brigades of not fewer than four regiments. Brigades formed into divisions, and the divisions constituted an army. Units seldom reached full strength in practice. A company usually contained fewer than the prescribed number of men, regiments seldom made full strength, and brigades rarely mustered the requisite four regiments. Depending on recruitment success in their respective districts, MSG units were much less likely to be at fully organized strength than the Union regiments, like the Home Guard U.S. Volunteer regiments in St. Louis, for example. Moreover, divisions in the case of the Missouri State Guard meant political subdivisions, not military troop strength.

MSG companies elected their respective officers, same as Union volunteers did. However, unlike the federal model in which companies elected their senior officers, Governor Jackson appointed the field commanding officers of the MSG because he served as commander in chief by the authority of the state legislature. He immediately offered the overall field command of the Missouri State Guard to Major General Sterling Price.[38]

News of the massacre in St. Louis spread rapidly throughout the state. The Union invasion swayed previously neutral Missourians toward the South and inflamed latent secessionist sentiments. Countless moderate Missourians, once inclined toward the Union, now switched to side with Governor Jackson and answered his call for support. Among the most prominent of them was Major General Price, former governor and recent president of the Missouri State Convention that had earlier rejected secession. Although he was a slave owner, he had been an unconditional unionist until Camp Jackson.[39]

The actions of Lyon and Blair at Camp Jackson outraged Price. He happened to be in St. Louis on the day of the massacre. His eldest son Edwin Price was among those assembled as a member of the Missouri militia. Young Price avoided capture in Lyon's action by donning civilian clothes and melting into with the crowd gathered around the camp. He leisurely drove a carriage between the lines of the Federals to the nearest railway station and left St. Louis.[40]

Incensed by the treatment of Missouri citizens, General Price switched from his influential moderate stance toward the Union to one decidedly sympathetic to the South. Up until the events at St. Louis, he had been an avowed Union man, trying sedulously to avert an impending conflict. He now abandoned his arguments for state neutrality and readily accepted Governor Jackson's call to service as commander of the newly constituted Missouri State Guard.[41] The affair at Camp Jackson crushed all hopes of averting a conflict. Price left St. Louis for Jefferson City the day after Camp Jackson. He confided in a friend, "All is lost; there is no hope now."[42]

The actions of Lyon, and more explicitly those of Frank Blair, Price's old political enemy, infuriated Price. Blair was nothing more to Price than a local antislavery politician who stooped to treason against the state when he allied himself with Lyon and personally led a regiment of German immigrants in the attack against his fellow Missourians.

The animosity toward Blair dated to the Mexican War in a confrontation between the two of them that amounted to a festering personal feud. Price had arrested Blair over a civil matter when Price was then U.S. military governor of New Mexico. Blair considered this arrest a piece of tyranny and a malicious personal outrage.[43] The bitterness between the two hardened when Price ran for the U.S. Senate in 1844 against Thomas Hart Benton. At that time, state legislatures selected senators. Blair, a political friend of Benton, obtained permission to say a few words about the candidates. He poured out his wrath toward Price in an excoriation that pronounced Price "worth the genius of a convict artist, and fit subject for a penitentiary print!"[44] Price suffered defeat in the election, and the political rupture never healed.

Price's personal resentment of Blair deepened after Camp Jackson. Angered by his son Edwin's treatment and that of his fellow militiamen, Price eagerly accepted Governor Jackson's appointment as commander of the MSG. When Price switched allegiance, reconciliation with the Union appeared lost. The impetuous affair at Camp Jackson crushed all hopes of averting more bloodshed in Missouri. It not only precipitated action on the part of the legislature, it drove many men into the ranks of the secessionists who heretofore had been conditional in support of the Union cause. E.M. Violette wrote, "A great many people who, uncertain as to what they should do, now joined the secessionists just because Price had done so."[45]

Unionists in St. Louis continued to press their advantage. Authorities obtained federal warrants that authorized searches within the city for articles of contraband of war, and to confiscate any found. Searchers found arms in the State Tobacco Warehouse on Washington Avenue and the Central Metropolitan Police Station on Chestnut Street.[46] A U.S. Marshal conducted the searches with U.S. soldiers under Captain Sweeny. They confiscated several hundred rifles and muskets to go with at least two cannons and a good supply of ammunition.[47] One observer ruefully remarked, "If this had been done at Camp Jackson, the slaughter of innocent men, women, and children never would have taken place on the 10th of May."[48]

Thus, the federal government commenced its program of subjugation of St. Louis with a high-handed piece of usurpation.[49] The government seized all the arms and ammunition in the city and freely searched the houses of citizens for concealed munitions of war. Secessionists saw the government crackdown as a reign of tyranny. St. Louis resident Lucy Hutchinson wrote an angry scathing letter to her brother: "We hardly dare say our souls are our own for fear some loved one may be cut off for even an expression of opinion in favor of the South.... Oh! I would we were under any despot on earth than this despotism. At this moment every avenue of the city is guarded by Dutch troops all our railroads are taken possession of by them; all our citizens are searched as they go out [and] come in; even those soldiers who were liberated on parole are threatened every day with rearrests. If a freeborn American raises his voice to cry out against these armed marauders as they march through the streets to their homes they are shot down like dogs. And this is what Missouri has gotten for sticking to the Union for allowing no word of secession to be spoken in the country all for the Union?"[50]

A ring of Union military posts soon surrounded the environs of St. Louis.[51]

As an ambience of terror spread throughout the state, the state government organized to resist invasion by the Union army. Lost was the opportunity, many said, to spare thousands of lives in Missouri because of actions by a single, hot-tempered, impetuous infantry commander whose ideology outstripped his political wisdom.

5

Harney and Price Truce

Lincoln's political solution to the command of federal forces in the Trans-Mississippi theater will go down as one of the curious lapses in presidential leadership of the war that followed. Even as the president was reinstating General William Harney to command military measures in St. Louis, a secret intrigue was unfolding to permanently replace Harney with Captain Lyon.

All during this time, Frank Blair was going and coming between St. Louis and Washington. In a striking example of presidential deference, Lincoln allowed Montgomery Blair to write out Special Order 135 on May 16, which placed General Harney on leave of absence and effectively gave Frank Blair the authority to remove Harney from command if and when Blair saw fit.[1] F.A. Dick, Blair's brother-in-law, described what happened: "Judge [Montgomery] Blair wrote out a memorandum for an order removing Harney and appointing Lyon Brigadier General [and] presented it to the President for his signature…. Bates objected…. Lincoln wrote a note to General Scott asking his opinion…. Cameron thought Lyon a rash man and not at all impressed with his real worth and ability."[2] Nevertheless, Secretary of War Cameron agreed to the order, concluding it better to mortify Harney with his removal than to endanger the lives of many men and the position of Missouri in the Union. General Scott reluctantly agreed.

Washington insiders generally understood that Montgomery Blair orchestrated Harney's removal and Lyon's appointment.[3] In the scheme of Missouri politics, Harney was in the way. In the larger scheme of Washington politics, he stood as an impediment to the enginery of a talented and ambitious family who held high places—the Blairs. Some observers claimed that the elder Francis Blair, Sr., a fixture in presidential matters going back to Andrew Jackson, was at the root of the intrigue to overthrow General Harney. He had presidential hopes for one of his sons. A firm hand in the Missouri conflict could yield a promise of Blair family distinction. The notable St. Louis historian Logan Reavis wrote, "His sons inherited

5. Harney and Price Truce

the traits of the father, and with that cunning that is always found associated with selfish ambition."[4] Lincoln remarked at one time that he could hear but little about Missouri. It was in the hands of the Blair family, he said.[5] Nevertheless, the president indicated his support for Lyon over Harney by promoting Lyon from captain to brigadier general of the brigade that had elected him, partly because by regulation a Regular captain could not serve as commander of volunteer forces.[6] Moreover, for the first time, the administration also raised the prospect of making the governor of Missouri a prisoner. "The capture of Caleb Jackson will be regarded with great favor by the administration," said F.A. Dick.[7]

In the meantime, the presidential directive left General Harney in charge of St. Louis, unless and until Frank Blair decided to remove him.[8]

A couple of days later, a vacillating Lincoln wrote privately to Blair on May 18, doubting the appropriateness of the impending order to remove Harney.[9] "We have a good deal of anxiety here about St. Louis," Lincoln wrote. "I understand an order has gone from the War Department to you to be delivered or withheld in your discretion relieving General Harney from his command. I was not quite satisfied with the order when it was made, though on the whole I thought it best to make it; but since then I have become more doubtful of its propriety. I do not write to countermand it, but to say I wish you would withhold it, unless in your judgment the necessity to the contrary is very urgent. There are several reasons for this. We had better have him as a friend than an enemy. It will dissatisfy a good many who otherwise would be quiet. More than all, we first relieve him, then restore him, and now if we relieve him again the public will ask, why all this vacillation? Still, if in your judgment it is indispensable, let it be so."[10]

Lincoln's personal letter to Blair underscored the president's reliance on Blair's judgment. It was not so much because it was a personal letter—Lincoln wrote thousands of letters in his own hand and seldom dictated anything—but because the one-page letter clearly outlined the likely course of events.[11]

Meanwhile, General Harney, oblivious to the scheme playing out behind his back, went about the impossible task of trying to reconcile the conflict between secessionists and unionists.

Animosity toward the Germans threatened to reignite hostilities in St. Louis. General Harney made a hurried request to the War Department on May 17 for authorization to raise another regiment of troops made up exclusively of Irishmen to dampen the hostility against the German federal troops. He asked that 10,000 stand of arms be placed at his disposal for issue to reliable Union men in Missouri. He did so knowing that Lyon had already armed five regiments of German volunteers and about as many reserves. Moreover, Lyon had given away 21,000 muskets to Illinois. When the arms shipment went across the river, he kept enough weapons to arm his 10 regiments but no more. Now, the numbers of recruits in St. Louis were growing to such numbers that there were not enough arms for them. Alternatively, Harney advised Washington to place another 9,000 men from Iowa and Minnesota under his command for operations in Missouri.

General Harney saw the threat before him. The 9,000 out-of-state federal troops were as much an antidote to the German Home Guards as a protectorate against secessionist rebellion. Captain Lyon and the Germans, in Harney's opinion, posed a major obstacle to keeping the peace in Missouri. General Harney's request to the War Department for more troops went unanswered. Washington had enough on its hands without putting down a sectarian revolt, let alone one clouded by ethnic strife, too.

On May 21, Brigadier General Harney met with Major General Price to confront the dangerous rift of animosity that divided the state.[12] The two men reached an agreement.[13] Harney consented to respect the neutrality of the state under certain conditions. For his part, he would carefully abstain from the exercise of any unnecessary powers against Missourians, and not use any troops outside his own Regulars to keep the peace, and then only as a last resort.[14] In exchange for federal recognition of the state's right to remain uncommitted in the impending war, General Price committed to suspend the state military buildup. Both men concurred in a joint effort to preserve the peace.[15]

There were weaknesses in the pact from the beginning. The two commanders agreed to terms that called for Missouri to remain neutral in exchange for a suspension of Union military action, "so long as no federal laws were broken." The secessionists had no respect for federal law, so that clause of the agreement was unlikely to hold up. At the same time, General Price agreed to stand down the expansion of the Missouri State Guard, which so far existed mostly on paper anyway. On the same day that Harney and Price reached their agreement, Governor Jackson activated the Missouri State Guard, an indication that suspension of military affairs by the state would face resistance. Many saw the Price-Harney agreement as little more than a delaying tactic on Governor Jackson's part to allow Price time to organize and train the Missouri State Guard.[16] Nevertheless, the agreement proposed to soften Missouri's stance from one of direct confrontation with the federal government and return it to its original position of armed neutrality. It was the same position taken by Kentucky, which kept that state out of the conflict in the crucial summer of 1861. Actions in Missouri did not appear to be on that same path.

Almost immediately, the agreement between Price and Harney met with criticism from both sides. Secessionist and Minute Men leader Basil

Duke said, "This agreement [Price-Harney] was undoubtedly a grave mistake on the part of the Southern men, for the slightest reflection might have convinced them that it was one which would not be maintained."[17] Unionists responded to the deal by chastising the federal government, which they saw as unwilling to resist those who would cut its throat for fear of exasperating them.[18] Frank Blair criticized it as an "accomplice to traitors."[19] While there was general public satisfaction with the agreement for the preservation of peace and nonintervention by the army of the United States, the more strident voices on both sides saw it as an ill-starred covenant with the enemy.[20] Washington did not weigh in on the Price-Harney agreement immediately, and Lincoln refused to sanction it.[21]

In a good faith act of compliance with the agreement, General Price ordered the troops that had assembled at the capital back to their respective districts, except for Captain Joseph Kelly's St. Louis Blues, who remained in Jefferson City.[22] Kelly and his company of a hundred young Irishmen spearheaded a band of nearly a thousand militia assembled at the capital from across the state, the greater part of them camped at the fairground under command of Kelly. Kelly was a veteran of the English army, a good soldier intolerant of slackness or negligence in his ranks. His Irishmen were intelligent, educated young fellows drawn from responsible business positions in the city.[23]

Secessionist leaders immediately expressed dissatisfaction with Price's order to disband the Jefferson City militia. Basil Duke thought, "Price virtually disbanded his troops under its terms. He surrendered a great advantage never to be fully recovered."[24]

A critical component of the Price-Harney agreement was the preservation of the peace among Missouri citizens. General Harney had pledged himself to desist from military movements so long as the command of General Price was able to preserve order in the state.[25] Nevertheless, confrontations between secessionists and unionists escalated. To those on the Union side, every successive day, treason showed a bolder front in the state of Missouri.[26] A circular went out asking people for recounts of outrages against citizens.[27] Despite the efforts of General Harney to broker a truce, secessionist activity in the state surged. Pro–South strongmen identified anyone professing Union sentiments, rudely drove them from their homes, and escorted them out of town. Frank Blair sent telegrams outside St. Louis to all parts of the state seeking reports that pro-secessionist factions had violated the Price-Harney agreement, namely that General Price would keep the peace in Missouri if Harney stopped the incursions of federal troops. Protesters soon littered Blair's desk with replies of statewide harassment of pro–Union men by secessionists. Complaints of abuse came in from all parts of the state alleging that loyal citizens were outraged and driven from their homes.[28] Letters told of atrocities across the state.[29]

Harney became convinced that many of the letters originated in St. Louis to intentionally discredit the Price-Harney agreement. Many turned out to be baseless. For example, a rumor surfaced that partisans had driven former Governor Stewart from his home in St. Joseph. Stewart posted a letter in the *St. Joseph News*: "Neither I nor any other Union man has been driven out of St. Joe."[30] Nevertheless, Blair used these letters to discredit Harney in Washington.[31] He saw to it that stories of outrages against Union citizens reached Lincoln, along with reports that General Harney had not acted vigorously to contain the mayhem. Amid the rancor, Harney entertained the idea of sending Blair and his regiment of volunteers to Virginia and ordering other German regiments out of St. Louis.[32]

Lincoln let Harney know of his feelings on the matter. In a scolding admonishment, the White House sent Harney a letter: "The President observes with concern that, notwithstanding the pledge of the State authorities to cooperate on preserving the peace of Missouri, loyal citizens on great numbers continue to be driven from their homes. It is immaterial whether the outrages continue from inactivity or indisposition on the part of the State authorities to prevent them. It is enough that they continue and it will devolve on you the duty of putting a stop to them summarily by the force under your command, to be aided by such troops as you may require from Kansas, Iowa, and Illinois. The authority of the Unites States is paramount, and, whenever it is apparent that a movement, whether by order of State authority or not, is hostile, you will not hesitate to put it down.[33]

"The professions of loyalty to the Union by the State authorities of Missouri are not to be relied upon. They have already falsified their professions too often, and are too far committed to secession to be submitted to your confidence, and you can only be sure of their desisting from their wicked purposes when it is out of their power to prosecute them."[34]

Harney wrote to Washington, essentially rebuking the president's message by affirming his confidence in the integrity of General Price.[35] He wrote to the War Department expressing his assurance in the preservation of peace in Missouri.[36] He included in his report the telling phrase, "interference by unauthorized parties as to the course I shall pursue can alone prevent the realization of these hopes."[37] General Harney pleaded with the Lincoln administration to cooperate in good faith with General Price and warned against those who clamored for blood, a clear reference to Blair and Lyon. Washington ignored his pleadings. On May 29, relations between Harney and Washington stood at an impasse.

5. Harney and Price Truce

General Harney's stormy relationship with Blair and the abolitionists seeking his removal cast a tempestuous cloud of distrust wrought by Harney's position on slavery. Harney privately reassured slave owners in St. Louis that the federal government had no interest in interfering with slavery, a position that appealed to secessionists but did not play well among unionist Republicans. He supported slavery and openly vowed to protect slave property. As events intensified in St. Louis and across the state, he received a letter on May 14 from Thomas Gant, a St. Louis lawyer. Gant wrote on behalf of a prominent Greene County slave owner who had written to him wanting to know, "Is it the intention of the United States Government to interfere with the institution of Negro slavery in Missouri or any Slave state, or impair the security of that description of property." Gant shared with Harney his reply to the concerned slave master: "Of course, my answer was most unqualifiedly and almost indignantly in the negative." Gant now sought a more authoritative answer form General Harney, asking if indeed the force of the United States military extended to the protection of slave property as with any other kind of property. Harney wrote back the same day, assuring Gant that he completely agreed with him and would have answered the slave master with the very same indignant feeling; that is, that anyone would think otherwise. Harney replied he would uphold the Fugitive Slave Law and return runaway slaves.[38] Leading newspapers across the state immediately published Harney's reply to Gant's letter, causing many slave owners who before were leaning toward secession to pause and adopt a conditional pro–Union position. If the institution of slavery were to continue in Missouri, they asked, what would be the reason to secede? Without the slave issue, secession diminished in importance. The threat of rebellion in Missouri teetered on Harney's remarks because proslavery advocates fueled the secessionist movement.[39]

General Harney's support of slavery rested on firm legal grounds. As the number of seceding states mounted in the South, many slaves fled to the North seeking protection, but none was forthcoming. The Fugitive Slave Act of Congress, passed in 1850, mandated the return of all slaves to their rightful owners, regardless of where they came from. The Act was controversial in most states and ignored in a few. Nevertheless, it was the law. Slaves who escaped from their owners and sought refuge in Northern camps under Northern generals had no protection even later as the Civil War raged. Repeated orders emanated from Washington, reminding Union commanders that fugitive slaves could not enter the Union lines and camps. The behavior of the North was a cold reminder that secession was not just about slavery but as much about the Union and states' rights, of which the right to keep slaves was but one issue and not always the foremost one on either side. Freedom for Black people would have to wait until the politics of the war dictated it. Meanwhile, commanders had permission to feed and clothe fugitive slaves, but only outside the lines.

Harney's avowed public position on slavery and the Fugitive Slave Act inflamed Northern sentiments. His apparent alignment with secessionist policies was the last straw that Blair needed to deliver his ill-fated letter of dismissal.[40]

6

Ascent of Lyon

The capture of Camp Jackson was no great military victory for Nathaniel Lyon; however, it did advance his military career. Unionists saw it as the right thing done at the right time "to stay the surging sweep of the waves of secession."[1] Union volunteers, fresh from their success at Camp Jackson and amid great celebration, elected Lyon to be brigadier general of the First Brigade of Missouri Volunteers. Lyon's election had no standing in the Regular Army, but, in making his report of the Camp Jackson campaign to Washington, Lyon made a point to call attention to his election, with the hint that the War Department might want to confirm it. Four days later, on May 16, unknown to Lyon or General Harney, his commanding officer, President Lincoln endorsed Lyon's election, elevating him officially to the rank of brigadier general of United States Volunteers effective May 18.[2] However, Lincoln withheld the order pending further developments on the ground in St. Louis, thus denying for the time being the full force of the presidency behind Lyon.

Meanwhile, Lyon wasted no time in putting down secessionist activity wherever he found it. On May 24, he sent a hundred volunteers to seize the Confederate steamer *J.C. Swon* at Harlow's Landing, 35 miles below St. Louis, and take it in tow to the arsenal.[3] The weapons captured at Camp Jackson had shipped from Baton Rouge on this boat after it slipped through casual inspection at Cairo and proceeded to St. Louis.[4] At the same time, a few miles away at Ironton, five thousand pounds of lead destined for rebel use was confiscated.[5] Shots were exchanged but without personal injury on either side. The Federals took 60 prisoners, and released them all except for five who refused to take the oath and ended up imprisoned at the arsenal.[6]

As Lyon stepped up his actions against the rebellion, so did the rebels against the Union. Secessionists seized 15,000 pounds of lead at Lebanon for future arms use. A pro–South mob tore down a U.S. flag at the St. Joseph post office and ripped it into shreds, replacing it with a states' rights banner.

The Price-Harney truce called for Missouri to stay in the Union as a neutral party in any armed conflict that might arise between the federal government and seceding states. The truce had the intent of restoring peace and order. Notwithstanding Lyon's soirees, the agreement said that Union forces would refrain from incursions into the state so long as the citizens of Missouri obeyed the law. Even Governor Jackson surprisingly agreed to a charade and swore allegiance to the Union in the deal. It had the promise of temporarily halting the buildup of the Missouri State Guard, and for a time things quieted down in St. Louis.

Meanwhile, General Harney dumbfounded his Washington superiors with what they saw as an ill-advised agreement with General Price. Price was buying time to recruit his army, they said; the Confederacy was steadily gaining strength in the state. General Harney's apparent weak fervor for the Union was less than they expected of a Union general.

Moreover, he had not yet delivered any Missouri volunteers to Lincoln's Army, a charge going back to the moment when Governor Jackson refused to answer Lincoln's call for troops. The German regiments did not count because they were strictly for affairs in Missouri and not the rest of the country. Warned by the War Department of this failure, General Harney hastily dispatched a regiment of Missouri Union Volunteers on May 28, but not soon enough to placate the political and military forces aligned against him.

Judge Samuel T. Glover, Lincoln's sometime contact in St. Louis, wrote to the president to express his regret at the Price-Harney pact, telling Lincoln, "The arrangement made between Price & Harney was very unfortunate. At that moment, he [Harney] had secession down and could have disarmed it. He would not do it—Jackson & Reynolds were ready to resign. He prevented it—they would have left the state as exiles. He prevented it. Instead of demanding a renunciation of the Military Bill, he recognized and established it. Instead of putting down the state forces, he conceded their legality by providing they shall cooperate with him in maintaining the constitution and laws—by his arrangement the military officers of the state may go on & organize their forces to maintain the government! In making the arrangement he did he had the counsel of the whole brood of semi secessionists, and of not one single friend of the government.... The rank & file of the secessionists repudiate the whole thing—and I tell you sir most solemnly if their counsels prevail we shall have things worse and worse—secession is looking up. They denounced his proclamation—but now they sing his praise—they are plotting and have never ceased—they are organizing and getting arms—they are lying in wait for our blood—and these movements ought to be put down."[7]

Glover was correct. The State Guard continued to organize in spite of the Price-Harney agreement.[8] Even before Price took command as major general of the State Guard, more than a thousand troops had gathered at Jefferson City waiting to muster into the MSG. As events unfolded, more units began to show up at the capital. The Independence Blues and Grays from Jackson County that had organized at the first hint of trouble brought with them two companies of light infantry, a company of cavalry, and a company of light artillery containing the four brass six-pounders taken from the Liberty Arsenal.[9] Companies from Clay and Lafayette counties brandished U.S. pieces, pistols, and sabers, all taken from Liberty.[10] Several companies from Cooper County came, along with several more from Callaway County. The Callaway Guard from Fulton had the distinction of being one of the few uniformed companies in the MSG. A large portion of the company comprised Westminster College students captained by D.H. McIntyre, a senior at the college. The only company better drilled with a more soldierly showing was the Warsaw Grays.[11] Meanwhile, Captain Kelly's company of Irishmen, sent to accompany arms from Camp Jackson, was still in the city to defend the capital.

The first Missouri regiment of the MSG to organize under the new military bill comprised eight companies from the counties close around Jefferson City. It was designated the First Regiment of Rifles, and its commander was John S. Marmaduke—grandson of a former Missouri governor and nephew of Governor Jackson.[12] He was also the son of a father strongly against secession.[13] His relationship with his father mirrored that of many Missouri families severed by the politics of the Civil War.

Overt instances of rebel organization ignored the Price-Harney document and multiplied. A supply order forwarded from Lexington to Jefferson City in amounts needed to feed an army, including 5,000 pounds of coffee and 10,000 pounds of bacon, hardly indicated the rations of a disbanding military.[14] Only recently, Jackson had appointed James S. Rains and Alexander W. Doniphan as brigadier generals under the Military Bill. General Rains, who strongly favored arming Missouri, was raising troops in upstate Missouri.[15] Doniphan, of Mexican War fame, had second thoughts and resigned his commission after two weeks.[16]

At first, MSG troops assembled at the capital and refused to disband under Price-Harney. General Price made a speech that policy, not principle, was at stake; a number left Jefferson City only to go to the South and enroll in the Confederacy. Missouri troops that were already organized across the state under the requisition of Governor Jackson remained active and refused to disperse.[17]

One of the most telling instances of duplicity was Lieutenant Governor Reynolds. When the Price-Harney agreement came out, Reynolds announced he was going to Canada, when in reality he crossed the Ozarks and went to Arkansas, where Confederate forces were assembling on Missouri's southern border.[18]

Judge Glover urged Lincoln to take action. "In mercy to our state these chiefs of rebellion should be dealt with—they who are now moving again should be promptly seized and 'shot' or 'imprisoned.' All this may be called rash—be it so—such rashness has saved this city despite of a treasonable government and police and so far saved the state—but for the courage and intrepidity in arming our citizens Missouri would be this moment out of the Union."[19]

Disagreement between General Harney and Washington reached an irreconcilable level. Blair's campaign to undermine the Price-Harney agreement by inundating Washington with reports of secessionist outrages across Missouri blinded the Lincoln cabinet, which was already reeling from threatened secessionist attacks on Washington.[20] General Scott had ordered the seizure and fortifications of Arlington Heights as a caution against rebel batteries that Washington feared could speedily reduce the whole city to ruins in a single night at commanding points on the southern bank of the Potomac. On May 24, Union forces crossed the Potomac River into Virginia and threw up earthworks in a ten-mile long defense of the Capitol, the first military campaign of the federal army into the rebellious South.[21]

Amid the anxiety in Washington, on May 30 Blair delivered Special Order Number 135, the letter of removal of General Harney as commander of the Department of the West that he had carried for two weeks.[22] Blair had convinced Lincoln to replace Harney earlier in the month, but waited for an opportune

Francis P. Blair, Jr. Frank Blair and his brother Montgomery undermined the Price-Harney agreement, which led to the dismissal of General Harney and the elevation of Captain Lyon to command of the Army of the West. Blair's political ties to the Lincoln administration, through his role as a U.S representative from Missouri, gave him unprecedented power over proceedings in Missouri. Photograph by Julian Vannerson, 1859. Library of Congress Prints and Photographs Division, Washington, D.C. (LC-2010649404).

moment to do it. Pressured by events in Washington, Lincoln permanently removed Harney from command of the Department of the West on the charge that he had not secured Missouri's assistance in putting down the rebellion of the South and had failed to deliver Missouri soldiers to the Union cause.[23]

The dismissal order granted Harney a leave of absence until further orders. Lincoln later said that the removal of General Harney was one of the greatest mistakes of his administration. General Scott boldly estimated that the removal of General Harney would cost the government 100,000 men and $100 million of treasure.[24]

Those who reviewed General Harney's military affairs at St. Louis characterized his removal as one of the great blunders of the Lincoln administration. In hindsight, Harney's removal was the work of intrigue stimulated by the ambition of designing men. It happened in disregard of the judgment of President Lincoln and General Scott.[25] General Harney left his command and later retired from the military in 1863. The War Department awarded and breveted him to major general in 1865 in recognition of his long and distinguished career. The claim that the Blairs and Lyon both "liked and admired Harney" was never true.[26] Montgomery Blair confided to an associate in St. Louis that Harney's intention was good but his judgment was weak.[27]

Montgomery P. Blair. The elder brother of Frank Blair, Jr., he directed affairs in St. Louis and Missouri as a member of the Lincoln cabinet. He used his Washington connections to have Captain Nathaniel Lyon assume command of military operations in Missouri. Brady-Handy Collection, ca. 1860. Library of Congress Prints and Photographs Division, Washington, D.C. (LC-BH82-5169).

According to Blair, Harney believed that "these men did not mean anything by all this business they were carrying on, but would agree to some compromise, lay down their arms, and become good citizens again if we did not do anything to irritate them." It was a position the Blairs strongly contested.

Command of the Department of the West fell to the newly promoted Brigadier General Nathaniel Lyon.[28] The order relieving Harney came with a companion order elevating Captain Lyon to the rank of brigadier general effective retroactively to May 18 by authority of Secretary of War Simon Cameron who, ironically, opposed both the removal of Harney and the appointment of Lyon.[29] Nevertheless, Lyon's commission as brigadier general was for the duration of the war and not just the three months that governed enlistees.[30] With the stroke of a pen, Lyon went from a decade-long service as a captain without promotion in command of a company of Regular U.S. troops to become a brigadier general of a brigade of U.S. volunteers.[31] Lyon and Blair were now in control of the federal cause in Missouri.[32] They were in the saddle for good, and the radical wing of the Republican Party massed behind them.[33]

Before that, however, the War Department had first asked Brigadier General William Tecumseh Sherman to replace General Harney, but Sherman declined the commission. Lincoln knew Sherman through his brother, U.S. Senator John Sherman, and had met the future general on Inauguration Day. A West Point graduate, Sherman had earlier left the army for civilian life, dabbled unsuccessfully in the legal profession in his brother-in-law's Leavenworth, Kansas, office, and had been in St. Louis only a short time since January when the call came from Lincoln to take over the Department of the West. He had given up an academic post in Louisiana when that state seceded and felt obliged to move back north. He worked as head of a St. Louis streetcar company at the time of Washington's invitation to take charge of matters in Missouri.[34] His brief interlude at St. Louis taught him it was no place to restart his military career. He absolutely refused to allow anyone to draw him into St. Louis politics. Sherman knew the purpose of war was to destroy armies, not capture cities.[35]

Notwithstanding the War Department's decision to name Lyon as its third choice behind Harney and Sherman to head the Department of the West, Frank Blair's well-oiled political machine was in motion in Washington. It had hastened the removal of General Harney and all but secured St. Louis and Missouri for the Union.

General Lyon seemed the logical replacement for General Harney. Relying heavily on the help of German immigrants in St. Louis, Lyon had secured the arsenal and placed it under federal control. St. Louis remained firmly in Union hands. His decisive temperament was exactly what the army needed to chase the Confederacy out of Missouri and preserve the state for the Union. The Blair brothers thought he was the best man to command and insisted that he head the Department of the West.[36] In a period of less than three weeks, Lyon went from the rank of captain to commanding general of the Department of the West. The time for Southern intrigue in Missouri was at an end.

General Price tried to put a good face on the change of Union commanders. He hoped that Lyon would honor the agreement of neutrality struck between himself and General Harney. He still hoped for a peaceful solution. At the same time, however, he assured his new MSG brigade commanders that he would resist any attempt to force Missourians under the terror of military force to accept a position other than one they chose for themselves. Both sides had made efforts to reconcile State and Union differences. Missouri was, after all, still in the Union. The legislature temporarily halted the buildup of the State Guard as a gesture of good faith. Negotiations broke down, however, and all trust dissolved when the army promoted Lyon to brigadier general and at the urging of the Blairs placed him in command of Union troops in Missouri. Lyon promptly ignored the Price-Harney agreement. Washington likewise disavowed it and threw unrestricted federal support behind Lyon.[37] The succession of General Lyon to the command of the United States troops fell like a bomb upon the fabric of rebel hopes.[38] Secessionist leaders assailed the effective cancellation of Price-Harney and the appointment of the militant Lyon as a flagrant violation of good faith.[39] General Price privately reiterated his position on states' rights. "The people of Missouri cannot be forced, under the terrors of a military invasion, into a position not of their free choice," he said.[40] Blair wrote to the president to urge him to send more troops. "Other states where there are no domestic enemies have larger forces authorized," Blair wrote, "while Missouri is inadequate." The scope of the Missouri conflict took on new dimensions.

The riots in St. Louis and events that followed fueled the rebellion in Missouri. In a touching reminder of the Camp Jackson disaster that began Lyon's meteoric rise to power, Captain Constantin Blandowski, a company commander in Sigel's Third Regiment, died on May 28 from a wound received in the carnage.[41] Surgeons had amputated his shattered leg, ending his career as a fencing instructor. The public did not know until later that medical evidence showed that a rifle Minié ball, which only federal troops possessed, had struck Blandowski.[42] Authorities kept the evidence that he died as the result of friendly fire secret and his status as a martyr for the Union cause went uncontested.[43]

Up to this point, most Missourians had striven to maintain genuine neutrality, although many elected officials leaned decidedly toward the Southern cause. There were pockets of unrest in the state but not everywhere. When Lincoln sided with Lyon and his Radical Republican supporters in St. Louis, however, great numbers of uncommitted Missourians went over to the South. Events in St. Louis did much throughout the state to solidify Southern sentiment. The veil of neutrality Missourians hoped to wear dropped aside. The state split. Families and communities divided, some choosing rebellion, others opting to support the Union. Those of secessionist leanings, finding it no longer possible to negotiate or delay the contest, prepared to fight. The escalation of violence across Missouri threatened to plunge the whole state into anarchy. Lawlessness increased throughout the state. Both sides feared the worst. Events that led up to the riots in St. Louis had begun when armed federal troops suppressed the duly elected government of the state and had soon progressed to much more oppressive actions by the federal government, in the eyes of pro-South Missourians. Outstate Missourians saw St. Louis as a captive city, and they were right. A line of military posts ringed the city. The Federals seized all arms and ammunition, and searched homes of citizens for concealed weapons. Cooperation between state and federal authorities quickly deteriorated after General Harney left. With Harney out of the picture, Lyon ignored the Price-Harney agreement. Both he and Blair found its disagreeable provisions reprehensible to the Union. Meanwhile, General Price stepped up enlistments of the Missouri State Guard and ordered his division commanders to prepare for action. Reports circulated that Confederate troops in Arkansas were massing on the Missouri-Arkansas border for a planned incursion into southwest Missouri.

    The national interests started to show the ominous face of a divided Union. Lincoln had said in his inaugural address, "The mails, unless repelled, will continue to be furnished in all parts of the Union." On May 31, Postmaster Montgomery Blair ordered suspension of mail in the seceding states.[44] The order routed all mail addressed to these states to the dead letter office. Two post office departments, one belonging to the Union and the other to the Confederate states, separated themselves from each other. However, even after Blair's order of suspension, mail still managed to cross the border until the U.S. banned the exchange of mail between North and South in August 1861, although some still managed to get through for the duration of the war.

7

Planter's House

On June 1, 1861, troop strength of the full command of General Lyon stood at 10,780, the whole of the force raised in St. Louis.[1] Upon his assumption of command, Lyon took occasion to issue a proclamation to the people of Missouri, assuring them that he intended to carry out the Price-Harney agreement in good faith and restrain the use of federal troops, a pledge that had little foundation in reality because he telegraphed Washington for permission to add another 5,000 troops.[2]

Perhaps foreseeing a larger role for himself as commander of the Department of the West, Lyon cut an order on June 1 to relinquish command of the St. Louis Arsenal. To make his new position more palatable to Washington, he placed Frank Blair in charge of the arsenal and all U.S. volunteers enlisted for federal service outside Missouri. On June 6, the War Department gave Lyon permission to enlist 5,000 more troops for service to the larger army of the U.S.[3] These three-year volunteers became the Sixth, Seventh, and Eighth Missouri U.S. Regiments, with a ninth regiment in the works.

Meanwhile, half a continent away, on June 10, 1861, a corps of 1,200 Confederate soldiers clashed with a federal force twice its size at Big Bethel, Virginia. The War Between the States officially began. The Union lost 18 men, the South only one.

As Washington buzzed with war fever and Lincoln awaited reports of the fight at Big Bethel, a small group of men met in St. Louis to discuss the fate of Missouri. The good citizens of St. Louis made one last attempt to avert war. Prominent men from the city persuaded both sides to meet. Governor Jackson and General Price jointly agreed to a meeting and sought an interview with General Lyon and Frank Blair. Lyon neither requested such a meeting nor desired it.[4] He saw no immediate value to such a conclave but was not necessarily averse to the idea. If the parties could arrive at a peaceful solution to the domestic troubles in Missouri, it was worth a try. He invited Jackson and Price to come to St. Louis. Because Jackson faced possible federal charges over the Confederate arms deal that had brought stolen weapons into Camp Jackson, he risked possible arrest inside the Union-held city of St. Louis. Lyon wrote out a safe passage order guaranteeing the governor's safety and that of Price from arrest or molestation during their visit as long as they arrived sometime before June 12.[5] On June 11, Jackson and Price arrived at the St. Louis station by special train from Jefferson City. They took a room at the Planter's House hotel and sent a message to Lyon informing him of their arrival.[6]

A fuss erupted over protocol before the meeting even began. Who should call upon the other? Lyon chose the arsenal as the meeting site. Jackson refused.[7] He felt that as the governor of the sovereign and independent state of Missouri, and Price being a major general, that Lyon, a mere little captain of artillery and lately brigadier general, should visit them at the Planter's House rather than they go to him at the arsenal.[8] They had, after all, come by special train all the way from Jefferson City. The least Lyon could do would be to come the Planter's House.[9] Lyon was not interested in these niceties and impatiently agreed that the meeting would take place at the Planter's House.[10]

Tension in Missouri politics was nothing new. The key players knew each other from past encounters. In the period leading up to the Mexican War, for example, Blair served as attorney general for the New Mexico territory. He came to know Sterling Price, then territorial governor of New Mexico, and held no affection for him. Blair hated Price and vice versa.[11] Their dislike for each other traced to events after the Taos uprising, which Price successfully ended to quiet unrest in New Mexico.[12] The Mexican War broke out during Price's term in the U.S. House of Representatives. He resigned his seat in Congress to accept a regiment command as colonel of Missouri volunteers to participate in the war. He gained a reputation as an able and well-liked commander. A person of great personal courage, Price had the faculty of holding his troops under fire and inspiring them to new heights. His followers loved him for it. He distinguished himself in New Mexico during the Taos Revolt, a performance that rewarded him with promotion as brigadier general and the governorship of the New Mexico Territory. He owned the ignominious distinction of fighting the last battle of the Mexican War at Santa Cruz; unfortunately, this occurred six days after the United States and Mexico, unbeknownst to him, had signed the Treaty of Guadalupe Hidalgo, ending the war. He returned everything captured in the Santa Cruz battle to the Mexicans.

After the Taos uprising, Frank Blair prosecuted the leaders of the rebellion. Justice for the accused amounted to a kangaroo court that hanged a defendant a day. Price intervened to pardon one offender and Blair objected so hotly that Price had him arrested. Blair resigned as prosecutor, thus beginning a longstanding feud that carried over to Missouri

7. Planter's House

Planter's House Hotel. Federal representatives and Missouri government officials met at the Planter's House in a standoff that led to open hostilities in the state. The hotel is in the background, past the columns of the east front of the courthouse. Photograph by Robert Benecke, 1876. Courtesy Missouri Historical Society St. Louis (N22438).

politics. Their hatred for each other was as much personal as political. The two men now positioned to enact the struggle for Missouri at the Planter's House hotel.

The fashionable Planter's House, reputed to be the largest hotel in the country—or at least the largest west of the Alleghenies—anchored the market district of St. Louis. Here the business of the city and county took place alongside a once active slave trade. The four-story hotel faced east on Fourth Street between Chestnut and Pine, a block from the Minute Man secessionist headquarters at the Berthold Mansion, and one block north of the courthouse in which Dred Scott first pled his case to be free from slavery.[13]

Sufficiently removed from the odor and frenetic activity of the riverfront, the Planter's House had an air of dignity and classical elegance that stood in stark contrast to the rough politics and violence of recent days. It was a symbol of St. Louis hospitality and a beacon to the wealthy and well connected. It was the finest hotel in the West and already a longtime gathering place for politicians wanting to bask in luxury and good service. The hotel had played host to visitors from both the North and the South. Jefferson Davis and Abraham Lincoln graced a long list of its famous guests. The normally acerbic Charles Dickens had stayed there once and wrote about the Planter's House as a highlight of his otherwise lackluster American tour, comparing its architecture to an English hospital. It had long hallways and transom skylights above the doors to allow light and air passage. The entire building lit up in the evening with its windows illuminating the street below. Streetcars ran regularly in front of it, and buggy and carriage traffic bustled about at all hours. A room cost $4.25, including four extravagant meals. A hungry traveler could feast on saddle of antelope and tasty custard pudding. A full meal might see 14 different dishes on the table at once.

None of this history or gaudy opulence mattered, however, to the men set to meet there that fateful day to decide the next course in Missouri's journey into war. The men who held the future of Missouri in their hands prepared to face off at the Planter's House.

Lyon and his delegation made their way up Fourth Street, passing the courthouse at about the time of day where a few months before a small crowd would have gathered outside in anticipation of the upcoming slave auction at noon.[14] For years, slave dealers sold their property on the steps of the St. Louis courthouse beneath its imposing Greek columns that marked the building as a symbol of democratic American justice.

St. Louis was the biggest slave market in Missouri going into 1861. Slave patrols operated throughout the city on the lookout for runaways and unlawful conduct by slaves. Ordinances of the city forbade slaves to read or write, smoke in public, ride in a carriage, or walk with a cane lest it become a weapon against a white master. No Black person could attend church without a white person present. Free Blacks who had settled in Missouri must leave or be reduced to slavery once more. Some thought slavery to be mild in Missouri, but nowhere in the country was the barbarity toward slaves more noted than in St. Louis. The last public auction of slaves in the city had taken place on New Year's Day just five months before. A mob of young Republican Wide-Awakes forced it to shut down, beginning the slide of events leading up to the meeting about to take place at the Planter's House.

Slave traders still plied their trade throughout the city. Lynch's Slave Pen on Fifth Street kept slaves as they awaited shipment to the Kentucky auctions. Corbin Thompson operated Thompson's Slave Pen near the county jail. Others operated under more businesslike names. Bolton, Dickens, and Company had an office on Chestnut Street not far from the Planter's House and another on Second Street where a sign read, "Negroes Bought Here." A good field hand sold for upwards of $1,300; women went for $1,000. Another dealer on South Fifth specialized in the sale of children, ages 5–16. Two blocks east at the terminus of Market Street, the St. Louis waterfront was a favorite place for a slave trader to market his slaves. Traders sold large gangs of slaves into the Southern slave trade and shipped them downriver to Natchez or New Orleans, and more recently to Kentucky.

On slave auction days before the crackdown by the Wide-Awakes, the city teemed with professional slave traders. They always stayed at the Planter's House hotel, where they drank their mint juleps at the Planter's bar, the most aristocratic drinking place in town. Small brick stores lined the east side of Fourth Street near the courthouse. Jewelry and notions firms crowded in among an assortment of other wares. Fine dining was discreetly available at John Bonnet's French restaurant across the street from the Planter's House. The French chef-owned establishment was the hangout of people who were careful of what they ate and circumspect in the matter of where and by whom they were seen.[15] The bars and restaurants were mostly empty now. The once thriving entertainment businesses had noticed a decided downturn since January. Slave traders continued to sell slaves in the city discreetly, and traders sent slaves to the auctions in Kentucky, but the days of open slave trade in St. Louis were over.

The action of the Wide-Awakes to shut down the slave auction had surprised some in the city. The auctions were a regular occurrence, and the passing public took little notice of them. The trade in human capital attracted no heightened concern in the general populace of St. Louis. The traders bought and sold people as diffidently as if they were swapping horses.

Such was the state of the institution of slavery in St. Louis in 1861, as the men who would decide the future of Missouri and with it the fate of slavery prepared to meet at the Planter's House.[16]

8

This Means War

The meeting at the Planter's House hotel convened shortly after 11:00 a.m. General Sterling Price and Governor Claiborne Jackson represented the state of Missouri and were accompanied by Colonel Thomas L. Snead, the governor's secretary. Colonel Frank Blair joined General Nathaniel Lyon on the part of the United States, along with Major Horace A. Conant, Lyon's aide.[1] This small group of leaders was the last demarcation between an uneasy peace and outright war between secessionists and unionists. General Price came to the meeting dressed in his Mexican War uniform, sporting cocked and plumed hat, curved sword, and high cavalry boots. General Lyon uncharacteristically showed up in his dress uniform, sash, and gold-trimmed epaulets. It was a stretch for the field-savvy Lyon because his common dress was the private soldier's blouse with the single star of his rank and a slouch hat.[2] Lyon's aide was in uniform; the other parties wore civilian clothes.[3]

The four principal participants in the meeting sat around a large mahogany table. The two aides sat elsewhere in the room. The room of the grand hotel gave off an airy rustic feeling with the blinds closed and the door and windows wide open. A calm breeze rustled quietly through the room, giving it a refreshing coolness.

Governor Jackson brought the insights of a seasoned politician to the table. Convinced that states' rights trumped the Constitution, his confidence as the elected leader of a sovereign state gave him a degree of self-importance not entirely borne out by his accomplishments. On the other side of the table, Frank Blair was Governor Jackson's political equal, and then some. Blair's tall, sinewy figure, alert face, and dignified pose revealed the persona of a natural leader.

Sterling Price, for his part, possessed the salient attributes of great personal courage and strength of conviction, both political and military. White-haired and large of frame, he presented an imposing if paternal character. Endowed with rare graces of mind and person, he was possessed of a clear and imposing dignity. Always the soul of kindness, he nevertheless had a stubborn streak that made him inflexible at times as to what he considered principle.[4]

Nathaniel Lyon was small in stature, of less than medium height, slender and angular, but large in self-confidence. With hair of a sandy color, and a coarse, reddish-brown beard, he was in his prime. His features were rough and homely, with the weather-beaten aspect of a man who had seen hard service on the frontier. He had deep-set, light blue eyes, whose lynx-like gaze was both arresting and unsettling.[5] His face reddened when angry.[6] He stood ramrod straight, the perfect specimen of a career soldier.

If neither side had much hope for the meeting, it did not show in the earnest confrontation that ensued on that fateful day for the state and nation. Lyon advanced into the room, sat down, and crossed one leg over the other stiffly, his face serious and stern. He spoke first. "Colonel Blair will speak for the Government," he said; "He enjoys its confidence in the very highest degree, and is authorized to speak for it."[7] He was alluding, of course, to Blair's Washington connections that included access to the president of the United States.

Governor Jackson opened the discussion on the state side. He proposed the suspension of

Major General Sterling Price. An advocate for sovereign states' rights, he unsuccessfully argued that federal troops should leave Missouri and allow the Missouri State Guard to maintain the state's position of neutrality. He served as chair of the state convention that rejected secession but switched to support of the South following the bloodshed at Camp Jackson. He served as field commanding general of the Missouri State Guard. Photograph by Saunders, ca. 1862. Courtesy Missouri Historical Society St. Louis (P0084-0367).

all military preparations in the state as a first step. He offered to halt the buildup of the Missouri State Guard if Lyon would do the same for the burgeoning Union army.

General Price reinforced Jackson's proposal, adding, "We will disband the state militia. I pledge to protect the citizens of Missouri regardless of their sentiment, maintain law and order, and repel any attempts to invade Missouri along its southern border." His statement was in essence the policy he and General Harney had agreed upon in the defunct Price-Harney truce. Jackson tried to get Lyon to acknowledge its previous terms.

Blair and Lyon looked at each other knowingly. Not only had they heard it all before, but Price had apparently overlooked the inconsistencies of how he might resist a Confederate incursion into the state if he disbanded the state militia.

Blair had barely opened his mouth to respond when Lyon interrupted. Despite the modesty of his beginning statement, the Union firebrand was too zealous and opinionated on the subject to let Blair speak for the United States federal government. In less than half an hour, he—Lyon—was conducting the meeting.[8] He knew Missouri's political history well. While in Kansas, he once said that he despaired of living peaceably with the South without constantly making disgraceful concessions. Now, these same sentiments flooded his mind again.

Colonel Snead, the governor's secretary who attended the meeting, said, "Lyon advanced into that room; a little, red-bearded, red-haired, precise, positive, plain man.... He spoke each word separate from the other, pronouncing the little words like *my* and *to* with as much emphasis as the longer words. He raised his right arm automatically as the conversation proceeded, and brought it down with a jerk, the forefinger extended, yet never speaking higher or lower than at first. We felt the sense of war and government in all his bearing ... 'I shall take small part in this conference,' said Lyon. 'Mr. Blair is familiar with this question, and knows the views of my Government, and has its full confidence. What he has to say will have my support' ... Yet in half an hour he took the case out of Blair's mouth and advanced to the front, and Frank Blair was as dumb as he had been."[9]

Jackson and Price represented the epitome of Missouri politics. They had been directing and controlling the state for years. Nevertheless, Lyon held the power to repudiate their politics. He began systematically to dispute their defense of armed neutrality point by point. It was soon clear that this was no mere infantry soldier of the Great Plains but an earnest student of the questions before the nation. He comprehended the matter of slavery and abolition as well as any man, and saw in the two opposing ideas the roots of the conflict that now bound up the country. Yet, he was a soldier and not a politician. He used a sword to cut the knots he could not otherwise untie.[10]

Lyon refused to accept Jackson's terms. He was too shrewd to fall for the governor's duplicity. He regarded the doctrine of neutrality in a war waged avowedly for the overthrow of the general government as the rankest political heresy.[11] "I will not bargain with a known secessionist whose conduct tramples on the U.S. Constitution," he said. "There will be no compromise of Federal authority." All the while as he spoke, he looked squarely at General Price as if he and not Jackson were more closely his equal in this discussion.

The meeting soon became a parley between Lyon and Price. Price had no use for Frank Blair and Lyon had no respect for Claiborne Jackson. The politics of Blair and Jackson shrouded irreparable differences between the two of them. All others sat in silence as Lyon and Price unlimbered on each other.

These two strongmen drew their verbal swords as prelude to unleashing their weapons of war. Governor Jackson, the facile politician used to a more sympathetic audience, had little to say as the meeting went on. From time to time, he injected a repeated opinion: "The United States troops must leave the State and not enter it. I will then disband my own troops and we shall certainly have peace," he said. The conciliatory statement did little to cut through the angry exchanges mounting between Price and Lyon as the meeting wore on into the afternoon.

After the first few minutes of the meeting, Blair took little further part, obscured by Lyon's aggressive earnestness. The debate devolved on Price and Lyon.[12] They looked into one another's eyes with set determination. Each weighed their words carefully and deliberately, not wanting to give the other the advantage of a misstep in the argument.[13]

General Price stated his proposals at length, claiming that General Harney had agreed to the state's neutrality and that both he and Harney had meticulously adhered to the principles it outlined. He thought it incumbent upon federal authorities to recognize the prior truce. Lyon sharply questioned him about the efficacy of the agreement when General Harney's second proclamation denounced the Military Bill passed by the Missouri legislature as unconstitutional and treasonable.[14] Price lamely replied that the agreement did not include the enforcement or carrying out of the Military Bill. Lyon's manner grew from stern to ominous when he followed up with a copy of a statement by Harney that clearly outlined Harney's objections to the Military Bill.[15] Moreover, the copy carried an annotation stating that a member of Harney's staff had read the proclamation to General Price on May 21, in the presence of witnesses. The normally unflappable Price, caught off guard for a moment, lost his prepossessing manner as his face reddened with mortification. Lyon's inquiring gaze never softened.

After what seemed like several minutes, Price said, "I do not remember hearing the paper read."[16] He admitted remembering a visit from Harney's staff but could recall nothing of the reading of any such paper.[17]

Lyon grew increasingly exasperated. The discussion grew more heated as he pressed General Price for a better answer. Ordinarily clear of mind, strong in his perceptions, and prompt in his conclusions, Price was an acute judge of men. He saw that Lyon had no intention of meeting the state on conciliatory terms, that he was merely looking for an excuse to tell his superiors that he had tried to avert war. At this point, Price took on a more threatening tone. He insisted "no armed bodies of Union troops should pass through or be stationed in Missouri."[18] "Such actions," he added, "would occasion civil war." As if to give Lyon a choice, he asserted that Missouri must remain neutral, absent of all armed troops on her soil.

Lyon replied, "Such removal of Union forces is impossible." He reiterated, "In times of unrest and civil strife, the Federal Government is obligated to protect its citizens.[19] To rely on the government of Missouri, a state already deeply implicated in secessionist sympathies, is an intolerable concession that I cannot and will not make." Lyon demanded unrestricted right to move and station its troops throughout the state, whenever and wherever that might, in the opinion of its officers, be necessary.[20] He went on at some length to explain the government position.[21] Blair remembered, "General Lyon told them they need not be apprehensive of any man being molested in any way so long as he made no effort against the government and the country. He told them that he believed in the supremacy of the general government, and that it was his duty to maintain that supremacy, and he would do it, and would allow nothing to stand in his way of doing it.... He told them that if they had any designs against the government they had better prepare."[22]

The impasse rested on the presence of Union troops in Missouri. Major General Price wanted them out; Brigadier General Lyon insisted they stay. On this point, the two men stood unmoved by anything the other said. The time passed 3:00 p.m. The meeting had lasted for more than four hours, with neither side willing to compromise. At this time, Governor Jackson entered into the discussion again. He said Missouri would prevent Confederate forces from entering the state if Lyon agreed that the Union would not recruit in Missouri. He wanted Lyon to disarm home guard units and freeze the movement of federal troops where they stood.[23] He suggested that they adjourn and continue to communicate by correspondence. Lyon immediately rejected the idea. He had suspected from the beginning that the main purpose of the conference was to allow the secessionists to gain time to organize. Agreeing to a prolonged discussion played into that plan.

Lyon closed the conference as he had opened it. Still seated, he spoke deliberately and slowly with a peculiar emphasis, as if to imprint his words on the minds of his adversaries.[24] "Rather than concede to the State of Missouri for one single instant the right to dictate to my Government in any matter however unimportant, better, sir, far better," he swore, "that the blood of every man, woman, and child within the limits of the state should flow, than that she should defy the Federal government." Lyon's volcanic temper finally got the best of him. One commentator observed it was "impossible for him to understand how there could be two opinions on a subject upon which he had made up his mind."[25] The time for talking was at an end. Getting slowly to his feet and pointing in turn to each of the five men in the room, his voice rising, he said: "I would see you, and you, and you, and you, and every man, woman, and child in the State, dead and buried."[26] The audience in the room cringed at the neurotic tone of his remarks because he pointed at each person in the room—friend and foe alike.[27] The words echoed in tone those spoken by Ralph Waldo Emerson upon the arrest of John Brown when Emerson said, "Better that a whole generation of men, women, and children should pass away by a violent death, than that one word of either should be violated in this country."[28] As Lyon rose to leave, he turned to Governor Jackson and said, "This means war. In an hour one of my officers will call for you and conduct you safely out of my lines."[29] Looking stiffly at his watch, he said, "Meantime, you can get your dinner."[30] Without another word or nod of the head, without even a glance at the others in the room, he turned on his heel and strode out of the room, the stunned silence broken only by the sound of his footsteps.[31]

Thomas Snead said afterwards, "Lyon was the greatest man I ever saw. That has been my statement everywhere. I felt it and said it the day we held that memorable interview of six hours with him at the Planter's House, St. Louis.... He was Jeff Davis over again, but not as narrow and prejudiced as Davis. He was Davis, however, in intensity and tenacity, and about of the weight and leanness of Davis...[S]uch was his [Lyon's] clearness, force and real genius that he met those old politicians at every point, conceding nothing, but never discourteous, his reason and his will equal. The whole party felt him to be the master mind, and the Federal historians do not err when they put him down as the greatest man they produced—greater than any produced on both sides west of the Mississippi River.... The United States never could have been typified by a more invincible mind and presence."[32] Snead lived in New York at the time he made his public comments to a New York correspondent, which may account for his complimentary tone toward General Lyon, an East Coast Union hero of the war.

The meeting broke up about three o'clock. After Lyon departed, the meeting ended kindly and politely.[33] With Lyon's words still hanging in the air, those left in the room exchanged uncomfortable glances, then rose and courteously bade each other farewell.[34]

The much-anticipated conference between national and state authorities had lasted several hours, resulting in nothing to stem the tide of conflict sweeping over Missouri.[35] Views of the parties flowed freely at the meeting, given sometimes in heated discussion, but neither party wavered and compromise was impossible.[36] Missourians went to war with Missourians on June 11, 1861, at the Planter's House hotel.[37]

Governor Jackson and General Price hurriedly took their dinner and left St. Louis by an express train. Within an hour, they were on a train back to Jefferson City.[38]

PART TWO

Gathering Storm

9

A Plan to Punish the Governor

Still reeling from the intense argument that had erupted and the abrupt ending of the meeting at the Planter's House hotel, Governor Jackson and General Price contemplated their next step. Uppermost in their minds was getting safely out of St. Louis and back to Jefferson City. Lyon's hot-tempered threat of war seemed to Price and Jackson to come from a man angry enough to break his promise of safe conduct, but he did not. The Union general kept his word. He dispatched a detachment of soldiers to the hotel to escort the governor's party to a waiting train that would take them safely out of St. Louis. Jackson and Price did not wait for Lyon's escort. They made their way alone to the train station and boarded the governor's private coach for the trip back to Jefferson City that afternoon.[1]

The two men formulated a plan on the train ride.[2] Price was sure Lyon would follow them to the capital next. The newly constituted State Guard needed time to organize. The Guard could not resist the Union invaders at its present strength.[3]

Price also knew the strategic value of the Missouri River. It was important to hold it in order to keep lines of communication open between the northern and southern portions of the state. The plan was to abandon Jefferson City, which they did not have the forces to hold; check the advance of the Federals at Boonville; and then make a determined stand at Lexington. Failing that, the next best option appeared to be a calculated withdrawal to the south to stall the federal advance while MSG recruits gathered in southwest Missouri under cover of elements of the Confederate army encamped in Arkansas near the Missouri border. Price never doubted that when the Confederate authorities learned there was an army friendly to their cause struggling to hold Missouri, the Confederate forces massed along the southern border of the state would march to its relief.

Jackson and Price rushed back to Jefferson City expecting immediate pursuit by federal troops. The party stopped at the Gasconade River

Bridge long enough to set fire to it in an attempt to slow the Union troops and hold off Lyon's chase from St. Louis. At the Gasconade, General Price stepped from the train and with his own hands proceeded to cut the telegraph wires.[4] They paused briefly at the Osage River crossing to finish burning it, too, to add to the assurance that Lyon could not follow them.[5]

The Gasconade River Bridge was a relatively new six-span railroad bridge. The attempt to destroy the bridge recalled a disaster just a few years earlier, in November 1855, when a train of ten passenger cars collapsed. It had been crowded with guests specifically invited to participate in the commemorative festivities marking the completion of the Pacific Railroad from St. Louis to the state capital.[6] The engine and several cars plummeted 30 feet into the water, killing many well-known, prominent citizens.[7]

Jackson and Price arrived back in Jefferson City around two o'clock on the morning of June 12.[8] A large crowd filled the train station platform, waiting for news despite the late hour. A commotion of excited anticipation greeted the travelers. The meeting with General Lyon clearly had not gone well. An announcement of the outcome of the meeting was unnecessary. Hasty messengers departed in every direction. One went to alert the nucleus of the State Guard encamped in the suburbs; another hastened off to hoist the rebel flag above the capitol.

Price drew up a list of actions to stall Lyon's likely pursuit of the departing state government. One of the first things to do was to disrupt Lyon's troop movements. He ordered Brigadier General Mosby Parsons, one of his recently appointed division commanders who had overseen the defense of Jefferson City, to leave the city and finish destruction of the bridges over the Osage and Gasconade rivers between St. Louis and Jefferson City.[9] Captain Joseph Kelly's command soon took up the urgent orders from Parsons to make all possible speed to eliminate the bridges. In a twist of irony, the order passed to Edwin Price, General Price's eldest son, to take a band of militia to finish the job of destroying the bridges and telegraph lines connecting St. Louis to the state capital.[10]

The detachment procured a locomotive and left immediately to carry out their mission, hauling the necessary implements and enough gunpowder to do the deed. They bypassed the intended targets and rode all the way to Franklin, 37 miles from St. Louis, just to see if the railroad was still intact. Finding it in good order and assuming it serviceable all the way to St. Louis, they determined to cut it as ordered at the two bridges. They went first to the Gasconade Bridge and there placed seven kegs of powder on it and touched it off, without much effect. The open work of the bridge span caused the power of the explosion to dissipate into the open air without as much as a splinter.[11] The result was perhaps to be expected. Edwin Price had a reputation of being less than fully dependable; worthless, some

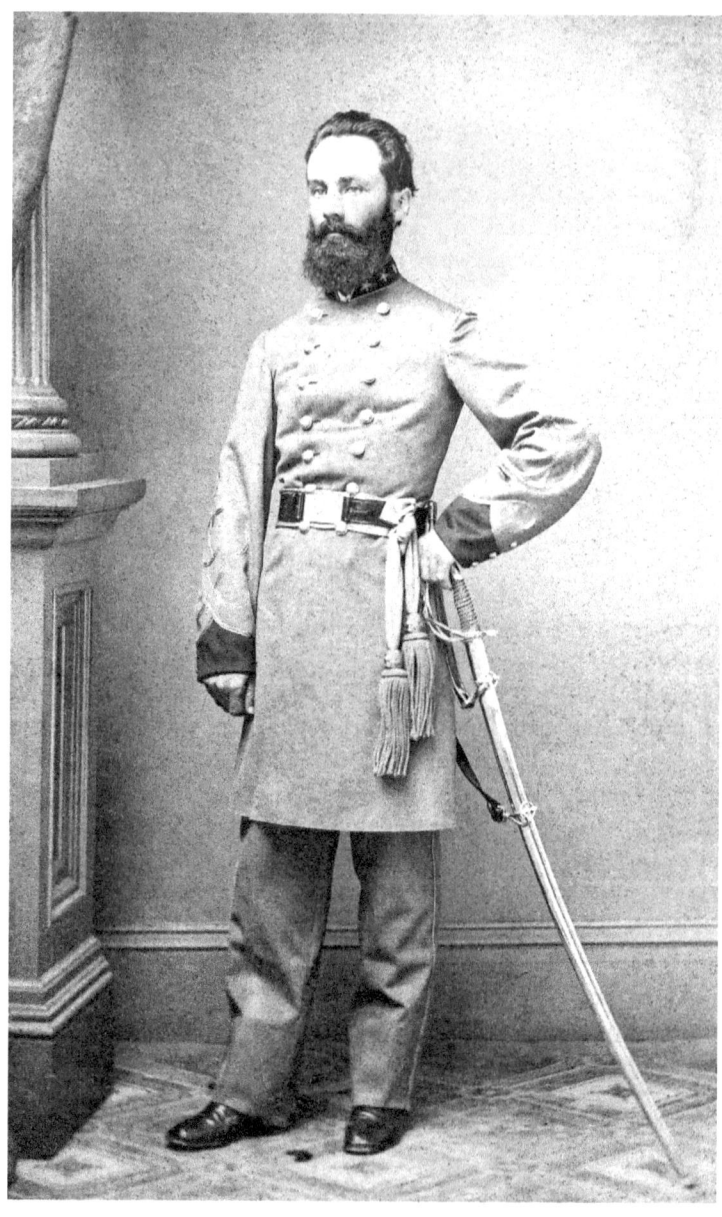

Edwin Waller Price. Eldest son of General Sterling Price, he escaped Union capture at Camp Jackson and later commanded the Third Regiment Missouri State Guard. He quickly rose to the rank of brigadier general. Union forces captured him in 1862, and he subsequently renounced the Confederacy and returned to Missouri, later obtaining a pardon from President Lincoln. Courtesy Missouri Historical Society St. Louis (P0084-0358).

9. A Plan to Punish the Governor 79

of the old-timers said. They called him Stump Price and allowed that without his famous father, the military would not have him.[12] Union soldiers captured him a few months later, and he sat out the remainder of the war.

After some discussion about the best way to disable the bridge, someone adopted a more direct method and applied a torch. The bridge collapsed into the river. They next turned their attention to the bridge over the Osage River. Governor Jackson and General Price had commenced its destruction the day before. The party finished burning the west span. In a short time, the Osage Bridge, too, was in ruin.[13]

Governor Jackson immediately went to work on the political side. He went to the capitol, where he called newspaper reporters together before dawn to warn the public of the anticipated federal offensive. He urged patriotic Missourians to rally to the defense of the state. He then called the General Assembly into emergency session, those who happened to be in town. He urgently tumbled the legislators out of bed and called them to the capitol despite the late hour. Ever the consummate politician, he issued a carefully worded proclamation designed at once to mollify Democrats, chastise the Lincoln administration in Washington, and vilify Lyon and Blair in St. Louis.[14] Before sunrise, the governor issued his proclamation, which went to all parts of the state. It outlined the irreconcilable differences between the federal government and the state.[15] The proclamation said nothing about slavery, the issue originally at the root of the rebellion. Slavery went from being the sole cause of secession to being a pawn of states' rights. Camp Jackson had changed everything. On one side, preservation of the Union was the rallying cry; on the other, the defense of states' rights. Slavery became entirely incidental in Missouri.[16] Missouri senator Charles Drake said, "Missouri's politicians were willing to commit the issue of slavery to the hands of an all-wise and gracious Providence." Nevertheless, slavery would be the single life principle and the great sustaining power of the Civil War.[17]

"All Missourians must obey the Constitutional requirement of the Federal Government," Jackson counseled in his proclamation. However, he added, "You are under no obligation whatever to obey the edicts of military despotism and its wicked minions now gripping the State." He called on Missourians to drive the federal invaders from the State. "A series of unprovoked and unparalleled outrages have been inflicted on the peace and dignity of this Commonwealth and upon the rights and liberties of its people by wicked and unprincipled men professing to act under the authority of the United States Government."[18] Jackson believed that Lyon's attack on the state militia at Camp Jackson and the killing of peaceful citizens was a wrong that it was the duty of Missourians to resent and to avenge.[19]

In light of recent events in St. Louis, the General Assembly handily passed Jackson's resolution of protest and sent it to Lincoln, who ignored it. It is not surprising that the governor found little support from Washington for his arguments for state neutrality, given his earlier diatribe against Lincoln's call for troops to put down the rebellion. Rebuffed by the Lincoln administration as a Southern sympathizer, Jackson took a more forthright action. He implemented the provision of the Military Bill that called for 50,000 Missouri volunteers to repel the U.S. Army.[20] It was a large number. Lincoln had only asked for 75,000 volunteers for the whole Union army. Many more would be necessary before the Civil War ended because the call soon went out for a national force of 400,000 U.S. troops, and climbed from there.

Nevertheless, in the beginning, the two leaders—the president and the governor—had very different views of the rebellion. Jackson's call for 50,000 troops in Missouri stepped up the urgency of settling the Missouri question as the state prepared to join the rebellion. Anyone paying close attention saw that Jackson's proclamation was the signal for civil war in Missouri.[21]

Lyon interpreted Jackson's proclamation calling for troops as tantamount to a declaration of war. He showed no sympathy for Missouri's neutrality or independence in the looming conflict. He vowed to catch the two traitors, Jackson and Price, and put an end to the rebellion in Missouri for good. His old religious philosophy of mesmerism stirred in him. He made it his mission to punish the governor and Price for their treacherous insults hurled at the Union at the Planter's House.[22] It was his design to maintain the supremacy of the general government at all hazards.[23]

When negotiations ended at the Planter's House meeting, Lyon had what he apparently wanted, an opportunity to squelch the rebellion in Missouri with the full blessing of the federal government. He planned a three-pronged campaign. He would lead an attack force west out of St. Louis, securing the Missouri River and the northern part of the state.[24] Meanwhile, a detachment of U.S. Regulars and Kansas Volunteers would start east from the Missouri-Kansas border and then swing south. The two planned to link up at Clinton, Missouri. Lyon planned to send a third arm of his command by rail to Rolla. From there it would proceed overland to southwest Missouri and then move north. The mission of the three-pronged attack was to flush the governor out of the central part of the state, trap him and his State Guard somewhere below Jefferson City, and force him to surrender. Lyon meant to crush the state government, and Price and Jackson knew it.

Frank Blair wrote a letter to the president to outline the plan. The Federals would advance into the state and take and hold Jefferson City.

The army would then advance to Lexington, St. Joseph, Hannibal, Macon, Springfield, and other points if needed. Blair thought the troops raised in the state and reinforced by Regular troops at Fort Leavenworth, Kansas, along with volunteer troops elsewhere in Kansas, would be sufficient. There were two regiments nearly 2,000 strong in Kansas. Nevertheless, Lyon also wanted federal troops from Illinois and Iowa that Washington had previously authorized for General Harney. Five Iowa regiments were on the northern border of the state ready to drop down at any time, and Illinois was concentrating troops at Cairo, Alton, and Quincy, readily available to move into the state.[25] The authorities at Washington complied, as Lyon wanted.[26]

Lyon had 500 Regulars in St. Louis, along with ten regiments of volunteer infantry, a battalion of artillery, a company of sappers and miners, and a company of riflemen, totaling about 10,000 officers and men. He also had several thousand home guards in other parts of the state where the Germans were numerous. Lyon telegraphed for 5,000 more muskets and the authority to enlist more Missourians.[27] The War Department approved immediately. This meant home guards outside St. Louis wherever there was strong Union sentiment would have arms to fight the Missouri State Guard.[28]

Lyon wasted no time in pressing his war agenda. As Price had predicted, he was almost immediately on their path. Now firmly in charge of Union affairs in Missouri, he set his plan in motion to capture the rebel government.[29] He quickly assembled a strike force of some 2,000 federal volunteers and U.S. Regulars at St. Louis. Within hours of the Planter's House meeting, his army prepared to move on Jefferson City, seize Jackson if possible, and disperse the Missouri State Guard before it could organize. Lyon understood the value of time in the outset of a war.[30]

Simultaneously with his preparations to move on Jefferson City, Lyon ordered a portion of his command to the southwestern part of the state to intercept the retreat of Governor Jackson and Price's State Guard should they get away and move in that direction toward Arkansas. Union officials had known for some time that Confederate troops were massing in northwestern Arkansas adjacent to the Missouri border.[31] Rumors were that 5,000 Confederate soldiers had entrenched themselves on the Missouri line at Harmony Springs, near Maysville, Arkansas.[32] Their presence there plainly indicated an early invasion of Missouri. Lieutenant Governor Reynolds was in Arkansas urging that the forces move into Missouri. Witnesses reported that he was in Little Rock making secessionist speeches.[33] While the welfare of Missouri was uppermost in the mind of Governor Jackson, Reynolds's main concern was the welfare of the Confederacy.[34]

On June 14, Governor Jackson sent a message to Fort Smith urging Brigadier General Ben McCulloch to advance a column into Missouri.[35] McCulloch stood in command in Arkansas, embracing the Indian Territory lying west of Arkansas and south of Kansas. Recently promoted to brigadier general by the Confederate government for his part in the capture of the arsenal at San Antonio earlier in the spring, he was a colorful and popular figure of the southwestern frontier.[36] The redoubtable Texas Ranger had lately left the vicinity of the Potomac to take charge of military affairs in Arkansas and all of Indian Territory, both places known to be overwhelmingly sympathetic to the Confederacy.[37] The Indians despised the Union, citing previous treaty grudges that had pushed them continuously to the frontier. They suddenly found an ally in the rebellious Southern states. Negotiations were under way with the Cherokee Nation to induce them to enter the conflict on the secession side.[38] McCulloch set up his headquarters at Fort Smith, Arkansas, and began organizing his forces.

Anticipating that Governor Jackson and General Price might move their force southward toward McCulloch's Confederates, Lyon dispatched troops to southwest Missouri to stage from there an operation to cut off the southern movement of the two leaders and their men, and to break up any rebel organizations in that direction. He ordered them to take up a position at Springfield, near which he believed other hostile organizations had formed that were bent on resisting the authority of the government. Lyon would push his river campaign west

Benjamin McCulloch. The army of General McCulloch, commander of Confederate forces in northwest Arkansas, posed a threat to federal occupation of Missouri. The Missouri State Guard could potentially have united with the Confederates into a sizable military organization. Collection of Dr. Tom and Karen Sweeney, ca. 1861. Courtesy Wilson's Creek National Battlefield (WICR 31514).

9. A Plan to Punish the Governor

in pursuit of Governor Jackson while the southwest detachment of federal troops moved south to intercept the governor, should he attempt to escape to the southwestern part of the State. The remainder of Lyon's army would stay in St. Louis to guard the arsenal, with orders to follow up the advance units at a suitable time and distance as reserve forces.

At the same time Lyon readied his forces in St. Louis, the third arm of his pincer movement began moving east into Missouri out of Kansas. Blair sent a request to Washington asking to use the Kansas Regulars in the southwest part of the state, and Lincoln immediately approved it.[39] This part of the plan called for a detachment of light dragoons to come southward rapidly down from Kansas City on the west side of the state to try to intercept any southbound rebel troops at the Osage River crossing near Warsaw. The overall long-term strategy of the pincer plan was for the Kansas army to link up with Lyon's force, and then the two of them to join the army at Springfield for a campaign against McCulloch's Confederates in Arkansas. It was an ambitious plan, but then Nathaniel Lyon was an ambitious man.

The plan had been in the works for some time, even before Camp Jackson. In congressional testimony before the Joint Committee on the Conduct of the War, in February 1862, Montgomery Blair revealed that he and not Lincoln was the one who had written the orders for arming the German troops in St. Louis and for superseding Harney in the first instance, recalling him to Washington and placing Lyon in charge. His intent, according to Blair, was to clear the way purposely for Lyon to march on Camp Jackson. Under Montgomery Blair's orders, Lyon "was about to capture Governor Jackson and his legislature at Jefferson [sic], when Harney was permitted, without my knowledge, to reappear on the scene, supersede Lyon, and suspend his operation for about a month, and 'til Harney could be again got rid of. Harney, on being superseded the first time, came on to Washington and wrote and published a letter protesting his loyalty. It was most unfortunate that just after Lyon struck his first blow [Camp Jackson], and before he could finish the work by the capture of the conspirators at Jefferson City, that Harney was sent back to supersede him by Mr. Cameron, without the knowledge of the President."[40]

From the beginning, Lyon had determined upon a movement as far as Springfield when Harney was first relieved. He decided now to push forward with his plan.[41] The first leg of the plan was to take Jefferson City.[42]

A U.S. Commissioner in St. Louis, upon affidavits filed with the commissioner, issued a warrant for the arrest of Governor Jackson for treason.[43]

10

Rock Creek

Seven companies of the First Kansas Regular Infantry left Fort Leavenworth, Kansas, for Missouri on June 13 under orders from General Lyon to rendezvous with the Second Kansas Volunteer Regiment coming out of Lawrence. This was the second arm of Lyon's army to capture Governor Jackson.[1] The Kansans marched under the command of the indefatigable Major Samuel Davis Sturgis. Major Sturgis possessed the usual soldierly credentials: U.S. Military Academy graduate, Mexican War veteran, and Indian fighter. Promoted to the rank of major just a month previously, this harsh-faced, bowlegged equestrian sported the look of an entire military life as a cavalryman. He pled no good sentiments toward the South, having recently fought his way out of Arkansas when his officers had resigned their posts at Fort Smith and joined the Confederacy. Nevertheless, he came into Missouri surrounded by mild controversy concerning his dedication to the Union. According to a story that circulated, an Arkansas private climbed a flagpole to take down a southern palmetto flag. Sturgis ordered him to put it back, and the private refused. Sturgis had him arrested and confined. When he tore up the flag in Sturgis's presence, Sturgis ordered him placed in irons. A blacksmith refused to put the man in irons, and that ended the story.[2] Notwithstanding his questionable behavior, though, Sturgis was a Union man. Known for his fondness of drink—brandy being his favorite—his reputation as a fighter gained him a place in General Lyon's command. As Union troops gathered in St. Louis, his federal force of 2,300 Kansas and Missouri volunteers and U.S. Regulars stood ready on the western border to join forces with Lyon in the drive to capture Governor Jackson and the Missouri State Guard. It seemed as if the ill-fated meeting at the Planter's House hotel had barely concluded when the Kansas Federals began to march upon Missouri. It was almost as if General Lyon had anticipated the failed outcome of the Price-Jackson meeting and set his plan in motion ahead of time.

There were other reasons besides conditions in St. Louis for federal troops in the western part of the state. Ever since the secessionist raid on the U.S. Arsenal at Liberty, rebel bands had continued to roam the region. Shortly after the government military stores at Liberty and Kansas City fell into rebel hands in April, a detachment of Regular federal troops, alerted by telegraph of the takeover at Liberty, moved down from Fort Leavenworth to occupy the Liberty Arsenal. Three companies of U.S. Regular infantry, two companies of Regular cavalry, and two pieces of field artillery under the command of Major W.E. Prince went into position at Liberty. After staying there for a few days and learning of secessionist movements at Rock Creek, Prince and his detachment moved down to Kansas City, arriving the day after the arms were taken from the Choteau warehouse.[3] They threw up a breastworks defense around Kansas City and had remained there since.[4] Meanwhile, unionists already in the region had worked to recruit home guard volunteers around St. Joseph to counter the secessionist presence in that part of the State.

Samuel Davis Sturgis. A graduate of West Point and a Mexican War veteran, Major Sturgis commanded Kansas federal troops coming into Missouri as part of a Union plan to capture Governor Claiborne Jackson. He pushed Missouri State Guard troops out of Jackson County, east to their rally point at Lexington. Brady-Handy Collection, before 1865. Library of Congress Prints and Photographs Division, Washington, D.C. (LC-2017896672).

The added soldiers out of Kansas served to quiet the rebels in the area and kept them out of Kansas City, although the rebels posed no great immediate threat. The state militia on the Missouri-Kansas border, as in other parts of the state, was little more than a loosely ordered gang of men bearing small resemblance to an army of soldiers. They had little organization and limited arms and ammunition. However, the new push to reorganize as the new Missouri State Guard provided a structure for them to coalesce into a more formidable fighting force.

The first well-fitted MSG unit in Missouri was that of Captain Joseph O. Shelby. He raised a cavalry company in Lafayette County, a bulwark of secessionist sentiment and the county with more slaves than any other Missouri county.[5] Shelby was the cousin of Frank Blair who had tried to get him to remain with the Union, to no avail.[6] Shelby rapidly deployed his force to the vicinity of Little Blue River in Jackson County, where Major Sturgis's federal dragoons from Kansas threatened the sovereignty of the state at Kansas City.[7] Shelby's effort notwithstanding, the force set to withstand Union troops in western Missouri had less than a thousand organized men, armed mostly with shotguns and hunting rifles.[8]

The first armed conflict of the rebellion in western Missouri took place on June 13, 1861, in Jackson County; not with Captain Shelby's crack outfit, as fate would have it, but with a decidedly less capable group and with tragic consequences. The incident happened at Independence, Missouri, not far from the Kansas border.

Independence was the most important town in western Missouri. Large wagon trains left from there for Santa Fe and Salt Lake City and for the forts and trading posts westward to the Rocky Mountains. Along with St. Joseph and Westport, it was the jumping-off place for all points west. Trappers and traders from distant Indian tribes brought their furs and buffalo robes to Independence for sale and shipment to the east. It was the town from which Missourians had brutally expelled the Mormons in 1838, and the town to which the Mormons expected to return in the future and build their temple, as soon as they were strong enough.[9] Missourians seldom mentioned the infamous Mormon issue at Hawn's Mill, where state militia butchered innocent people and forced survivors to leave the state.[10]

Independence sat on a high ridge of ground four miles south of the Missouri River. Located in the center of a fertile region, luxuriant blue grass covered all the uncultivated lands. It had been one of the Missouri staging grounds during the border conflicts over Kansas statehood. The wealthy and prominent men of Independence quickly threw the weight of their influence to the cause of secession when efforts to make Kansas a slave state failed and rebellion followed. A few companies of new Missouri State Guard recruits with warm pro–South feeling gathered across the area. Two of the state's old militia companies formed the core of rebel resistance. Known as the Blues and Grays from the color of their uniforms, two Independence merchants commanded them. Captain Thomas W. Arnold kept a store on the south side of the Independence square; Captain

George Whitehead's shoe store was a few doors east. It had been Arnold and his Grays that had taken the federal arms from the Choteau warehouse at Kansas City.

A camp was set up at nearby Rock Creek on the Westport-Independence Road to begin mustering the old militia troops into the new Missouri State Guard. Colonel Edmund Ballard Holloway soon arrived to take command of the rebel camp, making it a rendezvous destination for State Guard volunteers from surrounding counties. A West Point graduate and former U.S. Army officer, Colonel Holloway was a rising star in Missouri's quest for neutrality in the budding conflict, and a popular figure among secessionists of western Missouri.[11] He made his home in Jackson County, and had only days before resigned his commission in the U.S. Army, with a view of accepting service under the Confederate government. His immediate duty was to organize the First Infantry Regiment, Eighth Division of the Missouri State Guard. He still wore his old blue federal uniform. Holloway planned to counter the growing presence of government troops in the region with the formation of the First Infantry at Rock Creek. He assembled 10 to 15 companies in no time, including the companies organized at Independence, and dispatched orders for the companies in his district of counties to hurry to Rock Creek with the intention to capture or dislodge the Federals encamped at Kansas City.[12] Tensions began to escalate as more U.S. Regulars moved from Fort Leavenworth down to Kansas City to reinforce the troops already entrenched there.[13]

On June 13, seeing the buildup of Colonel Holloway's forces, thinking them easily dispersed, Major Prince sent a detachment to Rock Creek to confront them. Prince suspected that the group had its eye on government property stored at Fort Leavenworth.[14] Lieutenant David Sloan Stanley took a company of the Fourth Cavalry to investigate MSG activities at the Rock Creek camp and to ascertain the intentions of the camp. His orders from Major Prince were to stay short of a military confrontation. Lieutenant Stanley moved east out of Kansas City and proceeded about eight miles down the Kansas City and Independence Road until, descending the east side of Blue Ridge, he came in view of the rebel camp.

The new MSG recruits watched nervously as the well-disciplined Federals approached. Stanley halted his men about 300 yards from the camp and rode ahead with a sergeant carrying a white flag of truce, hoping to talk to someone to ascertain the intentions of the camp of armed secessionists gathering at Rock Creek. He soon spotted Colonel Holloway riding out to meet him. Holloway and his adjutant, Lieutenant Bud McClannahan, came up; the men saluted and courteously greeted each other. Lieutenant Stanley stated his mission. The two had been in conversation but a short time when Stanley noticed that several companies of rebel cavalry were making movements on each side of the road that threatened to flank him and cut him off. He called Colonel Holloway's attention to these movements but Holloway assured him there was no danger. Nevertheless, Stanley noticed that the movements continued and were becoming more threatening. They were starting to surround him. He broke off the meeting, galloped back to his men, and headed back to Kansas City.

Colonel Holloway and Lieutenant McClannahan turned at the same time to head back to their camp. Holloway raised his hand to motion his troops back to their positions. Some of them mistook his gesture as coming from a federal commander. An intoxicated Independence youth named Patsy McDonnell yelled, "Shoot the damn bastards," raised his musket, and fired at the retiring Federals. The raw MSG recruits thought it was a signal to fire and commenced firing in every direction. Holloway in his blue uniform and McClannahan, mistaken by their own men for the federal troops, fell mortally wounded, fired upon by the impetuous recruits.[15] They both died hours later.[16] The poorly organized rebels then opened fire on each other, thinking the Union troops were among them. The fusillade, which lasted a good ten minutes, left two dead and at least 17 wounded. A farmer from Lees Summit, Charles Harbaugh, died instantly, and a man named Stonestreet later succumbed to his wounds. Lieutenant Stanley and the Federals hastened away from the melee and retreated to Kansas City without having fired a shot.[17]

Edmund B. Holloway. Missouri State Guard troops, wary of approaching federal troops in Jackson County, accidentally shot Colonel Holloway and his adjutant. The death of Holloway, an accomplished officer who resigned from the U.S. Army to join the secessionists' movement, struck a blow to the military leadership of the Missouri State Guard. This 1848 portrait pictures him in his Mexican War uniform. Courtesy DeGolyer Library, SMU, Lawrence T. Jones III Texas Photographs.

10. Rock Creek

Richard Hanson Weightman. When rebel cavalry accidentally killed their Missouri State Guard commander, Colonel Edmund Holloway, Colonel Weightman took command of Holloway's regiment and led it out of Jackson County to a rendezvous with other units of the Guard. This engraving pictures him in 1848 as a young captain of light artillery at the time of the Mexican War, in which he served with distinction. Library of Congress Prints and Photographs Division, Washington, D.C. (LC-2003656303).

The rebels gathered their dead and wounded, carrying Colonel Holloway's body back to Independence. Colonel Richard Hanson Weightman, next in rank, assumed command and that night about 10:00 moved all the companies through Independence to a point on the east side of the Little Blue River, seven miles east of Independence, on a bluff overlooking the Little Blue.[18] Here St. Louis native Weightman, a former battalion commander of light artillery in the Mexican War, threw up some temporary earthworks. The command soon diminished considerably in numbers as men returned to their homes, greatly discouraged at the sequence of events.[19] Through their nervous friendly fire, they had killed their own commander, who had been in command only three days. A federal artillery officer wrote in his journal that he had seen the first blood of war.[20]

Expecting Major Sturgis and the Federals to attack with superior numbers of troops, Colonel Weightman prepared to relocate the Rock Creek volunteers further east to meet up with other elements of the Eighth Division now organizing in the region. Together they would collect at Lexington, a known safe house of rebel followers.[21] Since the beginning of May, Lexington had been in the hands of secessionists. The secession flag waved in front of the courthouse.[22]

Lieutenant Stanley returned to Kansas City and reported to Major Prince. The next morning, Major Prince's Fort Leavenworth Union cavalry marched down to the secessionist camp. Finding the camp empty, he continued on to Independence. In an abundance of caution, he ordered his men to load their muskets and fix bayonets. In an audacious show of military strength, the cavalry entered the town marching in columns of four. The drum corps followed them, playing a rousing rendition of "Yankee Doodle." The infantry came next, marching in platoons. Two six-pounder field pieces brought up the rear. The Stars and Stripes borne high, the column circled the courthouse square and returned to Rock Creek. The Federals camped there for the night and then returned to Kansas City the next morning.[23]

Secessionists tried to cover up the blunder of killing their own men. They blamed Colonel Holloway's death on federal troops. They characterized it as "an outrageous attack by the federal power upon the peaceable citizens of the state."[24] State Guard recruiters used the tragedy of Holloway's mistaken death to passionately appeal to pro–South men to rally to arms and fight for Southern independence.

11

Riverboats and Gunpowder

The bridges across the Gasconade and Osage rivers were out. Governor Jackson and General Price had burned them to try to deny Union troops the use of the railroad.[1] General Lyon sent a detachment out of St. Louis by rail as far as the Gasconade River to prevent further damage by the rebels and to decoy his opponents into thinking that he was following the railway line.[2] He found work crews busy repairing the crossings.

It did not take a tactical genius to see that the Missouri River connected St. Louis and Jefferson City. Undeterred by the interruption of the railroad, Lyon commandeered riverboats to transport his men upriver. In doing so, he inaugurated the tactic of river warfare that would characterize many campaigns of the approaching war.[3]

After some resistance from their owners, Lyon seized four steamboats and prepared to load his troops for the 125-mile trip upriver to Jefferson City. The city of St. Louis once again buzzed with talk of the impetuous general's high-handed action in taking the ships, and the audacity to use them with the intent of attacking the state government.

Samuel Clemens (aka Mark Twain), a Missouri River pilot working at St. Louis at the time, nearly had his boat conscripted. Clemens was by no means a Union man nor was he an avid secessionist partisan. His nearest hostile encounter during the Civil War was as a civilian passenger riding a steamboat down the Mississippi River. Someone from Jefferson Barracks fired a warning shot across the bow of his boat because the ship was in a restricted area. He enlisted in the pro–South Ralls County Rangers but found soldering so miserable he resigned.

Lyon's river campaign consisted of Frank Blair's First Regiment U.S. Missouri Volunteers, Lyon's original Second Infantry Company B U.S. Regulars, and a couple of companies of Regular Army service recruits commanded by Lieutenant W.L. Lothrop. Captain James Totten's Second Light Artillery, recently reconstituted after Arkansas secessionists pushed it out of the Little Rock Arsenal, and nine companies of the Second Missouri Regiment under Colonel Henry Börnstein rounded out a strike force of some 2,000 federal troops.[4]

Lyon outfitted two of the four appropriated steamers—the *Iatan* and the *J.C. Swon*—to lead his river campaign, the latter previously confiscated for its part in furnishing Confederate arms to Governor Jackson's Camp Jackson arsenal. He loaded his small army on to the two craft, and the first boat steamed out of St. Louis late on the morning of June 13.[5] The *Iatan* left St. Louis first, carrying the second battalion left wing of Blair's First Regiment under Lieutenant Colonel George L. Andrews, a section of Totten's Light Artillery, and two companies of U.S. Regulars. The *Iatan* paddled up the Mississippi River, turned into the mouth of the Missouri around noon, and started up the Big Muddy toward the state capital.

The *J.C. Swon* followed the *Iatan* transporting the right wing of Blair's First Regiment, another section of Totten's battery, and a detachment of pioneers. Onboard the *Swon* were General Lyon and his staff. They started upriver around two o'clock amid wild cheering and enthusiasm of the soldiers.[6]

The first phase of the movement numbered about 1,500 men.[7] They carried with them horses, wagons, and the necessary equipage of ammunition and provisions for a long march.[8] Meanwhile, Börnstein's Second Regiment U.S. Missouri Volunteers prepared to follow the lead force by boat as a reserve.

The *J.C. Swon* got off to an inauspicious start when it passed the mouth of the Missouri River shortly after four o'clock and had trouble finding the channel. It righted its course and around seven o'clock, the *Swon* passed the *Iatan* lying at anchor and waiting. Making up time, the big boat flew along, "with her furnaces crammed full, the smoke roaring out of her funnels, and the steam hissing and snapping from her escape pipes."[9] The *Swon* took the lead and by 8:30 p.m., the party was just above St. Charles. Around 11 o'clock, the *Swon* tied up at Murphy's landing to await the *Iatan*. The two ships tied up on the right bank, and Lyon decided to remain there until dawn the next day, having completed the first leg of his riverboat excursion.[10]

Meanwhile, the call went out from Jefferson City for volunteers for the new Missouri State Guard with disappointing results. Expecting a wave of indignant Missourians to answer the call, scarcely a thousand recruits rallied around Governor Jackson and General Price's banner. It became immediately clear that Jefferson City was indefensible against Lyon's army. Surprised by Lyon's unexpected river movement and that he was beginning his advance on Jefferson City by boat, the state government officials and the legislature prepared to evacuate the capital, fearing for their safety.[11]

11. Riverboats and Gunpowder

Governor Jackson wanted to make a stand against Lyon at Jefferson City, but General Price concluded that the capital was indefensible against a federal attack and soon persuaded the governor that there were not enough troops to hold it.[12] In an epic move never before witnessed in the United States, they decided to abandon the seat of state government to the Union army. Walter Barlow Stevens, *St. Louis Globe-Democrat* journalist and Civil War historian, wrote, "The entire official organization of a State still in the Union was preparing to evacuate the seat of government, not to escape a foreign enemy but the authority of the national government of which it was a part."[13] Jefferson Davis later said it amounted to the "subversion of the State government of Missouri by the Government of the United States."[14]

General Price ordered Brigadier General John B. Clark, commander of the MSG Third Division, to rendezvous his men at Boonville, 40 miles upriver from Jefferson City.[15] The State Guard would make a stand there.

General Clark was a study in contrasts when it came to Governor Jackson. They had been bitter political enemies going back to 1840, when Clark ran for governor of Missouri. The two became embroiled in a dispute that might have led to a duel,[16] but authorities arrested both of them before the duel could take place.[17] In the two decades since, the two had become friends and now found themselves with a common interest in defending the state. Clark had favored a non-secessionist neutral position at the state convention but after the Camp Jackson affair aligned himself firmly against the Union.[18]

Clark was a picturesque character, a large man

John Bullock Clark, Sr. A member of the U.S. House of Representatives from Missouri, General Clark commanded the Missouri State Guard Third Division. He went on to serve as both a senator and representative in the Congress of the Confederate States. Photograph by McClees' Gallery of Photographic Portraits, 1859. Library of Congress Prints and Photographs Division, Washington, D.C. (LC-2010649406).

with an unusually large head; he was a good storyteller who always attracted a crowd. As a boy, he lived with the Indians for a year as a hostage to guarantee a treaty with white settlers. He fought in the Black Hawk war and had a hand in expelling the Mormons from Missouri.[19] A consummate politician, his name once surfaced as a possible candidate for the presidency. An ardent country lawyer, he was known by opponents to shed tears in the courtroom to appeal to the emotions of a jury. In one typical case, he hired a man to ride all over the county to gather signed petitions asking the judge to free his client. The evidence against his client was strong and few signed the petitions. He asked those who did not sign the petition to sign a remonstrance. By the time the case came to court, every man in the county except one had already declared the man innocent or guilty by evidence of the signatures on one petition or another. The court could not find a jury to try the case.[20] Clark's detractors liked to characterize him as a slow thinker who never wore out many pairs of trousers upon the benches of a country school.[21]

Clark readied his small Third Division of the MSG to proceed to the defense of Boonville. General Price, meanwhile, instructed his other district commanders to assemble at some convenient place in their respective districts and hold their divisions ready for immediate service. Brigadier General Mosby Parsons, Sixth Division commander, directed his small force of 530 men to a place along the Pacific Railroad west of Jefferson City, in the event Lyon would try to advance by that route.[22]

Mosby Monroe Parsons. A state senator from Cole County, Missouri, General Parsons set aside political animosities with Missouri governor Claiborne Jackson to command the Missouri State Guard Sixth Division. Jackson summoned him to bring his troops to the defense of Boonville. Photograph, ca. 1860. Courtesy Wilson's Creek National Battlefield (WICR-32048).

Strongly in favor of secession from the start, Mosby Parsons was a zealous outspoken advocate of slavery and states' rights.[23] He supported Jackson's position on arming Missouri.[24] When Jackson made him brigadier general of the Sixth District, he showed up at camp in a neatly pressed new uniform, adorned with new State Guard buttons and all the necessary trimmings, one of the few officers of the State Guard who dressed like a military man.[25] He thrived on controversy. Like General Clark, he was a onetime political enemy of Governor Jackson. He had campaigned hard against Jackson in the 1860 election, writing about Jackson's decision to support Douglas and not the secessionist Breckinridge in the presidential race, Parsons said, "Our party, and its principles demands that we should discard him without hesitation."[26] Furthermore, he opposed Price as president of the state convention that had decided against secession. Now he put differences aside and placed his considerable reputation behind the governor's drive for secession. A sitting Missouri state senator, Parsons was the principal architect and writer of the Military Bill, the act that gave Jackson sweeping powers to prepare for war.[27]

General Price looked to make a stand at Boonville and not Jefferson City for good reason. The population of Jefferson City, like St. Louis, was largely Germans who were unfriendly if not positively hostile to the state government. It was a predominantly Union town of some 3,500 people, mostly loyal Union citizens.[28] The residents of Boonville, on the other hand, sympathized with Governor Jackson's stand against federal occupation.[29] Boonville, in the heart of Little Dixie, was the center of strong state sovereignty sentiment. Boonville also stood closer to the counties expected to respond more promptly to Jackson's call for troops.[30]

For months, as unrest mounted in Missouri, Governor Jackson had stockpiled a large cache of gunpowder. James Harding, the governor's quartermaster general, procured some 70 tons in St. Louis and from a variety of other sources across the country, including the Confederacy.[31]

The role of James Harding in the conflict not only spoke to his work as quartermaster, but also typified one of the many examples of families divided by the Civil War and the national turmoil that followed. He was the brother of Chester Harding, General Lyon's adjutant. The two brothers, divided in their allegiance, did not see each other for more than a decade. James Harding wrote, "When I left home for Boonville, I expected to be absent for a week or two, but I did not see Jefferson City again for ten years."[32]

Part of Jackson's supply of gunpowder, now securely in the hands of secessionists, was the powder that came from Camp Jackson, moved to Jefferson City under escort of Captains Joseph Kelly and Basil Duke on May 7, prior to the Union capture of the camp. Kelly and Duke had proceeded with two companies of Missouri Volunteer militia to the state capital to deposit the supplies. They had remained at the capital to act as a guard for Governor Jackson and the state government, should the need arise.

Jackson ordered kegs of powder distributed out of the capital and concealed across the state, conceivably out of the reach of the Federals. Over the intervening weeks, military stores brought up from St. Louis arrived at Jefferson City marked for destinations at various points in the state.[33] Jackson had anticipated that the differences between Missouri and the Union were irreconcilable and took steps to secret the powder for safety and future use.

Captain Kelly's men set about distributing it. A portion of it went upriver, shipped by steamboat as everyday cargo. Suspicions in the state were not yet sufficiently high to warrant close inspection of a package's contents. Shipping examiners who happened to be unionists allowed freight to pass if the shipment indicated nothing suspicious. For example, a large number of boxes marked as soap went upriver to Lexington. They turned out to be canisters of powder. Someone from St. Louis later sardonically remarked, "So much soap going into central Missouri was decidedly suspicious, as the people of the interior do not make extensive use of the article."

The conditions of trade in Missouri mirrored that of most of the country. This policy of relaxed trade

Joseph M. Kelly. A native of Ireland, Captain Kelly commanded the St. Louis Blues, a well-drilled unit of the Missouri State Guard that served as Governor Jackson's bodyguard. He was instrumental in hiding caches of gunpowder in strategic locations across Missouri. As colonel, he later commanded the First Missouri Infantry Regiment of the Sixth Division, C.S.A. Photograph 1862. Courtesy Maureen McGrath and Wilson's Creek National Battlefield. (WICR-12214).

11. Riverboats and Gunpowder

between warring factions went on all through the Civil War. Lincoln supported a policy of open commerce between North and South that prolonged a war that might have ended sooner had the North not continued to supply the South. Many a profiteer lined his pockets because of Lincoln's course of action.

In any event, supplies of powder ended up in Camden, Carroll, Cooper, Greene, Marion, Miller, and Phelps Counties, to name a few, and from those places went out to State Guard units. Wagons took it to many hiding places, often secreted there under guard of Captain Kelly and his detachment of State Guards.

When Kelly took charge of hiding the powder, it became widely known as Kelly's Powder. Some 6,000 kegs of it ended up concealed on different farms in Saline County, where it remained until gradually collected by MSG soldiers.[34] Saline County represented the heart of secessionist rebellion. Not only was it the home county of Governor Jackson and Colonel John Marmaduke, nine of ten citizens in Saline County were from Virginia, Kentucky, or Tennessee.[35] At the first sign of discord, the county had organized the Saline Jackson Guards.[36]

Several kegs of powder went to points up and down the Osage River by railroad in small lots to secessionist companies. Some 330 kegs wound up at Hannibal in Marion County. A company of volunteers led by Harry R. Mills picked up a large supply of it, carried it to Palmyra, and stored it in the local jail for safekeeping. From the jail under cover of night, it went out to all parts of the county. Rebel volunteers delivered a large supply to Linn Creek in Camden County. Secessionist men distributed it from there to MSG units throughout southwest Missouri. A large supply went by stagecoach to Greene County, where locals hid it in John Polk Campbell's barn outside Springfield, which was mostly pro–Union.[37] Federal troops later found the powder and confiscated most of it but not before a good amount found its way into the cartridge boxes and powder horns of the State Guard soldiers.[38]

Some counties did not wait for delivery of their supply of powder. Hiram Wilcoxson went to Jefferson City to obtain arms for his organization of secession militia units in Carroll County. He picked up a large quantity and loaded it on a steamer for the trip upriver. Volunteers unloaded the cargo at Hill's Landing, and from there sent it to various points around the county, storing it in hemp shacks and cellars until needed. Ex-state senator Mosby Parsons, the same Brigadier General Parsons now of the Sixth Division, hid 30 kegs of powder in his hog pen at Miami. He dug up a corner where the hogs usually slept, buried the powder, and covered it with straw and fodder.[39]

Every farmer had his own method of concealing a share, often using considerable stealth. Most secessionist followers owned slaves, and hiding the powder meant keeping it away from the curiosity of the slaves who kept a close watch on any suspicious movements of their masters and immediately reported the same to federal partisans. A great deal of the clandestine operation took place in the wee hours of the morning.

Wagons carried more powder to other places south of Jefferson City, some more than 100 miles distant. Governor Jackson wrote out a commission appointing Judge James H. McBride, of Texas County, brigadier general to command the Seventh Division of the Missouri State Guard and sent a delegation to deliver the commission, along with three large wagonloads of Kelly's Powder in the care of Edgar Asbury, a young MSG volunteer. The destination lay some 120 miles south of Jefferson City, a difficult journey, especially with a secret cargo of gunpowder.[40] The carriers hitched teams to large covered wagons, secreted the powder in salt barrels and tin cans, and started south. The kegs burst on the rough stony roads and streamed a trail of powder, leaking along the flint roadside, keeping the watchful teamsters fearful of an explosion. Going downhill, they avoided the hazard of striking sparks by keeping the wagon wheels unlocked, hurtling full speed down a slope. Union men moved everywhere around them. Two of the drivers and guards quit out of fear for their safety and returned to their homes, leaving one person to continue the hair-raising mission. The powder and Brigadier

James H. McBride. Circuit Judge McBride of Texas County, Missouri, dissolved court at Rolla, Missouri, amid partisan rancor when Union forces occupied the heavily secessionist town. He chose to follow the Confederate cause. Governor Jackson named him brigadier general in command of the Seventh District of the Missouri State Guard. Courtesy Missouri Historical Society St. Louis (N42580).

General McBride's commission arrived safely in Texas County without incident.[41]

The supplies of secreted powder proved handy many times. When companies of the MSG began to form, volunteers hauled it out and distributed it. The Federals uncovered some of it, but the major part went to supply the rebels. Union soldiers discovered the powder in only a few cases. Unionists found some piled up in the courthouse in Miller County, some of it in houses and barns, and some in caves around the region. Anyone found hiding a supply of powder on their property had to answer to Union authorities and could expect to end up a prisoner of the Union army.

Before deserting Jefferson City to Union occupation, workers loaded the last of the gunpowder on a boat and sent it out of the capital upriver for use at Boonville.

When Governor Jackson left the capital, he took with him the official great seal of the state of Missouri, packed the papers and currency of the Missouri state treasury, and hurriedly made his way northwest to Boonville,[42] convinced of the intent of the federal army at St. Louis to march on Jefferson City to take control of state government. Certain that Lyon and his Union troops would attack Jefferson City, Jackson and state government officials fled.[43] Many had already left the city with their families for safer ground north of the Missouri River.[44] When the House of Representatives voted to condemn Lyon for his actions at Camp Jackson, 44 members of the legislature were already conspicuously absent when the vote was taken, on their way out of Jefferson City.[45]

Meanwhile, on the same day that Lyon and federal forces steamed up the Missouri River and Governor Jackson abandoned the capital, Major Sturgis began moving federal troops east out of Kansas, and the southwest column left by rail from St. Louis for Springfield. Major Sturgis had about 2,000 Federals converging from the west. The southwest column fielded a force of approximately the same size.

Jackson and the other state officers went on board the steamboat *White Cloud* and went up the river to Boonville.[46] On board with Jackson were Lieutenant Governor Reynolds, ex-U.S. senator David Rice Atchison, and about 120 people of varying status.[47] Captain Kelly's company left Jefferson City by rail, burning the railroad bridge at Gray's Creek behind them.[48]

General Mosby Parsons took charge of the militiamen at Jefferson City and prepared to move them by land out of the capital to Tipton.[49] His orders from Governor Jackson were to retire along the Pacific Railroad west of Jefferson City, burning bridges and destroying telegraph lines behind them to delay the Federals if they attempted to advance by rail on the Pacific line.[50]

Parsons burned the Moreau Bridge, and General Price took care of the demolition of the telegraph lines. They took all the cars and locomotives available and operating in their flight. As fast as they crossed streams, they secured themselves from pursuit by burning the bridges.

As Lyon slowly made his way up the Missouri River and while Major Sturgis stood poised to bring more federal troops into Missouri at the Kansas border, the state government set a destination for Boonville. As the capital vacated, elements of the State Guard followed from the rear, destroying bridges in the wake of their exodus to slow Lyon's pursuit, intent on keeping Lyon off the ground but allowing him to freely move his forces by boat.

State officials tried to conceal their destination from the citizens of Jefferson City. However, it was certain that they were bound for Boonville, 40 miles upriver.[51] General Price deemed Boonville not only politically friendly but also more defensible from a military standpoint.[52] He hoped to buy enough time there to gather recruits and stall Lyon's advance until commanders of the State Guard divisions could organize around the state. As a last resort, they would retreat to southwest Missouri and seek Confederate aid from Arkansas.[53] Defense of the state had a better chance in that location.

Meanwhile, officials at Washington watched with knowing suspicion about the movement toward southwest Missouri. John Nicolay and John Hay wrote, "The spirit and impulse of revolution were at fever heat, and all the fire of the Border-Ruffian days smoldered along the frontier."[54]

When the governor and state officials left the state capital, it effectively ended the rule of state government in Missouri. The state treasurer, auditor, and land registrar later returned to their duties and took an oath as the only remnant of the duly elected state government.[55] When Jackson left Jefferson City, he never saw it again.[56] Missouri was a battleground state as the Civil War began. As the two sides contrived to claim a military advantage, the citizens of Missouri waited in anticipation of the carnage that was sure to follow. One observer wrote, "Then began those movements of troops within the borders of Missouri which continued almost incessantly during the entire period of the war, with the most disastrous results to the peace and prosperity of the State."[57] What started as state neutrality became a sort of unionism that caused Missouri to become a battlefield of untold miseries, trampled and ravaged by contending armies.[58]

12

Union Regiments Everywhere

As night came on, the Federals stopped at the landing above St. Charles. They spent the night there, ready to resume the next morning at first light. Getting an early start on June 14, the *J.C. Swon* in the lead, Lyon's troops arrived near Augusta. The Stars and Stripes greeted them from a cheering crowd of 50 to 60 citizens gathered on the wharf. They proceeded upriver past Washington, Missouri, and on the second night laid up a few miles below St. Aubert.[1]

General Lyon's efforts to put down rebellion in Missouri got some help on June 14, as U.S. troops from Illinois crossed into Missouri. The 16th Illinois Regiment seized the town of Utica in north central Missouri. They made prisoners of a few citizens and fugitives of many others, ripping down secession flags in the process. Further to the north, Ohio prepared to send national forces into Missouri, as other federal troops gathered on the Kansas border. What began as a measured response to protect federal property in St. Louis was fast turning into a full-scale federal takeover of the state.

On the evening of June 14, word reached General Lyon around half past nine o'clock that Governor Jackson and state officers were no longer in Jefferson City but had abandoned the capital for Boonville, taking with them several wagonloads of state paraphernalia.[2]

On the morning of June 15, General Lyon stopped about five miles below the town of Osage and went ashore to use the telegraph lines. A detachment of men went up by railroad to the Osage Bridge to check its condition. Governor Jackson's party had wrecked it, burning the western span and causing it to drop from the bank abutment into the water. Sliding down a plank from the draw to the wreck on the western span, the federal soldiers found a gang of railroad men already engaged in the work of repairing it.[3]

Ten miles below Jefferson City, Lyon transferred his U.S. Regulars from the *J.C. Swon* to the steamer *Iatan* with five companies of the left wing of Blair's regiment and Totten's artillery. Crowds of Union sympathizers began to gather on the levee as the boats approached the city.[4] An enthusiastic cheer from a large gathering of mostly Germans went up for the Union soldiers as they prepared to go ashore.[5]

The boats stopped on the south bank of the Missouri River, opposite the mouth of Cedar Creek, at a place just below the penitentiary where a large quantity of loose stone put there by the railroad company formed a makeshift landing.[6] A sandbar prevented them from using the regular levee. Deck hands pushed the gangplank of the *Iatan* against the bank, and around 2 o'clock in the afternoon Lyon stepped across, the first to go ashore with his company of U.S. Regulars.[7] Another hurrah from the locals greeted him as the Regular soldiers scampered up the steep bank and quickly occupied a high bluff commanding a view of the town near the railroad depot. Within minutes they formed a defense perimeter, ready

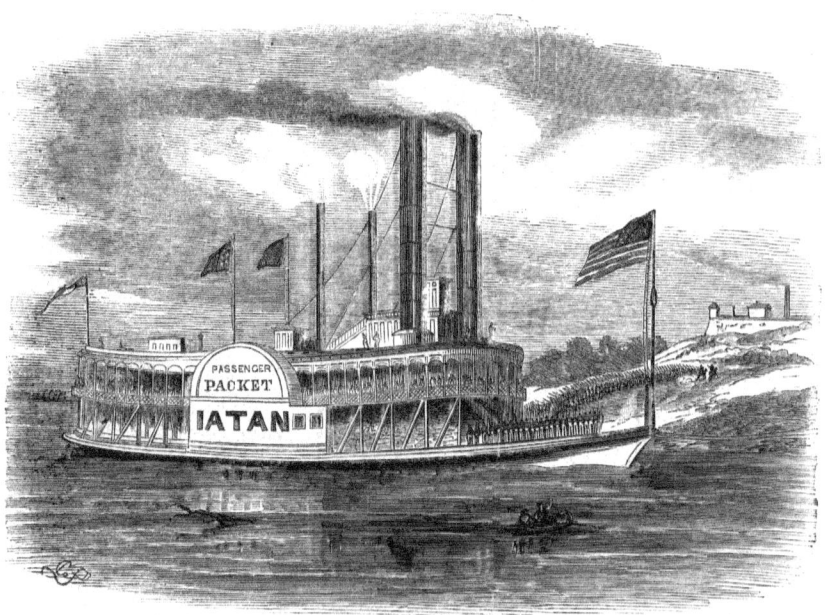

Landing of U.S. volunteers at Jefferson City. Union soldiers disembarked from the riverboat *Iatan* and entered the Missouri state capital at Jefferson City on June 15, 1861, without resistance. Federal troops took control of the capitol building and sent state officials fleeing up the Missouri River to the safety of Boonville. Sketch by Orlando C. Richardson, *Harper's Weekly*, Vol. 5, No. 236, page 420 (July 6, 1861). Courtesy Missouri Historical Society St. Louis (P0084-1255).

12. Union Regiments Everywhere

to repel an attack from MSG troops should it come. Next, the left wing of Blair's First Volunteer Regiment, 500 strong, disembarked.[8]

A band struck up the tune of "Yankee Doodle" as the Union troops marched conspicuously under the Stars and Stripes up the road fronting the penitentiary and on through the streets of Jefferson City to the State House amid more cheers at several points along the way.[9] The men stacked arms in front of the capitol and relaxed. It was a hot June day. One soldier wrote in his journal, "It is decidedly pleasant to sit here, in the shade of the cupola, where cool breezes fan the heated brow."[10] A party hoisted the national flag above the capitol, and the city band struck up a rendition of "The Star-Spangled Banner."[11]

After some delay in locating the keys to the capitol, the Federals entered the building around 3:30 on a Sunday afternoon. Lyon quietly took possession of Jefferson City.[12] The American flag was hoisted above the cupola, saluted by a hearty rendition of the national anthem and the enthusiastic applause of the onlookers. The seat of Missouri's government now belonged to the Union. The national troops had taken the place without firing a shot.[13]

The timeline stunned observers. Just two days after the state government abandoned the capital, Lyon took possession of it without opposition. Only three days after the meeting at the Planter's House hotel, Missouri's governor was in Boonville, and Jefferson City was in the possession of the Federals.[14]

Lyon ousted the entire state government. His occupation of Jefferson City expelled not only the duly elected governor of Missouri, but also the members of the Missouri General Assembly, the state supreme court, district judges, and state officers. Only two state officers remained at the capital by the time the Union troops entered. Lyon jailed one of them for refusing to take an oath to Abraham Lincoln.

Jefferson City, Missouri. Two riverboats steam up the Missouri River along the waterfront at Jefferson City. The state capitol building is visible in the background. Federal troops landed here and took control of the capitol building vacated by the state government. Sketch by Orlando C. Richardson, *Harper's Weekly*, Vol. 5, No. 236, page 420 (July 6, 1861). Courtesy Missouri Historical Society St. Louis (P0084-1257).

Lyon proclaimed his right to occupy the capital as a federal officer of the U.S. government. He read from General Harney's proclamation condemning Governor Jackson and the legislature. He said Jackson's actions had precipitated a conflict between the State and United States troops, a charge noticeably dismissive of the Union slaughter of Missourians at Camp Jackson.[15]

It was not long until Colonel Henry Börnstein's Second Regiment U.S. Missouri Volunteers caught up with Lyon's garrison at Jefferson City, reinforced it, and placed the city and capital peaceably and firmly in Union hands. The scene at the capitol was that of an invading army displacing a vanquished foe. One of Börnstein's men described the Union presence: "The soldiers were cooking upon the grass in the rear of the capitol, standing in the shade of its portico and rotunda, lying on beds of hay in its passages, and upon carpets in the legislative halls. They reposed in all its rooms, from the subterranean vaults to the little circular chamber in the dome."[16]

All signs pointed to a government abandoning the capital. One soldier wrote, "I went through the executive mansion, which had been deserted in hot haste. Sofas were overturned, carpets torn up and littered with letters and public documents. Tables, chairs, damask curtains, cigar-boxes, champagne bottles, inkstands, books, private letters, and family knick-knacks, were scattered everywhere in chaotic confusion."[17]

Heinrich Börnstein. Börnstein was the publisher of the influential German newspaper *Anzeiger des Westens* in St. Louis and an avid anti-slavery advocate. He led the Second Battalion of Union Volunteers at Camp Jackson and at Jefferson City. General Lyon put him in charge of the abandoned capital. Photograph by Jean Baptiste Feilner, Bremen, 1873. Courtesy Missouri Historical Society St. Louis (N11676).

12. Union Regiments Everywhere

Lyon took the presumptuous liberty of establishing Colonel Börnstein as acting provisional governor of the state of Missouri, with the intention to lay groundwork to form a unionist state government and replace the pro-South elected governor of the state, ousted and now on the run. The politically powerful Börnstein was the publisher of the German newspaper *Anzeiger des Westens* in St. Louis, and a strong vocal advocate of the Union presence in Missouri. The Federals now held undisputed control of St. Louis and Jefferson City, almost entirely through the work of the Germans.

Meanwhile, as Lyon and his men advanced into the state capital, another Union column, under the temporary command of Acting Brigadier General Thomas W. Sweeny, left St. Louis for southwest Missouri.[18] A Regular U.S. Army captain, whose rank as brigadier general of volunteers was questionable, Sweeny had been the first to nix Governor Jackson's plans to occupy the St. Louis Arsenal. The redoubtable one-armed Union loyalist had ridden beside General Lyon at Camp Jackson as second in command. Nevertheless, the expedition to southwest Missouri was the first independent campaign that Sweeny had directed. His column of federal troops represented the third arm of Lyon's three-pronged plan to capture Governor Jackson and take over the state.

The southwest column began boarding cars of the Pacific Railroad at St. Louis on the evening of June 11, the same day talks at the Planter's House hotel collapsed. Destined for Rolla, Missouri, the Federals aimed to occupy the terminus of the southwest branch of the railroad.[19] Lyon's plan was in motion even before anyone knew the full outcome of the Planter's House talks.[20]

The first of Sweeny's command to leave St. Louis was the First Battalion of the Third Missouri Regiment of Volunteers, commanded by Colonel Franz Hassendeubel. About 300 men broke camp late in the evening and marched to the 14th Street depot, where they boarded seven cars for the overnight trip to secure the Pacific Railroad leading to Rolla. Civilians in the surrounding German communities cheered the train despite the late hour as the first Union troops left for southwest Missouri. About 11:00 p.m., the train moved off quietly, its destination known to very few people in the city.[21]

Another battalion of the Third Regiment left the arsenal about 9 o'clock the following evening under the regimental commander colonel, soon to be General Franz Sigel. Brigadier general as of May 17 but ranked as colonel until August, he was ordered to commandeer the railroad from St. Louis to the Gasconade River. The remainder of the Third followed over the next two days. Major Henry Bischoff's battalion left St. Louis the next day, and Major Franz Backoff's battalion of artillery departed on June 13.[22]

Thomas W. Sweeny. As a U.S. Regular Army captain, Sweeny blocked an early attempt by Missouri secessionists to take over the St. Louis Arsenal. He commanded the Union incursion into southwest Missouri. His missing arm was the result of military action in the Mexican War. Photograph by Mathew Brady Studio, ca. 1861. National Portrait Gallery, Smithsonian Institution, Frederick Hill Meserve Collection (NPG.81.M3298.1).

The Fifth Missouri Regiment of Colonel Charles Salomon and Colonel B. Gratz Brown's Fourth Regiment Reserve Corps of Home Guards trailed the Third Regiment of the southwest column over the course of a few days.[23] Altogether, some 3,000 men made up the column ordered to intercept anyone retreating from Jefferson City and to prevent General McCulloch from joining the Missourians on the border.[24]

Lyon's decision to send Colonel Brown's Home Guard Reserves with the southwest column came as a surprise to Union supporters in St. Louis. Almost everyone generally supposed that the Home Guard Reserves would remain in the city and not go into the interior. Nevertheless, orders came to send Colonel Brown's regiment out on the Pacific Railroad to follow Colonel Sigel's forces into southwest Missouri. Brown's regiment would become instrumental in securing the route through Rolla to Springfield and would later add an important reserve to the Springfield garrison. Before long, three companies of Colonel John McNeil's Third Regiment Reserve Home Guards joined them. Lyon intended to use every man available in his fight to keep Missouri in the Union. The fight fast developed into a statewide campaign that sent St. Louis volunteers to all parts of the state.

B. Gratz Brown. A prominent member of the Missouri legislature and editor of the *Missouri Democrat*, he was instrumental in helping to organize Union forces in Missouri. He led the Fourth Regiment Reserve Corps of Home Guards into southwest Missouri. Missourians elected him governor of the state in 1870. B. Gratz Brown Papers. Courtesy Missouri Historical Society St. Louis (A0184).

Union volunteers came in two types: the U.S. Regiments of Missouri Volunteers and the Home Guard U.S. Reserve Corps. Lyon's brigade, now at Jefferson City, consisted mainly of the first type; that is, Blair's First Missouri Regiment of U.S.

Volunteers and Colonel Henry Börnstein's Second Missouri Regiment, along with companies of U.S. Regulars and a battery of artillery. The Fifth Regiment Home Guard Reserves under St. Louis brewmaster Colonel Charles G. Stifel joined Lyon's river campaign and later guarded important points upriver as far as Lexington. Meanwhile, the Third Regiment of Missouri Volunteers under Colonel Franz Sigel, Colonel Salomon's Fifth Regiment Volunteers, and Colonel Benjamin Gratz Brown's regiment of Home Guard Reserves made up the column sent to southwest Missouri. At the same time, a sizable force of U.S. Regulars and Kansas Volunteers occupied the western part of the state. Altogether, it was an army of more than 7,000 men in pursuit of Governor Jackson and the Missouri government. Lyon used Missouri Volunteer regiments for the heavy lifting but did not hesitate to employ the reserve corps wherever he considered it useful.

Not all troops were in pursuit of Jackson. Lyon stationed the Fourth Regiment Missouri Volunteers—Colonel Shuttner's Black Guards—at Bird's Point, the northern terminus of the Cotton Belt. Bird's Point had been the South's gateway to the North for many years.[25] Here the railroad met the river terminus for cotton distribution. Planters as far away as Texarkana, Texas, shipped their cotton bales there by rail, and from Bird's Point by steamer to markets in the Midwest.

Bird's Point sat in southeast Missouri on the west bank of the Mississippi River, a little above the mouth of the Ohio River, and directly across from Cairo, Illinois. One of the Missouri rail lines that served Bird's Point was the Cairo and Fulton Railroad. Lyon thought it important to keep this line open but to deny transport of war materials from the South through Bird's Point into Missouri, Arkansas, and Texas. Cairo and Bird's Point were keys to the lower Mississippi valley and an important strategic point in the West.[26]

He took additional steps to secure the state's other railroads. He detached a portion of the Fourth Missouri from Bird's Point to the western part of the state, there to assist a company of Hannibal Home Guards and a detachment of Illinois troops to guard the Hannibal and St. Joseph Railroad, St. Joseph being headquarters for Union forces in northwest Missouri and for troops coming out of Kansas. At the same time, several hundred mounted men under the Kansas Jayhawker Colonel James Montgomery, armed with Sharps rifles, reached Wyandotte, Kansas, from Lawrence to secure the Kansas side of the Missouri line in case Governor Jackson's forces might make a movement from Independence toward Kansas City.[27]

Lyon left the recently formed Sixth, Seventh, and Eighth Missouri Regiments of U.S. Volunteers stationed at Jefferson Barracks to keep an eye on the St. Louis Arsenal and any movement of Confederate troops to the south. The Sixth Regiment later oversaw protection of the Iron Mountain Railroad, one of the early trouble spots in the state. The Iron Mountain rails ran south from St. Louis and provided Missouri's only southward rail access to St. Louis.

Lyon made skillful use of the Home Guard Reserve Corps regiments. Some stayed at St. Louis; others he pressed into service across the state. The First Regiment Reserve Corps, almost entirely made up of Germans and commanded by Colonel Henry Olmstead, guarded Union property, garrisoned critical points around St. Louis, and eventually extended its guard duty as far upriver as Jefferson City. Olmstead's regiment had received the brunt of the abuse in the St. Louis massacre. Some said his men actually fired first into the crowd.

The Second Regiment Reserves, Colonel H. Hallman commanding, added to Olmstead's St. Louis defenses, as did most of Colonel John McNeil's Third Regiment Reserve Corps, not counting the three companies of McNeil's Third Regiment that joined the southwest Missouri campaign with the already mentioned Fourth Regiment Reserve Corps of the politically ambitious B. Gratz Brown. For Brown, southwest Missouri offered a chance to mix politics with military bravado.[28]

Colonel Brown, a St. Louis lawyer known as "Boozy Gratz" by his detractors, had an ample amount of political shrewdness, which he parlayed into a stint as U.S. senator and later governor of Missouri, ultimately to run as a candidate for vice president of the United States. He had been a delegate to the Republican National Convention that put Lincoln at the top of the ticket for president.

The Union success in Jefferson City and German pride in the expedition to southwest Missouri immediately boosted federal recruitment. More than 8,000 men answered the Union call for U.S. troops in St. Louis by the middle of June, filling eight U.S. Missouri Volunteer regiments, with a ninth in the process of organizing. In addition, there were the five regiments of three-month U.S. Home Guard Reserve Corps sworn into service in early May. The reserve regiments added another 5,000 men to the Union total, pushing the overall troop strength from St. Louis to more than 13,000 soldiers. The Ninth Regiment of U.S. Volunteers, in the process of forming, brought the total to nearly 14,000 men. The nine Missouri Volunteer regiments accounted for the number of regiments formed since Lincoln's proclamation in April, when he asked the state for four regiments.

The unanticipated resolve of the Confederacy to separate from the Union changed the Lincoln army. Shortly after the bombardment of Fort Sumter, William H. Seward, Lincoln's secretary of state, famously said, "It will all be over within ninety days."[29] Ulysses Grant held the same view as

Seward, that the war would not last more than three months.[30] However, it soon became evident that this was to be no short-term rebellion. When it became clear that the war would last beyond the initial ninety-day enlistment time, regiments began to reorganize as three-year volunteers or for the duration of the war.[31] Recruitment in St. Louis and elsewhere shifted to longer terms of service.

The Sixth Infantry Regiment U.S. Missouri Volunteers, under Colonel Peter E. Bland; the Seventh Regiment of Colonel John D. Stevenson, known as the Bates Guards; and the Eighth Regiment, commanded by Colonel Morgan L. Smith, were of the long-term kind. These Missouri units, and many more like them across the nation, left their home states to join other states in the major battles of the Civil War, some to fight and die in places far from their native soil. In one notable instance, the Missouri Eighth Infantry Regiment went on to great distinction in the larger war. This regiment took the name the Fighting Irish Zouaves, or American Zouaves of Missouri, organized in St. Louis by Morgan Smith and his brother, Captain Giles Alexander Smith. It was planned as the Fifth Missouri Regiment U.S. Volunteers, but Lyon moved so quickly to fill another German regiment as the Fifth that the Eighth Irish Regiment came later.

The Fighting Irish Zouaves had a reputation for colorful elaborate uniforms and fearless fighting ability. Such regiments were popular in other states, especially in the Smith brothers' native state of New York, where the Zouave tradition ran high. It was the first St. Louis regiment of either U.S. Volunteers or Home Guard Reserve Corps not overwhelmingly of German nationality. President Lincoln, who had first rejected such an idea of an Irish regiment from General Harney, personally ordered its formation to counter prejudice against the Irish, who many in St. Louis and across Missouri regarded as pro-secessionist. Many men who pledged loyalty to the Confederacy were Irish; few were German.

More than 600 Irish boatmen and deck hands answered Lincoln's call to form the Irish regiment and left their jobs on the St. Louis riverfront to fight for the Union. All through the months of June, July, and August, specially picked men from Illinois and other parts of Missouri joined the St. Louis recruits to form the Fighting Irish American Zouaves. The regiment went on to be a vital part of the campaigns of General Sherman and General Grant, gaining special mention in both generals' memoirs for the bravery and tenacious fighting skills of its soldiers. For gallantry during the Siege of Vicksburg, 11 soldiers of the Irish Missouri Eighth received the Congressional Medal of Honor in one day.

Notwithstanding the Fighting Irish, 80 percent of the Union regiments from St. Louis were German or of German parentage; about 8 percent were Irish, French, Bohemian, and other nationalities. Fewer than 12

12. Union Regiments Everywhere

percent were native-born Americans. As General Lyon deployed his army to different parts of the state in pursuit of Governor Jackson, it did not go unnoticed in the German ranks that although more than four-fifths of General Lyon's command were foreign-born citizens or their sons, not one of his seven staff officers was of foreign heritage. Many Germans were men of merit and military experience, but apparently not to the General's likes.

As springtime gave way to the summer of 1861, Lyon's army to capture Governor Jackson and his rebel force of Missouri State Guard troops fanned out from St. Louis to all parts of the state. Four regiments of Home Guards remained in St. Louis to help protect the city. St. Louis could spare another 5,000 men to Lyon's outstate campaign if necessary. Should these Missouri men be pressed into service elsewhere in the state outside St. Louis, 11,000 Illinois troops were within easy reach of Missouri at places along the Mississippi River; eight regiments of Illinois troops stood within two hours' distance, ready to come at a moment's notice. Union troops from Iowa were already on their way; 4,000 Union men stood ready at Keokuk, Iowa. The Union presence in and around Missouri was altogether a formidable force, lacking only leadership and mobilization. Nathaniel Lyon believed he possessed such leadership.

Many Missourians saw Governor Jackson's forlorn plan to keep Union troops out of Missouri as the failed policy of a naive politician. Lyon's rapid deployment of federal troops across the state had an immediate effect on Jackson's ability to recruit men to the Missouri State Guard.

13

The Southwest Missouri Column

Acting Brigadier General Sweeny—the "Irish Brigadier," his men liked to call him—took charge of the southwest Missouri arm of Lyon's army but did not immediately accompany Lyon's brigade to southwest Missouri. Instead, Sweeny had trouble from the outset gathering wagons, horses, mules, and rail cars for the brigade's departure to Rolla.[1] He remained in St. Louis several days to arrange to have the necessary supplies forwarded to his command. He had not anticipated the difficulty of piecing together an overland supply system across a vast expanse of largely unsettled country. He needed large numbers of horses and wagons, which proved difficult to come by in St. Louis where tensions still ran high. The job became even more difficult when Chief Army Quartermaster Justus McKinstry, irritated by Sweeny's unsanctioned acquisition techniques, kept reversing his orders and cancelling his contracts. McKinstry, always the archetypal administrator, revoked Sweeny's non-regulation arrangements, cancelled his wagons, discharged the drivers, and generally upset the planning of the entire southwest Missouri campaign. Sweeny knew McKinstry from their Mexican War days. He knew him also to be a West Point classmate of P.G.T. Beauregard, the Confederate general who had ordered the bombardment of Fort Sumter. McKinstry had been in the quartermaster job only a few months.[2]

Leaving Sweeny in St. Louis with his supply problems, it fell to Colonel Franz Sigel to take temporary field command of the southwest brigade. Sigel, a seasoned veteran of the German Revolution, carried the manner of an experienced military officer. He gained his military standing in Germany where he had built a reputation as a daring if unsuccessful infantry officer in the Baden Revolution of 1848–1849. Slightly built, he stood five feet seven inches tall, weighed 140 pounds, was clean-shaven, and had coal-black hair and piercing black eyes. His stiff posture betrayed the same firebrand tendencies as Nathaniel Lyon exhibited. As a young lieutenant in

13. The Southwest Missouri Column

Franz Sigel. A veteran of the 1848 German Revolution, he commanded the Third Regiment U.S. Missouri Volunteer Infantry, dispatched to southwest Missouri to block unification of the Missouri State Guard and Confederate forces in Arkansas. Photograph ca. 1861. Library of Congress Prints and Photographs Division, Washington, D.C., Gift of Mrs. Norman P. Mason (LC-2005683059).

the German army, Sigel had assailed the army in public writings with such acerbic rhetoric that he often found himself at odds with his fellow officers. His rebellion against the standing German army reached a low point when a duel resulted in the death of a rival.[3] Sigel resigned from the German army and entered the cause of the German Revolution, raising a volunteer corps of opposition soldiers. Royal troops defeated him in two battles before driving him out of Germany. He returned to fight in several more battles before superior numbers eventually forced him to conduct his army of 15,000 revolutionaries in a retreat through three hostile royal corps to escape into Switzerland.[4]

Driven from his homeland and into involuntary exile along with thousands of other German nationals, Sigel made his way to New York in 1852. He became a teacher and writer, eventually settling in St. Louis in the summer of 1857. A sensitive and intelligent scholar, he spoke five languages; was an accomplished pianist; was active in chess club, library club, and choir; and taught Sunday school. He gave fencing lessons at the Turner Society, the German educational organization devoted to physical fitness and gymnastics. His subsequent election as director of the St. Louis public school system and appointment to the committee on public safety affirmed his status as an educator and political activist popular among German immigrants. He had been in the city three years, serving as a teacher of mathematics and history at the German Institute, when events came to a head at the St. Louis Arsenal.[5]

Sigel took sides against rebellion this time as the secession crisis in the United States grew. His previous outspoken opposition to the royal standing army of Germany made him no stranger to political strife and civil war. Perhaps mellowed in his political outlook about revolution, the 37-year-old academic vigorously defended northern Union principles in newspaper articles. Seeing a threat to St. Louis and the future of Missouri in the Union, Sigel organized one of the first Wide-Awake Home Guard regiments of infantry and, more than any other person, influenced the Germans to take the side of the Union.[6] He joined Frank Blair and Nathaniel Lyon in defense of the arsenal and led his Third Regiment of Volunteers in the capture of Camp Jackson. Sigel's troops were among those who opened fire on St. Louis citizens, causing the riots that followed, and sustained most of the casualties including the death of Captain Constantin Blandowski, a Polish nobleman immigrant and the first Union officer to die in the rebellion.[7] In Brigadier General Sweeny's absence, the expedition to southwest Missouri was in Colonel Sigel's hands, as the troop train rolled south toward Rolla.

It was a day's ride by rail from St. Louis to Rolla. The troops that filled the rail cars presented a strange and motley group. Nearly all were fresh from civilian life. Those with uniforms wore them uneasily, as someone unaccustomed to dressing up might wear his Sunday suit.[8] A few carried sabers and awkwardly tried to adjust to walking with a three-foot long piece of steel dangling from the waist. One officer looked upon the soldiers with a mix of contempt mingled with admiration for their earnest outpouring of patriotism. With a punctuation of mild diatribe, he pronounced it a damned proud day.

Sigel and his Third Regiment of Missouri Volunteers headed into uncertain territory. Many of his soldiers had never been much beyond the outskirts of St. Louis. The entire unit was German. Many spoke no English, and Sigel issued instructions in German or English as the need arose. These volunteers to the Union cause had not anticipated that the cause extended beyond the politics of St. Louis. The men exchanged excited chatter over this new adventure, as the train rolled steadily toward its destination.

Reporters from the Eastern press rode with the Federals to send news of the expedition back to St. Louis and the Eastern papers. Their descriptions of outstate Missouri and the people they found living there were often generally derisive. They fabricated many a story to add color and entertainment to their dispatches, trying to interest their readers in events in a part of the state that no one knew much about and cared less.

Rolla was born of the railroad.[9] One writer told how the name Rolla came about before he even set foot in the place. When it came time for a committee to name the town, he said, it came down between Hardscrabble and Raleigh.[10] A North Carolinian who had settled in those parts suggested the name should honor the capital of his native state—Raleigh. The scribe of the committee reduced the request to writing and sent it to the Missouri legislature for approval.[11] Unfortunately, the scribe wrote out the name phonetically as best he could, and Raleigh became Rolla, although the inhabitants continued to pronounce its intended spelling. It made an amusing footnote to a news dispatch but hardly chronicled anything of much literary value.

Another story told of the first days of the railroad. The land between St. Louis and Rolla had few inhabitants, being generally unsuitable for agriculture. The natives refused to use the railroad for a time after it opened, declaring that the old way of travel by horseback was better. The rail company ran a daily freight train each way in the first week the road was open, but few patronized it. The only haul local residents could remember was a bear and a keg of honey. The mistake was made of placing the bear in the same car as the honey, and the company had to pay for the damage.[12]

The railroad had its own story to tell in the burgeoning conflict. The issue of westward expansion of the railroad contributed much to the tensions in Missouri between the various political factions. Business interests in cities like St. Louis and elsewhere saw rail commerce as a way to develop markets in the west. They wanted railroads everywhere. Slavery played a part in the debate about which companies should build the rails and where. It took large amounts of labor to construct a railroad. A new route through a slave state as opposed to a free state obviously stood to gain more profit.

During his term as governor, General Sterling Price divided his political priorities between the slavery question and the demands of the railroads, which under his predecessor had grown to an unsustainable extravagance because the state picked up a large part of the cost. Price vetoed numerous railroad bills and in the process further aggravated the Eastern industrial interests that were promoting them. However, Price did not always place good government above his own special interest. His home at Keytesville Station sat on the railroad that he was instrumental in bringing through the area. Railroad barons built the line mostly with slave labor, and largely at state expense.

It took a long time to get a railroad into southwest Missouri. Anyone traveling by train from St. Louis to Springfield after 1876 rode on the Frisco Line. However, for a long time before 1876, there was no railroad to Springfield at all. By 1861 construction efforts to build one had advanced as far as Rolla before sectional strife stopped it. Section men dropped their shovels and picked up muskets to join either North or South. Plans to link St. Louis to Springfield by rail wound up on hold.

The railroad to southwest Missouri had its beginning as far back as 1849, when the Missouri legislature authorized the Pacific Railroad, an ambitious idea to make St. Louis the "Gateway to the West." It was an idea spurred on by the recent rush to the gold fields of the Pacific West Coast and the perceived urgency of need for more rapid transportation to the West. "We will build a railroad from St. Louis to the western boundary of Missouri and thence to the Pacific Ocean," declared its builders.[13] The project had the ambitious name of the Southwest Branch of the Pacific Railroad, known otherwise as the St. Louis and San Francisco branch, locally called the Frisco.[14]

Several railroad lines in eastern Missouri began about the same time to fulfill this grand idea under the Pacific Railroad charter. The line that terminated at Tipton, Missouri, for example, linked up with the Overland Mail Stagecoach, which ran from Tipton to San Francisco. St. Louis and San Francisco were less than 25 days apart via this route, faster than the old Isthmus of Panama route by some 10 days.

The planned Southwest Branch of the railroad extended 120 miles from St. Louis to Rolla, where it linked up with the Butterfield Stage Line, another overland mail service. Grading of the roadbed was complete between Rolla and the Gasconade River at the outbreak of hostilities, but no rails went down for another five years. Rolla was the end of the line, the terminus of the railroad into southwest Missouri.

As the railroad pushed westward away from St. Louis, there came with it a certain urgency of need for more and better civil services along its route. Rolla sprang up with this in mind. People had begun settling along the streams and tributaries of the Gasconade and Meramec rivers in the rolling hills of the Missouri outlands as early as the 1820s. However, the town of Rolla and the area around it were relatively new to political geography. Phelps County was established only in late 1857. The Missouri legislature named Rolla the county seat in 1860, following a legal protest from a rival city that went all the way to the Missouri Supreme Court before the state legislature intervened. The first train did not pull into Rolla until December 22, 1860, and the first passenger train of cars on the afternoon of New Year's Day, 1861.[15] The town in its brief existence now stood poised in the summer of 1861 to become a major player in Nathaniel Lyon's drive into southwest Missouri.

The entire population of Phelps County gathered at Rolla at the first town council meeting in February 1861 to determine whether to join the Confederate secessionists. The people decided to remain neutral and await further developments. However, when the South made its intentions clear by firing on Fort Sumter in April 1861, some of the citizens of Rolla wasted no time in declaring their support for the rebellion. During a meeting of the circuit court at the courthouse on May 10, proceedings broke down after a heated debate over secession. The secessionists soon took charge of the town. A Confederate flag made by the women of Rolla flew outside the courthouse in place of the Stars and Stripes. Angry men marched on the newspaper office and forced its pro–Union editor to cease publishing. Rebel sympathizers patrolled the town around the clock. They ordered Union partisans to get out of town or face the consequences. Circuit Judge James McBride, whose court had dissolved amid partisan rancor, departed for Texas County to become Sterling Price's brigadier general of the Seventh District of the Missouri State Guard. By the end of May 1861, all of Rolla and most of Phelps County was strongly in favor of secession. Ironically, Phelps County took its name from John S. Phelps, a popular U.S. congressman and strong Union man living in Springfield.[16]

General Lyon was quick to recognize the strategic importance of Rolla. It represented a needed military supply point for federal troops operating in southwest Missouri and elsewhere, eventually along the Arkansas and Kansas borders. The first task of Colonel Sigel's southwest expedition was to secure Rolla as a Union outpost. The politics of the town did not matter much to the trainloads of German soldiers coming out of St. Louis.

There had not been a train for three days because, unbeknownst to anyone at Rolla, the trains had been busy transporting Union troops into the outskirts of Phelps County. Excited men filled the town. Rebels crowded into Graves and Faulkner's large commission house seeking news of the Lincoln army. A trio of Union men up from Greene County on their way to St. Louis hired a hack at the commission house to take them out of town up the road to St. James. About four miles out of town, they came on Sigel's troop train coming slowly up the Dillon grade. It carried the first of the St. Louis Germans on their way into Rolla. The travelers soon located Sigel and apprised him of the rebel situation. Sigel unloaded his troops and prepared to surround the town. They made a splendid sight with their gleaming muskets, moving in close order through the woods toward the town.

Some three to four hundred rebels had gathered around the commission house. A handful of braggarts boasted how the Rolla men could whip all the Dutch in St. Louis. One old fellow said he hoped the Germans did come so the men of Phelps County could teach them a lesson. He had no more than finished when someone rushed into the room and said, "Holy damn! The Dutch are here now upon us!" The old man and several others stepped out on the platform and sure enough, down the road about four hundred yards from town through a break in the woods, they saw Sigel's troops bearing down on them. Without a word, the whole crowd broke and ran, dissolving into the countryside. A witness described the scene. "There was a good deal of sensation created in Rolla on Friday last [June 14, 1861] by the unexpected appearance of glistening bayonets at various points commanding the town, and before the people were aware of it the town was filled with armed men. Our 'braves' very soon made themselves scarce.... Lieut. Trigg's head looked like a fiery meteor as it shot swiftly through the black-jacks. Those wonderful men who were ready to eat Dutchmen without salt couldn't' be found. No person had any idea of the movement. The flag of the Confederate States, which had been swinging to the breeze since the great secession camp-meeting here some weeks since, was summarily taken down by a small detachment of German volunteers from Col. F. Sigel's regiment, and the glorious stars and stripes now float where the Confederate flag had waved."[17]

The Germans quickly swept aside the secessionists congregated at Rolla, taking several prisoners in a swift descent on the town. Sigel's men handily dissuaded the disorganized secessionist protagonists from resisting. The German troops pitched their tents on the James' Addition, which appears to have been a municipal tract of land near the courthouse.[18] From

13. The Southwest Missouri Column

June 14, 1861, Rolla was under federal control. It was the same day Lyon and his men took control of Jefferson City.[19]

The first troop train from St. Louis pulled into Rolla about midday. Its driving wheels were five feet in diameter; the 15-ton diamond-stack locomotive wore #3. The name "Pacific" arched along its side. The train could go no further. From here, goods went by wagon train and horseback along roads and trails to Springfield, and all other destinations south and west.

Used to the busy life of St. Louis, the Germans found most of the natives to be easygoing and not overly excited about their presence. They looked on Rolla as a town of barefooted backwoodsmen living in hillbilly shacks. However, the new two-story stone courthouse did impress them, although some wondered who might have built it.[20]

For the time being, the lone Union presence at Rolla consisted of Colonel Sigel and his Third Regiment of Volunteers, a regiment unaccustomed to the rigors of field duty. It had garrisoned briefly at the St. Louis Arsenal after an inauspicious presence at Camp Jackson. It had moved out to Rock Springs on the western suburbs of St. Louis, and then headed by rail for Rolla.[21]

The Third Missouri was a poorly provisioned regiment. The men had no blankets, no military issue knapsacks, and barely any camp equipment. Each company was fitted with half a dozen kettles, mess pans, and a few Sibley tents. Field gear for a soldier consisted of a bare tin canteen and a homemade white sheeting haversack. Uniforms, if they had them, were old and held at the waist by rotten white belts condemned since the Mexican War. The uniform consisted of a gray flannel blouse, gray trousers, and a gray woolen hat. The colors of the opposing ideologies had not yet gained their legendary blue and gray status because the Union wore gray, a color soon to be the fabled gray of the rebel cause. Soldiers regularly performed duty with rations of hard bread, coffee, sugar, and salt. Troops relied heavily on the surrounding countryside for food. Subsistence in addition to the meager army mess came from the local population, seized preferably from rebel citizens identified as disloyal to the Union.

Sigel established his camp at Rolla, named it Camp Lyon, and there awaited the rest of his brigade.[22] The Fifth Missouri Volunteers left the arsenal late on the evening of June 15 and proceeded by train to Rolla.[23] Major Charles Eberhardt Salomon commanded the Fifth Missouri.[24] He was the brother of Lieutenant Governor Edward Salomon of Wisconsin, both refugees of the German Revolution.

The Salomon brothers came to the United States in 1849 among the many political exiles of the German uprising. Charles was an officer in the Prussian army and received a sentence of two years in prison for his part in the 1848 rebellion, but escaped capture when authorities mistook his brother Frederich for him. Both managed to evade authorities and together emigrated to America. Four brothers of the family eventually settled in Manitowoc, Wisconsin.

Charles had studied surveying in Germany and held jobs there in railroad and other engineering work before coming to the United States. He moved to St. Louis and took a job in the city engineer's office. He won election as county surveyor for St. Louis County, outpolling Ulysses S. Grant in the contest for the popular vote.

Salomon was among the first to respond to President Lincoln's call for volunteers after the bombardment of Fort Sumter and helped organize the Fifth Missouri Volunteer infantry. His men elected him colonel. Now age 49, he kept a close eye on his younger brother Frederich, who commanded Company C of his regiment.

The Fifth Missouri fared no better than the Third when it came to field duty. The Fifth had initially

Charles Eberhardt Salomon. Major Salomon—later Colonel Solomon—accompanied Colonel Franz Sigel to southwest Missouri in command of the Fifth Regiment of U.S. Missouri Volunteers. In 1862, he took command of the Ninth Wisconsin Infantry volunteers from his home state, and served in that position as a Union officer for the duration of the war. Courtesy Kent Salomon.

backed up the original four regiments enlisted in response to President Lincoln's call for volunteers and had participated in the Camp Jackson raid. The regiment comprised about 65 percent German, with the balance American, Bohemian, and Irish. It became part of Sigel's Second Brigade when President Lincoln increased the Missouri troop authorization from four regiments to 10,000 men.

Shortly after Sigel and Salomon's infantry settled at Rolla, the remainder of the Brigade arrived. Captain Christian Essig's battery of four 12-pound howitzers joined them, along with Captain Theodore Wilkins's battery of two 12-pounders and a couple of 6-pound field pieces. Captain

John Diederich Voerster's company of pioneers rounded out Sigel's brigade, now made up mainly of two regiments of poorly equipped volunteers armed altogether with about 2,000 obsolete muskets and eight untried artillery pieces.[25] This was the contingent of General Nathanial Lyon's army whose mission it was to block the escape of Governor Jackson, roust General Price out of southwest Missouri if need be, and in so doing preserve Missouri for the Union.

More federal soldiers soon arrived at Rolla close behind Sigel and Major Salomon. These were the troops of Colonel B. Gratz Brown's Fourth Regiment Reserve Corps of 825 men and officers in 10 companies. The regiment rolled into Rolla about midnight to find "neither provisions, water, tents, cartridge boxes, nor any other material." Brown immediately sent word to Sweeny in St. Louis, urging him to send supplies.[26] Brown's men had the responsibility to stay at Rolla and keep the road to St. Louis open until reinforcements arrived, and to establish a military depot at that point. President Lincoln soon issued a personal order to hold Rolla at all costs. The 13th Illinois Infantry Regiment from the president's home state followed Colonel Sigel's brigade in due time to guard Rolla and the railroad terminal.

The entire area from town to countryside overnight became a military post. The Union built Fort Wyman with its powder magazine of stone-block walls five feet thick.[27] At one time during the war, more than 20,000 Union soldiers garrisoned at the fort. It was the principal staging and evacuation point for troops engaged in the southern and western parts of Missouri and in northern Arkansas. The Phelps County courthouse that once hosted the bold secessionist sentiments of Judge McBride became a Union hospital. Rolla's Southern sympathizers fled to the countryside, where they formed small guerrilla bands with other southwest Missourians to harass the Union supply line from Rolla to Springfield and beyond. The Phelps County jail became a guardhouse for recalcitrant citizens who refused to retract ugly statements made against Union men.[28]

Phelps County split three ways in the war. Most entered the Confederate service. Some entered the federal army. Many did not enter either army but engaged in bushwhacking.[29]

As soon as Major Salomon's regiment arrived in Rolla on June 16, Sigel left for Springfield. Leaving Rolla well garrisoned, he outfitted a train of wagons and struck out with his Third Regiment, accompanied by a half dozen pieces of artillery marching southwest toward Springfield, a distance of 100 miles. The trip would take about a week because beyond Rolla, transportation was by foot and horse. Sigel ordered Major Salomon to follow him with the Fifth as soon as possible.

Civil War wagons. Federal troops rode by rail from St. Louis to the railroad terminus at Rolla, Missouri, where they loaded military supplies into wagons for the 120-mile overland trip to Springfield. Steady rains slowed the heavy wagons and added to the misery of the reluctant German foot soldiers. Civil War Photographs, 1861–1865, Library of Congress Prints and Photographs Division, Washington, D.C. (LC-2018666197).

Sigel sat astride a huge black stallion, looking more the part of a German schoolmaster than a dashing soldier does. On horseback, he appeared diminutive and always had a fixed death-like expression that West Pointers referred to as "a block of ice," not the look of a daring soldier. Nevertheless, his stiff, nervous, and unyielding personality—terse and overbearing in character, consumed with energy and ambition—subverted an unflinching courage and willingness to fight to the death; "a fool in action," as one observer put it.[30]

14

Blunder at Boonville

Before Governor Claiborne Jackson fled Jefferson City for Boonville and abandoned the capital to the Federals, he took steps to organize his Missouri forces. His brigadier generals were already in the field beginning to assemble and train the anticipated force of 50,000 men that they would lead against the Union army. Brigadier General John B. Clark, Sr., had already been busy assembling his division in the counties of the Third District north of the Missouri River. At the same time, State Guard troops under Brigadier General James S. Rains in the western Missouri Eighth District were converging on Lexington to resist Union Major Sturgis's anticipated move out of Independence. The generals had instructions to form their several brigades as quickly as possible and bring them to Boonville and Lexington. Jackson had a seasoned field commander to lead them in the person of Major General Sterling Price.

The governor planned to flee upriver to Boonville, and there to rest a little before retreating further on to join the others at Lexington.[1] He hoped by then to have a force of sufficient size to turn Sturgis back and meet the advancing Federals of General Lyon.

Governor Jackson and his entourage of state officers arrived by boat at Boonville on June 12, as Lyon's Union troops moved to occupy the abandoned state capital behind them. General Price and the Jefferson City troops arrived at Boonville by land soon thereafter.

General Price knew he had but a short time to organize resistance to Lyon. He immediately sent for Colonel John Sappington Marmaduke from nearby Saline County to assist in organizing a force at Boonville.[2] Marmaduke had suspended his military activity during the Price-Harney talks and returned to his home in Arrow Rock. Price then ordered Brigadier General Mosby Parsons and his MSG Sixth Division to take up a position near Tipton along the Pacific Railroad, 20 miles south of Boonville.[3] Meanwhile, Brigadier General Rains's Guard units were coming together at Lexington. If Lyon marched on Boonville, the State Guard could retreat to the safety of either Tipton or Lexington.

Price had doubts about trying to defend Boonville against what he believed to be Lyon's superior force. Nevertheless, he began to put together an army as rapidly as possible. Four or five hundred loyal MSG volunteers were already at Boonville when Governor Jackson arrived, and as many more came by the time General Price got there. A somewhat lesser number of troops made up Price's contingent of the Guard from Jefferson City. Together, these would serve as an escort to protect Jackson and the state government from what the governor and many other fellow Missourians saw as foreign troops recklessly invading the state by the thousands. Messengers went out to nearby towns to urge state guards to meet at Boonville and to bring arms and ammunition.[4]

Brigadier General Clark, coming down from the Third District with his division of about 700 men, reached Boonville shortly after Price did to help organize the volunteers pouring into the town.[5] They set up a camp outside the city about four and a half miles east of Boonville, named it Camp Vest (or Camp Bacon, as the citizens preferred to call it, from the name of a gentleman owning a house nearby), and there awaited additional recruits.[6] Many of the volunteers wandering into Boonville had heard of the government massacre in St. Louis and did not wait for organization in their home districts, instead heading straight for Boonville to help rescue the governor.

Fifteen hundred men assembled at Camp Bacon by Saturday, June 15, but fully half of them were without arms.[7] One private in General Clark's division remembered his company had about eight guns, mostly common rifles and double-barreled shot guns. There were no arms to distribute at Boonville.[8] When the federal raid on Camp Jackson confiscated all the arms at the camp, Governor Jackson and his secessionist followers had only what few arms remained stored in the basement of the state capital. The capitol arsenal comprised two six-pounders mounted, 310 rifled muskets, 553 flintlocks, 224 rifles, 40 sabers, and 58 swords. Brigadier General Parsons fielded four bronze six-pounders, pistols, muskets, and sabers captured from the Liberty Arsenal; altogether, hardly the firepower needed to defend against Lyon and his army.[9] When State Guard volunteers first showed up at Jefferson City, the quartermaster had invited them to go down to the capitol basement and select whatever weapon they could find there. Stored alongside the muskets was a carload of artillery manuals. Apparently, the new soldiers thought the best way to prepare themselves for war was to arm themselves with a musket and a copy of light artillery tactics because they helped themselves to each. Any kind of realistic military training had little chance of success in the hurried assembly of new recruits. The quartermaster said, "The order to 'charge bayonets' lost its formidable looking potential when carried out by a platoon armed with squirrel rifles."[10] Watching a company of shotgun-wielding privates stack arms was equally uninspiring. It was a situation where events compelled the formalities of military art to yield to the force of circumstance.[11] The state stood on the brink of war essentially unarmed and defenseless.[12]

About the time the MSG was assembling at Boonville, word reached them of the death of Colonel Edmund B. Holloway, the popular and accomplished West Point officer who had recently resigned his commission to lead a Missouri force in Jackson County.[13] Messengers told how Holloway had fallen at the crossing of the Little Blue River, along with several of his men, accidentally shot by his own soldiers while engaging Union troops from Fort Leavenworth. A report said there was fighting between state troops and federal cavalry near Independence. Intelligence said Kansas regiments and Major Sturgis's dragoons were advancing from the west.[14]

The deeply felt loss of Holloway and the exaggerated details of the skirmish alarmed General Price to the point that he determined to leave Boonville and go to Lexington.[15] He would take command of the troops there, now rapidly coming together from various places north and south of the Missouri River. Lexington was a rich territory of strong pro–South people and a logical place to assemble the Missouri State Guard. Price intended that if a stand against Lyon should occur, it should be at Lexington and not at Boonville.[16]

No sooner did General Price arrive at Boonville and set things in motion than he became violently ill.[17] He had a chronic health condition that aggravated him his entire life. At the outset of the Mexican War, he had contracted cholera on the march to Mexico and suffered from intestinal disorders the rest of his days. One of his most serious bouts with the disease came at this inopportune moment at Boonville, when his military leadership was crucial. He came down with severe dysentery and left Boonville on the steamer *White Cloud* the following day for his home upriver at Keytesville, in Chariton County, hopefully to recover enough later to join the MSG forces further on at Lexington 130, miles above Boonville.[18]

When Price became ill and left Boonville, he placed Brigadier General Clark in command with orders to fight a delaying action, and then retreat toward Tipton or Lexington if necessary.[19] Clark collected several hundred men at Boonville and welcomed Colonel Marmaduke and his regiment back from furlough.[20] Marmaduke possessed somewhat better military credentials than the politician Clark did.

With General Price out of the picture, Governor Jackson brushed Clark aside, and as commander in chief of the MSG assumed the defense of Boonville, placing himself directly in charge of military strategy.[21] Jackson formed a loosely styled joint command with Colonel Marmaduke, who happened to be his nephew and the beneficiary of his uncle's recent commission as a colonel.[22] Together, they presented an unlikely military duo. Jackson had no military training at all, and Marmaduke—a student of Yale and Harvard—while a recent West Point graduate, was not a stellar student and had very limited military experience. The credentials of the 28-year-old officer lacked much in the way of a recommendation except for a stint in the Mormon War. His politics were conflicted, too. The son of a former Missouri governor, he broke allegiance with his father, who favored the Union. The young Marmaduke resigned his U.S. Army commission and joined the MSG against his father's wishes.[23] Two of his brothers followed him into the Confederacy. Their unionist father died before the war ended and did not live to see his son serve Missouri as governor 20 years later. Colonel Marmaduke's destiny, however, was in the future; the task at Boonville now was to stop General Lyon and deny the U.S. government a takeover of the state.[24]

General Lyon hardly stopped in Jefferson City. Bent on capturing or killing Jackson and eliminating secessionist rebellion from the state, he allowed no time for his troops to celebrate the capture of the state capital.[25] At

John S. Marmaduke. He strongly advised against a defense of Boonville. He relented under pressure from Governor Jackson to lead a small band of Missourians into battle. He left the Missouri State Guard to accept a commission as brigadier general in the Confederate Army. Photograph, ca. 1862. Library of Congress Prints and Photographs Division, Washington, D.C. (LC-2018668909).

noon the next day, Sunday June 16, just as the first troop train of the southwest column pulled into Rolla, the zealous Lyon loaded his men back on steamboats and set out in pursuit of the rebel governor at Boonville, 48 miles upstream from Jefferson City.[26] With characteristic promptness, at two o'clock he started upriver on the steamers *A. McDowell*, *Iatan*, and *City of Louisiana*.[27]

Lyon's river command amounted now to about 1,700 infantry and artillery, including Colonel Frank Blair's First Missouri Regiment, Captain Totten's Artillery Battery, and two rifle companies of the Second Missouri Regiment.[28] Three companies of the Second Missouri and a detachment of the Fifth Regiment Reserve Corps stayed behind to secure the state capital with Colonel Henry Börnstein in charge of the city.[29] Before Lyon left Jefferson City, he sent out a call for Union columns out of Iowa and Kansas to converge toward Boonville.[30]

Meanwhile, Börnstein issued a proclamation defending his purpose at the state capital. "The precipitous abandonment of Jeff City," he said, "would have produced lawlessness and anarchy and all their consequent evils." He assured slave owners, "Slave property will not be interfered with by any part of my command, nor will slaves be allowed to enter my lines without written authority from their masters."[31] The mention of slaveholders was a diplomatic sojourn. Missouri was a slave state, although increasingly so in name only. As it became apparent that federal troops intended to occupy Missouri, people began sending their slaves south in the hope of saving them from the hands of Northerners.[32] The traffic in human beings suddenly ceased and slave pens closed.[33] Owning property in slaves grew precarious. Slaves abandoned their masters in large numbers, exiting Missouri for the freedom found in the North. One abolitionist publication wrote, "Slaves are running away from Missouri at the present time in battalions.... It would be a glorious thing for Missouri, if all her slaves should take it into their heads to run away."[34] Many slaves whose owners thought they would never leave crossed into Illinois and Ohio. The Fugitive Slave Law, having suddenly become irrelevant, was no longer a way to catch them. Slaves had a clear idea of the meaning of the looming war. Their bondage was the real cause of the dispute. Moreover, they believed the end of slavery was in sight and they would soon be free.[35] When it came to a choice between slavery and the preservation of the nation, the Constitution was not inviolate.

As Lyon and his troops began to head upriver, eager to catch the Missourians, Union spies reported that Governor Jackson intended to defend Boonville with a force of anywhere from 2,000 to 4,000 state troops, a number that turned out to be greatly exaggerated by the unionist swanker.[36] As the boats went upriver, the soldiers crowded the decks and boisterously talked about the coming campaign, naively looking forward to an early opportunity to win glory in battle. Lyon sat in the cabin aboard his flagship, calm, quiet, and thoughtful, occasionally venturing out to station himself on the bow of the boat.[37] No one approached him except Colonel Blair. The two men had much to talk about and conversed long and freely. Lyon had shelved his old captain's coat and general's dress uniform. He wore a long, light gray linen duster and on his head was a coarsely woven wide-brimmed straw hat.[38]

As Lyon eased up the river, officials in Washington were busy plotting his future. Ever since Lyon had superseded General Harney in command of the Department of the West at the end of May, Union leaders in Missouri and Washington continued to oppose his aggressive policy and objected to his ongoing command of the Department of the West.[39] Moreover, the War Department wanted a Regular general officer to head the department. This prejudice against Lyon as a breveted brigadier general added to the prevention of his appointment to assume permanent command of the department. The conservative elements in Lincoln's cabinet and General Scott contrived to hold Lyon in check by reorganizing the Department of the West to remove Missouri from the department and add it to the Department of the Ohio. Consequently, command of Missouri passed from Brigadier General Lyon to Major General George B. McClellan, commander of the Department of the Ohio. Secretary Montgomery Blair, greatly displeased by the change, tried along with Secretary of the Treasury Salmon Chase to get Lincoln to revoke this order, but the order stood.[40] Colonel Frank Blair likely knew the change was imminent. It is unknown if Lyon was aware of the change at the time. In any event, it did not alter his plans to pursue Governor Jackson.

McClellan was at that time a rising star in the military. In mid–May, he had gone from the rank of captain to major general of the Regular Army and accepted command of the Department of the Ohio, with headquarters at Cincinnati.[41] The department included the bellwether northern states of Ohio, Indiana, Illinois, Western Virginia, and, since June 6, Missouri.[42] At the same time, Washington removed headquarters of the Department of the West from St. Louis to Fort Leavenworth, Kansas.

Because of an unexplained hiatus in communication, McClellan did not receive immediate notice of his command of Missouri.[43] He was at the time occupied in Western Virginia. He did not even know the location of Missouri counties and confessed that he had no county map of the state.[44] Embarrassed in the matter, he objected to having Missouri in his command.[45]

Lyon and McClellan had an on-again, off-again relationship. Before his ascent to command of the Department of the Ohio, McClellan had offered to send Ohio troops to aid Lyon in Missouri on June 13. He was then in charge of the Ohio militia. However, coincidental with the unfolding of events at Boonville, he revoked the order and informed Union Adjutant Chester Harding that no troops would be forthcoming.[46] However, he committed to trying to keep in touch with Lyon by telegraph.

Union progress up the Missouri River was tedious. The rugged, turbid stream was usually a quarter to half a mile wide in the spring and early summer; this year, the water was low and the troops frequently had to disembark in order to allow the boats to go over the shoals.[47] Along the way, careful to remove any secessionist activity, a boat would pause at a riverboat landing. Soldiers went ashore to arrest any anti–Union men that might be in the vicinity. Occasionally, a small squad of cavalry went into the countryside to pick up pro–South men and return with them as prisoners.[48] About 15 miles out of Jefferson City, they passed the little town of Marion. The inhabitants turned out to express their loyalty to the cause with hearty cheering of the expedition.[49]

The troop boats pushed ahead, with engines chugging, paddle wheels slap-slapping, water rushing past the bows of the boats as they plied through cotton fields on both sides of the river.[50]

At Boonville on Sunday morning, even before Lyon left Jefferson City, a report came in from the MSG picket guards that seven boats were coming up the river, loaded with federal troops. Rumors quickly circulated of Lyon's mounting force advancing to attack Boonville. An alarm went out that he was descending on Boonville with perhaps as many as 7,000 men. This turned out to be a rumor without fact. Nevertheless, thinking that the actual strength of the Federals was nearly ten times his own force of armed and ready men, Colonel Marmaduke saw that he could not hope to defend his ground at Boonville. He strongly advised Governor Jackson to take General Price's advice and not attempt any engagement with Lyon should the Federals choose to march on the city. Jackson's other officers agreed and wanted to withdraw all the way to Warsaw on the Osage River, there to take advantage of better defensive terrain, they said, and to pull Lyon away from his supply line on the Missouri River.

At first, the governor agreed and gave his assurance not to risk a battle.[51] He sent orders to stand down the MSG forces and reassemble at Lexington. They could not hope to defend themselves against such an army as Lyon appeared to have. The MSG recruits, however, disagreed and expressed considerable displeasure with the governor's order.[52] They were determined to have a fight. The more passionate among them thought it nothing less than a fight for their homes and loved ones. The time had come to send a message to the U.S. government and show local Southern sympathizers that Missouri intended to make a stand. Many volunteers were local men. Pride stood in their way of returning home without trying at least to resist the Federals.[53] "This is as much a fight about honor as politics," one grizzled private loudly remarked, jabbing his finger in the air to punctuate his patriotic words.

The local citizens of Boonville fanned the flames of rebellion. That Sunday afternoon, the Rev. Frank Mitchell took it upon himself to circulate among the troops at Camp Bacon, passionately egging them on to fight, pressing them to do their duty, and admonishing them about the consequences if they did not. The justice of their cause, he intoned, meant God was on their side.

When the reports about the seven steamboats turned out to be untrue, it was not long until hot-blooded secessionists spoiling for trouble persuaded Jackson to revoke his order to disband. Local politicians convinced him that it would be a serious blow to the pro–South cause if yet another Missouri city fell to the federal troops. Without further consultation with General Clark or Colonel Marmaduke, the governor declared his intention to fight.[54]

Colonel Marmaduke argued strongly against a battle.[55] He protested that an engagement with Lyon would be ruinous and risk complete overthrow of state government.[56] He knew that the Boonville force was no match for Lyon's army and counseled Jackson that a defeat of state troops at this early date in the conflict would greatly discourage the secessionist movement across the state and impede further recruitment to the poorly organized State Guard.

The governor insisted on a fight at Boonville anyway. In his capacity as commander in chief, Jackson ordered his subordinate to offer Lyon battle and check the federal advance until Brigadier General Parsons could come up from Tipton with reinforcements.[57] Governor Jackson was a political leader and a true son of the South. A symbol of the old established order, earnest and experienced at 55 years of age, he was a policy maker but not a soldier.[58]

Nevertheless, at the urging of local citizens and the awaiting young recruits eager for action, Colonel Marmaduke reluctantly consented to the governor's order. Marmaduke took charge and began preparing for a fight as General Lyon's government troops bore down on the town.

Colonel Marmaduke still held his initial impression in the back of his mind that his small band of untrained men would be no match for Lyon's army of well-trained and well-drilled troops.[59] The largest number of defending Missourians he could put in the field was less than 800, armed with ordinary hunting rifles and shotguns. They had scant ammunition and no functioning artillery. They had a couple of pieces of six-pounder artillery but no ammunition for the guns, against Lyon's artillery and better small arms. The untrained and untried recruits had no appreciation of the peril they faced.[60] Still, the Union force that threatened them was relatively small. A well-prepared defense might be successful. The bluffs and hilly terrain around Boonville gave the Missourians a good defensive advantage.

Marmaduke marched out of Camp Bacon with about 500 men "full of fight" and advanced downriver to meet Lyon.[61] Captain Kelly's Infantry stayed back to protect the governor, while several hundred unarmed recruits remained in camp with nothing to do.[62]

Not far away, in Pettis County, near Syracuse five miles west of Tipton, Brigadier General Parsons had the beginnings of another regiment of the MSG and four pieces of artillery.[63] When General Lyon departed from Jefferson City for Boonville, General Parsons and his force was only 20 miles south, where General Price had stationed him. Governor Jackson sent word to him to come to Boonville at once to assist Colonel Marmaduke: "Proceed in all haste to Boonville."[64] Perhaps based on the same assessment of futility that Marmaduke saw in the defense of Boonville, Parsons did not respond directly.[65] For reasons never explained, Parsons ignored the governor's order—although he was but a day's march away—leaving Marmaduke to face Lyon alone.[66]

15

Skirmish on Rocheport Road

Riverboat travel up the Missouri River posed an element of danger, even for experienced pilots. Feeling their way upriver was slow work, as the steamers loaded with federal troops strained against the strong current. They had less than 50 miles to go but by nightfall had covered less than 30. The boats stopped for the night at a landing on the left bank of the river about a mile below Providence, in Boone County, west of Boonville with still some 15 miles yet to go to Boonville.[1] Here at this small shipping point they landed and lay up for the evening until daybreak.[2]

Giddy excitement ran high among the young national troops. Soldiers talked animatedly with each other in a buzz of chatter over the prospects of tomorrow's battle. Conversation turned noticeably more somber onboard Lyon's flagship when the surgeons silently hauled forth the horrible instruments of their trade and busily arranged them for the bloody work of the coming day. Watching the surgeons prepare for the earnest work to come, cold reality crept over the scene on the eve of the first battle in Missouri on that early day of the coming Civil War.

The steamers got underway before sunrise the next morning, Monday, June 17. Daybreak found General Lyon seated forward of the steamer's cabin, his glass in hand, closely scanning both banks of the river. Sandbags lined the open deck of the boat. Riflemen stood posted and ready to react quickly to any threat of ambush as the slow-moving steamboats worked upriver. Lyon knew they were easy targets for state guns.

They reached Rocheport around 6:00 a.m. and paused to gain information.[3] Rocheport was a small town of about 800 residents situated on the river at the mouth of Mountain Creek.[4] "The people were surly, and not disposed to be communicative," wrote a soldier in his journal. The resentment of the people of Rocheport indicated that the federal forces were in a part of the state where they were unwelcome.[5] Nevertheless, they determined from the inhabitants that State Guard troops were in force a few miles below Boonville ready to make a vigorous defense.[6]

Scouts took the steam ferry *Paul Wilcox* to a point a few miles below

15. Skirmish on Rocheport Road

Boonville, where they spotted two pieces of artillery positioned on a high embankment behind a clump of trees, partially concealed and trained on the channel, which the troop boats would slowly have to pass.[7] They did not know the guns were inoperative pieces placed there as decoys against a river assault. They could see the rebel camp in the distance and scouts hurrying to report their arrival.[8]

The engines reversed at once and the troop boats moved back downriver about three miles, stopping about a mile short of Rocheport to bring the army ashore and approach Boonville by land.[9] The boats edged behind a large channel island to shield them from view. Lyon, Blair, and John Schofield walked across the narrow island and cautiously examined the landing site on the south bank of the river.[10] Rich bottomland extended in the distance for a mile and a half from the river's edge to a line of steep bluffs to the south.[11] The Rocheport Road ran parallel to the edge of the water for a ways, dipped south, and then angled westward toward Camp Bacon. It offered a handy approach for the Federals to follow on foot.

Sure that the landing was free of rebels, Lyon disembarked his troops on the south bank of the river around seven o'clock, a mile or so above Rocheport and some seven miles below Boonville.[12] Upon going ashore, he left one company of Blair's First Missouri and one eight-inch siege howitzer onboard the *A. McDowell* under Captain Henry Richardson to guard the boats, with the additional instruction to advance upriver to a position that would place the rebel camp within range of the siege howitzer.[13] Once in position, Richardson was to order the artillery party to open up on the camp. A conspicuous movement of the boats upriver would also divert attention from Lyon's land approach.

Lyon landed his force at a wood-yard about three miles below the State Guard encampment, which stood between Boonville and the Union troops. Locals informed Lyon that a force of state troops of unknown size were in position below the camp, ready to make a defense of Boonville. He was about two miles from the reported State Guard position east of town.

Preparations swung into place for the ground attack. Officers immediately formed their units, and by 8:00 a.m., the column of Federals marched off toward the state camp. The ground forces stepped out and advanced up the sandy Rocheport Road. The boats moved steadily along the river beside them.[14]

Two companies of Second Missouri Volunteers went ahead as skirmishers. They moved out under Major Peter Osterhaus, who stood in as commander of the Second Missouri replacing Colonel Börnstein, now in Jefferson City with the balance of the Second Regiment. Major Osterhaus and Captain Schadt's Company A, along with Captain Klohr's Company B, led the advance column. At a proper distance behind them followed

Lyon's old company of the Second Regular Infantry Company B under Sergeant William Griffin. Captain Totten's battery came next, followed by two companies of Regular recruits under Lieutenant Lothrop, and then Colonel Blair's First Regiment of Missouri Volunteers. At the rear guard were four more companies of the Second Missouri, commanded by Lieutenant Colonel Schaefer. All the while, the boats moved up the river to keep even with the marching troops.[15]

Colonel Marmaduke on the MSG side had led his small band southeast out of Boonville toward the Union force. They were 500 poorly armed militia with little ammunition and no artillery.[16] About a mile beyond Camp Bacon down the Rocheport Road, in Cooper County, he deployed his main line of battle. He placed his men along a narrow dirt lane that intersected the Rocheport Road and ran at a right angle north toward the river along a low ridge of ground. A lone brick house belonging to William M. Adams stood on the northeast corner of the isolated intersection. The Adamses vacated the house, and a number of Missouri sharpshooters moved in to occupy it.[17]

The rest of the rebels faced east from behind the house, extending their line south and north along the river path. A rail fence at one side of an adjoining wheat field provided modest shelter for a few soldiers, while others deployed in a fringe of woods. Most, however, stood in open ground, their thin ranks lining the field. Marmaduke put out his pickets and waited to meet the advancing government troops.

The Federals moved cautiously because Lyon operated under narrow intelligence limitations. He thought Governor Jackson had collected three or four thousand men to throw up a defense against his advancing army. Instead, behind a low swell of land awaited Colonel Marmaduke and a small army of 400–500 ill equipped and hastily organized Missourians.[18]

The Federal column proceeded quietly up the river road for a little over a mile and a half to the spot where it began to ascend the bluff.[19] Where the bottomland narrowed, just before the road climbed into the wooded bluffs, the nationals met the advance pickets of the State Guard. Before rebel reinforcements could arrive, Lyon was on the MSG recruits. His advance guard of skirmishers drove the state picket line in.[20] Major Osterhaus collected his Company A skirmishers to the right of the road; Captain Schadt hurriedly brought Company B up to Osterhaus's left, and all opened fire. The Marmaduke pickets fired off a few rounds, and then hurriedly fell back.[21]

Two army correspondents, zealous to see the first battle, found a place on a hill to survey the conflict through their field glasses. They narrowly escaped with their lives when Lyon mistook them for enemy scouts and

15. Skirmish on Rocheport Road

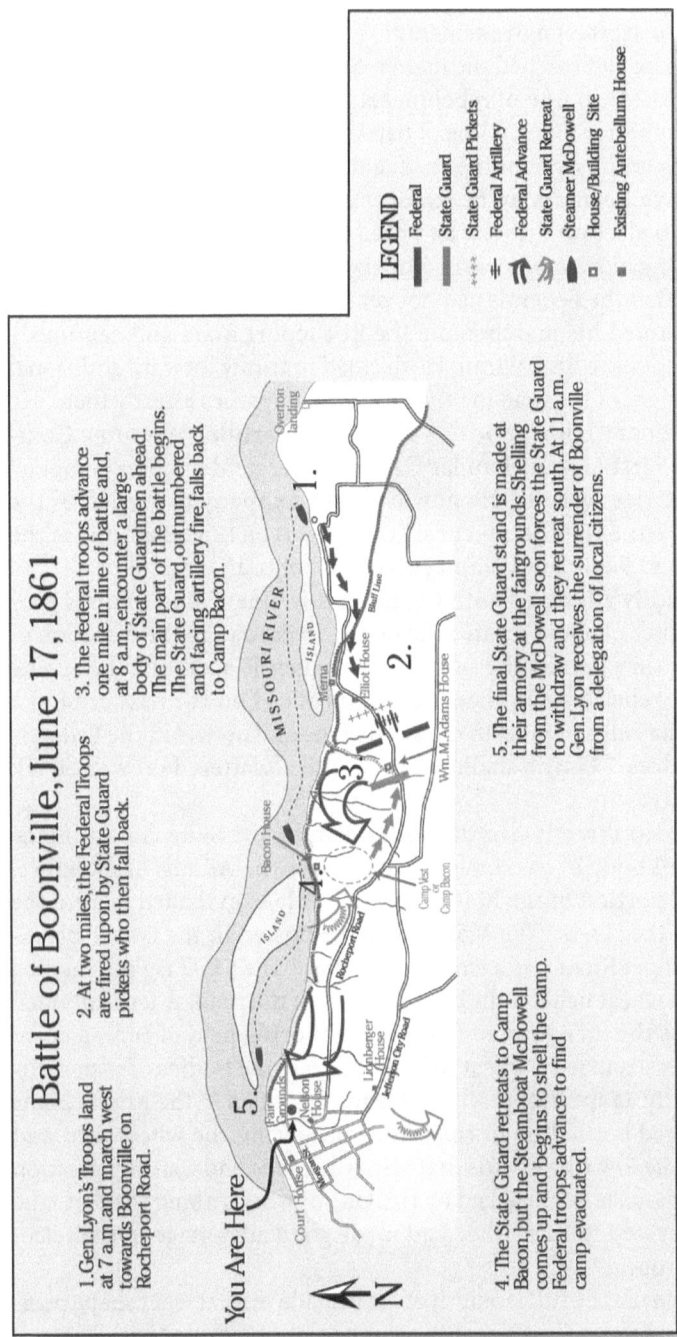

Engagement at Boonville, June 17, 1861. Federal troops land at 7 a.m. and march west on Rocheport Road before taking fire from State Guard pickets who then fall back. The main battle begins at 8 a.m. with a body of State Guardsmen positioned at the Adams house. The State Guard retreats to Camp Bacon where the steamboat A. McDowell shells the camp, forcing the Guard to retreat and make a final stand at the fairgrounds armory. Courtesy of Missouri State Parks.

ordered his sharpshooters to target them.²² One of his aides recognized them in time to avert an ugly incident.²³

Thinking he had reached the main rebel line of defense, General Lyon pushed aside the thin line of rebel pickets at the bluffs and immediately deployed his superior force in line of battle.²⁴ He deployed two companies of skirmishers to the right of the road, and positioned Company B of the Second Infantry Regulars to the left of the road. Captain Totten brought his battery into place on the road and fired a few rounds in the direction of the withdrawing pickets, who were quickly falling back to the west. It soon became clear that the Federals had not yet reached the main state force.²⁵

Lyon resumed his march along the Rocheport Road and cautiously continued to advance his column. He decided to throw forward additional troops to the right of the road to reinforce the companies already there. He sent out Lieutenant Lothrop with a company of artillery recruits, Company H of the First Missouri under Captain Yates, and another company of Regular Service recruits. He now had one company to the left of the road and five to the right, a total of six companies on line. Elements of the First and Second Regiment Volunteers trailed behind.

Lyon steadily advanced both flanks on line. The Union soldiers proceeded a distance of about a half-mile up the river road in the direction of Boonville. As they gained the summit of the gentle acclivity, they came in sight of the rebels posted about 300 yards ahead on the next crest of a long undulating ridge parallel to the swell of ground on which the Federals found themselves.²⁶ Only a shallow valley with a scattered growth of oak separated the two lines.²⁷

The road led directly over the ridge held by the State Guard infantry and a small body of cavalry. On the left was the Adams brick house, occupied by a portion of the MSG soldiers.²⁸ A lane extended behind the house toward the river.²⁹ The MSG main line posted in the lane.³⁰ Blocking the Rocheport Road was a troop of cavalry.³¹ The MSG right wing had a position in a wheat field on the opposite side of the road. A fence divided the field where the men formed from a neighboring field of Indian corn. Behind all this stretched a wheat field in which small bodies of men gathered, apparently as spectators without arms or orders.³² The Missourians formed a ragged battle line in the woods bordering the wheat field and spread along the low ridge.³³ The State Guard troops had a strong position behind the Adams house, backed by thickets of woods along the dirt lane on slightly elevated terrain. They had made good advantage in the selection of their ground.³⁴

Lyon deployed the full strength of his brigade in a crescent shape positioned obliquely along the ridge, nine companies of infantry with Totten's battery in the rear.³⁵ The Federals stood arrayed with elements of Blair's

15. Skirmish on Rocheport Road

Boonville Defense. Federal forces met the Missouri State Guard in line of battle along this ridge, which ran perpendicular to the Missouri River across the Rocheport Road. The two forces engaged each other in a brief exchange of fire before Union artillery drove the Guard back to their camp on the Missouri River. Historic American Buildings Survey, Library of Congress Prints and Photographs Division, Washington, D.C. (LC-mo0574).

First Regiment Volunteers on the left and the German volunteers of Börnstein's Second Regiment on the right. The field of Indian corn on their left and trees on their right framed the battlefield.[36] The government troops took up a position on the facing ridge of ground parallel to the rebel line. A witness said, "It was a momentous period big with Missouri's future."[37]

Totten's light artillery opened the fight, throwing a few nine-pounder explosives into the MSG ranks.[38] The thunderous roar of the cannon announced the opening salvo of the fight to the people of Boonville. The deep tone of the guns rolled over the hills, echoing fainter and fainter till it died away in the distance, and then another.[39] A shell fell in the midst of the throngs gathered in the wheat field, forcing the loose groups to hastily retreat.[40] The Missourians replied with a barrage of musketry delivered with a good deal of determination. A close volley opened on the advancing Federals.[41] In a few moments, the two opposing lines engaged in a noisy exchange.[42] Minié balls flew thick and fast about the Federals' ears, occasionally wounding a man on the Union side.[43]

The Federals had not expected such a determined stand by the state troops.⁴⁴ For a moment, it looked dubious.⁴⁵ Most of the Union casualties occurred here.⁴⁶ To approach the rebel line to within gunshot range, the Federals had to cross over open ground, exposed to heavy fire. After a short skirmish, the federal troops fell back.⁴⁷ Conflicting reports even said Lyon ordered a hasty retreat to the boats. The state troops followed in hot pursuit, thinking they had the advantage.⁴⁸

State Guard troops were raw recruits fresh from the farm. Most wore only the everyday clothing that they had on when they left home.⁴⁹ They had no inkling of military service.⁵⁰ MSG recruits had no organized training, but they were nearly all accustomed from their childhood to use a rifle or a double-barreled fowling piece.⁵¹ Men who owned muskets loaded their hunting rifles, placed a piece of cotton over the muzzle, and pressed down the ball a little. An old pocketknife cut off the extra patching. A rod rammed the ball down gently. The shooter put on a percussion cap, and then gazed under the smoke to look for a shot.⁵²

The federal withdrawal into the field worked as a stratagem to draw the rebels into the open. The Federals formed obliquely, withdrawing the center of their line and advancing the points of the wings to clear a path for Totten's artillery.⁵³ Captain Totten rapidly brought up the guns of his lone battery to fill the center of the line and opened fire. The Regulars led the charge, boldly marching along the field of Indian corn until they reached the ascent of the grade on which the rebels poised. They moved slowly, while the volunteers moved up to support them and spiritedly joined the attack. The Germans on the right advanced at the same time, persistently engaging the MSG line.⁵⁴

Some of the Federals dropped to the ground and fired from the prone position.⁵⁵ Staggered by their initial losses, the Federals quickly saw that they had superior numbers and advanced, firing as they attacked. They closed with the Missourians and fired a few volleys into them, opening a destructive fire, confusing and routing the MSG recruits.⁵⁶

In the heat of the engagement, General Lyon attempted to dismount his horse and proceed on foot, not wishing to present quite so conspicuous a target for MSG sharpshooters. The horse at the same instant broke away from fright and threw Lyon to the ground. When the solders saw him fall, the rumor soon flew along the lines that assassins had shot the general. Shouts for vengeance were loud and angry until the truth ascertained that their leader had simply fallen off his horse.⁵⁷

The State Guard troops faltered and fell back in order but stood their ground; several volleys rang out with balls "flying thick and fast," one rebel private remembered.⁵⁸

The Missourians checked the Federals' progress. Lyon deployed more infantry and brought up his artillery. Company B of the First Missouri under

Captain Thomas D. Maurice guided to the left in support of the Second Regular Infantry Company. Lyon sent Captain Nelson Cole's Company E First Missouri to extend the right flank in the direction of Camp Bacon.

Discovering that Marmaduke had no artillery, the Union gunners shelled the rebels at will from long range. Three hundred yards away, Totten's guns belched columns of smoke, white at first, but rapidly changing to blue, shooting out 25 or 30 feet from the muzzle before sounding the echoing report.[59] Totten's Mexican War experience kicked into full gear; this was his first chance to fight since his surrender of the federal arsenal at Little Rock. He was a West Point graduate and classmate of General Lyon of the class of 1841.[60] A genial character when not on the battlefield, Totten enjoyed a good conversation. He could ramble on seemingly forever on almost any subject before

James Totten. Secessionists in Arkansas forced Captain Totten to withdraw from his command of the U.S. arsenal at Little Rock. He joined federal forces at St. Louis, where he participated in the Camp Jackson affair. His artillery on the Rocheport Road quickly turned the engagement at Boonville into a federal rout of Missouri State Guard forces. Courtesy Wilson's Creek National Battlefield (WICR-31808).

finally getting to the point. His nickname was "Bottlenose" because of a tendency toward heavy drinking. He liked a good card game, and some of his friends said he talked too much. However, when he aimed a gun in battle, the results were flawless. Two shots from Totten's guns smashed through the east brick wall of the Adams house, scattering the state sharpshooters inside.[61] The rebel line answered with a smattering of small-arms fire.

William M. Adams House. Missouri State Guard formed along the ridge on which the house stood, in the adjoining fields, and in a lane that ran behind the house. Federal artillery damaged the house in the engagement between Union and Missouri State Guard forces. Photograph, after 1933. Historic American Buildings Survey, Library of Congress Prints and Photographs Division, Washington, D.C. (LC-mo0574).

The federal infantry then opened up with a withering musket discharge. A few more rounds of shell from Totten's guns dislodged the rebels and pushed them back.[62] Small bands began to abandon the line, throwing down their weapons and taking to their heels. However, a few held their ground, then clambered over the fence and slowly retreated through the wheat field, falling back to a small rise behind them.[63] They reorganized on the brow of the hill and prepared to make a determined stand.[64]

Governor Jackson, watching the fight from a hill a couple of miles distant, sent orders for the Missourians to fall back and form a line of battle nearer Boonville.[65] Colonel Marmaduke decided simultaneously on his own to call off the engagement and to withdraw his men. Still the Missourians stood their ground. A considerable number had already taken up a position and formed a new line of battle. They were eager to continue the fight and had gone too far to retreat. They refused to move back without exchanging more shots with the Federals.

Marmaduke told his men they could not reasonably hope to defend the position and ordered them to retreat. "If the Yankees catch you in here, they'll kill half of you," he warned. "Orders are to retreat, and every man takes care of himself." With that, he strode off in a huff, miffed and frustrated by this mutiny. The men decided to disobey orders, determined that they would not leave the ground without engaging the Federals. The men remained on the field under the command of Lieutenant Colonel Horace Brand.[66]

The Federals kept up a steady pressure. General Lyon advanced his ranks. Both flanks pushed forward. Totten continued to work his guns.[67]

The Missourians advanced their thin line a few paces toward the Federals and opened fire on them.[68] Lyon brought up his line of battle a second time and another sharp exchange followed. The rebels opened a galling fire from a grove of trees on the left of Lyon's center and from a shed still further on to the left.[69] The skirmish took on the shape of a battle.[70]

One partisan unionist writer said Lyon exhibited remarkable coolness leading the advancing column. "Forward on the extreme right. Give them another shot, Capt. Totten."[71] This same writer claimed Lyon's force numbered about 500 men against some 1,500 MSG soldiers when the numbers actually were the reverse of that, although neither force participated in the fight at full strength.[72] James Peckham, a Union soldier who joined in the skirmish, went to even greater lengths to trumpet the Union success. "The Union force was 2,000 in all," he said, "but not over 500 participated at any one time in the battle.... The enemy were over 4,000 strong."[73] Civil War historians Duyckinck and Switzler both later copied Peckham's numbers, adding to the confusion of exactly how many men participated in the Boonville affair.[74]

Knowing the Federals greatly outnumbered them, the Missourians broke and fell back in confusion.[75] Lyon had more than three times as many volunteers and trained Regulars on the field as the MSG had green recruits. After a few more discharges of cannon, the entire rebel force except for one company fled the field. Captain William Brown's company fought intelligently and well until it fell prisoner to the advancing force of Lyon.[76]

As Marmaduke predicted, so it happened. When his troops fled, Boonville was left without a defense and Governor Jackson practically without an escort. Many of the recruits hardly knew what was happening, let alone why they were there in the first place. Governor Jackson's personal rage against the Federals had not yet settled on the young militia. They were attracted more to the defense of Missouri's independence than to any continued engagement with Union troops.

After 20 minutes from the time the first gun fired, the rebels were in full retreat and the Federals stood on the ground the MSG once claimed.[77]

16

Occupation of Boonville

The Federals steadily pressed forward, giving the rebels no time to rally or strengthen their positions. The defeated State Guard scattered and melted gradually away, leaving the field in possession of the national troops. Rebels went by any path in a race for the rear. Many sprinted back to Camp Bacon to gather possessions and evacuate the area. A man rushed into the camp, shot through the arm in the Boonville fight. He said that some of Lyon's men charged them and fired, and then loaded "lying on the ground…. That's what whipped us," he said. He declared he had had enough of war, and "damn the Dutch."[1]

After the Federals advanced about a mile or so, a determined handful of MSG soldiers made a last stand in some woods near their encampment about a mile west of the Adams house where they had first posted.[2] Taking advantage of a good knowledge of the steep and rugged terrain, hidden behind bushes and clumps of trees, they opened a heavy skirmishing fire from right and left to defend the approaches to Camp Bacon.[3]

As the federal infantry pressed the ground attack, the Union boats moved upriver to bring the siege howitzer within range of the rebel camp.[4] The unarmed Missouri State Guard that congregated there quickly dispersed when the iron howitzer on the *A. McDowell* dropped a couple of shells into the Guard position, which was on the federal right near the river.[5] Captain Voerster with his artillery and Captain Richardson's company of infantry onboard the lead steamboat opened fire, scattering the stunned and dispirited Missourians. Totten gave them a few more rounds to hasten the rout.[6] The rebel retreat became a general stampede. They quickly abandoned their camp and joined the rush to the rear. About 20 horses appeared in the federal lines with vacant saddles.[7] The retreat turned into a tumult. The rebel Missourians took flight in every direction.

Camp Bacon lay in the line of retreat. The retiring rebel army fled right past it without stopping, not halting until well out of harm's way, back to Boonville and beyond. Some swam the river, or disappeared into the countryside. Many piled on board John Porter's ferry and crossed over

Battle of Boonville. The Northern press characterized the engagement at Boonville as a full-scale battle. This sketch shows cannons and crews firing toward the tree line in the background. Sketch by Orlando C. Richardson, *Harper's Weekly,* Vol. 5, No. 237, Cover (July 13, 1861). Courtesy Missouri Historical Society St. Louis (P0084-0596).

to Howard County. A sizable number headed south, but most of them went westward by boat toward Lexington.[8]

The short skirmish and quick retreat of the rebels went into Civil War lore as "The Boonville Races."[9] One Guard trooper said it was a "helter-skelter, pell-mell sort of affair." A trail of MSG recruits started showing up in Boonville shortly after the skirmish began and continued over the next three hours.[10]

Captain Nelson Cole of the First Missouri, who had moved his company up to the right to strengthen the federal line, slipped his men around the left flank of the retreating rebels and took possession of Camp Bacon.[11] State Guard officers tried to rally their men but Cole's Federals rapidly outflanked them. The action lasted a very short time before the Union guns completely routed the poorly prepared Missourians and seized their camp.

The abandoned camp had all the signs of a hurried exit. Campfires burned beneath frying pans full of breakfast. One filled with meat had fried to a crisp due to the cook's hasty exodus. Dozens of coffee pots sat unattended.[12] A camp table spread with plates and utensils carefully arranged belied a leisurely meal unexpectedly interrupted.[13] A couple of overturned chairs at the table told of the hasty departure of the diners only a few moments before. Blankets strewn about on the ground before the empty tents indicated late sleepers caught up in the sudden retreat. Several copies of Sir Walter Scott's novels, then the prevalent romantic literature, were in evidence.[14] Tobacco remnants of a relaxing evening lay strewn about. In those days, nearly everybody used tobacco; nine out of ten men chewed tobacco or smoked. Long, coarse cigars were plentiful for a cent apiece.[15]

The Missourians abandoned large amounts of military provisions, arms, and ammunition, as well as secessionist flags of various designs.[16] The Confederacy had not yet fully imprinted its symbol on the State Guard. The Federals collected banners of the St. Louis Minute Men secessionist movement, a Lone Star flag, and one state flag with 15 stars representing the Confederate states.[17] The State Guard flag of blue merino with the arms of the state emblazoned in gold in each side had not yet made its appearance, despite General Price's order laying out the design on June 5 and urging units to have it ready.[18] Neither did his order apply that day that each company of MSG infantry have one drum and one fife. The organization of the Boonville defense fell noticeably short on military pomp.

Everything at Camp Bacon pointed to a gathering of inexperienced recruits thinking a few of them could go out before breakfast and chase Lyon and his troops back down the river. The Missourians retreated in such a hurry that few of them paused long enough to saddle their horses before they skedaddled back to Boonville. The pursuing column of Federals discovered numerous saddles, but there were no horses. Most of them had bolted into Union lines. One tent contained a sidesaddle, a fancy pair of garters, and a hoopskirt, calling into question how focused some of the camp occupants were on the battlefield.

The rebel troops left in their flight two six-pounder artillery pieces, most of their camp gear, and a large assortment of all sorts of arms, all of it material the strapped young Guard could hardly afford to lose.[19] Upwards of 80 Guard soldiers became prisoners, the ones who had remained stubbornly on the field and chosen not to run. In one unlikely instance, the chaplain of the First Regiment took 26 prisoners. He had charge of a party of four men, two mounted and two on foot, with orders to take charge of the wounded. A witness described what happened. "Ascending the brow of a hill, he suddenly came upon a company of twenty-four rebels, armed with revolvers, and fully bent upon securing a place of safety. Their intentions, however, changed when the parson ordered them to halt, which they did, surrendering their arms. Surrounded by the squad of five men, they were marched on board the *City of Louisiana* as prisoners of war."[20]

Governor Jackson watched the debacle from a distance, surrounded by Captain Kelly's company. Seeing the young Guard recruits crushed by Lyon's troops, Jackson's own men angrily reprimanded him for his cowardice and bad judgment in starting the engagement. When Jackson stepped into General Price's vacated role as field commander, he did so without any actionable military experience. Aside from his brief stint as a captain in the Blackhawk War, his services had been as uneventful and brief as those of Abraham Lincoln, who was two years his junior.[21] Jackson made what appeared to his followers to be a cowardly decision that proved to be disastrous. He placed his least disciplined troops at the front while inexplicably holding the best-prepared command of Captain Kelly in reserve as his bodyguard, unavailable for battle.[22] Jackson took no part in the fight himself but watched the conflict unfold from a mile away.[23]

The State Guard troops fled Boonville, part going south by land with Governor Jackson and General Clark and the balance on a steamer headed toward Lexington. Some of the Boonville recruits went back home, having experienced all the war they wanted. Their allegiance to Governor Jackson diminished. One observer wrote, "When the fate of the contest became apparent, he [Governor Jackson] rode to town and shortly after disappeared without indicating the place of his destination."[24]

A good number of recruits, however, caught up with the fleeing governor, scurrying out of town with Captain Kelly and the remnants of the MSG to begin a hasty retreat toward southwest Missouri. A disappointed and humbled Colonel Marmaduke resigned from the Missouri State Guard and, disaffected, left the state to seek a Confederate commission.[25]

Leaving Captain Cole in command of Camp Bacon, Lyon reformed the national troops in column and proceeded on toward Boonville.[26] The *A. McDowell* paddled along on the river to the rear and off to the right.[27] The Federals on the boat had a clearer view of the MSG men from the river and saw their intent to make another stand at the fairgrounds, about three-quarters of a mile beyond the eastern edge of Boonville, where the state had set up a temporary armory. Another shell from Captain Voerster's howitzer onboard the *A. McDowell* and a couple of discharges from Captain Totten's guns, followed by a volley from Lothrop's detachment of rifles, scattered the defenders in all directions for a third time.[28]

The fairgrounds occupied the site of the original Boonville settlement where Widow Hannah Cole and her nine children built their fort in 1810. The old settlement had long since vanished. Organizers held the first Missouri State Fair there in the fall of 1853. People from all over the state came to enjoy the thoroughbred horse races. So many spectators came one year that the hastily built wooden bleachers collapsed under their weight. Regional fairs after a few years undercut attendance, and the founders of the State Fair went bankrupt. The Boonville fairgrounds fell abandoned.

Immediately south of the fairgrounds, a fine grove of walnut trees marked the Walnut Grove Cemetery, a four-acre rural park-like setting. Rebel lookouts crouched behind the very large headstones watched the approaching Federals. Some who were wiry enough to climb on top of the biggest stones could survey the entire neighborhood. An ornately fenced circular burial site that belonged to the late David Barton anchored the center of the cemetery, with other lots spreading out concentrically from the 20-foot marble obelisk that marked his grave. Little Red Barton, as he was known, chaired the 1820 state constitutional convention, and many said he wrote the constitution that brought Missouri into the Union. One could not help but wonder what he would think now about the determination of the secessionists of his hometown to remove Missouri from the Union.

Lyon's interest in the fairgrounds was not in the history of the State Fair, or in a few lingering rebels cowered behind David Barton's grave, but instead in the rudimentary armory established on the grounds. The Federals easily pushed aside a small group of rebels vainly blocking the road and took possession of the facility. They found large numbers of old rusty arms and cartridges, and a huge store of shoes, items sorely missed by the rebels going forward. Lyon seized all the State Guard's supplies and equipment kept at the armory, including some 500 old flintlock muskets and 1,200 pairs of shoes awaiting distribution to new recruits.[29] The Union troops afterwards derisively referred to the Missourians as "the barefoot rebel militia."[30]

More significant than the loss of logistical items, however, was the effect of the federal victory on rebel morale. The bloody affair at the Rocheport Road took its heaviest toll on the pride of the stubborn Missourians. Lyon left a company to guard the stores at the fairgrounds armory and marched his army slowly into Boonville.[31]

Boonville lay along a bluff overlooking the Missouri River, elevated a good hundred feet above the water's edge. A town of some 3,000 residents, it lay a comfortable distance away from St. Louis, 150 miles west. Several stage routes emanated from the city, connecting to St. Joseph, Syracuse, Tipton, and the North Missouri Railroad.[32]

By happenstance, Mary Todd Lincoln had family in Boonville, but they had lost touch. Her husband, the president, was usually circumspect about his in-laws but remembered his sister-in-law. Writing to a friend, he said, "Ann Todd was married to a fellow by the name of Campbell, and who, Mary says, is pretty much of a 'dunce,' though he has a little money and property. They live in Boonville, Missouri, and have not been heard from lately."[33]

Boonville was the county seat of Cooper County, set at the very heart of Boonslick country. The oldest town in central Missouri, Boonville at the time represented the best of Little Dixie, a rich, fertile farm region where locals claimed, "If you plant a ten penny nail there at night, it'll sprout crowbars by morning."[34] Residents of Cooper County did not mirror other parts of Missouri in their divided loyalties. The whole county supported the South. The wealthier inhabitants openly entertained strong secessionist sympathies. Cooper County slave owners had helped raise money for proslavery factions in Kansas during the Border Ruffian days. Slaves accounted for more than one-third of the county's population. Only a few poorer folks tended to favor the Union. A few who voted for Lincoln for president found their names listed in the local Boonville newspaper as a matter of curiosity.

The rout of Governor Jackson's troops caused much excitement in Boonville. As General Lyon approached the city about 2:00 p.m., a group of cowed citizens met him at the creek that ran along the eastern edge of town.[35] District Court Judge G.W. Miller and Acting Mayor James H. O'Brien led the delegation on behalf of the people. They carried a flag of truce.[36] Major O'Brien, who was also a military officer, surrendered Boonville to Lyon.[37] The delegation pleaded with Lyon to spare the town from violence and plunder by his troops.[38] The secessionists had imparted a dire expectation in the event of a federal victory.[39] Lyon informed them that they could go about their business as usual without fear of consequences from his men. Lyon and Blair cordially assured them that if no resistance occurred, they had nothing to fear. "No harm will come to civilians," Lyon said.[40]

Nevertheless, aware of the secessionist sentiments of the town, Lyon required the mayor and city council to accompany him into the city, which he entered without incident.[41] The federal entourage made its way down Main Street toward the courthouse. Aides took note of suitable places to quarter troops along the way.

The triumphant entry of the Federals was absent much cheering.[42] They marched silently past the new opera house, a magnificent four-story Greek Revival building on the corner of Main and Vine Streets.

The St. Louis German soldiers felt mildly welcomed by not one but two fledgling Turner Societies recently established by young Germans at Boonville. Some soldiers thought it strange to find Turners that far west of St. Louis in the middle of a proslavery enclave. The Turners would later purchase the Baptist Church across from the opera house and turn it into Turner Hall. Just now, however, the church looked like a good place to house a few companies of Federals.

Surprisingly, a few cheers began to emerge from the crowd that gathered along the streets, lustily returned by a hearty response from the Federals. The Stars and Stripes began to appear from house windows, and someone ran one up the church steeple, as Boonville grudgingly proclaimed itself a loyal town.[43] The proprietor of the City Hotel denounced the secessionist movement as "the greatest crime committed since the crucifixion of our Savior."[44] Lyon discovered that had he entered the town much later, Jackson and his followers who had been forcing unionists to leave would have fortified it.

Down Chestnut Street a block west of Main at Fourth Street, an aide spotted George Hain's house, a nice-sized walnut log structure with a neatly kept lawn nestled behind a white picket fence. A pecan tree growing alongside the house gave the place a pleasant domestic look. The house might make a good headquarters. A couple of blocks past the opera house, they came to the Kemper Military School at the corner of Spring Street and Main. The sign in front of the academy carried the school's motto: *Nunquam Non Paratus* [Never Not Prepared], which seemed oddly inapplicable. The academy master, Frederick Kemper, pleaded innocent neutrality in the conflict; however, everyone knew that his brother James firmly favored the Confederacy. Many Kemper graduates and a few students were among the State Guard troops that Lyon had routed.

A block past the academy, on Morgan Street east of Main, sat the Cooper County Jail and Hanging Barn, a formidable two-story structure built of huge limestone blocks quarried by slaves. Along with the prisoners and criminals, slaves who were destined for the auction block on Main Street were penned here by their traders. Many an unfortunate soul came to a bad end here. Not until the twentieth century, in 1978, did a federal court declare the jail cruel and unusual punishment and order it closed.

Lyon soon covered the short distance to the courthouse, which stood at the north end of Main on the public square overlooking the river. A large two-story brick structure of plain design and simple ornamentation, it afforded an excellent view of the river from the cupola. Boonville was firmly in federal hands by midafternoon, thus ending the first land fight of the Civil War on Missouri soil.

Lyon quartered part of his force in the city, some camped at the fairgrounds, and the remainder returned to the boats, now stationed just below Boonville opposite the fairgrounds.[45] The Federals paused and took time to inspect the details of the fight. They reported two killed and nine wounded, two of them mortally. One chap was missing and not accounted for. The figures were less precise on the rebel side. Union officers guessed 10 rebels killed and some 20 wounded; local sources, however, claimed anywhere from three to 15 killed and five to nine wounded. Contrary to federal claims, they said only 20 prisoners were taken.[46]

The actual number of casualties suffered in the Boonville affair remains clouded in mystery.[47] Greatly exaggerated at the time, no reliable official report exists. One excited secessionist report called the melee "very bloody and our loss very heavy—the federal artillery mowed our men down; at one point on the road where it had played upon them the field was covered with dead, and one of the gullies at its side was running blood."[48] However, calmer reports said losses were small. The accepted number of dead and wounded made credible by repetitious publication was two killed and nine wounded on the Union side, and two or three killed with about 20 to 25 wounded on the MSG side.[49] Depending on the sectional bias of the reporter, Union dead ran as high as 100 and MSG casualties even higher.[50] St. Louis papers reported Lyon had defeated the sate troops with their loss of 300 killed, 600 prisoners, and 1,500 stand of arms taken![51]

The Missourians tried to put an equally positive spin on the affair, claiming to have inflicted heavy casualties on the Federals. They estimated that they killed or wounded more than a hundred of the Federals. Some pro–South newspapers placed the count as high as 300. Several others, they said, later died of their wounds. Only three Missourians died on the field, they reported. The count of the Missouri wounded was somewhere between 17 and 25, according to pro–South accounts.[52]

Actual casualties were in fact light on both sides. Using best estimates, with the mortally wounded factored in, the Federals had four dead and seven others injured. A handful of rebels died, with maybe a dozen wounded. The battle ended in such disarray that there was no reliable count of Guard losses.

Lyon pardoned the prisoners and liberated them upon their promise not to take any part against the government. Many were young men, several under the military age. Lyon characterized them as misguided youths, misled by the statements of the secessionists, in his words: "ingeniously devised and industriously inculcated by designing leaders, who seek to devolve upon unreflecting and deluded followers the task of securing the object of their own false ambition."[53]

Partly to correct the impressions created by "unscrupulous calumniators," he released everyone on their oaths to obey the laws of the general government and not serve in the impending hostilities against the U.S.[54] They said they would and went back to their homes, most of them. Many pleaded themselves duped and misled by their leaders, and did return home. A core of them, however, soon caught up with Governor Jackson's fleeing MSG forces to continue their resistance to the Union invasion.

PART THREE

Forcing Move

17

Muster at Lexington

Boonville became a clarion call of Northern sentiment demanding more such action to throttle the rising Southern Confederacy. Occurring more than a month before the Battle of Bull Run, Boonville was the first conflict of the Civil War judged not because of the numbers engaged and the losses incurred but for the far-reaching consequences of its decisive military and political results. Boonville decided the final political lineup in Missouri and with it the definitive course of the Civil War.[1] The effect of the battle was national in scope. The Northern press heralded it as a great Union victory. Soon after occupying Boonville, Frank Blair took a riverboat back to St. Louis and from there went by train to Washington to claim his seat in Congress.[2] All along his route through Illinois, Indiana, and Ohio, he received a continual ovation. The first land victory since the fall of Fort Sumter boosted the morale of the Northern states and had a corresponding depressing effect on the spirits of the people of the South.[3] Boonville dealt a stunning blow to the Southern rights men of Missouri, and in the process weakened the Confederacy. It consummated Blair's scheme to make it impossible for Missouri to secede, thus denying state resources to contribute liberally of men and matériel to the South.[4]

The press tried to magnify the skirmish as a significant battlefield engagement, but it fell short of that.[5] There were a handful of casualties on both sides but no significant losses. The entire affair from start to finish lasted less than three hours; the fight itself lasted barely 20 minutes.[6] The half-organized and poorly armed state troops melted before the better-armed Federals and their artillery.[7] Nevertheless, it was the first hostile collision in the state in the form of armed combat that pitted the authority of the United States against the state government of Missouri.[8] The Lincoln administration saw it that way. The president's biographers wrote, "This affair at Boonville was the outbreak of open warfare in Missouri."[9]

Confederate historian Thomas Snead acknowledged Boonville as "the most brilliant of Lyon's well-conceived campaign." It was high praise coming from the St. Louis newspaperman many considered the best authority on Missouri in 1861 from the Southern rights point of view. Snead wrote, "The capture of Camp Jackson had disarmed the State, and completed the conquest of St. Louis and all the adjacent counties. The advance upon Jefferson City had put the state government to flight and taken away from the Governor the prestige, which sustains established and acknowledged authority. The dispersion of the volunteers that were flocking to Boonville to fight under Price for Missouri and the South extended Lyon's conquest at once to the borders of Iowa [and] closed the avenues by which the South-minded men of north Missouri could get to Price and Jackson."[10] The Missouri River became an unobstructed federal highway from its source to its mouth—except for the lone remaining rebel rallying point at Lexington.

For several weeks, MSG volunteers had concentrated at Lexington, a strong proslavery town 40 miles east of Kansas City. A moderately wealthy town of about 4,000 people, it was the county seat of Lafayette County, which boasted the largest slave population of any county in the state. One-third of the residents of Lafayette County were slaves.

Lexington was the last stronghold standing between Lyon and total dominance of the northern half of the state. Located strategically on the bluffs overlooking the south bank of the Missouri River, it was a hub of river commerce and one of the most important towns in western Missouri. Its occupation by either side would represent a significant victory in the control of the state.

The defense of Lexington had been General Price's objective from the start. Orders had gone out to rally the State Guard there. Captain Jo Shelby's Calvary and elements of Colonel Richard Weightman's newly formed force from Blue Mills had orders from Price to rendezvous with the Eighth Division of Brigadier General James S. Rains at Lexington and to take up a position between Major Sturgis's Kansas federal troops and the army of Lyon at Boonville. Price intended for Lexington to interrupt the junction between the two Union armies.

The Blue Mills camp had planned originally to oppose Sturgis's movement of Union troops at Independence. However, after brief skirmishes around the Little Blue River, the anticipated attack failed to materialize, and Weightman decided to withdraw to Lexington.[11] The unfortunate death of Colonel Holloway at Rock Creek and the choice of Colonel Weightman to replace him hastened the decision to leave the Kansas City area and move further east to consolidate the State Guard troops.

Recruits poured into Lexington. General Rains worked Lafayette County enrolling volunteers for his Eighth Division. The state senator made his home in Sarcoxie, in southwest Missouri, but recruited up and down the western border. Governor Jackson courted Rains as a division commander because of his broad political popularity. His recruiting efforts had never let up from the time the governor called for troops to repel federal invasion. Even as the Price-Harney agreement ostensibly halted military buildup, Rains continued to organize in preparation for a military rebellion. When hostilities erupted at Boonville, General Rains and his division were already near Lexington.[12]

Across the Missouri River, Brigadier General William Y. Slack amassed another body of men awaiting the opportunity to cross the river.[13] Slack represented the epitome of Missourians struggling with the politics of secession. He was Kentucky-born and a 40-year citizen of his adopted state of Missouri. He parlayed a common school education into the study of law at Columbia, Missouri, and became a prominent member of the state bar. He built a home and reared his family at Chillicothe.

James Spencer Rains. A perceptive politician and prolific recruiter to the secessionist cause, General Rains commanded the Missouri State Guard Eighth Division. He led the Eighth out of Lexington into southwest Missouri. He fought at the Battle of Carthage and the Battle of Wilson's Creek. A strong proponent of states' rights, he joined the Confederacy and after the war retired to Texas. Courtesy Richard K. Rains, Jr.

He got into politics, attended Democratic conventions, made campaign speeches, and served in the Missouri General Assembly. He was a Southern rights Democrat opposed to the popular sovereignty doctrine that made Kansas a free state. He had the lean, hard features of a determined man, with the set lips and aggressive jaw of a fighter. He served

17. Muster at Lexington

in the Mexican War with Sterling Price. When it came time to select commanders of the MSG divisions, Governor Jackson quickly turned to Slack to lead the Fourth Division.

Union authorities watched Slack's ascent into the secessionist ranks. The War Department sent a detachment of the 16th Illinois Regiment by way of the Hannibal and St. Joseph Railroad into Livingston County to arrest him. These were the first federal volunteer out-of-state troops to enter Missouri outside of Kansas. When they arrived in Chillicothe on June 14 with the intent of capturing Slack, he barely escaped by a narrow margin and crossed the river with about 250 of his men destined for Lexington.[14]

William Yarnell Slack. A resident of Livingston County, he commanded the Fourth Division of the Missouri State Guard. He recruited several hundred volunteers from his home north of the Missouri River and led them across the river to Lexington before federal forces closed off the northern half of the state. This image, taken from an original glass negative, is the lone surviving photograph of him. Photograph attributed to Mathew Brady, ca. 1860. Library of Congress Prints and Photographs Division Washington, D.C. (LC-B812-3026).

Meanwhile, when Lyon initially chased Governor Jackson out of Jefferson City, many of the MSG units that had gathered in defense of the capital retreated to Lexington, adding more men to the rebel center. These Missourians had little in the way of arms and training, including artillery and men to operate it. Hiram Bledsoe was a Cass County farmer and Mexican War veteran with a record of involvement in the Kansas troubles, and he was an experienced military man. He took up the secessionist cause on behalf of first the cavalry and then the artillery.[15] He gave up on the cavalry after he organized a company at Jefferson City of about 60 mounted riflemen only to learn they had no horses.[16] When he got to Lexington, he found three pieces of artillery, a bronze nine-pounder captured by Missourians in Mexico, an iron six-pounder cast at Lexington, and a brass six-pounder taken from the arsenal at Liberty.[17] With some difficulty, officers at Lexington persuaded Bledsoe to take temporary charge of these guns.

The nine-pounder, called Old Sacramento after the battle where U.S. forces captured it, had a story to tell. For years, the gun had lain around Lexington, used for Fourth of July celebrations. Bledsoe had it bored out and converted to a 12-pounder howitzer. The smooth chase reduced the thickness of the metal, which gave the cannon a peculiar sound when fired. Oral tradition said the Mexicans used a quantity of silver in casting it. The piece became a familiar sound in battle to both North and South alike. Before the war ended, Bledsoe's Battery became one of the most famous and effective batteries of the Civil War.[18]

Hiram Miller Bledsoe, Jr. The light artillery battery he salvaged from discarded guns at Lexington, Missouri, formed the core of the Missouri State Guard artillery. The Bledsoe Battery became one of the celebrated batteries of the Civil War. After the war, he returned to Cass County and resumed his life as a farmer. Photograph ca. 1880. Courtesy Missouri Historical Society St. Louis (N20930).

Meanwhile, there were three brass guns in General Parsons' Sixth Division at Tipton, the three Model 1841 six-pounder field guns taken from the Liberty Arsenal in April along with the fourth brass gun in Bledsoe's battery. No one knew how to use them.[19] These guns lay buried in a dense thicket after the Liberty raid to hide them from the Federals. Pro–South men dug them up and gave them to Parsons and the MSG in what their guardians called "a glorious resurrection."[20] There were four caissons, a battery wagon, and mobile forge, each pulled by a four-mule team in plough harness.[21] There was a half-supply of ammunition and no equipment, except for one sponge-staff, which rounded out the assets. This, along with Bledsoe's makeshift battery at Lexington, was the only artillery in the entire Missouri State Guard.[22]

Volunteers came into Lexington from all parts of the state, informed that it was the State Guard rendezvous point. A few came armed with the familiar shotguns and squirrel rifles, but the majority of them had no weapons. Some of them joined the Guard with mixed feelings about the conflict. Salem Ford, for example, came from his home in Platte County. Like most of his compatriots, he mustered into the Guard for a period of nine months, "thinking and hoping the trouble would be over by that time."[23]

General Lyon learned from Union sympathizers at Boonville that State troops were massing at Lexington. At that point, he might have garrisoned Boonville as he had Jefferson City and steamed back to St. Louis. His strategic victories had secured important points on the Missouri River from Kansas City to St. Louis. The rebels at Lexington were in no position to mount a counteroffensive, and whatever happened in the southwest part of the state would be of little consequence in the outcome of the Civil War. The region posed no immediate threat to wrest Missouri from Union control. However, instead of retiring to consolidate his military gains for whatever campaigns lay ahead, Lyon pursued his determination to unleash his ostentatiously named "Army of the West" on Governor Jackson. He planned to encircle and capture not only Jackson, but also General Price and any MSG forces they could muster.

Lyon planned first to lead his attack force of Regulars and Home Guards west out of Boonville to flush the rebels out of Lexington. From there, he would link up with Major Sturgis's Kansas volunteers and together carry out the pursuit of Jackson. Meanwhile, a sizable force of men under Colonel Sigel was already moving overland from Rolla to block the governor near Neosho, with more Union troops to follow out of St. Louis. The secessionist army, caught between these three wings of the Union army, must either surrender or face annihilation, according to Lyon's plan. He expected to catch the fleeing fugitive governor and his army somewhere above Springfield.

As General Lyon laid plans to capture or destroy the Missouri rebels, General Price's steamboat docked beneath the bluffs at Lexington. Weakened by his illness but recovered sufficiently to travel, he made his way to join the gathering MSG troops. He took a carriage to the outskirts of town to meet Brigadier General Rains and Brigadier General Slack.

Price knew General Slack as an aggressive and highly partisan pro-South officer recognized for his energy and decisiveness; General Rains he knew less for his military experience and more for his oratory skills and success in persuading others to the Southern cause. Both men had been busily recruiting in their heavily pro–South central Missouri counties.

The troops in General Rains's Eighth Division came from the pro-slavery counties along the western border. The largest of the MSG military districts, the 19-county Eighth District ran from the Arkansas line all the way up to the Missouri River. When Rains called for volunteers under Governor Jackson's proclamation, hundreds of Southern empathizers responded. He recruited strongly in Jackson and Lafayette counties and divided his time between hostilities around Independence, Lexington, and the growing unrest in southwest Missouri.

Meanwhile, the Fourth Division of Brigadier General Slack came from the 11 counties of the Fourth Military District north of the Missouri River, in the region of the state popularly known as Little Dixie. Together, Rains and Slack had raised about 2,000 men, mostly unarmed and many shoeless; the recruits expected to receive arms and equipment from the State Guard.

The Union possession of Boonville gave General Lyon a strategic point on the Missouri River from which to attack Lexington. The federal occupation and control of the river put an end to Price's hope of holding the rich and friendly counties in the vicinity of Lexington until the Confederacy could send an army to his support with arms and supplies for the men he was concentrating there.[24] He had neither trained men nor the resources of war to make a stand. Federal soldiers advanced along the river from two directions, threatening to catch the state units in the middle. Lyon threatened them from the east and a sizable force under Major Sturgis was descending on them from the west. At the same time, another Union regiment from Iowa stood ready to bear down on Missouri from the north in answer to Lyon's plea to Washington for more reinforcements.

Aware of the dire situation that faced his Missouri army, Price looked to buy time to organize and train a force capable of staving off Lyon's troops. Otherwise, Missouri was lost. Upon learning of the debacle at Boonville, he knew Lexington was next. He saw the imminent peril in trying to defend against the river-borne troops of Lyon.

It became clear to General Price that the State Guard could not defend Lexington against a federal attack.[25] Their best hope was to seek shelter under the umbrella of Confederate troops in Arkansas until the rebel volunteers were strong enough to mount a show of force in Missouri. At the same time, a retreat to southwest Missouri would draw Lyon's army away from his baseline of support, the Missouri River.[26]

Price needed time to form the MSG recruits into a fighting force, in his words, to defend the state against invasion. His best hope of doing that lay in southwest Missouri where the State Guard could join up, if possible, with the regular Confederate army of Brigadier General Ben McCulloch, known to be making his way from the interior of Arkansas toward Missouri with a well-organized force. Price hoped to induce General McCulloch to bring his Confederate troops to the assistance of the Missourians.

He gathered a small escort as soon as he was well enough to travel, left General Rains in charge at Lexington, and struck out immediately for southwest Missouri. He placed Rains in command despite Rains's lack of military background compared to General Slack because Rains had the largest recruiting success.

Price ordered the Guard to proceed south and regroup beyond the Osage River. The Osage enters Missouri from Kansas about 60 miles south of Kansas City. It flows in an easterly and northeasterly direction and empties into the Missouri River a few miles below Jefferson City. The river formed a natural line of defense behind which the counties of western Missouri were almost totally secessionist.[27]

When Price placed Brigadier General Rains in charge of the troops at Lexington, he left instructions to abandon the town and meet up with the retreating troops of Governor Jackson at Lamar, in Barton County, 110 miles to the south. There seemed little doubt now that the legions of North and South would settle the contest on the prairies of southwest Missouri.

18

Rising Unrest

Sectional unrest continued in St. Louis in sporadic incidents across the city. On the day that Lyon steamed up the Missouri River to capture the town of Boonville, and the southwest column took Rolla by rail, another street affair was unfolding in St. Louis. Several citizens lost their lives and at least four soldiers were hurt when gunfire erupted, reminiscent of the unrest that had gripped the city a week earlier.[1]

The Union troops that remained in St. Louis had orders to guard the various railroads leading in and out of the city. At about 10 o'clock on the morning of June 17, at about the time Lyon was landing his force at Boonville, a company of Home Guards was returning from a trip to the North Missouri Railroad to investigate a couple of bridge burnings by secessionists. Elements of the Second Missouri U.S. Reserve Corps had formed at the depot and were marching quietly down Broadway and Seventh Street. When Company B reached St. Charles Street, a man described as a crazed individual insulted the troops with language so abusive and threatening that they took him into custody. The captain ordered him released, and the troops moved on toward Olive Street.

As the troops marched down Seventh Street toward their headquarters, they passed an engine house on the east side of the street between Olive and Pine. A pistol shot rang out from a second-story window on the east side of the street just south of Olive, wounding one of the men in the shoulder. Almost simultaneously, a second shot came from near the pavement curb, and then a third shot from the window above.

Fearing an attack, the soldiers hurriedly prepared their muskets to return fire. Captain Herman Kallman halted the company, pistol shots still firing from the windows. An officer was shot and disabled and a soldier at the rear fell senseless.

Captain Kallman quickly reformed his unit from marching four abreast to wheel westward and realign in double file fronting east. In the haste of arming, one of the muskets accidentally exploded. Without an order to do so, the company faced about and fired into the buildings.

The troops began firing briskly up at the windows of the Missouri engine house, toward the recorder's courtroom, and into the second story of the building adjoining it on the north.

The balls went through windows and doors, killing three men and wounding two others. The perpetrator was among the dead, identified as the rowdy secessionist bent on stirring up trouble. A large crowd soon gathered and for a moment, it looked like tensions might erupt into a much bigger confrontation. However, the pistol fire ceased. The melee, which lasted less than two minutes, ended and the troops moved on.

A county meeting had been under way inside the engine house, and some of the dead and wounded were apparently innocent bystanders. The troops marched off a couple of blocks, where they formed into line and reloaded their weapons. The excited crowd did not follow, and after a while, the company of Federals marched quietly on to its quarters.

Collision between federal troops and citizens of St. Louis. Troops fired into a crowd after receiving shots from agitators. They fired on the Recorder's Court, which was then in session on the second floor of the engine house. Casualties resulted on both sides. "From a sketch by a special correspondent taken on the spot" in *Frank Leslie's Illustrated Newspaper*, Vol 12, No. 293, Cover (June 29, 1861). Courtesy Missouri Historical Society St. Louis (P0084-1317).

Reports of casualties listed anywhere from six to nine victims, including the recorder who was in his office at the time. The local press claimed six citizens died while the soldiers escaped with slight wounds. The county coroner, however, said nine people died in the melee. A coroner's jury exonerated citizens of any responsibility, and military officers laid the blame on the undisciplined soldiers.[2] The jury could find no one specifically to charge and the incident became part of the sectional chaos that shrouded St. Louis and threatened to engulf all of Missouri.

Immediately following Lyon's successes at Jefferson City and Boonville, the Blair brothers—Frank and Montgomery—tried again to get the War Department to supersede McClellan and have Lyon placed back in charge of Missouri. They thought he was the "right man in the right place."[3] They argued without success that Lyon was in Missouri while McClellan was out of touch in Virginia. Moreover, they reasoned that Lyon was an older officer and more experienced commander in the field than McClellan was. There was no sufficient reason for subjecting his operations in Missouri to any intermediate supervision.[4] However, if not Lyon, they implored Washington to make Missouri a separate department and appoint someone familiar with Missouri politics to oversee it—perhaps someone like John Charles Frémont, the son-in-law of the late senator Thomas Hart Benton. Both Frank and Montgomery Blair supported the appointment of Frémont but then lost confidence in him. Lincoln offered his opinion. "The Blairs have to an unusual degree the spirit of clan," he said. Their family was a close corporation. Frank was their hope and pride. "They have a way of going with a rush for anything they undertake; especially have Montgomery and the old gentleman."[5]

Notwithstanding the intrigue in Washington, General Lyon went about the duties of his latest conquest. He set up camp at Boonville and named it Camp Cameron, a name purposefully chosen in honor of Lincoln's secretary of war. There he attended to the organization of his contemplated expedition into the interior of the state.

He issued a proclamation to the people of Boonville, assuring them that his mission was not to invade or interfere in their private rights as citizens.[6] He implored them to go about their business as if nothing had happened, and the national government would do its part to protect them from the scourge of the secessionist menace. It was a naive pleading because Boonville occupied one of the most intensely pro–South locations in the state, near the heart of Little Dixie. He cautiously omitted any mention of slavery in his proclamation.[7] However, Lyon finished off his statement with a stern reminder that the clemency of the government did not extend to those arrayed against its authority. At the same time, he sent out a message to local home guard organizations located to the south of

Boonville to be on the lookout for Governor Jackson and his army of rebel Missourians who were marching in that direction.

Lyon knew the emerging challenges of his situation. His reputation for violence and high-handed action preceded him. People of outstate Missouri held the fearful impression that great violence would be perpetrated upon persons and property by Lyon and his troops. He sent a communique to Washington: "I have been engaged more or less in removing this impression. I regret much that my proclamation was not published promptly, so that I could have had it here for distribution. I get no news of what is going on around us, but much fear the movement from Texas, and hope the subject will engage the attention of the general government. Keep McClellan advised upon the matter. I had hoped some of our Iowa troops would have been in this region by this time, but hear nothing of them. My suspense just now is painful."

The fear expressed about the movement from Texas referred to General McCulloch, now gathering forces in Arkansas on the Missouri border. These were the forces General Price hoped would join the Missouri State Guard in a concerted effort to repel Lyon and federal troops.

When General Price left Lexington, he struck out down the Warrensburg road. Still laboring from his recent illness, he rode ahead, taking only a small escort of about 100 men with him. He hurriedly rode as rapidly as possible toward Arkansas to find General McCulloch.[8] Price expected to forge an alliance with McCulloch and then rejoin the Missourians somewhere in southwest Missouri, hopefully with a reinforcement of Arkansas troops.[9]

He reached Warrensburg on June 18. Unionists in town recognized him and set a plan in motion to kidnap him. He avoided capture by escaping in an ambulance and took up his journey on toward the southwest.[10] As he hurried south, word came that Major Sturgis's army, believed erroneously to consist now of four to five thousand federal troops collected from Kansas, was moving southeast with a view to meeting General Lyon at Clinton and cutting off the Missourians. Price sent orders back for the State Guard to hurry and consolidate its forces at Montevallo. His plan was to outdistance the Federals and gain the relative safety of southwest Missouri, where he could organize and train his young corps of Missourians under the protective gaze of the Arkansas Confederacy and a sympathetic Indian Nation.

Price did not know at the time that Jefferson Davis was unenthusiastic about coming to the aid of Missouri. Any assistance was likely to have to come from Arkansas state militia forces and not from McCulloch's Confederate troops, unless Price could convince McCulloch to act on his own initiative. However, McCulloch was having his own difficulty procuring arms through the Confederate leaders for the defense of Arkansas. He had three moderately armed regiments approximately 1,000 strong altogether, two of cavalry and one of infantry of Louisiana troops. However, there were no arms for the Indian regiments that he hoped to enlist, and no tents in the entire state of Arkansas. Nevertheless, he believed that he would soon find himself "obliged to act on the northwestern corner of the State to repel an attack from the North."[11] He requested permission of the Confederate secretary of war for permission to go north and cross into Missouri if necessary. He did so with reservations because he looked upon the MSG as a hapless military organization. An acquaintance quoted him saying, "There is no concert of action among them, and will not be until a competent military man is put in command of the entire force."[12] Price, in McCulloch's view, might not have been that man.

The loss of Jefferson City and then Boonville effectively ended the administration of Governor Jackson. Pro–South supporters blamed Jackson for what was widely seen as a first-class humiliation. Newspapers criticized him for watching from the rear rather than leading the Guard into battle personally. To the Northern states in particular—and many in the South as well—Jackson became a fugitive pretender devoid of honor and authority. Caught in a political no-man's-land, the Lincoln administration saw him as an open traitor while the Jefferson Davis Confederacy had no confidence in his ability to deliver Missouri to the Confederate ranks.[13] Jackson's boast to furnish 100,000 men in service to the Confederacy if Missouri seceded seemed increasingly unlikely.[14]

Davis was never a strong supporter of adding Missouri to the Confederacy anyway. Surrounded on three sides by free states, he saw the defense of the long Missouri border as impractical despite the attractive value of the state's rivers and mining resources.[15] At the time, Missouri had more horses and mules than any state, was the principal lead- and zinc-producing area of the nation, and had a considerable iron mining industry—all of which would have met critical supply shortages in the Confederacy.[16]

Davis did not like Jackson or Price. He considered the policy of Missouri neutrality an affront to the Confederacy. An associate once heard him express himself "as being highly suspicious" of Governor Jackson.[17] Although he had agreed to send Confederate arms in support of Camp Jackson to take the St. Louis Arsenal, he refused to come to the state's defense otherwise because, he said, Missouri was still in the Union. To do so would be a double-dealing insult.

Davis tempered his decisions about Missouri with a personal dislike of Price that dated to their respective assignments in the Mexican War. The two argued over the conduct of the war. Price gained a reputation for putting down the revolt at Taos as his main claim to fame but not without incurring the contempt of Davis, who thought Price acted in a brutal and inhumane way in putting down the insurgency.[18] Price fired cannon into the center of the town, and those who the guns did not kill faced a kangaroo court that hanged a man a day. From that time on, Davis expressed profound contempt for Price.[19] When he became president of the Southern Confederacy, he more than once voiced his loathing for Price, a dislike that very well may have contributed to keeping Missouri in the Union because Davis never supported the idea of Missouri as a Confederate state with much enthusiasm. Furthermore, Davis had a dislike of any officer not a West Point graduate, which Price was not.[20]

Davis had a deeply flawed view of the confrontation at Boonville. He was of the opinion that Lyon and Blair's Boonville force amounted to 7,000 well-armed federal troops and eight pieces of artillery against about 800 poorly armed Missourians and one piece of artillery. Those who knew Jefferson Davis knew him as a man of scholarly attainments. Nevertheless, his understanding of the Boonville conflict from his vantage point in the South was substantially different from the opinion of the North. Davis wrote in his memoir, "With courage which must be commended at the expense of their discretion, they [the MSG] resolved to engage the enemy, and, after a combat of an hour and a half or more, retired having inflicted heavy loss upon the enemy, and suffering but little themselves. ... This first skirmish between the Federal troops and the Missouri militia inspired confidence in their fellow-citizens, and checked the contemptuous terms in which the militia had been spoke of by the enemy."[21] The result of the fracas at Boonville was, of course, just the opposite. The reputation of Davis as a man of integrity of purpose and dedication suffered at times from a made-up narrative growing out of a redefined patriotism.

The State Guard men at Lexington armed themselves with a generous supply of the gunpowder that Governor Jackson had secreted there and prepared to exit the town. General Rains, General Slack, and Colonel Weightman united their divisions and marched out of Lexington. The generals gathered their forces of some 2,500 Guard volunteers—one-third of them unarmed—and angled for the southwest corner of the state following behind Price, expecting to meet the governor and the combined divisions of General Clark and General Parsons coming down from Boonville.[22] Those men who were armed carried their personal hunting rifles and shotguns that they depended on to provide food for their households. They had gunpowder but no cartridge boxes, canteens, or any other supplies usually associated with a military expedition.

The green recruits turned their backs on Lexington and left in the midst of a driving rainstorm. When they did, they took the first steps that would forever link their destinies to the Confederacy of the South.[23] With the inherent courage of their growing convictions, they marched out of Lexington and headed south.

They marched in three columns. General Slack went by way of the Warrensburg road, Colonel Weightman took the Columbus road, and General Rains took the Wellington and Pleasant Hill road.

The column marched with few wagons or provisions to support an army. They had no blankets or military issue clothing of any kind, no tents, and without anything usually reckoned among the comforts of an army.[24] The commissary wagons were mostly empty. They left with little in the way of supplies, intending to travel under the good will and sympathy of the people along the way, meaning the men faced a diet of green corn taken from fields along the roadside, whatever the land yielded to feed an army on the move.[25] They had to rely entirely on the country through which they marched. It was friendly territory, but there was no time for hospitality.[26]

The fall of Boonville crippled the MSG recruiting effort. Southern sympathizers had confidently hoped that the State Guard would stop Lyon and the Federals at Boonville, and if not Boonville, then Lexington. When this did not happen, much of the ardor of pro-secessionists subsided. It put a check on the volunteer enlistments in Price's army for the time being.[27] Marmaduke's warning proved accurate. The federal victory had a devastating effect on the morale of the young rebel army and depressed enthusiasm among the Southern rights element.

The Union success at Boonville forced the State Guard to abandon the Missouri River. From this strategic point, the river fell under Union control. The turbid water of the Missouri River divided the state. In the spring and early summer, its width and turbulent current made it a natural boundary between the upper and lower parts of the state, cutting it in two and throwing up a barrier to State Guard volunteers on the north side trying to reach General Price's army.

Lyon had moved quickly to neutralize the strategic points of Missouri's defense. In rapid order, St. Louis, Jefferson City, and Boonville passed into federal hands. The Union victory at Boonville ensured federal dominance over the Missouri River and effectively cut off resources from the northern part of the state. Union troops cleared the Missouri River of all ferryboats and skiffs up and down its length, confiscating or sinking anything usable as transport across the river. The only ferries not destroyed were at towns heavily garrisoned by federal soldiers. The northern part of the state above the river completely lost contact with the counties south of the river.[28]

19

Rebels and Federals

In the summer of 1861, every man in Missouri of military age was a rebel or a federal.[1] Robert J. Christie, a State Guard soldier from north Missouri, wrote, "No one who did not participate in the excitement of those days, just before hostilities began, can realize the intensity of passion, even frenzy that impelled people onward until nothing but actual combat could follow. No one could resist the pressure that forced them to take sides. Persons who had been lifelong neighbors and friends were alienated from each other, and went into respective parties of Union and Secession. All idea of compromise was soon lost in the determination of the one party to save the Union and of the other to defend the sovereignty and rights of the states against invasion."[2]

The fighting elements on both sides seemed by common consent to make up their minds to attach themselves to the Regular Army organizations of one side or the other before they should do any fighting. On both sides, men quietly went away, singly and in small squads, to find recruiting stations and to face each other on the battlefield.[3]

When hostilities erupted between federal and state troops, people quickly divided their loyalties between secession and Union. In many counties, joining the MSG signaled treason against the United States. However, in the counties of Little Dixie and places of similar political persuasion, the response was just the opposite.

Families divided. Animosities among kin sometimes eclipsed the enmities felt between soldiers of the North and South. Bitterness between relatives and old neighbors, now enemies, was often greater than between the opposing sides.[4] Wife and husband often came down on different sides of the issue.[5] Men and boys left home to pursue some deeply felt allegiance, many never to return home. Fathers and sons died and went to rest buried together. In one case described by Confederate politician Robert Y. Toombs, "His short grave barely reaching down to his father's knees as they lay side by side."[6]

In many parts of the state a destructive guerrilla warfare broke out,

Border Ruffians. Many of the young men who joined the Missouri State Guard were proslavery activists who had crossed from Missouri into Kansas Territory to promote slavery in the fight for Kansas statehood. These two unidentified volunteers with swords were typical of the recruits who followed General Price into southwest Missouri. Photograph, ca. 1860. Library of Congress Prints and Photographs Division, Washington, D.C., Liljenquist Family Collection of Civil War Photographs (LC-2016646192).

degenerating into neighborhood family feuds, bloody personal reprisals, and revenge, collectively known as "bushwhacking." Paramilitary bands burned houses and bridges, plundered farms, obstructed railroads, and kidnapped and assassinated men. During the whole period of the war unrepressed disorder, lawlessness, crime, and almost anarchy enveloped the state.[7]

When Governor Jackson issued his call for 50,000 volunteers, thousands of Missourians responded. Many more tried to join but could not because of the rapid progression of events. Potential recruits faced a tough journey. Lyon's swift pursuit of the State Guard and the cutoff of large sections of the state made it difficult for would-be MSG recruits to enroll. Joining Price's army was an arduous task, made doubly difficult by Lyon's occupation of central Missouri and the isolation of the northern counties. Because of General Lyon's rapid action, the retreat of MSG forces literally outran recruits attempting to join up. The patrolling army of the federal government controlled the Missouri valley, for the most part ending military recruiting in that heavily pro-secession part of the state.[8] Southern sympathizers north of the river found it almost impossible to get past the Union occupation. Northern Missouri suppliers friendly to the Confederacy were unable to send needed resources south. Communications between the two parts of the state practically ceased.[9] Nevertheless, the incursion of armed Union troops drew a large response from Missourians eager to teach the interlopers a lesson in Missouri independence.

Young men wound up on different sides of the conflict, often through no choice of their own. If a family held slaves, everyone understood such circumstances meant taking sides with the South. Anyone whose father owned slaves quickly found himself a member of a local militia made up of young men of similar circumstances.

The armies on both sides catered to no specific class. They came from many places and all backgrounds. Men reared in luxury who had worn fine clothes shouldered against poor boys who had never been far from the meager gleanings of their homesteads. It is a mistake to suppose that only the lower class enlisted. Many of the most respectable young men took up their respective causes. All met hardship cheerfully together, bearing the burden of camp life and the forced marches through scorching summer sun without complaint. The one malady each could expect at one time or another was a bout of homesickness. They bore the long marches in good spirits. One private joked, "All the day I long for night, and all the night I long for its continuance."

Henry Martyn Cheavens cast his lot with the state. He saw no reason to abide a federal invasion of his adopted Missouri. A native of

Philadelphia, student of Yale University and Amherst, with a degree from the latter, he made his home in Boone County off and on for 20 of his 31 years.

Private Cheavens was not someone easily characterized by pro-unionists as an example of rebel rabble. Well educated, thoughtful, and strongly principled, he spent much of his youth in pursuit of knowledge, greatly influenced by the teachings of Edward Wyman's renowned English and Classical High School in St. Louis. It was said of Wyman, "He taught more than books contained. He taught character."

Cheavens followed his mentor into education and was a schoolteacher in Boone County when Governor Jackson issued his proclamation against the federal presence in the state. Cheavens opposed the high-handed tactics used by the central government. He also saw a threat to respectable slave owners like his friend Eli Bass, the prosperous Boone County landowner whose family Cheavens had once served as a private tutor. The Bass Forest Hill Plantation was the largest plantation west of the Mississippi River and the quintessential model of Little Dixie.

Henry Martyn Cheavens. He gave up a teaching job to answer Governor Jackson's call for volunteers to defend Missouri against federal takeover. A student of Yale University and Amherst, with a degree from the latter, Private Cheavens caught up with Missouri State Guard forces near Warsaw, Missouri. Courtesy State Historical Society of Missouri Photograph Collection (P0295 ID22995).

In the late spring of 1861, Cheavens answered the call for volunteers to protect Missouri from the "outrages of the federal government." He gave up his teaching job, left his home in Ashland in southern Boone County, and struck out to join Price's army and fight for the sovereignty of his home state.

Private Cheavens started on his journey to join the Guard on June 16,

1861, with a number of other men excited to respond to the call for volunteers to resist the Federals at Boonville. Cheavens lived only a few miles from Boonville, but by the time his band arrived there, the Federals had already dispersed the MSG and taken control of the town.

Disillusioned by the turn of events, many in the group found the job of catching up with Governor Jackson too difficult, gave up, and went back home. The quitters gave their weapons and equipment to those who continued. Someone gave Cheavens a white blanket to substitute for the coat he lost the first day out. He got a Mississippi rifle and a Bowie knife, climbed on his horse, and started in earnest to catch up to the rebel army.

The weapons Cheavens carried made him well-armed compared to most State Guard recruits. His U.S. Model 1841 rifle was an effective if not accurate long-range weapon. Most men had no arms. The MSG came together so rapidly that those able to respond joined the army with only the clothing on their back and whatever weapon they could bring from home. If a man had a weapon, it was a shotgun, fowling piece, or Kentucky hunting rifle. Some came with nothing more than a scythe or pitchfork for a weapon. Others owned nothing at all. Yet they joined to fight. Whatever they needed to defend the state, they acquired on their own. It was an army of individuals, true citizen soldiers.

The Guard was an unlikely looking army. They had no uniforms, or hardly any. Mostly they wore the simple farm clothes of day-to-day life. A few uniformed companies enlisted but soon discarded old standard clothing when it quickly wore out. With none to replace it, men took cloth, needle, and thread to make their own.

When the Missouri State Guard companies began first to form across the state, it became immediately apparent that they suffered from a lack of qualified officers.[10] The country had known peace for so long that only old men knew the art of military drill.[11] It became necessary to hunt up those who had been colonels or captains. Where such rank did not exist, organizers created it on the spot. Military titles of captain, major, or colonel were upon everyone's lips. These were often the same men who weeks before as plain "misters" had until recently been held in light esteem.[12] In the beginning, almost every officer appointed for political reasons and through favoritism or relationship had under him men who were his superiors in military ability. Before a regiment could do much service, it had to unload its make-believe officers and get new ones.[13]

Companies drilled often, with dismal and sometimes humorous results. One fellow tried urgently to impress on the recruits the use of the bayonet, how to stand firmly and receive a charge of cavalry. The potential menace of the drill got lost, however, because the gun with which he enthusiastically demonstrated the trick was a small double-barrel shotgun.

Neither Private Cheavens nor any of the men in his small band owned any camping equipment. They slept on the ground beneath a tree or with sympathetic families who provided a floor for their beds. They ate bread and dried beef. Hundreds of men like Henry Cheavens and his friends shouldered the hardships of rebellion and volunteered for the MSG to swell its ranks to a sizable fighting force. Lincoln's army owned better weapons than the Missourians and had the strength of experience and training, but Missourians had a saying: "An army of ants can kill a horse."

The Union victory at Boonville was militarily decisive because it denied the use of the river to state forces, opened the way for a campaign against Price at Lexington, and forced the State Guard to flee southward.[14] The Boonville action cleared the Missouri River of all formidable hostile forces, isolated the counties north of the river, and drove Jackson and his army into the southwest corner of the state.[15] The federal government now controlled the entire state, except for southwest Missouri, up to that point the last outpost of rebel resistance.[16]

In just one week from the Planter's House meeting, federal forces had taken the state capital, routed the state army in the first Civil War engagement on Missouri soil, and taken possession of the Missouri River, all in rapid succession.[17] Lyon's prompt action swept the eastern part of Missouri clear of secessionist resistance from St. Louis to Boonville and forced the abandonment of their stronghold at Lexington.[18] The governor of the state was in flight, his state troops scattered in the first collision, and control of the Missouri River was in federal hands. The enormous morale effect of falling in defeat to the "St. Louis Dutch" added to the uncertain future of the Missouri State Guard.[19]

Boonville might have been a terminal military disaster for the secessionists, ending in the capture of the state government. Instead, it turned out to be little more than incidental contact in General Lyon's chase of Jackson and his followers out of central Missouri. The greatest importance of the river campaign aside from its overwhelming military success was the unceremonious removal of a duly elected sitting government by force of arms; that and the evident resolve of Governor Jackson that he did not intend to give up Missouri without a fight. His little army of raw recruits, overpowered by numbers, fled in disarray, but the first fight of the Civil War west of the Mississippi made a memorable impression on the Federals of the determined resistance of the Missourians.

Lyon's base of operation now extended from Boonville up and down the Missouri River and claimed all of eastern Missouri along the Mississippi River down to Bird's Point, with the rivers and railroads as a means of transportation. In addition to his troops at Boonville, he counted 2,500 men stationed at Herman and Jefferson City, some 3,200 soon to be at Rolla, 1,000 on

19. Rebels and Federals

the North Missouri Railroad, another 1,000 at Bird's Point, and 2,500 in St. Louis. An army stood ready in Illinois to increase the St. Louis garrison by 10,000 men within a few hours if necessary. With these troops, the Federals held the entire portion of the state north of the river and all of the southeast quarter between the Mississippi and a line drawn southward from Jefferson City to the Arkansas border. They held the strategic points of St. Louis and Bird's Point, as well as Hannibal and St. Joseph, once two of the most dangerous ends of the secessionist-dominated region north of the river along with the railroad town of Palmyra. They owned the towns and with them the rivers and railroads.[20] Only the southwest quarter remained to make Lyon's conquest of the state complete.[21]

The elements of Lyon's three-pronged plan of pursuit of Governor Jackson were in place. He began immediately to organize a supply train at Boonville to take his army into southwest Missouri.[22] A trip into the interior of the state meant abandonment of river transport and no access to railroads. Supply would have to be by horse and wagon. The country around Boonville was of such a character that he anticipated no difficulty in impressing teams and wagons enough to support his column. The land surrounding Boonville was among the wealthiest and best cultivated in the state. He reasoned they could always count on getting subsistence along the way.[23]

Meanwhile, Colonel Sigel and the southwest column had already begun their overland journey toward Springfield. Having reached the end of the Pacific Railroad line at Rolla, the column began a difficult 110-mile trek. They marched along the Wire Road, so called because the telegraph lines ran beside the road.[24] The Rolla-to-Springfield section of the road was part of a military project that began at Jefferson Barracks near St. Louis and continued to Fort Smith, Arkansas, passing through Springfield and the Ozarks. It was a relatively new project only completed a year ago in June 1860.[25]

The intention of Sigel's movement toward the southwestern part of the state was to prevent hostile concentration on the line of the Osage River and impede any move made toward the confederates in Arkansas.[26] About 30 miles below Neosho, Brigadier General Ben McCulloch waited at Camp Walker, Arkansas, with a growing formidable force composed of state militia and Confederate troops from Texas, Louisiana, and Arkansas.[27]

While Lyon and Sigel organized their forces, the third arm of the pincer plan stirred on the western side of the state. Major Sturgis readied the First and Second Kansas Volunteers, along with five companies of U.S. cavalry, two companies of rifle recruits armed with muskets, and Captain Du Bois's artillery battery. Four companies of Regular infantry troops from Fort Leavenworth, some recently arrived from guarding the nation's capital at Washington, added to the strength of the Sturgis column.[28]

The Lincoln administration watched with guarded expectations as events unfolded in Missouri.

On June 18, as General Lyon's plan took shape, he gathered his small army at Boonville. He pleaded with Washington for more troops to join him. The War Department, eager to hold Missouri in the Union, ordered the First Iowa Regiment U.S. Volunteers to join him immediately. The fight for Missouri took on a new national dimension.

20

Prelude to Catastrophe

The First Iowa Infantry U.S. Volunteers organized in the spring of 1861 in response to President Lincoln's first call for troops to put down the secession rebellion. Recruits enrolled as 90-day enlistees at the pay grade of seven dollars a month and departed for duty to rendezvous at Keokuk, Iowa. Their average age was 22.[1]

It looked for a while as if they would never leave Keokuk. Situated between the Mississippi and Des Moines rivers, Keokuk was a good trading city of about 8,000 residents. Nevertheless, the restless young soldiers garrisoned there thought of the town as a victim of arrested development. They feared that the war would end before anybody knew that the First Iowa existed.[2] Then, orders came to proceed to Lexington, Missouri, to break up secessionist rebel forces massing along the Missouri River.

The regiment left Keokuk on June 13 and arrived at Hannibal, Missouri, about midnight.[3] There they loaded on to stock cars and proceeded by rail to Macon. A pall of fear of Union troops hung over Macon. After Camp Jackson, a wave of rumors spread like a cloud over the state. One rumor said that the Dutch had taken Macon, killed the women and children there, and were then marching on Callao.[4] This rumor had no basis in fact. Nevertheless, the presence of federal troops in an avowed secessionist town threatened this normally peaceful community.

The First Iowa paused at Macon to take possession of *The Register*, a secession newspaper. The regiment happened to have among its ranks several printers who promptly issued a new journal called *Our Whole Union* that, instead of political issues, focused on a debate over economics, which challenged the widely held view of the Southern press that Northern soldiers were "ignorant mercenaries."[5]

General Price, his staff, and a small escort rode south, all the while gathering more recruits along the way. Price attracted new followers like a magnet. By the time he reached Nevada, he had some 1,200 men with him. Mostly unarmed and untrained, these were nonetheless citizen soldiers in every respect. His close friend and adjutant general, Colonel Lewis Henry

Little, took over the organization of the new enlistees. Once on the fence on the secession question, Colonel Little resigned as a U.S. Army officer to undertake the task of shaping the MSG volunteers into a fighting force.

Several hundred men had joined Price by the time he approached the Missouri-Arkansas border, all assembled behind him as he rode swiftly to meet General McCulloch. When he reached Cowskin Prairie deep in southwest Missouri, he had a large body of recruits, most of them without weapons. He immediately left Colonel Little in charge and proceeded to Arkansas to meet with McCulloch and Brigadier General N.B. Pearce, commander of Arkansas state troops at Maysville. McCulloch was not available to meet with Price, but Pearce loaned Price 600 muskets, enough to arm less than half of his growing army. No commitment was forthcoming for assistance from the Confederacy.

Meanwhile, some of the remaining State Guard troops at Boonville briefly considered whether to make a stand against Lyon's Federals. Quartermaster James Harding remembered, "They actually took a vote, sitting on their horses, as to whether they obey the order [to defend Boonville]." The "noes" had it, and the company galloped away, "to fight again some other day." Captain Kelly, now alone and unsupported with Governor Jackson, marched off as well.[6]

When Governor Jackson left Boonville, he detoured to his home in Arrow Rock, in Saline County, to see his family before proceeding south.[7] Soon thereafter, he gathered the remnants of his cabinet and with Brigadier General John B. Clark, Sr., rallied a small body of the Boonville defenders and moved southward. They headed directly for the southwest part of the state, there to join General Price within easy distance of Confederate forces in Arkansas.[8]

As Governor Jackson and his small band of MSG men hastened southward, the First Iowa Regiment advanced toward Lexington, keeping in touch by telegraph. When they learned the State Guard had exited Lexington, the Iowans diverted to Boonville to join Lyon, adding a welcome measure of new strength to his growing army. The Iowans came overland from Macon and Renick, headed south, stopped briefly at Fayette, and then crossed the Missouri River at Arrow Rick close behind Governor Jackson before easing downstream to Boonville.[9] Unknown to the Iowans, the MSG Callaway Guard was close behind them seeking to join Jackson's army. The Callaway Guards had heard the sounds of the Boonville fight from Columbia. However, by the time they arrived near Boonville, the battle was over, and Governor Jackson had left. They bypassed Boonville and marched along the north side of the river, reached Fayette while the First Iowa camped nearby, and followed the Iowans from Fayette to Arrow Rock before breaking off without contact to turn toward southwest Missouri and catch up with the division of General Clark and Governor Jackson now making their way toward Arkansas.[10]

State officials, soldiers, and civilians traveled side by side as Jackson's followers. They made an odd column of refugees. Among the party was ex-U.S. senator David Rice Atchison, the prominent proslavery advocate and Border Ruffian leader in the Bleeding Kansas era. A onetime militia member of the Liberty Blues and an avid secessionist, Senator Atchison became a footnote to history when he arguably became president of the United States for one day in 1849. That came about when the term of James Polk officially expired on Sunday and his successor, Zachary Taylor, refused to take the oath of office on the Sabbath. Atchison was next in line to be president as president pro tempore of the Senate, as there was not yet a vice president either. Atchison later remarked that his one-day administration had been the most honest one in history.

The senator now found himself a dozen years later in a much different circumstance.[11] He rode behind a governor whose infamy suddenly threatened to tarnish the reputation of anyone seen in his presence. Public opinion thought the affair at Boonville a first-class embarrassment. Vocal secessionists fixed responsibility on Jackson.[12] His standing as a state leader took a beating. Newspapers continued to ask sarcastically why he had watched the battle from the rear instead of leading his men in person. In the minds of many, anyone who followed him deserved the same scorn.

Up to this point, both sides had taken advantage of river and rail transport. However, as the contest moved into the interior of the state, all of that changed. Rail travel in outstate Missouri was in its first decade of development, and telegraphic facilities were meager. Missouri only possessed four trunk lines of railway in 1861, all starting from St. Louis. The first—the Missouri Pacific—followed a westerly direction along the line of the Missouri River, passed through Jefferson City, and stopped at the village of Sedalia. The North Missouri (later Wabash) went northwest to Macon, where it connected with the Hannibal and St. Joseph Railroad that ran west across the state but reached only about halfway across.[13] No railroad reached Kansas City. A third line out of St. Louis—the Iron Mountain Railroad—ran southward as far as the mines near Pilot Knob at Ironton. The fourth line, the Southwest Branch (later Frisco), angled southwest with its terminus at Rolla.[14] None of the railroads reached much more than halfway across the state. Western Missouri was beyond any quick reach of a military expedition from St. Louis.[15] Beyond the railheads at Pilot Knob, Sedalia, and Rolla, armies could only survive by living upon the country or by organizing long trains of convoys for their provisions.[16]

There were no railroads in southwest Missouri either. People moved by horse and wagon, or on foot. There were no speedy excursions by train for Union men back east and no quick means of troop movement for either North or South into southwest Missouri. The two opposing forces threatened each other, isolated from speedy reinforcements and potentially desperately needing material support. Moreover, the Union troops were distant from all principal depots at a time when the ability of the government to arm and equip an army was taxed to the utmost.[17]

At the same time, telegraph communication with southwest Missouri was mainly by the Stebbins line connecting St. Louis with Fort Scott, Kansas, by way of Springfield. There was a line, too, over the Hannibal and St. Joseph Railroad; another line connected St. Louis with Sedalia via Jefferson City and Syracuse following the path of the Pacific Railroad. It ran southwesterly to Fort Smith, Arkansas, through Warsaw, Bolivar, and Springfield, Missouri. However, all telegraph communication with southwest Missouri effectively ended when secessionists cut the lines at the outset of hostilities. Burning bridges, firing on passenger trains, and cutting the telegraph wires became a relentless occupation of marauding bands throughout Missouri. It may have been just as well, because few men had greater opportunities to betray a cause than the telegraph operators did.[18]

When Governor Jackson and the remnants of the Boonville State Guard took up the line of march for the southwestern portion of the state, the Guard had dwindled to fewer than 300 men.[19] As Jackson proceeded south, stragglers caught up with him, including the men of the Callaway Guard. On June 18, by the time he reached the vicinity of Syracuse about 25 miles south of Boonville, the number had grown to around 500 to 600 men.[20]

Brigadier General Mosby Monroe Parsons, commander of the Sixth Military District in the center of the state, caught up with Governor Jackson's party west of Tipton in the Syracuse area. The governor wanted some answers as to where Parsons was during the Boonville fracas. It seems that when Jackson's urgent call for help had gone out from Boonville, Parsons had elected to swing east from his base at Tipton toward Jefferson City, to come up on the rear of Lyon's troops. Parsons and his men consequently arrived too late to participate in the Boonville skirmish, arriving just as Jackson was leaving.

Parsons and General Clark united their troops and set a course to escort Governor Jackson toward Warsaw on the Osage River. Parson's command of several hundred infantry and cavalry from the central counties and three pieces of artillery more than doubled the size of the Boonville contingent. The chased Missourians' spirits soon lifted when they united with Parsons's division. The rebels marched south in the direction of sympathetic territory with high confidence in their growing numbers. They planned to rendezvous with the Lexington rebel force under

Brigadier General Rains, supposed to be on his way from Lexington to Roup's Point in Jasper County. They would then proceed together toward the ultimate goal of reaching Arkansas and General McCulloch.[21]

The column left Syracuse about daybreak on June 18. Outriders of men confiscated property of Union citizens as needed and commandeered the rolling stock of the Pacific Railroad as they moved south.[22] A detachment destroyed the costly rail bridge across the Lamine River six miles west of Syracuse.[23] With the addition of Parsons's division, a growing number of new recruits, and a large contingent of civilians, Jackson's entourage grew to a trail of about 1,600 followers.[24] General Parsons took charge of the supply of ammunition and gunpowder, supervising the troublesome task of transporting the guard's supply in an assortment of farm wagons.[25]

The governor's army steadily grew in size as he rode south, but it marched without much organization and was poorly supplied with arms and equipment. The usual shotguns and squirrel rifles were the principal weapons, mostly useful for close fighting, a questionable skill for the poorly trained men who carried them.[26] A third of the men had no guns of any kind.

Muddy roads and a train of surplus baggage added to the slow progress of the column. A sizable number of civilians had joined the train in its exodus out of Boonville. They carried wagonloads of feather beds, frying pans, and other household goods scarcely suited to an army in quick marching order.[27] The column lacked sufficient men to fill one division but trailed enough wagons to support a brigade.[28]

The dangerous political and cultural divisions that manifested in military conflict blanketed the entire state of Missouri. For example, the organization of the Union Home Guards by the Radical Republicans of St. Louis did not limit itself just to the environs of St. Louis. Unionist Home Guard units began to organize throughout Missouri soon after Governor Jackson issued his proclamation against federal intervention in the state. They formed largely in German communities, although not exclusively. For instance, a Home Guard company drilled in French southeast of Jefferson City at a French settlement in Osage County. The French camp guarded a stubborn bastion of Union sympathy in an overtly secessionist section of the Missouri River Valley. Elsewhere, the first Home Guard unit to form in central Missouri was a German company organized surprisingly at Boonville, although it took no part in the Boonville fight.

Other Home Guard units quickly organized all across Missouri. Like St. Louis, these were initially groups of armed neighborhood citizens sympathetic to the Union but operating autonomously and without government support. For the most part, Home Guards formed independently as political groups for self-protection and not as federal soldiers. The government-organized military Home Guards did not start up until immediately after hostilities began in St. Louis. The War Department in Washington encouraged these federal bands of volunteers and armed them in some cases. Units soon existed throughout the state wherever secessionist activity threatened local citizens.

Such was the case in Benton County, Missouri, a strongly pro–South secessionist region. Threatened by local rebel leaders, a contingent of volunteers made up mostly of German immigrants sympathetic to the Union came together to form a Benton County Home Guard unit.

Benton County had two political and cultural populations. The earliest settlers were Southerners, largely from Kentucky and Tennessee. Their culture remained Southern, including slavery. Most of central and southern Benton County came from Southern states; many were slave owners. Because a large part of the population was decidedly of Southern lineage, Benton County supported the South as might be expected, except for a section of German Americans who lived near the town of Cole Camp. A sizable population of German families stretched across a large farming community northeast of this small Missouri town. They were openly antislavery and steadfastly backed the Union. Everybody in Benton County knew the Germans were loyal unionists with a fervent dislike of slavery. Yet despite their cultural differences with their Southern-bred neighbors, relations in the Cole Camp community between the citizens of Southern heritage and those of German background had remained cordial up to this point, and had developed over the years into one of mutual tolerance.

For the last 25 years, a stream of new arrivals from the Hanover region of northern Germany had poured into this rich farmland region, bringing with them a strong farming work ethic, the Low German language, and the Lutheran religion. Many came persuaded by the writings of Gottfried Duden, whose book on Missouri led them to settle in the region where land sold for $1.25 an acre.[29] They called his book "Duden's Eden." However, his idyllic descriptions of rich Missouri farmland did not always measure up to his propaganda. They encountered a less than ideal existence in reality.[30] Many who came to escape the German Revolution found the labors of farming too difficult and retreated to more urban fortunes, mostly in St. Louis.[31] Nevertheless, by 1860 the German population across all of Missouri ranked it sixth among the states.[32] In Benton County, 14 percent of the population was foreign-born. There were only eight slaves in the entire county.[33]

The Cole Camp community represented the outliers of German immigration, die-hard tillers of the soil who refused to abandon farm life for easier work in the cities. By 1861, successful German farmers occupied much of the land around Cole Camp, giving a large swath of the

20. Prelude to Catastrophe

community a distinctly German character. Many were military refugees and talked of the German Revolution of 1848. There were colonels and majors among them, names from ranks they held in the German insurrection. They lived in their own community, there to best retain their language and customs, speak their native tongue, and pursue the religion of their native land.[34]

The general population of Benton County generally regarded the Germans as a good class of citizens, educated and fond of literary exercises, although the latter often seemed out of place in a frontier town like Cole Camp. Germans exhibited a particular fondness for balls and festivals, and were the ones most devoted to shooting.[35] Turkey shoots ranked high on the list of community pastimes; German target societies competed constantly.

The Germans did not easily integrate into the rest of the Benton County countryside. Historian Lucien Carr said, "Leading the isolated lives they did, they were not open to outside influences, and this, of course, had a tendency to keep them separate and apart from the rest of the community. It also aggravated the natural tenacity with which they clung to the language, the manners and customs, and habits of thought which they brought from the 'fatherland.'"[36]

They stayed apart both socially and religiously. Local preachers of more fundamental dogma characterized them as hard to move and given over to beer drinking, saloons, and masquerade balls. When sectional strife surfaced in Missouri and the Germans sided with the Union, the South-leaning faction of Benton County freely targeted them.

The secessionists did not tolerate advocates of the Union cause in their midst. Early in March, a delegation of them visited A.H.W. Cook and Alexander Mackey, two prominent Benton County Union men, and ordered them to leave the state. The two men lived in Cole Camp, in the north part of the county. Cook left right away for Springfield, Illinois, and from there went directly to Washington to apprise Lincoln of the deteriorating state of affairs in central Missouri. Cook knew Lincoln, having acquired a modest degree of notoriety as the brother of one of the men who rode with John Brown in the Harpers Ferry raid.[37]

Mr. Cook returned from Washington via St. Louis in time to participate in the capture of Camp Jackson. He came back to Cole Camp with a commission from the War Department to enroll and organize a troop of Union Home Guards in Benton County. What he did not have were the weapons to arm the troop. He appealed unsuccessfully to General Harney, who at the time was operating under the terms of the Price-Harney agreement. Governor Jackson refuted claims that he, too, had denied arms to Benton County factions.[38]

Cook set up headquarters at Squire John Brill's place about seven miles northeast of Cole Camp, in the midst of the pro–Union German settlement, and commenced to enlist men for the Union army. He established contact with General Lyon, who was still in St. Louis, and obtained from him the appointment of Captain Henry L. Mitchell as federal quartermaster of the Benton County troops, giving them access to federal arms.[39]

During late May and the first week of June, Cook, Mackey, and several other loyal Union men quietly visited as many of the German unionists as possible to encourage them to enlist as Union volunteers or Home Guards in their own self-defense.[40] About 300 enrolled in the active U.S. volunteer service but most chose to join the Home Guard.[41] June 11 was set as the appointed date to assemble at Harmon Harms barn four miles north of Cole Camp. Here they would perfect an organization and begin the process of military training.[42]

As the nation divided between North and South, so did Benton County and the Cole Camp community. There were almost six hundred German families living in this region at the time. The men of these families made up the core of the Benton County Home Guard. The official government name for this three-month band of volunteers was Benton County Home Guard Missouri Volunteers, but it quickly became known as the German Regiment because 95 percent were German-born or German descendants.

21

Cole Camp

The Benton County Home Guard Volunteers began to assemble at the appointed place at Harms barn northeast of Cole Camp on June 11, 1861, as planned. Captain Abel Hannibal Washington Cook, self-styled as Colonel Cook, commanded.

From New York originally, Cook was a native-born American of German descent whose grandfather served in the Revolutionary War. He came to Benton County from New York at an early age. Now in his 41st year, the organization and command of the German Home Guard fell to him. He had secured a commission to form the regiment, and it seemed proper that he serve as its first commander. His men elected him captain of Company A, but he served instead as commander of the whole regiment. The Germans signaled their loyalty to the Union and infuriated their secessionist neighbors by naming their encampment Camp Lyon, a clear signal that their movements were under the command of General Lyon.[1]

Nearly six hundred men showed up at Camp Lyon on the first day of training filled with enthusiasm for the national cause; about as many women and children accompanied them, all equally full of zeal. The Stars and Stripes flew conspicuously to signal their loyalty to the Union. Cook enrolled five companies of recruits that first day and swore them into service.[2] The next day, another large crowd gathered, and he swore four more companies into government service. Within two days, more than nine hundred men mustered into Union service at Camp Lyon.[3] The regiment included about two hundred Morgan County men, several others from Pettis County, and a few men from Henry County.[4] However, most came from Benton County, and most came without arms or ammunition.

Around five o'clock on the afternoon of June 12, some of the nine assembled companies left the rally point at Harms barn and marched about three hundred yards southeast to the Heisterberg farm. The two farms joined each other and shared a boundary. The Home Guard soldiers encamped in the barns and planned to spend the next week drilling and organizing the regiment.[5]

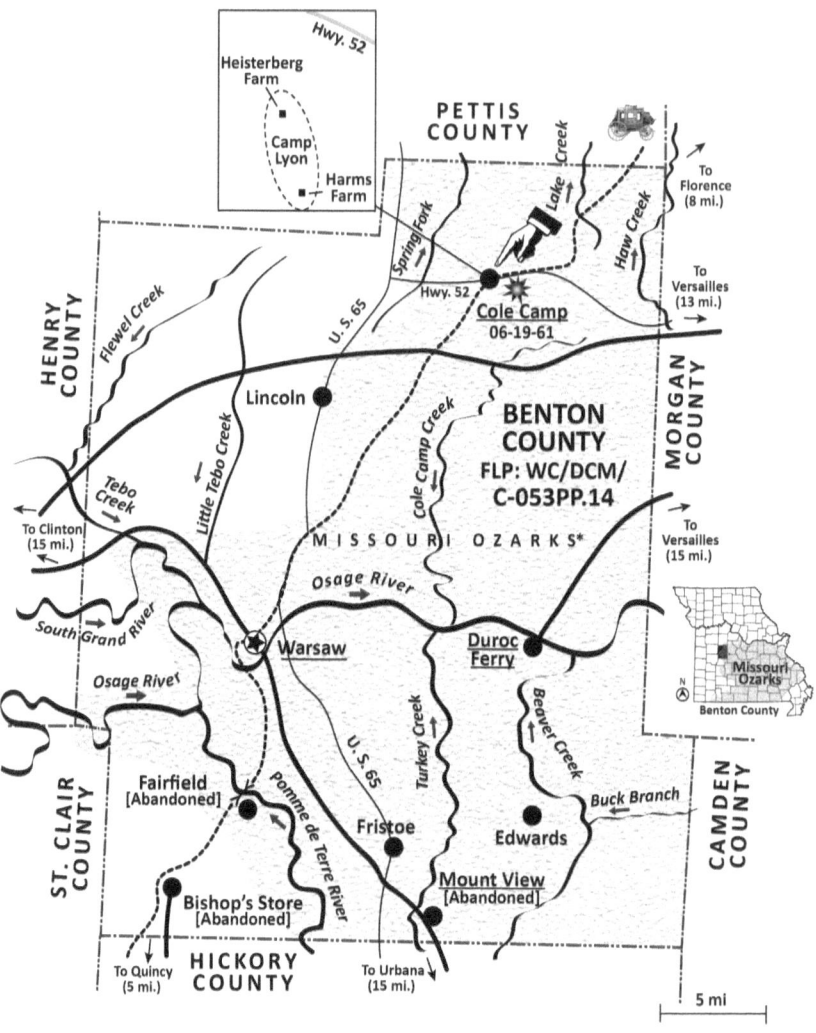

Map of Benton County. A large pro–Union settlement of German Americans lived at Cole Camp, in northern Benton County. The colony stood directly in the path of Governor Jackson's retreating Missouri State Guard. Heavy lines indicate the main roads in use in 1861. Modern Highway U.S. 65 runs north-south through Benton County on the western edge of the Missouri Ozarks. Map by Jackie Worth. Courtesy of Fry's Lyon Foundation, Inc. © 2018, https://mo-passport.org/cole-camp-massacre.

The two barns where the soldiers went into quarters sat about three hundred yards apart on the north and south sides of the Duroc and Cole Camp road. The dwelling houses were several yards west of the barns at the end of a lane that divided the two German-owned farms. The Versailles and Jefferson City road approached from the northeast and intersected the Duroc and Cole Camp road at a point halfway between the camp at the German barns and the town of Cole Camp a short distance to the west. The barns were heavily framed and bulletproof; the one on the north had portholes cut for small-arms fire. Both were close enough together for the men in them to assist each other in the event of an attack.[6]

The secessionists in the area became alarmed at the Home Guard activity and on June 16 sent the sheriff of Benton County to the German camp with a warrant for Cook's arrest. They gave as their reason the camp's threat to the governor of Missouri. Sheriff Bartholomew W. Keown made the trip to the Home Guard camp under the pretense of arresting the camp's leaders. He knew his mission had no chance of succeeding. His real purpose was to gather information about the camp. As expected, Captain Cook declined to go with the sheriff, the camp officers refused to comply with the arrest order, and Keown returned to Warsaw empty-handed. Before the sheriff left, Cook assured him he would make no hostile movements unless threatened by the secessionists.[7] Sheriff Keown delivered his intelligence about the count and condition of the Home Guard camp to the secessionist leaders at Warsaw.[8]

Following the sheriff's visit, Captain Cook leisurely set about the task of training his regiment. He had about four hundred old infantry muskets, not enough to arm his nine hundred recruits. Lacking enough weapons to equip all the volunteers and seeing no immediate prospects of securing additional ones, he furloughed about half of the men and sent them back home to tend their farms.[9] He allowed them to go home for three days unless sooner needed. This left around 450 guards, still poorly armed, quartered in and around the two barns.[10]

General Lyon, anticipating Governor Jackson's direction of flight out of Boonville, knew the Benton County German Regiment was in the governor's path. He sent a message to Captain Cook late on Monday, June 17, alerting him that Jackson was coming down the Boonville road. Lyon directed Cook to intercept Jackson's retreat and stop him. Cook realized that his Home Guards at Cole Camp stood directly in the governor's way.[11]

Governor Jackson's defeated rebel party out of Boonville marched about 25 miles south headed in the direction of Benton County, the fight of the morning at Boonville still in their minds. Governor Jackson knew about the German regiment at Cole Camp. While still at Boonville, he had sent a message to secessionist leaders in Benton County urging recruitment of a Missouri State Guard unit in that vicinity to counter the Union buildup at Cole Camp.

Governor Jackson and his MSG column arrived near Florence on the Butterfield Road about 12 miles north of Cole Camp, where he learned that several hundred Home Guards were at Cole Camp in force, set to block his escape.[12] He knew that an expedition for his relief was speedily coming together at Warsaw south of Cole Camp, ready to remove obstructions to his journey. He sent word ahead to Warsaw to come fast to help to open a corridor through the German camp. Expecting to encounter unknown trouble ahead from the German Home Guard, Governor Jackson halted his men for the night short of Cole Camp and took refuge outside the village of Florence to wait until their route opened. Jackson could not risk capture of what was left of the state government traveling with him, which included Lieutenant Governor Reynolds and many of the elected state officers. The divisions of General Parsons and General Clark had rapidly grown the MSG column to nearly two thousand individuals by now, more than three times the number of the blocking Home Guard regiment in front of them. However, not more than six hundred MSG men were armed. No one in Governor Jackson's party knew the state of readiness of the Home Guard at Cole Camp.

Meanwhile, the retreating State Guard had federal troops close on their heels from the time they left Boonville. A detachment of about 1,400 of the federal army under Captain James Totten closely pursued Jackson, looking to strike a blow against the trapped governor.[13] With instructions from General Lyon, Totten was to capture and bring Jackson back to Boonville.[14] He cautiously followed the retreating rebels from a distance almost to Florence, within striking distance of Jackson's column, before abandoning the chase and returning to Boonville.[15]

As Jackson contemplated his next move to get past the Home Guard at Cole Camp, a small force of Missourians quickly came together 20 miles south of Cole Camp and prepared to open the way for his entourage.[16] They rallied at Warsaw, where a rebel flag had flown on the east side of the courthouse lawn since April 23. A force of pro–South men assembled in a matter of hours to clear Governor Jackson's path. Captain Walter S. O'Kane gathered the Warsaw Grays, while longtime Benton County resident Dr. Stephen F. Hale organized the Blues under the command of Thomas W. Murray.[17] The Windsor Guards Cavalry under Captain John W. Gibbons augmented the Blue and Gray infantry.[18] O'Kane's Grays had only recently returned to Warsaw from a month-long stint of guard duty at the capitol building in Jefferson City. Responding to Governor Jackson's call for troops, they fulfilled their tour of duty uneventfully and had recently returned to Warsaw on June 1.[19] They now quickly answered Jackson's call for help, eager to serve the governor again. The Warsaw force numbered approximately 350 men, about one hundred of them mounted, armed, and equipped with two small cannon.[20]

21. Cole Camp

Captain O'Kane took command. A 28-year-old bachelor from St. Louis, the Indiana-born O'Kane rejected Union plans to dominate Missouri. He split family allegiances with his brother serving in the Union Navy and joined his exceptional planning and leadership abilities to the cause of Governor Jackson and the Missourians. He came from an educated family. His father was a minister, described by those who knew him as thoroughly versed in theology. His ancestors were of Irish nobility. The young O'Kane had lived in Kentucky, spent time prospecting and trading in California, and had recently rejoined his family in Missouri.[21]

While General Lyon was spreading his proclamation of Union reassurances to the citizens of Missouri at Boonville, O'Kane's secessionist rebels gathered at Warsaw, ready to clear the way for Governor Jackson and his defeated Missouri State Guard. Knowing from Sheriff Keown that his force of 350 was about equal in size to the German regiment encamped at Cole Camp and with the advantage of surprise, O'Kane set out with his band on the evening of June 18 up the Butterfield Trail north from Warsaw with the intent of attacking the Germans.

Cole Camp was a town of around two hundred people. Prospering from its crossroads location, the elegant Keeney hotel on the west edge of town, the Ferguson House hotel, and more than 40 businesses and shops, it was one of the better destinations in the state.[22] The Butterfield Mail route, which originated in the Tipton area and ran west, passed through Cole Camp en route to San Francisco. The Butterfield Mail left Tipton twice a week, Monday and Thursday mornings. Six to nine passengers piled on two-and-a-half-ton Concord coaches to begin the 2,700-mile ride into the Wild West, with numerous stops in Missouri. The full trip took less than 22 days. A ticket westbound cost $200; the return trip east was $100. Beginning as a two-horse stage mail route, John Butterfield worked a government contract with his newly formed American Express Company into one of the foremost business ventures of the time. The primary purpose was still to carry the mail—a letter cost 10 cents an envelope—but more importantly it symbolically and actually linked the East Coast with the West.

Cole Camp set on the Butterfield route at the hub of four main roads, each pointing toward different destinations in the state. The Butterfield road, known locally as the Duroc road, ran south to the Osage River crossing. The Jefferson City road, also known as the Versailles road, led east to the State Capitol, and the Boonville road came in from the north. It was along the Boonville road that Jackson and his men were proceeding. He intended to pass through Cole Camp to get to General Sterling Price's rendezvous point at Montevallo in southwest Missouri.

The German camp received two visitors on the evening of June 18 who brought disturbing information. John Tyree, a longtime respected citizen of Benton County and one of its earliest settlers, had witnessed the preparations of the secessionists at Warsaw. He went to the German camp accompanied by Porter Mitchell, son of Captain Cook's quartermaster, to report this information to the camp leaders. He warned in an exaggerated report that the secessionists were marching from Warsaw under Captain O'Kane fully one thousand strong and determined to attack the Union camp, probably by midnight that day. Cook met with his officers but decided to take no direct action, except to dispatch couriers to recall the furloughed troops sent home on the 16th, ordering them to return as quickly as possible, preferably that night. Three companies in addition to those already in camp could come within a few hours in time to meet the secessionists from Warsaw.[23]

Tyree's warning apparently did not greatly alarm Captain Cook, and he expected no attack.[24] He put out a handful of pickets to cover the roads into the camp, a total of seven men to stand as sentries, and a half dozen mounted patrol pickets to ride back and forth between these outposts. He meant for these sparse preparations to prevent a surprise assault mostly from Jackson's forces to the north; otherwise, he made minimal to no preparations for an attack.[25]

That night—the night of June 18, 1861—a force of approximately 400 German Home Guards settled down for the evening, enjoying a few cups of liquid refreshment before turning in. Mustered in just six days earlier, they were brand new citizen soldiers not yet acquainted with the rigors of military discipline. Oblivious to the danger of Walter O'Kane's band of approaching rebels, Captain Cook's men drank heavily into the night, several gathering at a nearby log house in what one witness later described as a party atmosphere. They were unaware that O'Kane's band was nearby.

Neither the Union outfit nor the secessionist band presented much of a military organization. Each was a hastily thrown together collection of Missouri citizens with no Regular Army officers and no battlefield experience.

As the rebels approached Cole Camp along the road near the Fordney School and not far from Ball Town, they met up with John Tyree around one o'clock in the morning returning to his home near Cole Camp Creek. He lived about where Williams Creek joined Cole Camp Creek. Under questioning, some of the men recognized him as having been in Warsaw earlier in the day and accused him of spying for the Union. Surmising that he had tipped the Germans, and after getting all the information they could from him, O'Kane had him tied to a tree and shot.[26] The Virginia-born Tyree was 65 years old and a slave owner but a Union man. The rebels left his body tied up for the animals. Neighbors later found his badly torn remains and took him home. His family buried him behind his house, where his stone still stands.[27]

The two adjoining farms occupied by the encampment of the German Home Guard belonged to Harmon Harms and Henry Heisterberg.[28] These barns, which housed the main elements of the camp, sat some three hundred or so yards apart. The men were staying in these two barns and other outbuildings. Captain Cook had his headquarters at Harmon Harms barn. Night shrouded the camp, the buildings silhouetted against a faintly moonlit landscape. Most of the Home Guard soldiers slept; a few were up waiting for the approaching dawn.

The Warsaw rebel force left the Butterfield Road and made its way along farm trails toward the Union camp situated a couple of miles north and slightly east of Cole Camp. Shortly after three o'clock on the morning of June 19, O'Kane's cavalry and infantry advanced on the Home Guard camp.[29] It was nearing dawn when O'Kane came upon the camp. A glint of twilight spread across the eastern sky. The Germans had only a handful of pickets out and only then on the northern perimeter. Expecting an attack to come from Governor Jackson's forces located to the north, only a few guards watched the southern perimeter. As O'Kane approached the camp, he employed a bit of treachery. His troops carried a Union flag.[30] The few pickets that stood guard on the southern perimeter of the camp mistook the rebels for friends and did not challenge them. O'Kane's men bayoneted the hapless guards to avoid alerting the slumbering men. The rebels killed the outside picket on the Cole Camp road, then quietly moved up the road and killed the two at the second station.[31] O'Kane's force easily overran the pickets without awakening anyone.[32] When they were almost upon the camp, they approached a fourth picket near the north barn. He saw them coming and fled without discharging his gun. The hapless sentry escaped and ran yelling into the camp, but it was too late.[33]

22

O'Kane's Night Attack

The rebels planned to divide their companies and attack the two barns of sleeping Home Guards simultaneously. However, Captain Gibbons's Windsor Cavalry arrived early at the Heisterberg barn.[1] The fleeing picket rushed into the barn, leaving the double doors wide open. Gibbons's soldiers were immediately behind him. More rebels followed close on the picket's heels, and finding no opposition came to within a few yards of the barn. Before the excited picket could wake the sleeping Home Guard soldiers and warn them, the secessionists rode up to the door and opened fire as the men inside were getting up. The Germans awoke to the clatter of hooves and the shouts of the attackers as their first notice of danger. Gibbons's men delivered another volley into the unsuspecting men, slaughtering some of the Union volunteers in their sleep. More volleys of rapid fire from double-barreled guns and fowling pieces took a fierce toll on the German troops. The brazen attack killed 21 men.[2] Completely surprised, the Germans faced near annihilation in an instant. Many had left their muskets outside the barn because there was hardly room inside. Left defenseless, the trapped men fell before the mounted assault.[3]

The rest of the Home Guard camp came alive. A Home Guard officer, Lieutenant Elsinger, heard the commotion and saw the attack from his position behind a fence not far north of the Heisterberg barn where his men had billeted for the night in three corncribs.[4] His platoon of 24 Home Guardsmen grabbed their muskets and fired into the flank of the attackers.[5] They fired several volleys into the ranks of the secessionists at short range until nearly out of ammunition, killing six secessionist leaders and wounding several more in the rebel ranks. The few unwounded men in the Heisterberg barn joined in the fire, and the rebels fell back. Protected by the fence and corncribs, Lieutenant Elsinger did not lose a single man. Seeing the men in the barn who were alive or not captured safely out of the barn, he withdrew his men toward the timber and in the direction of the Home Guards camped at the south Harms barn.[6]

22. O'Kane's Night Attack

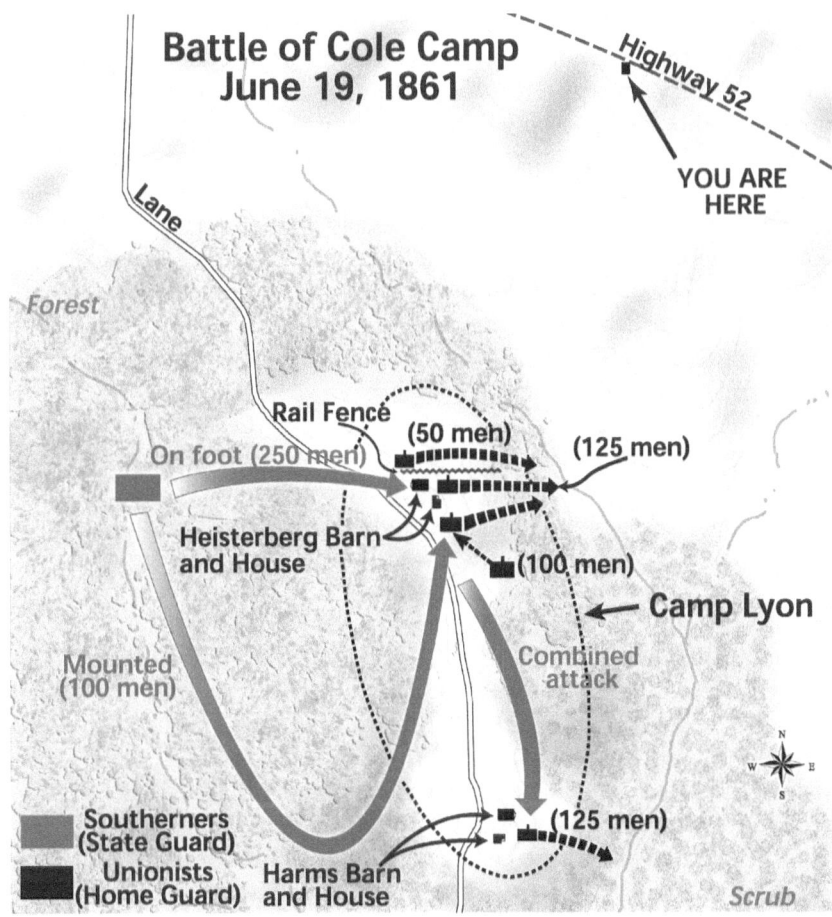

Cole Camp. A band of Missouri State Guard men from Warsaw, led by Colonel Walter S. O'Kane, raided a Union camp near Cole Camp in a surprise attack on the night of June 19, 1861, killing many German Home Guard troops. The raid cleared the way for Governor Claiborne Jackson to continue his march into southwest Missouri. Modified map courtesy Missouri State Parks.

Under heavy fire from the Home Guard soldiers, Captain Gibbons halted his attack, withdrew his men to the woods, and regrouped. He launched a second assault, overrunning the Heisterberg barn and farmhouse area. Using rails from a nearby rail fence, his men broke down the doors and routed the German defenders, most of whom had exhausted their ammunition and fled.

As daylight broke, the men escaping the attack at the Heisterberg barn withdrew southeast along the lane on the Cole Camp and Duroc road until they reached the end of the lane. With the rebel cavalry in pursuit, the Home Guard soldiers turned south toward the wood line southeast of the barn. They regrouped at the timber's edge and started back up the hill. Before they got very far, about 45 rebel cavalry intercepted them. The cavalry temporarily postponed its mission to attack the adjacent Harms barn to drive into the flank of this new target of opportunity and force the Union Guard back into the woods. The Germans attempted to form a defense, but Gibbons's mounted attackers slammed into them and drove the undisciplined men from the field. The rebel assault stalled at this point because the cavalry could not operate effectively in the woods. Under cover of underbrush and young timber, the Germans rallied and drove back the cavalry. When it was over, another Home Guard man lay dead, along with two or three rebels.[7]

By now, the Home Guard troops stationed at the south Harms barn some distance away had heard the gunfire at the north barn and formed to join the fight. Captain John Henry Mueller and Captain Henry Groteheier formed their companies in line in front of the barn and moved forward to engage the rebels. They saw a column of soldiers approaching. It surprised them to see that they carried a Union flag.[8] The rider at the head of the column carried the Stars and Stripes; others in the ranks also carried the national banner.[9] Seeing the flag in the twilight, the Union force waiting at the barn hesitated and held its fire.[10] Confused by the rebel subterfuge, the Germans did not open fire until the rebels fired upon them. A volley from the furtive secessionists killed four and wounded two, including Captain Mueller, who was badly shot in the neck.[11] It was too late to mount a counterattack. Amid a hail of bullets now directed on them, the Germans dropped their weapons and fled, leaving the battleground completely to the secessionists. The deceived Germans did not do any fighting. Well in command of the situation, the Warsaw rebels rode around the field shouting and firing their weapons, still carrying a Union flag.

Reports varied widely as to the number of casualties at Cole Camp. None of the units that met that morning had official military credentials, therefore there were no official casualty counts on either side. Curiously, the St. Louis newspapers did not immediately publish an account of the rebel raid.[12] The *Missouri Democrat* ran limited news coverage about Governor Jackson's whereabouts but did not pick up the news of Cole Camp until several days after the clash.[13] The *New York Times* ran a brief account based on local dispatches coming from the *Boonville Register*. The *New York Tribune* made brief mention of the affair, mostly to complain about the alleged bad treatment of prisoners and the killing of Mr. Tyree.[14] A couple of papers picked it up in the South, but largely it went unreported and forgotten.[15] Later published versions of the fight listed German Home

22. O'Kane's Night Attack

Guard losses at anywhere from 25 to 36 officers and men killed or mortally wounded, about 60 wounded, and some 25 captured.[16] The captors took the prisoners to Warsaw and there released them upon taking an oath not to bear arms against the Southern Confederacy.[17] Meanwhile, secessionists, according to published versions, lost six or seven killed and 25 to 30 wounded, notwithstanding Union claims of 44 men lost on the side of the rebels.[18] More extreme estimates of casualties appeared in subsequent years. Jefferson Davis and other pro–South historians claimed that over two hundred Germans died, slaughtered in their sleep, more than that wounded, and upward of 100 captured.[19] These numbers defy reality because, added up, the losses approach the entire number of German Home Guards encamped that morning at Camp Lyon. The truth probably lies somewhere in between. The secessionists gave no count of their casualties. However, Lieutenant Mitchell, the Home Guard quartermaster, returned to the Heisterberg barn later that day under a flag of truce to look after the killed and wounded Germans. He claimed to have seen three wagonloads of dead rebels awaiting burial. He estimated the number of dead to be not less than 100.[20]

Reports varied as to the actual number of men engaged at Cole Camp. Cook estimated the number of secessionists to be between 1,000 and 1,200. However, secessionists said their force was only 350. Cook had about 400 Union men. Of these, he claimed 23 killed, 20 wounded, and 30 taken prisoners. Pollard, the secessionist historian, insisted the Home Guards lost 206 killed, a large number wounded, and more than 100 taken prisoners.[21] He put secession losses at four killed and 15 or 20 wounded.[22] Jefferson Davis in his book on the Confederacy used Pollard's numbers for casualties, and other historians similarly based their accounts on Pollard.[23]

One thing was certain; the Cole Camp engagement signaled the growing personal cost of sectional hostilities. That Wednesday morning, the rebel dawn sneak attack on the Heisterberg barn alone instantly killed or wounded at least 34 or 35 of the 170 men billeted there, including Friedrich Detjen, Claus Hink, Theodor Bergman, and Friedrich Kranke, all members of the same small German church. Actual numbers remain unverified. Nevertheless, survivors allegedly buried 90 unidentified dead in Union-Williams Cemetery southwest of Cole Camp and another 17 in unmarked graves in Monsees Cemetery (Immanuel Lutheran), south of the battle site.[24] Many more lie buried at various places around the area. Family members buried many at home on the farms where they lived. The Union lamented the loss of some of its best officers. For example, Captain Carl Brühl's Company F was in the Heisterberg barn when the attack occurred, along with Lieutenant Colonel Henry Imhauser. Brühl died in the assault and Imhauser received a shot through the neck.[25]

Meanwhile, the rebels carried their casualties—whatever their number—back to Warsaw. Their dead included six of the most prominent residents of Warsaw, among them 24-year-old John H. Leach, publisher and printer of the *Warsaw Southwest Democrat*.[26] The newspaper ceased upon his death, ending a once strident and influential voice of secession.

The Cole Camp flight left a trail of muskets, knapsacks, and cartridge boxes. O'Kane's troops gathered up captured weapons and prisoners, then headed back to Warsaw. The once poorly armed rebel Missourians took away 362 muskets, almost the entire stand of arms of the German Home Guard. The bayonets, they thought, would be of particular use against the Union invaders.[27] These weapons, combined with another 150 muskets taken previously from a German company in a neighboring county, added significantly to the MSG cache of arms.[28]

The rebels wanted the prisoners executed. "Death to the Dutch," they shouted.[29] O'Kane refused and slowly marched the captives back to Warsaw. Away from the heat of battle, he liberated them upon each one taking an oath not to bear arms again against the state of Missouri.

The conduct of Captain O'Kane and his men in the Cole Camp raid drew considerable criticism. His breach of military conduct tainted the victory and reduced him in the minds of some to little more than a gratuitous murderer instead of an honorable knight of the Southern cause. To begin with, the murder of John Tyree was an arbitrary death sentence that many thought did not match the level of the crime, as traitorous as it may have appeared to secessionist sympathizers. Secondly, the rebels bayoneted the pickets, ostensibly to keep them from firing their weapons and alerting the camp. However, they stabbed one captured lad to death anyway, though he was already relieved of his weapon.[30]

Furthermore, O'Kane's troops had been able to approach both barns through the Union flag deception. The Germans dedicated themselves to defending the Union and hesitated to raise a weapon against its flag. By the time they detected the ruse, it was too late. Under a Union flag, the secessionists approached the Home Guard camp and fell upon the sleeping soldiers, killing many in cold blood. Finally, the commission of wanton murder apparently extended to innocent bystanders. Among the captives was a recent German immigrant by the name of Tomforte who complained that he was not a fighter but only a cook. Not understanding his broken English, the rebels mistook him for the Union Home Guard commander, Able Cook, and shot him dead.

The real Able Cook came under considerable criticism himself for his performance at the Cole Camp fight. His lack of preparation drew the most scrutiny. Sending half his force on furlough may have serendipitously saved lives; however, he was slow to recall them after a warning of impending danger. The sent-for reinforcements got within two miles of the camp when the attack started. Unsure about the circumstances of the assault, the untrained recruits stood by and did nothing.[31]

One newspaper account placed Cook in the Heisterberg barn when the attack began, but he apparently escaped uninjured and fled at the beginning of the fight.[32] He claimed later that he left to consult with Union forces in pursuit of Governor Jackson coming out of Boonville. Cook's men said otherwise and demanded his replacement as commander of the German regiment. One New York newspaper said Cook should have been court-martialed. Nevertheless, Captain Cook eluded court martial and took on new assignments in service to the Union.

The evening after the fight, Cook left his men in small defensive detachments in the timber around Cole Camp and started out to reach General Lyon. He found him at Boonville in the middle of organizing his southwest Missouri expedition. Lyon was not able to help in Benton County immediately due to lack of transportation. He asked Cook to send ten teams to Boonville to carry ammunition and equipment back to the Cole Camp defenders and said he would follow as soon as was practicable. In the meantime, he promised some important new assignments for the vanquished German Home Guards.[33]

Larger events of the Civil War overshadowed the war's opening skirmishes. The engagement at Cole Camp faded into more of a legend than a reality.[34] Eastern newspapers gave a brief report of it at the time, and the local press later characterized it as the first battle of the Civil War.[35] However, it soon dropped from the headlines as bigger, more costly battles vied for attention. Those in the fight, however, did not forget. Stories of atrocities that circulated among Union sympathizers frequently connected to Cole Camp. One story told how the Miller brothers, traveling cross country on their way to Ohio and having nothing to do with the assembly of Home Guards at Cole Camp, stopped for the night to seek lodging. They put up in the Heisterberg barn where Captain Cook's men had bedded down. When the secessionists descended on the camp and its unsuspecting sleepers, opened the doors of the barn, and commenced a deadly fire on the occupants, the Miller brothers escaped in the darkness, running in different directions. The rebels took one of them prisoner; the other brother was less fortunate. Met by a squad of secessionists, they shot him through the head without provocation and left his body on the prairie, where hogs tore it to shreds. The captors of the surviving brother roughed him up and then released him once he'd taken an oath of allegiance to the state of Missouri. The anger in his eyes and the revolver he carried afterward, peeking from the breast of his shirt, said that he would not long honor his oath or the law, although he was a lawyer by profession.

Tensions in the Cole Camp community continued with deadly results. Rebel bushwhackers shot Herman Sempke and Adolph Reiser while both were at work. The community was so outraged that people came to their funerals carrying guns. The bloodshed continued. Some rebels shot Arndt Cordes because he did not stop when ordered to do so.

The German community continued to suffer throughout the Civil War. Northern and Southern troops traversed back and forth through the area. The terrorism of the bushwhackers and marauding bands of guerrillas created a lasting hatred between sides that divided the town for many years after the War. Following the affair at Cole Camp, in the wake of events at Boonville and Jefferson City, longstanding local feuds erupted all over the state. Destructive guerrilla warfare emerged, degenerating into neighborhood conflicts that often ended in bloody personal reprisals and revenge in vigilante-style activity. Bushwhackers burned houses and bridges, plundered farms, tore up railroads—where there were railroads—and left a trail of kidnappings and assassinations. In the absence of organized law enforcement campaigns in Missouri, unrepressed lawlessness and crime turned the state into a place of near anarchy.[36] Reckless and violent men traveled in parties of 20 to 30, usually by horseback, wandering about and visiting mayhem on anyone whose sentiments they found displeasing. As soon as one of these bands of marauders found that troops were approaching, they dispersed, each man going to his home. When troops arrived, they found only law-abiding men working in the fields or in their offices or businesses. As soon as the troops left, they were again armed and on the prowl, menacing the community.

Captain O'Kane's rout of the German Home Guard at Cole Camp provided the Missourians with their first battlefield victory and a welcome morale boost to the rest of the struggling force. The rebel success at Cole Camp opened the way for the fleeing Governor Jackson and his men to continue their journey into southwest Missouri. There was now a clear path for Governor Jackson's forces. Two days after the action at Cole Camp, the governor and his entourage passed through the German camp, the blockade now removed. They proceeded toward Warsaw, in lower Benton County just north of the Osage River. There Jackson hoped to gather reinforcements and bask in the success of O'Kane's victorious Warsaw regiment.[37]

After the Cole Camp affair, Captain Totten broke off the federal chase. Based on the receipt of flawed information as to the strength of Jackson's forces, obtained from a German who escaped the destruction at Cole Camp, and misled by local Jackson sympathizers about the exaggerated size of Jackson's army, Totten abandoned his pursuit and returned to

Boonville and to General Lyon's preparations for the extended campaign into southwest Missouri.[38]

Governor Jackson knew nothing of Lyon's plans to capture him. He anticipated Union pursuit but had no knowledge of the federal force already descending on southwest Missouri from St. Louis by way of Rolla, intent on providing the anvil to Lyon's hammer to destroy the fledgling State Guard.

23

Into the Spider's Web

The heavy rains that drenched MSG troops marching out of Lexington extended down the river plain across Boonville, hampering General Lyon's efforts to organize a land campaign in pursuit of Jackson and the MSG. Moreover, bullet-ridden supply steamers coming into Boonville confirmed that hostile forces still operated along the Missouri River.[1]

Nevertheless, the Union now had undisputed control of the rivers and the central environs of the state and worked to root out any vestiges of rebellion there. On one occasion, Lyon received word of a force of State Guard volunteers gathering at Glasgow a few miles upriver from Boonville on the north side of the river. He put part of his infantry and a battery of artillery on steamers and set out to confront them.

It was not long until he landed his force and came up on the backside of the town, putting it between his men and the river. A young guardsman astride his horse saw the danger and took off at a full gallop. Someone yelled, "What are you running for?" He said, "Why, don't you see? They are going to fire a cannon."[2] The Federals wheeled the guns into position and with a few shots scattered the raw recruits. Those who could not get on ferryboats swam the river or escaped by any means at hand. Most of them abandoned the thought of war and went back home. Wherever the threat of a rebel rallying point existed, Union forces moved quickly to break it up.

To top off Lyon's frustration, McClellan was in western Virginia. Lyon hardly knew who commanded or where to turn.[3] He had no direct way to communicate with General McClellan from Boonville.[4] On June 20, he wrote a letter and sent it to Adjutant Harding at Jefferson City with instructions to transmit it by telegraph to McClellan.[5] He asked McClellan for more reinforcements at Boonville and Warsaw, "which is a nest of rebels who have massacred at Cole Camp Union men," he wrote.[6]

Almost simultaneously with Lyon's letter, reinforcements began to arrive at Boonville. Four companies of the Seventh Missouri U.S. Regiment arrived from St. Louis to bolster General Lyon's army. The First Iowa Infantry Regiment Volunteers joined them shortly thereafter on June 21,

23. Into the Spider's Web

Union and Missouri State Guard Troops. Federal forces captured the state capital at Jefferson City and drove the Missouri State Guard out of Boonville. In a coordinated pincer plan, Union regiments marched cross-country from Rolla, Missouri, deep into southwest Missouri, while troops coming out of Kansas threatened the rear of the State Guard. Governor Jackson abandoned Boonville to rendezvous in southwest Missouri with the main body of the Guard coming south out of Lexington. General Price waited in the far corner of the state under the shelter of Confederate forces in northern Arkansas. Modified map after Jacob Wells, *Battles and Leaders of the Civil War*, 1887–1888, page 263.

and the Fifth Missouri Volunteers came up a few days later, all substantially increasing the size of Lyon's Union force. These were the first of Lyon's hoped-for reinforcements. Unfortunately, the First Iowa came with the same enlistment time constraints as his own soldiers. In a few weeks, their tours of duty would end.

The men of the First Iowa came into Boonville from the west, traveling downriver from Arrow Rock by ferry. As they came upon the fairgrounds at Boonville, they caught their first glimpse of General Lyon, standing with Frank Blair beside the river, which was running nearly bank full from recent rains. A soldier onboard the ferry described the scene: "A large stone-quarry had been opened on the river bank, and about an acre of level stone uncovered. The river had risen to within six inches of this level ledge of rock. There were two men alone at its edge watching our boat come across; one had blue army pants, a line coat, and a black felt hat; it was Lyon. The other dressed in citizen's clothes with an army cap. He stooped and dipped a long black bottle into the raging Missouri. While he churned the bottle up and down he watched us and turned up his face now and then to talk with Lyon, who was gazing at us through a field glass." The two men stood on the white stone ledge, talking and looking out over the water; Blair and Lyon standing there, Blair dressed all in black. They appeared at a distance as two marooned figures, alone in a vast expanse of space in which no other living thing stirred. The swiftly moving current of the muddy Missouri lapped at the feet of the two figures to give the scene a chilling surrealism that left a lasting impression on the Iowans.

The Iowa soldiers came to dislike Lyon. They decried his cruelty toward privates, his favorite mode of punishment being a buck and gag technique that tied offending soldiers spread-eagled on a wagon wheel, leaving them in the sweltering hot sun to repent their transgressions.[7]

First Iowa Infantry Soldier. Private Lewis Creitz enlisted on April 18, 1861, in Company A, First Iowa Infantry, mustered in at Keokuk, Iowa. The First Iowa enlisted for 90 days under President Lincoln's first call for volunteers. Creitz was among the Iowans who joined General Lyon's forces at Boonville and accompanied him into southwest Missouri. Shown here as Lieutenant Creitz in this 1862 photograph by H.A. Balch, Memphis, Tennessee. Courtesy Wilson's Creek National Battlefield (WICR 11189).

Moreover, the Iowans despised the young Regular Army officers and railed against the Germans. One soldier said, "One feels as if we were sold to the Dutch in this army. Dutch is the prevailing language."[8] Many were the stories demeaning the federal Missourians. A sentinel hailed an intoxicated officer one night. "Who comes there?" inquired the sentinel. "You idiot," said the officer. "Advance, you idiot, and give the countersign," replied the sentinel.[9]

If the soldiers did not like Lyon, they did like Blair. They called Blair the bejesus colonel because he punctuated his conversation with a steady stream of "bejesus." Their fondness for Blair also came from a rumor that Blair did not like Lyon much either. Unfortunately, Blair left Boonville and went back to Washington, leaving the Iowans stuck with Lyon.[10]

The First Iowa was a well-educated regiment of young men, many of them scholars of some distinction. They had opinions on everything. The North stood divided on Lincoln; some thought he was going too slowly, some thought he should slow down. Within the First Iowa, however, Mr. Lincoln appeared friendless. The Iowa boys had no confidence in him whatsoever.[11]

Each Iowan carried the old-fashioned long, heavy musket that bore the stamp U.S. 1829, a flintlock altered over into a percussion. Its ammunition was the buck and ball, meaning one large round ball and three large buckshot in one cartridge. The guns had only a notch for a rear sight. Tinkering with the front sight got an approximation of a target, but the smoothbore weapons did not shoot straight.[12]

Ammunition for the muskets was equally archaic. Cartridges were tough paper with big charges of coarse black powder. The ball was a Minié bullet, conical at the front with a cavity in the rear filled with a pointed wooden plug. A pointed steel ramrod, rammed against the wooden plug, spread the ball to fit tightly in the smoothbore barrel. Accuracy was dubious. However, a shot could paralyze a man a mile away.[13]

The Iowans were much aware that when war broke out the rebels would have the best of everything. The South had prepared for war for years and had control of the government to deliver it. The South started with 150,000 of the best muskets while the Iowans waited, content with the old-fashioned guns and leavings. The South got a thousand of the best cannon while the Union got the old shopworn stuff. The old weapons did have at least one redeeming quality. The bayonets made excellent candlesticks. A bayonet stuck in the ground provided a socket that exactly fitted a candle.[14]

The First Iowa boys quickly found ways to amuse themselves at Camp Cameron while they waited at the fairgrounds for orders. Daily drills entertained local Boonville crowds. Major Osterhaus had a voice like a trumpet, shouting out orders sometimes in German, sometimes in English. At the same time, Captain Totten seemed always to carry a canteen of brandy, directing his battery between drinks, "Forward that caisson g—d d—n you, sir." Drills usually ended up at a nearby beer saloon for a treat of blackberry brandy, a favorite Missouri drink.[15]

Evenings brought a different kind of entertainment. When the Iowans marched out of Keokuk, officers stripped them down to the essentials. They consented to let their Bibles go but kept their poker decks.[16]

It seemed like every fifth man was a fiddler and would fiddle all night for two dollars. Charlie Stypes carried his accordion in a bag over his burly shoulders and could turn any sound into a musical composition. A group of soldiers sang "The Happy Land of Canaan." To top of an uneventful day, the campers could usually count on a serenade of the mules braying at precisely midnight.[17]

Soon after the action at Cole Camp, Governor Jackson's column resumed its steady march southward on the flight from Boonville. With the road ahead now cleared in Benton County, Governor Jackson moved his Missourians cautiously forward toward Warsaw. He expected to halt at Warsaw to pick up reinforcements.[18]

As the weary Missourians filed past the abandoned site of the carnage at Cole Camp, several miles to the northwest, elements of the Lexington wing of the Guard struggled to cross the Black River near Warrensburg, on the way to Clinton and a juncture with Jackson. The Lexington troops were more a loosely gathered collection of men, banded together under a common aversion to Union occupation, than they were a well-organized army of soldiers with a shared military mission. However, the Guard had the rough outline of a fighting force. Riding in command of the Lexington army was Brigadier General James Rains, acting on his appointment as interim commander of the MSG by General Price. At the core of the army were Brigadier General Slack's 700-man infantry and Colonel Benjamin Allen Rives's Ray County Regiment of 500 mounted cavalry. Hiram Bledsoe's three-piece artillery made up the heavy guns.

Colonel Rives's cavalry was perhaps the best armed of any of the units. Some of his men were among the participants in the raid on the Liberty Arsenal. He owned a large plantation east of Kansas City and owned more slaves than anyone else in Ray County. His reputation as a civic leader and his profession as a medical doctor seemed to make him an unlikely warrior.

Captain Joseph O. Shelby, at the head of his hard-riding rangers, led the Lexington column. Shelby, a wealthy businessperson from Waverly, in Lafayette County, had previously taken his men into the border wars with Kansas and experienced firsthand the dangers of sectional fighting. He witnessed Lyon's actions in St. Louis and immediately threw his support to Governor Jackson. His well-trained, disciplined men presented a model for the remainder of the MSG.

Besides Shelby's men, the infantry of Colonel John T. Hughes was by far the best trained of the lot. Hughes, a Clinton County farmer, began organizing a militia in his home county in April, even before the shelling of Fort Sumter. He took his men to Lexington to join General Price right after the events in St. Louis. His right-hand field commanders, Lieutenant Colonel James A. Pritchard and Major J.C. Thornton, were capable military men ready to take the fight to the Union interventionists.[19]

The size of the Lexington arm grew daily. Bands of new recruits came from all directions along the way. Missourians came individually and in groups. Colonel Francis M. McKinney joined with 16 men. Colonel John R. Graves attached his battalion of 271 infantry; Colonel Edgar V. Hurst, a farmer from Cass County, added about the same number. The Kentuckian Hurst was particularly welcomed for his good military knowledge and skills, attributes sorely lacking in the fledgling Missouri State Guard.

Colonel Richard Weightman undertook the task of trying to organize the growing infantry. All the different foot-soldier companies roughly formed the First Brigade. Meanwhile, Brigadier General Rains busied himself with the various cavalry commands also streaming into the State Guard column. Colonel Robert Yates Ludwell Peyton brought his 115 Lafayette County mounted; Colonel Jesse Lamb Cravens, Jr., contributed another 200 men. The rough-and-tumble Cravens made no attempt to disguise the fact that Brigadier General Rains was his brother-in-law and that he, Cravens, had more military background than the popular Rains. In Carthage where Cravens made his home and kept a store, people knew him as the acerbic merchant with all the slaves.

The first elements of the Lexington rebels passed Warrensburg on June 20, and after a 20-mile trek came to Clinton just north of the South Grand River. Bands of men continued to join the retreating column. Clinton Hunter, the town's founder, rode out to meet them with a small group of soldiers.

Even the women got into the excitement. Eliza Apperson and Minerva Conner, two patriotic Henry County citizens, volunteered to join as nurses. General Rains politely declined.

The crossing of the South Grand took the better part of two days. Most of the men and supplies crossed the swollen stream on homemade rafts. One man drowned when he slid off a raft. Ever mindful of the dangers of federal pursuit, patrols went up and down the river to destroy anything that might aid General Lyon in crossing the river. One Guard private wrote home, "Lyon will need magic to cross this river."

Meanwhile, the first elements of Governor Jackson's party arrived at Warsaw about midday on June 23. O'Kane's Warsaw battalion of 350 soldiers, give or take a few, instantly joined the growing MSG army. Governor Jackson rested his men at Warsaw for two days, waiting for news of General Price in southwest Missouri and of the main body of the army coming down from Lexington. During that time, MSG recruits continued to try to reach the defiant governor. Additional State Guard volunteers from the countryside quickly enlisted. Jackson's MSG force now numbered well above 2,300 men. Rebel volunteers across the state took many risks to try to catch up to the growing MSG army, some in vain but others successfully.

One Missourian who had trouble trying to join Governor Jackson's MSG troops was Henry Guibor, a St. Louis artilleryman hurrying across country with his compatriot William Barlow.

Joining the State Guard could be a risky proposition, especially if the origin of the effort was St. Louis. Nevertheless, after the Boonville clash, Minute Men and pro–South sympathizers, tired of Lyon's high-handed tactics, left the city to join the State Guard. Two of them, Henry Guibor and William P. Barlow, were experienced artillerymen. Guibor, of Northern birth but a staunch defender of Missouri and states' rights, had been active in the Kansas troubles, as had Barlow. They were also at Camp Jackson when that affair occurred, and were among the prisoners paroled by Lyon. Each wanted to get even for the Camp Jackson massacre. Their skills as battery gunners were

Henry Guibor. Paroled by General Lyon for the Camp Jackson affair, Captain Guibor and Lieutenant William Barlow set out to join the Missouri State Guard forces. They arrived at Jefferson City to find the state government deposed and federal volunteers in charge. They made contact with State Guard forces at Warsaw, where Guibor took charge of the MSG artillery. Courtesy Missouri Historical Society St. Louis (N12334).

23. Into the Spider's Web

William P. Barlow. Lieutenant Barlow turned down a Union commission, choosing instead to fight with the rebel Missouri State Guard Light Artillery Battery of Captain Henry Guibor. Paroled along with Guibor after Camp Jackson, Barlow caught up with Guard troops at Warsaw. Photograph by John A. Scholten, ca. 1890. Courtesy Missouri Historical Society St. Louis (N20997).

in demand; both of them turned down appointments as officers in the Union army. When Jackson's circumstances became dire at Boonville, they set out to join the MSG. To avoid suspicion of their movements, they split up in St. Louis and rendezvoused some 20 miles outside the city. Guibor told his family he was going to the country on a short trip, which turned out to last four years.[20]

Guibor was the deputy marshal of the criminal court in St. Louis and a first-generation American, whose father emigrated from Canada and once fought with the British in the War of 1812. When the Mexican War broke out, young Guibor left his work in the carpenter's trade and was with the first U.S. troops to cross the Rio Grande. He returned to St. Louis after the war to an on-again, off-again military career. He had returned recently from a campaign against the Kansas Jayhawkers on the western border when the crisis engulfed St. Louis. He had won a promotion to lieutenant in the Missouri state militia for his service in Kansas. As an officer in the state militia, he was at Camp Jackson when General Lyon led federal troops to place the whole camp under arrest. After Camp Jackson, and a few days short of the aborted meeting at the Planter's House hotel between Governor Jackson, Sterling Price, General Lyon, and Frank Blair, Lyon and Blair offered Guibor a commission as colonel of a federal regiment. Guibor refused. He said his sympathies lay with the South, but he did not intend to take part on either side. He had lately lost his father and his mother now depended on him for support. The bitter experience at Camp Jackson and his parole by Lyon under protest did little to endear Guibor to the Union. Soon after turning down the government offer, friends informed him that a warrant was out for his arrest. On what grounds no one knew. He immediately teamed up with Barlow, another alleged fugitive from the government, and the two started out on horseback to find Governor Jackson's troops, at that time organizing somewhere in the state. After an adventurous beginning, the duo reached Jefferson City only to find Jackson gone and Lyon and his Union forces in control of the capitol. Circumventing the federal pickets, they reached Versailles, only to face prompt arrest by secessionists as Union spies. The next day, they and their captors caught up with Governor Jackson's column at Warsaw. The governor promptly relieved the two men from arrest and put Guibor in charge of the battery of General Parsons's six-pound cannon, the same obtained by force from the Liberty Arsenal. Thus began Captain Guibor's Battery. Guibor soon discovered that the men operating the guns had no training and the guns had the unique appearance of military antiques, which they were. Nevertheless, he made his companion, Barlow, his first lieutenant and together they began drilling the men. They improvised whatever equipment the guns required to make them operational. Soon, the artillerists could fire each of their six-pounders three times a minute. The battle routine prepared them to discharge a gun, dismount it, lay it upon the ground, remove the wheels from the carriage, drop flat upon their faces, then spring up, remount the gun, ready for reloading or removing, all in 45 seconds.[21]

As Jackson and his weary Missourians rested on the banks of the Osage River at Warsaw, General Rains regrouped his Lexington men not far away on the south bank of the South Grand River and took up the march for the Osage. Neither Rains nor Jackson knew that their two State Guard armies were only about a day apart.

After a couple of days, hearing no news of the Lexington arm, the State Guard broke camp at Warsaw on June 25 and crossed the swollen Osage River. It had rained off and on since Boonville, and flooded streams and muddy roads added to the misery of the march. Colonel Marmaduke had acceded to Jackson's wishes and had accompanied the governor this far but left at this point to hitch his star to the Confederacy. At the same time, General Clark had returned to his home, supposedly to raise more troops. He would soon return, but Marmaduke would not. Several other officers left for various reasons as well, some not liking the politics of the MSG organization.

Nepotism ran rampant. Edwin Waller "Stump" Price, for example, son of the general, had no military credentials. Nevertheless, General Price appointed him captain over other more qualified men. General Clark likewise made his son a company commander, even though his experience at the time was more political than military. To add to the discontent, Governor Jackson's own disagreeable decisions on military matters fanned the dissent.[22]

The governor and his column continued south in a more leisurely manner once across the Osage River. The Missourians crossed the covered bridge over the Pomme de Terre River near Fairchild, angled past Bishop's Store, and came to Osceola 25 miles out of Warsaw. Osceola was the hub of several roads that fanned out in all directions and one of the last river ports on the Osage River. A mile or two south of Osceola, they struggled to cross the swift waters of Sac River, roiling from the rains.[23] Storms normally associated with the month of May had continued into June in an unseasonably wet spring.

Few ferries and hardly any bridges existed in this frontier part of Missouri. Some recruits trying to cross the streams drowned when the current swept them away. Roads, where they existed, formed a muddy quagmire, adding to the difficulty of flooded streams. Stragglers were a problem from the beginning. Recruits lagged behind, many without rest from sleeping on damp ground while rolled up in a quilt brought from home. The journey seemed to grow increasingly more difficult the further south they went. Wagons filled with the goods of prominent citizens trailing the army slowed the march. These refugees from Jefferson City and Boonville carried personal belongings that had no military value at all, but as they were loyal supporters, Jackson did not want to send them back.

24

At Wit's End

Bad weather continued to stall Lyon's departure from Boonville. Moreover, he had neither adequate supplies nor sufficient men to confidently undertake a campaign deep into the interior of the state. An impatient press criticized him for his slow progress in pursuing the rebel forces. The arrival of the First Iowa Volunteer Infantry added to the men General Lyon needed to bolster a launch of his pursuit of Governor Jackson.[1] However, his forces were constantly dwindling from the expiration of the three months for which the regiments enlisted.[2] He waited at Boonville, hampered by the rains, struggling to organize a supply train, and trying to repair his faltering political and military image.

A recurring impediment to gathering a supply train was Quartermaster Major Justus McKinstry.[3] Just as McKinstry had done previously, interfering in Sweeny's attempt to construct a similar supply train for the southwest convoy, he now actively interfered in Lyon's work to acquire the necessary equipment to go into the interior of the state. As fast as Lyon's people could make purchase agreements with local owners for wagons and horses, McKinstry would cancel the contracts, thus denying payments.[4] General Lyon urged Washington to replace him at once.[5] The War Department subsequently sacked McKinstry for graft, corruption, and fraud, and drummed him out of the army.

Faced with a growing sense of urgency for action, Lyon waited at Boonville. Isolated skirmishes between Union and secessionist forces took place at Little River on June 22 and at Jackson, Missouri, on the 24th. Both light engagements were in southeast Missouri near Cairo, Illinois, a strategic military post deemed critical to control of the lower Mississippi River. A befuddled Lyon contemplated shifting his campaign to the southeast but did not. Despite isolated pockets of rebellion across the state, the primary focus of military action remained on southwest Missouri.

Lyon saw it as his mission to punish Jackson and Price, who he felt had insulted the Union at the St. Louis meeting. Unwilling to relent, he prepared to take up the pursuit of what he considered to be a band of treacherous rebels. His determination as a self-proclaimed agent of punishment stemmed from his views that originated in the Kansas troubles. He once wrote, "It is the duty of government to guarantee to all its subjects protection from injustice and fraud, and at the same time redress the grievances of society, and punish the aggressions of lawless violence."[6] Governor Jackson was a duly elected state official, which caused Lyon's edict to beg the question of who the perpetrator of "lawless violence" was.

Lyon's plan for a strategic pincer movement to capture Governor Jackson was coming together. He was preparing to move out of Boonville toward Warsaw with 2,500 troops, Sigel had 1,500 men at Neosho with another 1,500 under Sweeny coming out of Rolla toward Springfield, and Sturgis had 2,200 more men moving toward Clinton. Sturgis reached the South Grand River on June 24. Swollen by recent rains, the river was too high to cross. After a few days' delay, a long detour took them to a suitable crossing of the river. Marching through deep passages of mud, they hoped to rendezvous with Lyon somewhere around Clinton before Independence Day.[7]

An anxious Lyon sent a string of telegrams reassuring his superiors that his pursuit of Governor Jackson was imminent. On June 25, he telegraphed from Boonville, "Hope to get off on the 26th." The 26th passed without any movement, and on June 27 he wrote, "Shall try to get off tomorrow but am not certain." June 28 came and still no movement. "The rains are terrible. I cannot get off," he telegraphed. Desperate for information, Lyon telegraphed Adjutant Harding at the arsenal on July 1, wanting to know where the troops were for reinforcing Missouri. With tensions rising, he demanded, "What is going on in the southeast?"[8]

A comet appeared on the night of July 1. It had come into view the night before, but on this night, its blazing tail arched across nearly half the sky.[9] Both sides saw it as a foreboding of what was to come.

The next day—July 2—Lyon telegraphed Harding, "I hope to move tomorrow." He weighed the possibility of postponing his movement into southwest Missouri to go instead to Cairo. Nevertheless, he told Harding, "I think it more important just now to go to Springfield." He reminded Harding to ready a sizable amount of provisions. "Our operations are becoming extensive," he wrote. "Cannot something be done for us from Washington?"[10]

Still, control of the rivers was essential. Before he started south, he ordered that no boats ply along the river between Boonville and Kansas City. He assigned the Seventh Missouri Infantry Regiment under Colonel John Dunlap Stevenson to take charge of Jefferson City and all points along the Missouri River from Kansas City to its mouth at St. Louis.[11] Stevenson was a solid Union man, notwithstanding his Southern roots. When the

Confederacy sent its secession commissioner from Mississippi to Missouri at the beginning of the rebellion to court state legislators to join the South, Stevenson had put his seat in the General Assembly on the line to protest Lieutenant Governor Reynolds's demand that the assembly honor the commissioner.[12] Union control of the Missouri River was now in his hands.

When Lyon first conceived his river campaign, he planned not only to control key centers of rebel activity along the rivers, but also to extend action to the southwest—not merely to control that part of the state and to protect it against invasion, but also, ultimately, to extend his march into Confederate territory in Arkansas.[13] The likelihood of a major confrontation gained momentum on June 26 when the Confederate Department of War finally wrote to General McCulloch, authorizing him to enter Missouri in support of Governor Jackson "as will subserve the main purpose of your command."[14] It now appeared that General McCulloch might come to General Lyon.

All through the spring of 1861, parties in Greene County, Missouri, prepared for the fight that everybody felt sure was to come but which everybody wished to evade and put off as long as possible. The lightly armed Home Guard at Springfield had only hunting rifles, shotguns, and revolvers. However, in this respect they were as well off as their secession neighbors.[15]

The buildup of both the State Guard and Union armies continued.

Jackson's forces rested at Warsaw for two days, after which they proceeded toward Montevallo, in Vernon County. The first elements of the Lexington column caught up with them in Cedar County. They then marched on to Vernon County and there halted for six days, waiting for the other MSG troops coming out of Lexington. On July 3, the last regiments came together and formed a junction with Jackson's column, now in force and moving toward Lamar.[16]

As the MSG columns began to arrive at Lamar, the first trial of the guns of Guibor's Battery celebrated the rendezvous of Jackson and the Lexington army. From here, they would proceed as one body to meet General Price encamped somewhere below Neosho near the Arkansas-Missouri border. The Missourians were only days from uniting with General McCulloch and the Confederacy of the South. Their combined armies together would exceed 10,000 men.

Meanwhile, difficulties of assembling a train at Boonville delayed Lyon's departure until July 3. By that time, the State Guard had rendezvoused at Lamar. Almost out of supplies, short of men, and short of wagons, Lyon nevertheless gave the order to leave Boonville to pursue the Missourians.[17] He left Boonville at his usual starting time of 3:30 in the morning.[18] Lyon did not know that on the same day—July 3—President Lincoln would authorize the reorganization of the Western Department and permanently remove him from command. With the earnest solicitations of Frank and Montgomery Blair, Lincoln reluctantly placed Missouri under the command of newly appointed Major General John C. Frémont. "I only think he is the prey of wicked and designing men," said Lincoln, "and I think he has absolutely no military capacity. He went to Missouri the pet and protégé of the Blairs."[19] Frémont dallied in Paris and New York, not reaching St. Louis to take command of the Western Department until July 25.[20]

Lyon's military exploits no longer mattered to Washington. The string of successes that had marked his rise to prominence was at stake. Since Camp Jackson, he had opened his military actions against secessionists at Potosi, ordered the seizure of the Confederate steamer *J.C. Swon*, sailed past the Price-Harney agreement to command the Department of the West, and with federal outposts in various locations, had captured the state capital at Jefferson City and routed Governor Jackson and the MSG at Boonville. At its height, the Lyon army swelled to as many as 14,000 men. However, the terms of enlistment of many of the soldiers would expire in less than a month, threatening to reduce his forces.[21]

When General Lyon left Boonville, he knew he had no telegraphic communication with any point of his campaign.[22] Nevertheless, on July 3,

Departure of General Lyon from Boonville. After several days of heavy rains, Lyon led his troops out of Boonville, destined for southwest Missouri. The delays prevented him from effectively springing his pincer trap on the fleeing Governor Jackson and the Missouri State Guard. Sketch by Orlando C. Richardson, *Harper's Weekly*, Vol. 5, No. 239, page 465 (July 27, 1861). Courtesy Missouri Historical Society St. Louis (P0084-1248).

he and his army, numbering 2,700 men, with four pieces of artillery and a long baggage-train, departed Boonville for Springfield.

The sun rose hot and oppressive.[23] At 1:00 p.m., the troops stopped to encamp on the banks of a small stream 16 miles from Boonville. At three o'clock on the morning of July 4, the roll of drums aroused the weary men to resume the march.[24] Lyon rode at the head of the column mounted on an iron-gray horse he had acquired at Boonville. His bodyguard of ten German soldiers from St. Louis, armed with revolvers and massive cavalry swords, rode beside him, mounted on powerful chargers.[25] The parade made a conspicuous sight, Lyon's diminutive size and the Germans' burly forms and expert horsemanship.[26]

Colonel Franz Sigel left Rolla on June 16, marching his brigade down the Wire Road toward southwest Missouri. He went cautiously. The country around Rolla, as in much of southwest Missouri, was alive with Southern sympathizers.[27] From Rolla, for at least 60 miles, the country was mountainous and barren. Teams had to take their own forage. Adjutant Harding telegraphed Quartermaster McKinstry: "It is absolutely necessary that a large amount of wagon transportation should be immediately provided."[28] None was forthcoming.

Following the road through Waynesville, Lebanon, and Marshfield, Sigel arrived at Springfield on June 27.[29] After a brief stop, the brigade continued in a southwesterly direction to Neosho, in Newton County, situated in the extreme southwest corner of the state, about 85 miles from Springfield. They arrived there on July 2, relaxed along the stream fed by a large spring, and awaited orders to intercept the forces of Governor Jackson coming down from the north.

The abundant water supply also gave the men of Sigel's brigade a chance to do some laundry. Soldiers possessed no clothes except what they wore. Marching in the hot summer sun made it imperative to strip down and wash out the perspiration from time to time. On Thursday, July 4, after learning that the MSG was in force with a reported 4,000 men 30 miles northwest of them, they gathered their belongings, garrisoned Neosho, and moved out to meet the governor.[30]

On July 5, 1861, Adjutant Chester Harding wrote to Washington from the St. Louis Arsenal: "General Lyon is moving down from Boonville toward Springfield, Greene County, Missouri, with 2,400 troops. Major Sturgis is on the way from Fort Leavenworth with 2,200.[31] There are 3,500 on the Southwest Branch of [the] Pacific Railroad and the line thence to Mount Vernon, beyond Springfield. In a day or two another regiment will be moved down. There is a depot for supplies at Rolla, the terminus of the Southwest Branch; another must be established at Springfield. All the supplies for, say, 10,000 troops must take that direction."[32]

24. At Wit's End

Harding did not know that when he sent his telegram to Washington on July 5, Sigel had already advanced his federal force to Carthage to meet the State Guard units of Governor Jackson on a collision course that would ignite hostilities in southwest Missouri for the duration of the war.

The Third Infantry U.S. Volunteers of Colonel Franz Sigel met the Missouri State Guard of Governor Jackson a few miles north of Carthage, Missouri. Greatly outnumbered, Sigel fought a daylong action that spread over several miles and included six separate engagements before the Union army withdrew under the cover of darkness. It was the largest full-scale land battle of the Civil War up to that point, occurring 11 days before the Battle of Bull Run. The *New York Times* called the engagement "by far the most serious battle of the war" and described it as the first serious conflict between the United States troops and the rebels.[33] For the first time, two armies from the same state met in the ultimate conflict over states' rights. Immigrant nationals fought native sons of Missouri in a state not seceded from the Union and not part of the Confederacy.[34] Arriving too late to join the battle at Carthage, General Lyon diverted his brigade east and went into camp outside Springfield.

Despite the turn of events in southwest Missouri, the military leadership in Washington remained focused on southeast Missouri. On July 5, General McClellan wrote to Adjutant Harding, "Do not lose sight of the importance of Cairo, and of its operations in southeastern Missouri." McClellan said nothing about southwest Missouri.[35]

On July 6, 1861, General McClellan finally acknowledged Lyon's letter of June 20 in which he had asked for reinforcements. McClellan gave him the support of General John Pope for operations on the line of the Southwest Branch of the Pacific Railroad.[36] However, by that time events had accelerated in southwest Missouri beyond the tardy assistance of McClellan and Washington politicians.

After Lincoln appointed General Frémont to command the Department of the West, Lyon sent several messages to Frémont, urging the general to send reinforcements to sustain him. He warned that "if he was not supported he could not hold his ground there successfully against such odds."[37] Frémont did not attempt to reinforce Lyon in southwest Missouri, although the president and the country by now held the region to be of critical concern.[38] In light of Sigel's retreat at the Battle of Carthage, headquarters assumed that General Lyon, with the force he had and three or four of his regiments having nearly expired, would not fight but would instead withdraw and let Sigel take command of the rear guard at Springfield.[39]

25

The Halfway Ground

On July 22, 1861, after the state capital at Jefferson City was securely in federal hands, a special state convention met to vote on withdrawal from the Union. Ignoring Governor Claiborne Jackson's call for secession, the convention voted to stay in the Union, and five days later declared the governor's office vacant. The following day, Republican Hamilton Gamble, a unionist, took office as provisional governor in Jackson's place.

On August 10, 1861, with the expiration of the terms of volunteer enlistments ravaging his dwindling army, General Lyon made a desperate decision to meet the combined forces of General Price and General McCulloch in the historic Battle of Wilson's Creek, the first major battle of the Trans-Mississippi Theater of the American Civil War. Each side claimed the daylong engagement as a victory. It was nevertheless the Confederates and the State Guard forces that drove the Union regiments into retreat. However, the victors were too disorganized and poorly armed to pursue the federal forces. The *New York Times* spun the battle as a Union conquest: "The report of the battle fought by General Lyon near Springfield, Mo., conveys the assurance of victory.... It is stated that our gallant Army, numbering about eight thousand, engaged the enemy, numbering about twenty-three thousand, at six o'clock on Saturday morning, fought them victoriously all day, and drove them from the field and back upon their encampment." As occurred often in the eastern press, the reporter exaggerated the outcome; the actual result of the battle was just the opposite.[1] The battle effectively gave General Price control of southwest Missouri. It also emboldened him to lead the State Guard north in a campaign to reclaim Lexington.

The foremost story of the Battle of Wilson's Creek was the death of General Lyon, killed in action by a sniper's bullet, as he led a charge of the First Iowa Regiment U.S. Volunteers.

After Wilson's Creek, the main body of the Missouri State Guard, some 7,000 men under General Price, marched toward the Missouri-Kansas border to repel incursions by Union troops coming out of Fort

Hamilton Rowan Gamble. The state constitutional convention named him provisional governor of Missouri to replace the deposed Claiborne Jackson. A former justice of the Missouri Supreme Court, he was the brother-in-law of Edward Bates of the Lincoln cabinet. Although he owned slaves, he often defended slaves in court and was instrumental in the decision to keep Missouri in the Union. Courtesy Special Collections, Fine Arts Library, Harvard University (FAL274485).

Battle of Wilson's Creek. General Lyon led the charge of the First Iowa Regiment at the Battle of Wilson's Creek, near Springfield, Missouri, August 10, 1861. The Missouri State Guard met Union troops in the first major battle of the Trans-Mississippi Theater. *Frank Leslie's Illustrated Newspaper*, Vol. 11, August 31, 1861, page 244. Library of Congress Prints and Photographs Division, Washington, D.C. (LC-USZ62-121404).

Scott. They repelled the Kansans in the Battle of Dry Wood Creek, sending them back to Kansas and out of Missouri. Price then led his army north along the Kansas border toward Lexington. He planned to oust the Federals garrisoned there to regain control of the Missouri River and open access to recruits north of the river. By the time he reached Lexington on September 11, 1861, he had collected around 15,000 men.[2] The Guard lay siege to the town for a week before launching an assault on September 20. The *New York Times* soberly reported the outcome: "We are sorry that we have nothing yet that looks like a redeeming feature in the loss of Lexington, Missouri. The more recent accounts rather add to, than diminish, the apparent value of the conquest to the rebels."[3] The victory won by the State Guard boosted pro–South sentiment and tentatively regained control of the western part of the Missouri River Valley.

However, Lexington was not to be the final word in the fight for Missouri. In a period of barely seven months, more than 60 battles and skirmishes took place between the contending forces in the determined struggle for Missouri, from Camp Jackson in the spring of 1861 to the fight at Mount Zion Church in late December 1861. Of the 157 Civil War

25. The Halfway Ground

engagements and battles listed in the *Army Register* in 1861, 66, or more than 42 percent, were in Missouri. In that period, Missouri saw more action than Virginia and West Virginia combined.

After Union forces ousted Governor Jackson from office, he went into exile in the southwest corner of the state, where he assembled a rump legislature from the remnants of his government. The rump assembly passed an act of secession in October 1861. The ordinance, adopted October 28, at Neosho, Missouri, lacked the force of law because the assembly lacked a majority of members present. The Confederate government nevertheless accepted the results. Missouri became the ad hoc twelfth state of the Confederacy and remained on the list of Confederate States of America for the duration of the war.

Governor Jackson, who had led a raid into Kansas in 1855 to overthrow civil authorities there, now became a hunted fugitive from his home and his chair of office, deserted by friends, ruined in fortune, and threatened by the prospect of the gallows.[4] Writer Francis Grierson described his maligned government as "wrecked mariners scanning the horizon for the smallest sign of a white sail of hope."[5]

Missouri continued to be a bloody battleground throughout the war.[6] Of the 2,261 battles of the Civil War, 244—or more than 10 percent—were in Missouri.[7] Missouri had fanned the fires of civil war in Kansas, and now the same fires blazed tenfold upon the state's own sovereignty. Civil process broke down, giving way to the bayonets of military confrontation and hordes of unchecked marauders sweeping across the countryside.[8]

If sympathizers could not organize officially with their chosen sides of Union or Confederate, they could form guerrilla bands in hit-and-run tactics to keep the military campaigns off balance. Marauding bands degenerated into lawless gangs of predators bent on visiting death and destruction on the population on thinly veiled pretexts of patriotism. Such groups earned the denigrated title of bushwhackers, men who hid in the bushes and ambushed or preyed on opposing and innocent people. Bushwhackers became any small group of renegades loyal to either the North or the South that worked at disrupting the opposing military presence by primarily attacking the civilian population. Armies needed elsewhere had to expend their men and resources trying to keep the bushwhackers in check.

Bushwhackers became nothing more than murderers and thieves preying on blameless citizens under the guise of their loyal duty.[9] Of either ilk, they were outlaws, robbers, arsonists, cutthroats, and nightriders skulking about under cover of masks and darkness. Old men left at home and unable to join the war stayed hidden or relied on a fast horse to outrun the raiders who would go into houses where only women and children were to take whatever they wanted, threateningly cursing and swearing as they did so. On one such occasion, George Laney, who lived in Christian County, heard riders approaching his house and ran out the back door. The bushwhackers opened fire on him as he raced toward the woods. A bullet penetrated his body and lodged against the skin of his chest. He made it to the woods and managed to hide as the invaders ransacked the house. Years later, his grandchildren heard stories of the bushwhackers and touched the bullet that he carried until his death, a lethal reminder of the cruelty that his neighbors visited on him in the name of patriotism. He never identified his assailants nor sought vengeance, although he shunned certain families thereafter and never again associated with them.

Southwest Missouri remained a place of conflicting sentiments for the duration of the war. The region saw scores of bloody little battles, skirmishes that lasted for an hour or only a few minutes. Mostly too small to catch the attention of historians, they were nevertheless part of the fabric of the war and memorable experiences for the people who were in the midst of them. Secessionists and unionists occupied the same ground, and the fortunes of the people rose and fell with the ebb and flow of the troops that in turn occupied the region. If you were a Southern sympathizer, you risked losing everything to the invading Northerners or their bushwhacking partisans. If you favored the Union, on the other hand, you and your family lived under constant threat from bushwhackers of the Border Ruffian kind.

Conditions reached a depth of misery seldom endured, even in wartime. George Cook described what it was like as a boy of ten to witness the brutalities of war on innocent people caught in the middle. He wrote, "I might tell of the church almost filled with the bodies of citizen prisoners who were shot down as they attempted to break from their captivity.

"One army took all in sight by way of tribute another army followed, hunting for more," Cook continued. "I might tell of the scores of men driven from home, hiding in caves and unused coal mines, their families living upon parched corn and roasted potatoes, with the vaulted dome of heaven for their covering at night. There was no rest, no safety, no peace, and no hope: only the dismal fear of the invasion tomorrow; only the dreary moan of cattle dying for want of food—every blade of grass, every stalk of corn, levied upon to feed the insatiate maw of the demon of battle. There was no food to buy, and little left with which to buy it. Oppression was on the one hand, death on the other. Such was the situation on the half way ground."[10] It was southwest Missouri's darkest hour for the civilian population. Bushwhackers and guerrilla bands murdered hundreds for either their political convictions or personal grudges. A known partisan in the war had about as much chance of being killed sitting at home as he did standing on the battlefield.

25. The Halfway Ground

Both sides eventually took steps to reign in the violence. The Union dismantled the Home Guard units because they fostered vigilantism and infringed on recruitment for federal service. The government created instead the Enrolled Missouri Militia: local militia organizations, mostly cavalry, operating under state control. All Missourians of military age had to enlist in either Union or State service to remain in the state. Instead of coming under local command of the organizing counties or cities, enrolled militia units came under state command. Anyone not enrolled in the EMM came under Union supervision. A man not enrolled in either was an assumed pro–South secessionist.

Captain Jo Shelby tried a similar thing on the rebel side to curtail vigilantes. Frustrated by the lawless disorganization of the secessionists, he tried to bring bushwhackers into the regular State Guard ranks and authorized his men to shoot them if they resisted. His effort to curb bushwhackers, however, went without much success despite such a severe penalty, and the excesses on both sides continued. Shelby himself eventually turned to a campaign of harassment and guerrilla warfare. His one hundred splendidly mounted men kept the entire countryside in fear and turmoil, but without the inhumane atrocities visited on civilians that characterized many of his plundering contemporaries.[11]

Missourians never wavered in their divided allegiances. Of the approximately 140,000 Missourians who fought in the Civil War, 110,000, or more than 75 percent, joined the Union army. Upward of 30,000 joined the Confederate forces.[12] When Missourians met each other at the Battle of Vicksburg, 25 Missouri units were Union and 17 were Confederate.[13] Official records show 25,885 Missourians died in the war, not counting another estimated 12,000 victims of local Home Guards and guerrillas operating within the state.[14]

Across the nation, the Union of 20 states and the Confederacy of 11 states, not including the five Border States, opposed each other. Approximately 19 million people confronted nine million, of which three and a half million were slaves.[15]

Chapter Notes

Introduction

1. Carr, *Missouri, a Bone of Contention*, 139–148; Axelrod, *Civil War*, 26.
2. Washburn, *The Issues*, 8–10; *Frank Leslie's Illustrated Newspaper*, 27 June 1857, 50.
3. Oates, *To Purge This Land*, 82–138; Carr, *Missouri, a Bone of Contention*, 241–266; Harvey, "Missouri," 30–31.
4. Sanborn, *The Life and Letters of John Brown*, 501.
5. Bordewich, "John Brown's Day of Reckoning," 62–69; Axelrod, *Civil War*, 27–29.
6. Herndon and Weik, *Herndon's Lincoln*, 466–468.
7. Connelley, *A Standard History*, 299–300; Webb, *Battles and Biographies of Missourians*, 298; Phillips, *Missouri's Confederate*, 170–172; Carr, *Missouri, a Bone of Contention*, 220–240; Harvey, "Missouri," 23–26; Shoemaker, "Missouri: Heir of Southern Tradition and Individuality," 435–446.
8. Violette, *A History of Missouri*, 327.
9. Catton, *Coming Fury*, 370; Missouri General Assembly, House of Representatives, *Missouri State Convention*, 132; Carr, *Missouri, a Bone of Contention*, 267–290. The State Convention met at Jefferson City and St. Louis in 19 sessions over a period of 23 days, beginning February 28, 1861, in Jefferson City. On the third day, March 4, 1861, it moved to the Mercantile Library Hall in St. Louis and concluded there on the afternoon of March 22, 1861.
10. Nicolay and Hay, "Abraham Lincoln: A History, the Advance," 294.
11. Lincoln, *The Collected Works*, 428.
12. Greene, Kremer, and Holland, *Missouri's Black Heritage*, 75.
13. Lincoln, "Proceedings of Congress," 4. Lincoln called them the middle states and not the Border States because he refused to recognize them as the southern border of the Union.
14. Davis, *The Rise and Fall of the Confederate Government*, 399–401.
15. Snead, *The Fight for Missouri*, 129; Carr, *Missouri, a Bone of Contention*, 291–323; Blum, "The Political and Military Activities of the German Element," 118.
16. U.S. Congress, *Report of the Joint Committee on the Conduct of the War*, 154, 156–161; Wurthman, "Frank Blair," 263–287; Blum, "The Political and Military Activities of the German Element," 115; Snead, *The Fight for Missouri*, 99; Anderson, *The Story of a Border City during the Civil War*, 63–85; Harvey, "Missouri," 31–37.
17. Drake, *Union and Anti-slavery Speeches Delivered during the Rebellion*, 106.
18. Rorvig, "The Significant Skirmish," 127–148.
19. Woodward, *The Life of General Nathaniel Lyon*, 221; Woodward, "Review of *The Life of General Lyon*," 151.
20. "Domestic Intelligence. The Alarm at Charleston." *Harper's Weekly*, 5 (April 20, 1861), 247.
21. Snead, *The Fight for Missouri*, 9; Lincoln, "Proceedings of Congress," 3.
22. Moore, *The Rebellion Record*, 1:78.
23. Peckham, *General Nathaniel Lyon and Missouri in 1861*, 138; Harvey, "Missouri," 39; Blum, "The Political and Military Activities of the German Element," 129.
24. Britton, *The Civil War on the Border*, 25.

25. Grant to Colonel H. K. Craig, May 3, 1861.
26. Parrish, *Frank Blair: Lincoln's Conservative*, 96.
27. Scharf, *History of Saint Louis City and County*, 492.
28. *Missouri's Sons of the South*, 707–710, 725.
29. *The American Annual Cyclopedia and Register*, 661; Ethier, "Firebrand in a Powder Keg," 56; McElroy, *The Struggle for Missouri*, 87. Documents vary as to the exact number of men encamped at Camp Jackson and subsequently made prisoners of war. The settled number is 639 privates and 50 officers as prisoners at Camp Jackson, according to Lyon's official report. Other sources give a number upwards of 1,000 and more, not including 50 to 75 officers.
30. Scharf, *History of Saint Louis City and County*, 495.
31. Buegel, "The Civil War Diary of John T. Buegel," 309–310.
32. Frost, "No. 2. Protest to Nathaniel Lyon," 7.
33. Leland, "General Lyon," 405–413.
34. Rorvig, "The Significant Skirmish, 127–148; Stevens, *Centennial History of Missouri*, 738.
35. Howison, "History of the War," 331. Conflicting accounts of the firing at Camp Jackson often depended on the political preference of the writer. Howison maintained that troops fired on the crowd without intimidation by the crowd and that the crowd assaulted them with stones and pistol shots only after the federals fired first.
36. Peckham, *General Nathaniel Lyon and Missouri in 1861*, 153–155; Rombauer, *The Union Cause in St. Louis in 1861*, 233; Faust, *The German Element in the United States*, 1:537; St. Louis County Coroner's Record Book, Missouri History Museum, 229–230.
37. Scharf, *History of Saint Louis City and County*, 498; Stevens, *Centennial History of Missouri*, 738.
38. Richardson, *The Secret Service, the Field, the Dungeon, the Escape*, 134; Rombauer, *The Union Cause in St. Louis in 1861*, 234; Snead, *The Fight for Missouri*, 171; Scharf, *History of Saint Louis City and County*, 497–498; Börnstein, *Memoirs of a Nobody*, 298; Anderson, *The Story of a Border City during the Civil War*, 97–98; Adamson, *Rebellion in Missouri*, 62–63; Covington, "The Camp Jackson Affair, 1861," 210; Peckham, *General Nathaniel Lyon and Missouri in 1861*, 156; "The Camp Jackson Incident." *Museum Gazette*, National Park Service, Jefferson National Expansion Memorial, 3; Gottschalk, *In Deadly Earnest*, 13; Winter, *Civil War in St. Louis*, 34; Scharf, *History of Saint Louis City and County*, 497; *The American Annual Cyclopedia and Register*, 661; Violette, *A History of Missouri*, 344. Richardson gave the numbers 20 killed and 11 wounded. Anderson reported about 25 killed and wounded. Börnstein, whose Second Regiment fired on the crowd, said there were 16 dead and 50 wounded. Snead counted 28 people dead or mortally wounded, including three prisoners. Peckham, citing his interpretation of the coroner's report, listed 28 dead and 10 officially wounded. Rombauer agreed with Peckham's numbers. Adamson used Peckham's count of 28 killed and 10 wounded. Covington used the number of 28 fatalities and a number of wounded that could not be estimated accurately. Winter put the count at nearly three dozen civilians, Missouri militia, and Union troops dead or mortally wounded and left on the field, including 27 citizens. Violette published a more conservative count of 15 dead, three of whom were Camp Jackson soldiers.
39. Violette, *A History of Missouri*, 348.
40. "The Camp Jackson Incident." *Museum Gazette*, May 1999, National Park Service, Jefferson National Expansion Memorial, 3.
41. Reavis, *The Life and Military Services of Gen. William Selby Harney*, 361.
42. Lademann, "The Capture of 'Camp Jackson," 73.
43. McElroy, *The Struggle for Missouri*, 87. McElroy did not give a source to support the efficacy of his claim.
44. *Official Record*, Report of Captain Nathaniel Lyon, Series I, 3:5.

Chapter 1

1. Gottschalk, *In Deadly Earnest*, 11; Peckham, *General Nathaniel Lyon and Missouri in 1861*, 140–142; Fiske, *The Mississippi Valley*, 17–18; Carr, *Missouri, a Bone of Contention*, 302; Smith, *The Borderland in the Civil War*, 235.

Notes—Chapter 1

2. Peckham, *General Nathaniel Lyon and Missouri in 1861*, 182.
3. Violette, *A History of Missouri*, 344.
4. *New York Times*, May 15, 1861; Winter, *Civil War in St. Louis*, 54.
5. "Valuable Arms Captured at Camp Jackson," *New York Times*, May 15, 1861, 1.
6. Stevens, *Missouri the Center State*, 268.
7. Duyckinck, *National History of the War for the Union*, 312; Barns, *Commonwealth of Missouri*, 355.
8. Stevens, *Missouri the Center State*, 268.
9. McElroy, *The Struggle for Missouri*, 79.
10. Stevens, *Centennial History of Missouri*, 738–739; Woodward, *The Life of General Nathaniel Lyon*, 254; Violette, *A History of Missouri*, 346.
11. Lademann, "The Capture of Camp Jackson," 73.
12. Barns, *Commonwealth of Missouri*, 354.
13. Stephenson, *The Civil War Memoir*, 3.
14. Drake, *Camp Jackson*, 3
15. Rombauer, *The Union Cause in St. Louis in 1861*, 236.
16. Rombauer, *The Union Cause in St. Louis in 1861*, 232.
17. Snead, *The Fight for Missouri*, 175.
18. Gamble and Yeatman to Abraham Lincoln, May 15, 1861.
19. Scharf, *History of Saint Louis City and County*, 498.
20. Anderson, *The Story of a Border City during the Civil War*, 99.
21. Rosengarten, *The German Soldier*, 138; Faust, *The German Element in the United States*, 537.
22. Lademann, "The Capture of Camp Jackson," 73; Rombauer, *The Union Cause in St. Louis in 1861*, 233; Peckham, *General Nathaniel Lyon and Missouri in 1861*, 152; Scharf, *History of Saint Louis City and County*, 463.
23. McElroy, *The Struggle for Missouri*, 79.
24. *Official Record*, Report of Captain Nathaniel Lyon, Series I, 3:4–5; Anderson, *The Story of a Border City during the Civil War*, 104.
25. *The American Annual Cyclopedia and Register*, 661.
26. Richardson, *The Secret Service, the Field, the Dungeon, the Escape*, 134.
27. *Official Record*, Report of Captain Nathaniel Lyon, Series I, 3:4–5.
28. McElroy, *The Struggle for Missouri*, 127. A letter found later at the office of the *St. Louis Bulletin*, proved Jackson's intent.
29. *Official Record*, Report of Captain Nathaniel Lyon, Series I, 3:4–5.
30. Winter, *Civil War in St. Louis*, 54.
31. Peckham, *General Nathaniel Lyon and Missouri in 1861*, 165.
32. Missouri, General Assembly, House of Representatives, *Journal of the House of Representatives, Called Session*, 38–041; Stevens, *Centennial History of Missouri*, 741; Anderson, *The Story of a Border City during the Civil War*, 102–103.
33. Snead, *The Fight for Missouri*, 173; Stevens, *Missouri the Center State*, 271; Switzler, et al., *Switzler's Illustrated History of Missouri*, 315; Viles, "Claiborne Fox Jackson." 324; Kirkpatrick, "Missouri in the Early Months of the Civil War," 240; *The American Annual Cyclopedia and Register*, 479; "Important from St. Louis," *New York Times*, May 14, 1861, 1; Barns, *Commonwealth of Missouri*, 315.
34. Switzler, et al., *Switzler's Illustrated History of Missouri*, 317, 344.
35. Ware, *The Lyon Campaign in Missouri*, 16.
36. Peckham, *General Nathaniel Lyon and Missouri in 1861*, 168
37. *History of Newton, Lawrence, Barry, etc.*, 100; Stevens, *Centennial History of Missouri*, 741.
38. Barns, *Commonwealth of Missouri*, 315.
39. Snead, *The Fight for Missouri*, 173; Anderson, *The Story of a Border City during the Civil War*, 104; *Jefferson City (MO) Daily Tribune*, 29 Aug 1893, 4.
40. Snead, *The Fight for Missouri*, 173; Duke, *Reminiscences of General Basil W. Duke*, 52.
41. Stevens, *Missouri the Center State*, 271; *History of Newton, Lawrence, Barry, etc.*, 100; McElroy, *The Struggle for Missouri*, 90; Switzler, et al., *Switzler's Illustrated History of Missouri*, 315–316; Stevens, *Centennial History of Missouri*, 741; Kirkpatrick, "Missouri in the Early Months of the Civil War," 240; Barns, *Commonwealth of Missouri*, 316.
42. Britton, *The Civil War on the Border*, 15; Switzler, et al., *Switzler's Illustrated History of Missouri*, 315–316; The

American Annual Cyclopedia and Register, 480; Howison, "History of the War," 331; Barns, *Commonwealth of Missouri*, 316.
43. Snead, *The Fight for Missouri*, 174.
44. Switzler, et al., *Switzler's Illustrated History of Missouri*, 315–316.
45. Anderson, *The Story of a Border City during the Civil War*, 103–104.
46. *The American Annual Cyclopedia and Register*, 480.
47. Missouri. General Assembly. *Journal of the Senate Extra Session of the Rebel Legislature*, 42–43; *The American Annual Cyclopedia and Register*, 480.
48. Carr, *Missouri, a Bone of Contention*, 307.
49. Peckham, *General Nathaniel Lyon and Missouri in 1861*, 23.
50. Missouri, General Assembly, House of Representatives, *Journal of the House of Representatives, Called Session*, 55.
51. Snead, "The First Year of the War in Missouri," 266; Viles, "Claiborne Fox Jackson." 324.
52. Carr, *Missouri, a Bone of Contention*, 313; Mudd, "What I Saw at Wilson's Creek," 89; Kirkpatrick, "Missouri in the Early Months of the Civil War," 244; Barns, *Commonwealth of Missouri*, 362.
53. Violette, *A History of Missouri*, 350; Musick, *Stories of Missouri*, 249.
54. Anderson, *The Story of a Border City during the Civil War*, 102–103; Stevens, *Centennial History of Missouri*, 741; Snead, *The Fight for Missouri*, 173.
55. Switzler, et al., *Switzler's Illustrated History of Missouri*, 314–315.
56. Switzler, et al., *Switzler's Illustrated History of Missouri*, 314–315.
57. "Important from St. Louis," *New York Times*, May 14, 1861, 1.
58. McElroy, *The Struggle for Missouri*, 89, 101.
59. Switzler, et al., *Switzler's Illustrated History of Missouri*, 314–315.
60. Anderson, *The Story of a Border City during the Civil War*, 103.
61. *The American Annual Cyclopedia and Register*, 480.
62. McElroy, *The Struggle for Missouri*, 92.
63. Lademann, "The Capture of Camp Jackson," 73–74.
64. Buegel, "The Civil War Diary of John T. Buegel,"309–310.
65. Lademann, "The Capture of Camp Jackson," 74–75.
66. Anderson, *The Story of a Border City during the Civil War*, 181.
67. Fiske, *The Mississippi Valley in the Civil War*, 19.
68. Lademann, "The Capture of Camp Jackson," 75.
69. *Official Record*, Report of Captain Nathaniel Lyon, Series I, 3:4–5.

Chapter 2

1. Ward, *The Slaves' War*, 55; Gamble and Yeatman to Abraham Lincoln, May 15, 1861.
2. Chauvenet, "St. Louis in the Early Days of the Civil War," 2.
3. Gottschalk, *In Deadly Earnest*, 13; Peckham, *General Nathaniel Lyon and Missouri in 1861*, 158.
4. Rombauer, *The Union Cause in St. Louis in 1861*, 232–239.
5. Stevens, *Centennial History of Missouri*, 740.
6. Violette, *A History of Missouri*, 348.
7. "Important from St. Louis," *New York Times*, May 14, 1861.
8. Duyckinck, *National History of the War for the Union*, 312; U.S. Congress, *Report of the Joint Committee on the Conduct of the War*, 158.
9. Peckham, *General Nathaniel Lyon and Missouri in 1861*, 181.
10. Moore, *The Rebellion Record*, Doc. 11, 9: 258.
11. McElroy, *The Struggle for Missouri*, 81.
12. U.S. Congress, *Report of the Joint Committee on the Conduct of the War*, 3, 154. This committee met during the course of the Civil War. The committee, writing about the Department of the West, was not able to obtain all the facts and was unwilling to ask the attendance of those in the military from so great a distance whose testimony was necessary to fully elucidate all the facts. The report is primarily an inquiry into the conduct of General Frémont in reinforcing Lyon before Wilson's Creek. It contains important information about Nathaniel Lyon's activities in Missouri.
13. Moore, *The Rebellion Record*, 404–405.

14. Anderson, *The Story of a Border City during the Civil War*, 108.
15. *The American Annual Cyclopedia and Register*, 480–482.
16. Snead, "The First Year of the War in Missouri," 266.
17. Drake, *Camp Jackson*, 7.
18. Frost, "No. 2. Protest to Nathaniel Lyon," 7.
19. Frost, "No. 2. Protest to Nathaniel Lyon," 8.
20. Harney, "No. 3. General Harney's Letter," 8–9.
21. Letter from [signature illegible], St. Louis, to Dear Friend, May 15, 1861, Missouri Historical Society.
22. Gottschalk, *In Deadly Earnest*, 13.
23. *Official Record*, Report of Captain Nathaniel Lyon, Series I, 3:4–5.
24. Winter, *Civil War in St. Louis*, 36. In a turn of historical irony, the brother of Emmet McDonald, James Wilson Alexander McDonald, sculpted the medallion on the red granite obelisk monument dedicated to Lyon in Lyon Park, St. Louis.
25. Gerteis, *Civil War St. Louis*, 114.
26. Winter, *Civil War in St. Louis*, 55; Peckham, *General Nathaniel Lyon and Missouri in 1861*, 161.
27. Peckham, *General Nathaniel Lyon and Missouri in 1861*, 190.
28. Winter, *Civil War in St. Louis*, 55.
29. Börnstein, *Memoirs of a Nobody*, 294n4.
30. Davis, *The Rise and Fall of the Confederate Government*, 1:415.
31. Gottschalk, *In Deadly Earnest*, 13.
32. Peckham, *General Nathaniel Lyon and Missouri in 1861*, 24.
33. Britton, *The Civil War on the Border*, 12; McElroy, *The Struggle for Missouri*, 80.
34. Stephenson, *The Civil War Memoir*, 8; Stevens, *Centennial History of Missouri*, 735.
35. Anderson, *The Story of a Border City during the Civil War*, 106–107.
36. Peckham, *General Nathaniel Lyon and Missouri in 1861*, 162.
37. Eben Richards, St. Louis, to his wife [Caroline B. Richards], May 13, 1861, Missouri History Museum; *The American Annual Cyclopedia and Register*, 661.
38. *The American Annual Cyclopedia and Register*, 661.
39. Stevens, *Missouri the Center State*, 269; Duyckinck, *National History of the War for the Union*, 312; Howison, "History of the War," 331. Howison's account is at odds with the facts.
40. Moore, *Missouri*, 35.
41. "News of the Rebellion: Events in Missouri," *New York Times*, May 25, 1861, 2; Stevens, *Centennial History of Missouri*, 740.
42. *Official Record*, Report of Captain Nathaniel Lyon, Series I, 3:9.
43. U.S. Congress, *Report of the Joint Committee on the Conduct of the War*, 161.
44. U.S. Congress, *Report of the Joint Committee on the Conduct of the War*, 154.
45. *Official Record*, Report of Captain Nathaniel Lyon, Series I, 3:9.
46. Gerteis, *Civil War St. Louis*, 116.
47. Peckham, *General Nathaniel Lyon and Missouri in 1861*, 114; U.S. Congress, *Report of the Joint Committee on the Conduct of the War*, 178.
48. Ethier, "Firebrand in a Powder Keg," 55.
49. Crumpler, "Yankee Avenger," 49.
50. Tomes and Smith, *The War with the South*, 250–251.
51. Snead, *The Fight for Missouri*, 175.
52. Börnstein, *Memoirs of a Nobody*, 303.
53. McElroy, *The Struggle for Missouri*, 80.
54. "Important from St. Louis, Investigation of the Camp Jackson Affair," *New York Times*, May 16, 1861, 1.
55. Peckham, *General Nathaniel Lyon and Missouri in 1861*, 144–145; Stevens, *Centennial History of Missouri*, 723.
56. "Great Excitement in St. Louis," *The Constitutional*, Alexandria, LA, May 18, 1861.

Chapter 3

1. Stevens, *Missouri the Center State*, 270; Switzler, et al., *Switzler's Illustrated History of Missouri*, 354.
2. Peckham, *General Nathaniel Lyon and Missouri in 1861*, 184.
3. Burks, *Thunder on the Right*, 357.
4. Gerteis, *Civil War St. Louis*, 115.
5. McElroy, *The Struggle for Missouri*, 82.
6. Peckham, *General Nathaniel Lyon and Missouri in 1861*, 185–187; Reavis, *The*

Life and Military Services of Gen. William Selby Harney, 361.
7. "Richards, Eben, St. Louis, to his wife [Caroline B. Richards]," May 13, 1861, D6196, Missouri History Museum.
8. Moore, *Missouri*, 35.
9. Violette, *A History of Missouri*, 348.
10. McElroy, *The Struggle for Missouri*, 81.
11. Faust, *The German Element in the United States*, 538.
12. "Important from St. Louis," *New York Times*, May 14, 1861, 1.
13. Switzler, et al., *Switzler's Illustrated History of Missouri*, 357.
14. Richardson, *The Secret Service, the Field, the Dungeon, the Escape*, 136.
15. Stevens, *Centennial History of Missouri*, 740.
16. Stevens, *Centennial History of Missouri*, 741.
17. Cayton, Alice E., to her brother [Alexander Badger], St. Louis, May 12, 1861.
18. Peckham, *General Nathaniel Lyon and Missouri in 1861*, 159; Violette, *A History of Missouri*, 340; Barns, *Commonwealth of Missouri*, 354.
19. Anderson, *The Story of a Border City during the Civil War*, 113.
20. Catton, *The Centennial History of the Civil War*, 381.
21. Gottschalk, *In Deadly Earnest*, 13; Boyce, "The Evacuation of Nashville," 60–61; Carr, *Missouri, a Bone of Contention*, 307; Smith, *The Borderland in the Civil War*, 241; Phillips, *Damned Yankee*, 198–199; Snead, *The Fight for Missouri*, 183; *History of Boone County*, 409.
22. Anderson, *The Story of a Border City during the Civil War*, 144.
23. *History of Carroll County*, 290–296.
24. Peckham, *General Nathaniel Lyon and Missouri in 1861*; Stevens, *Centennial History of Missouri*, 741.
25. Stevens, *Missouri the Center State*, 35.
26. McElroy, *The Struggle for Missouri*, 84.
27. Gamble and Yeatman to Abraham Lincoln, May 15, 1861.
28. Gerteis, *Civil War St. Louis*, 115; U.S. Congress, *Report of the Joint Committee on the Conduct of the War*, 158.
29. Nicolay and Hay, *Abraham Lincoln, a History*, 216–217.

30. Gamble and Yeatman to Abraham Lincoln, May 15, 1861.
31. Lyman Trumbull to Abraham Lincoln, May 15, 1861.
32. Stevens, *Centennial History of Missouri*, 741.
33. Peckham, *General Nathaniel Lyon and Missouri in 1861*, 193, 196.
34. Glover, Samuel T., to Abraham Lincoln, May 24, 1861, Abraham Lincoln papers, Library of Congress.
35. Gerteis, *Civil War St. Louis*, 117.
36. U.S. Congress, *Report of the Joint Committee on the Conduct of the War*, 161.
37. Nicolay and Hay, "Abraham Lincoln: A History, the Advance," 296.
38. McElroy, *The Struggle for Missouri*, 84.
39. Peckham, *General Nathaniel Lyon and Missouri in 1861*, 207.
40. Nicolay and Hay, *Abraham Lincoln, a History*, 216–217.
41. Sandburg, *Abraham Lincoln*, 1:399–400.
42. McElroy, *The Struggle for Missouri*, 100.
43. Burks, *Thunder on the Right*, 357.
44. Stevens, *Centennial History of Missouri*, 741.
45. Switzler, et al., *Switzler's Illustrated History of Missouri*, 357; "Important from St. Louis," *New York Times*, May 14, 1861, 1.
46. North, *History of Jasper County*, 43.
47. Moore, *The Rebellion Record*, Doc. 11, 9: 257–261.
48. Reavis, *The Life and Military Services of Gen. William Selby Harney*, 365.
49. McElroy, *The Struggle for Missouri*, 85.
50. Kirkpatrick, "Missouri in the Early Months of the Civil War," 241; *The American Annual Cyclopedia and Register*, 480.
51. Fiske, *The Mississippi Valley in the Civil War*, 14.
52. Anderson, *The Story of a Border City during the Civil War*, 115; Snead, *The Fight for Missouri*, 176–177.
53. *Official Record*, Military Department of the West, Series 1, 3:371, 374.

Chapter 4

1. *Official Record*, Report of Captain Nathaniel Lyon, Series I, 3:9–11.

Notes—Chapter 5

2. Richardson, *The Secret Service, the Field, the Dungeon, the Escape*, 147.
3. *Official Record*, Report of Captain Nathaniel Lyon, Series I, 3:9–11.
4. Woodward, *The Life of General Nathaniel Lyon*, 257–258.
5. Moore, *The Rebellion Record*, 253.
6. Leland, "General Lyon," 408; Duyckinck, *National History of the War for the Union*, 316.
7. Peckham, *General Nathaniel Lyon and Missouri in 1861*, 187–188.
8. Cole, "No. 2. Report of Captain Nelson Cole," 10.
9. Woodward, *The Life of General Nathaniel Lyon*, 258.
10. Cole, "No. 2. Report of Captain Nelson Cole," 10; Duyckinck, *National History of the War for the Union*, 316.
11. Cole, "No. 2. Report of Captain Nelson Cole," 10.
12. Woodward, *The Life of General Nathaniel Lyon*, 258–259; Cole, "No. 2. Report of Captain Nelson Cole," 10.
13. *Missouri State Gazetteer* [1860], 70.
14. Cole, "No. 2. Report of Captain Nelson Cole," 10.
15. Duyckinck, *National History of the War for the Union*, 316.
16. Anderson, *The Story of a Border City during the Civil War*, 142, 145.
17. Peckham, *General Nathaniel Lyon and Missouri in 1861*, 187–188.
18. Cole, "No. 2. Report of Captain Nelson Cole," 10.
19. Cole, "No. 2. Report of Captain Nelson Cole," 11.
20. Duyckinck, *National History of the War for the Union*, 316.
21. Tomes and Smith, *The War with the South*, 258.
22. Howison, "History of the War," 332.
23. Webb, *Battles and Biographies of Missourians*, 55.
24. Anderson, *The Story of a Border City during the Civil War*, 130.
25. Anderson, *The Story of a Border City during the Civil War*, 154.
26. Glover, Samuel T., to Abraham Lincoln, May 20, 1861, Abraham Lincoln papers, Library of Congress.
27. Missouri General Assembly, House, *Journal of the House of the State of Missouri*, 1861, 32.
28. Snead, *The Fight for Missouri*, 180.
29. *New York Times*, May 16, 1861.
30. Violette, *A History of Missouri*, 355.
31. McElroy, *The Struggle for Missouri*, 119.
32. Pollard, *Southern History of the War: The First Year of the War*, 128.
33. Howison, "History of the War," 330.
34. Stevens, *Missouri the Center State*, 271.
35. Anderson, *The Story of a Border City during the Civil War*, 117.
36. Piston and Sweeney, "Don't Yield An Inch! The Missouri State Guard," *North & South Magazine* 5 (June 1999): 10–26.
37. Howison, "History of the War," 331.
38. Howison, "History of the War," 332; Holcombe, *History of Greene County*, 45; North, *History of Jasper County*, 40.
39. Richardson, *The Secret Service, the Field, the Dungeon, the Escape*, 134.
40. Wallace, "Gen. E. W. Price," 208.
41. Snead, *The Fight for Missouri*, 183; Kirkpatrick, "Missouri in the Early Months of the Civil War."
42. Peckham, *General Nathaniel Lyon and Missouri in 1861*, 161; Edwards, *Shelby and His Men*, 21.
43. Stevens, *Missouri the Center State*, 96.
44. Richardson, *The Secret Service, the Field, the Dungeon, the Escape*, 134–135.
45. Violette, *A History of Missouri*, 350.
46. Anderson, *The Story of a Border City during the Civil War*, 116.
47. Moore, *The Rebellion Record*, 72.
48. Scharf, *History of Saint Louis City and County*, 398.
49. Asbury, *My Experiences in the War 1861–1865*, 3.
50. Hutchinson, Lucy, St. Louis, to brother Robert Randolph Hutchinson, May 22, 1861, Missouri History Museum.
51. Pollard, *Southern History of the War: The First Year of the War*, 127.

Chapter 5

1. Stevens, "Lincoln and Missouri," 75–76; McElroy, *The Struggle for Missouri*, 100; Reavis, *The Life and Military Services of Gen. William Selby Harney*, 375; Ware, *The Lyon Campaign in Missouri*, Frontis; Barns, *Commonwealth of Missouri*, 359.
2. Reavis, *The Life and Military Services of Gen. William Selby Harney*, 374–377.

3. Reavis, *The Life and Military Services of Gen. William Selby Harney*, 375; U.S. Congress, *Report of the Joint Committee on the Conduct of the War*, 154.
4. Reavis, *The Life and Military Services of Gen. William Selby Harney*, 379.
5. Reavis, *The Life and Military Services of Gen. William Selby Harney*, 380.
6. Gerteis, *Civil War St. Louis*, 20; Woodward, *The Life of General Nathaniel Lyon*, 257. Lincoln promoted Lyon to brigadier general of the first brigade of Missouri Volunteers on May 17, 1861.
7. Peckham, *General Nathaniel Lyon and Missouri in 1861*, 197; Reavis, *The Life and Military Services of Gen. William Selby Harney*, 376.
8. Nicolay and Hay, *Abraham Lincoln, a History*, 217.
9. Snead, *The Fight for Missouri*, 189.
10. Stevens, "Lincoln and Missouri," 75–76; Faust, *The German Element in the United States*, 538; Peckham, *General Nathaniel Lyon and Missouri in 1861*, 210; McElroy, *The Struggle for Missouri*, 100; Reavis, *The Life and Military Services of Gen. William Selby Harney*, 382.
11. Stevens, "Lincoln and Missouri," 115.
12. Miller, "General Mosby M. Parsons," 42.
13. *Official Record*, Operations in Missouri. Series I, 3:376; Barns, *Commonwealth of Missouri*, 359.
14. McElroy, *The Struggle for Missouri*, 97–99; Kirkpatrick, "Missouri in the Early Months of the Civil War," 242; Howison, "History of the War," 332; *History of Newton, Lawrence, Barry, etc.*, 98–99; Stevens, *Centennial History of Missouri*, 742; Duyckinck, *National History of the War for the Union*, 316–317; Switzler, et al., *Switzler's Illustrated History of Missouri*, 358–359; Stevens, *Missouri the Center State*, 271–273.
15. Peckham, *General Nathaniel Lyon and Missouri in 1861*, 203.
16. McGuire, *St. Louis Arsenal*, 94; Barns, *Commonwealth of Missouri*, 357–360.
17. Duke, *Reminiscences of General Basil W. Duke*, 55.
18. Woodward, *The Life of General Nathaniel Lyon*, 259–261.
19. Gerteis, *Civil War St. Louis*, 120.
20. Anderson, *The Story of a Border City during the Civil War*, 117; Davis, *The Rise and Fall of the Confederate Government*, 1:420.
21. Paris, *History of the Civil War in America*, 158.
22. Snead, *The Fight for Missouri*, 188.
23. Duke, *Reminiscences of General Basil W. Duke*, 52.
24. Duke, *Reminiscences of General Basil W. Duke*, 55.
25. Leland, "General Lyon," 405–413.
26. Woodward, *The Life of General Nathaniel Lyon*, 256.
27. Carr, *Missouri, a Bone of Contention*, 310.
28. Violette, *A History of Missouri*, 351.
29. Kirkpatrick, "Missouri in the Early Months of the Civil War," 242.
30. Reavis, *The Life and Military Services of Gen. William Selby Harney*, 373.
31. Peckham, *General Nathaniel Lyon and Missouri in 1861*, 211.
32. Switzler, et al., *Switzler's Illustrated History of Missouri*, 360; Engle, *Yankee Dutchman*, 61.
33. Gerteis, *Civil War St. Louis*, 121; Davis, *The Rise and Fall of the Confederate Government*, 2:474; Smith, *The Borderland in the Civil War*, 250.
34. Lincoln to Harney, May 27, 1861; Peckham, *General Nathaniel Lyon and Missouri in 1861*, 220; Nicolay and Hay, "Abraham Lincoln: A History, the Border States," 68; Woodward, *The Life of General Nathaniel Lyon*, 276; *The American Annual Cyclopedia and Register*, 482.
35. Nicolay and Hay, "Abraham Lincoln: A History, the Border States," 68.
36. Reavis, *The Life and Military Services of Gen. William Selby Harney*, 372.
37. Davis, *The Rise and Fall of the Confederate Government*, 1:420.
38. Britton, *The Civil War on the Border*, 16.
39. Gantt, Thomas T., to Brig. Genl. W. S. Harney, May 14, 1861 and Brig. Genl. W. S. Harney to Thomas T. Gantt, May 14, 1861, in Berlin, "Missouri," 413–414.
40. U.S. Congress, *Report of the Joint Committee on the Conduct of the War*, 159.

Chapter 6

1. McElroy, *The Struggle for Missouri*, 87.

2. *The American Annual Cyclopedia and Register*, 482.
3. Woodward, *The Life of General Nathaniel Lyon*, 262; *New York Times*, May 27, 1861, 3.
4. Woodward, *The Life of General Nathaniel Lyon*, 262; Duke, *Reminiscences of General Basil W. Duke*, 46.
5. Anderson, *The Story of a Border City during the Civil War*, 118.
6. *New York Times*, May 27, 1861, 3.
7. Glover, Samuel T., to Abraham Lincoln, May 24, 1861, Abraham Lincoln papers, Library of Congress.
8. Peckham, *General Nathaniel Lyon and Missouri in 1861*, 211.
9. Snead, *The Fight for Missouri*, 185; Britton, *The Civil War on the Border*, 23.
10. Burks, *Thunder on the Right*, 386.
11. Bell, "Price's Missouri Campaign," 271.
12. Moore, *Missouri*, 37; Snead, *The Fight for Missouri*, 186.
13. Stevens, *Missouri the Center State*, 31; Stevens, *Centennial History of Missouri*, 742.
14. Glover, Samuel T., to Abraham Lincoln, May 24, 1861, Abraham Lincoln papers, Library of Congress.
15. Snead, *The Fight for Missouri*, 68.
16. Alexander W. Doniphan, a Missouri lawyer and politician, gained fame during the Mexican War when he led an expedition that covered over 5,000 miles in less than one year. Doniphan was a delegate to the 1861 Washington Peace Conference and was also elected to the 1861 Missouri state convention, where he opposed secession. Doniphan briefly held a commission as major general in the Missouri State Guard in June 1861, but resigned after two weeks.
17. Moore, *The Rebellion Record*, 78.
18. Burks, *Thunder on the Right*, 405.
19. Glover, Samuel T., to Abraham Lincoln, May 24, 1861, Abraham Lincoln papers, Library of Congress.
20. Snead, *The Fight for Missouri*, 191–192.
21. Nicolay and Hay, "Abraham Lincoln: A History, the Advance," 281.
22. Smith, *The Borderland in the Civil War*, 250; Nicolay and Hay, "Abraham Lincoln: A History, the Border States," 68; Holcombe, *History of Greene County*, 47; Leland, "General Lyon," 408; Moore,

Missouri, 39; Stevens, *Missouri the Center State*, 273; McElroy, *The Struggle for Missouri*, 101; Violette, *A History of Missouri*, 352; Gerteis, *Civil War St. Louis*, 122; Ware, *The Lyon Campaign in Missouri*, Frontis, 100.
23. *The American Annual Cyclopedia and Register*, 482.
24. Reavis, *The Life and Military Services of Gen. William Selby Harney*, 381.
25. Reavis, *The Life and Military Services of Gen. William Selby Harney*, 387.
26. McElroy, *The Struggle for Missouri*, 100.
27. Reavis, *The Life and Military Services of Gen. William Selby Harney*, 377; U.S. Congress, *Report of the Joint Committee on the Conduct of the War*, 159.
28. Anderson, *The Story of a Border City during the Civil War*, 118, 198.
29. Peckham, *General Nathaniel Lyon and Missouri in 1861*, 209.
30. Peckham, *General Nathaniel Lyon and Missouri in 1861*, 198.
31. Woodward, *The Life of General Nathaniel Lyon*, 358.
32. Peckham, *General Nathaniel Lyon and Missouri in 1861*, 196.
33. McElroy, *The Struggle for Missouri*, 102.
34. Campbell, *The Rebellion Register*, 219. Sherman's military assignments led him to St. Louis in 1850. He resigned his commission in the army in 1853 and went to California, where he worked in a banking house. Invited to take up the presidency of the Louisiana Military Academy, he promptly resigned the position upon Louisiana passing the secession ordinance.
35. General Sherman's brother-in-law in Leavenworth, Kansas, was the soon to be infamous Civil War Brigadier General Thomas Ewing, Jr. When atrocities spread throughout the border counties of Missouri, Ewing promulgated Order 11, which harshly and inhumanely drove families from the counties of western Missouri and eastern Kansas, arbitrarily turning the territory into a wasteland to rid it of pro-Confederate guerrillas. To this day, Order 11 remains one of the most drastic and repressive military measures ever directed against a civilian population.
36. U.S. Congress, *Report of the Joint Committee on the Conduct of the War*, 161.
37. Viles, "Claiborne Fox Jackson," 325.

38. Woodward, *The Life of General Nathaniel Lyon*, 262.
39. Duke, *Reminiscences of General Basil W. Duke*, 56.
40. Woodward, The Life of General Nathaniel Lyon, 263.
41. Blandowshy [sic], Constantin, 3rd Regiment, Missouri Infantry (3 months, 1861), Company: H, F, National Archives and Records Administration, M390 Roll 4.
42. Winter, *Civil War in St. Louis*, 66; Gerteis, *Civil War St. Louis*, 350n26.
43. Gerteis, *Civil War St. Louis*, 122.
44. Moore, *The Rebellion Record*, 37; Sandburg, *Abraham Lincoln*, 1:261.

Chapter 7

1. Missouri, *Adjutant General's Report of th State Militia for 1861*, 6.
2. Leland, "General Lyon," 405–407.
3. *Official Record*, Operations in Missouri. Series I, 3:382–384.
4. Woodward, *The Life of General Nathaniel Lyon*, 264.
5. McElroy, *The Struggle for Missouri*, 109; Anderson, *The Story of a Border City during the Civil War*, 199–201.
6. Crumpler, "Yankee Avenger," 47–51; *Missouri State Gazetteer* [1860], 729; Snead, "The First Year of the War in Missouri," 267. Planter's House appears in documents alternately spelled Planter's, Planters', and Planters without an apostrophe. The most common spelling and the one presently used is Planter's.
7. Peckham, *General Nathaniel Lyon and Missouri in 1861*, 243.
8. Hammond, "Recollections of Gen. Nathaniel Lyon," 415.
9. Peckham, *General Nathaniel Lyon and Missouri in 1861*, 245.
10. Snead, *The Fight for Missouri*, 198.
11. Snead, "The First Year of the War in Missouri," 266.
12. Switzler, et al., *Switzler's Illustrated History of Missouri*, 262.
13. Winter, *Civil War in St. Louis*, 14; Grierson, *The Valley of Shadows* [description of Planter's House].
14. Gerteis, *Civil War St. Louis*, 7–10.
15. "St. Louisan Recalls Days when Slaves Were Sold at Auction," 1.
16. Moore, *Missouri*, 40.

Chapter 8

1. Kirkpatrick, "Missouri in the Early Months of the Civil War," 243–244.
2. McElroy, *The Struggle for Missouri*, 103; Howison, "History of the War," 332–333; Peckham, *General Nathaniel Lyon and Missouri in 1861*, 231–232.
3. Gottschalk, *In Deadly Earnest*, 19; *History of Newton, Lawrence, Barry, etc.*, 99.
4. Violette, *A History of Missouri*, 332.
5. Anderson, *The Story of a Border City during the Civil War*, 202; Carr, *Missouri, a Bone of Contention*, 294–295.
6. Hammond, "Recollections of Gen. Nathaniel Lyon," 417.
7. Switzler, et al., *Switzler's Illustrated History of Missouri*, 361; Crumpler, "Yankee Avenger," 47–51.
8. Snead, *The Fight for Missouri*, 199, 262; Switzler, et al., *Switzler's Illustrated History of Missouri*, 361. General Price made Snead the custodian of his private and official papers.
9. Barns, *Commonwealth of Missouri*, 361n1.
10. Snead, *The Fight for Missouri*, 199.
11. Woodward, *The Life of General Nathaniel Lyon*, 266.
12. Crumpler, "Yankee Avenger," 47–51.
13. Switzler, et al., *Switzler's Illustrated History of Missouri*, 361.
14. Duyckinck, *National History of the War for the Union*, 318.
15. McElroy, *The Struggle for Missouri*, 112.
16. McElroy, *The Struggle for Missouri*, 114.
17. Peckham, *General Nathaniel Lyon and Missouri in 1861*, 247.
18. Peckham, *General Nathaniel Lyon and Missouri in 1861*, 247.
19. Peckham, *General Nathaniel Lyon and Missouri in 1861*, 247.
20. Duyckinck, *National History of the War for the Union*, 318.
21. Leland, "General Lyon," 405–407; Crumpler, "Yankee Avenger," 47–51.
22. U.S. Congress, *Report of the Joint Committee on the Conduct of the War*, 159.
23. Crumpler, "Yankee Avenger," 47–51.
24. Anderson, *The Story of a Border City during the Civil War*, 201.
25. Carr, *Missouri, a Bone of Contention*, 295.

26. Switzler, et al., *Switzler's Illustrated History of Missouri*, 361; Stevens, *Missouri the Center State*, 278; Crumpler, "Yankee Avenger," 49.
27. Stevens, *Centennial History of Missouri*, 75.
28. Sanborn, *The Life and Letters of John Brown*, 502
29. Stevens, *Missouri the Center State*, 278; Snead, *The Fight for Missouri*, 199–200; Kirkpatrick, "Missouri in the Early Months of the Civil War," 243.
30. Switzler, et al., *Switzler's Illustrated History of Missouri*, 361; Barns, *Commonwealth of Missouri*, 361n1.
31. Snead, "The First Year of the War in Missouri," 267; Crumpler, "Yankee Avenger," 47–51.
32. Barns, *Commonwealth of Missouri*, 361n1. Snead gave his interview in the summer of 1877 to a New York correspondent of the Cincinnati *Enquirer*, more than a decade and a half after the event had occurred.
33. Snead, *The Fight for Missouri*, 200; Moore, *Missouri*, 41.
34. Carr, *Missouri, a Bone of Contention*, 312–313.
35. *The American Annual Cyclopedia and Register*, 481.
36. Peckham, *General Nathaniel Lyon and Missouri in 1861*, 245; North, *History of Jasper County*, 43; Anderson, *The Story of a Border City during the Civil War*, 199–201; Switzler, et al., *Switzler's Illustrated History of Missouri*, 360. No official record exists of this meeting. Varying accounts surfaced after the meeting occurred. The details presented here are based largely on "The Meeting at the Planters House" by John McElroy excerpted from his book, *The Struggle for Missouri*, 1909. Claims about the length of the meeting varied from three to six hours.
37. Stevens, *Missouri the Center State*, 277.
38. Woodward, *The Life of General Nathaniel Lyon*, 268.

Chapter 9

1. Crumpler, "Yankee Avenger," 47–51.
2. Stevens, *Missouri the Center State*, 278.
3. Anderson, *Memoirs: Historical and Personal*, 1–15.
4. Holcombe, *History of Greene County*, 48.
5. McElroy, *The Struggle for Missouri*, 118; Crumpler, "Yankee Avenger," 47–51; U.S. Congress, *Report of the Joint Committee on the Conduct of the War*, 159.
6. Violette, *A History of Missouri*, 239–240.
7. Barns, *Commonwealth of Missouri*, 278–279; Switzler, et al., *Switzler's Illustrated History of Missouri*, 278–279.
8. McElroy, *The Struggle for Missouri*, 118.
9. Peckham, *General Nathaniel Lyon and Missouri in 1861*, 167; Kirkpatrick, "Missouri in the Early Months of the Civil War," 244; Miller, "General Mosby M. Parsons," 49; Barns, *Commonwealth of Missouri*, 360.
10. Lossing, *A History of the Civil War*, 172.
11. Peckham, *General Nathaniel Lyon and Missouri in 1861*, 259.
12. Ware, *The Lyon Campaign in Missouri*, 150.
13. Peckham, *General Nathaniel Lyon and Missouri in 1861*, 259.
14. Burks, *Thunder on the Right*, 392–394. Thomas L. Snead, Governor Jackson's aide, wrote the lengthy proclamation that the governor delivered.
15. Stevens, *Missouri the Center State*, 278; McElroy, *The Struggle for Missouri*, 118.
16. Christie, "The Memoirs of Dr. Robert J. Christie," Chap. 6.
17. Drake, *Union and Anti-slavery Speeches Delivered during the Rebellion*, 130, 176.
18. Woodward, *The Life of General Nathaniel Lyon*, 269.
19. Snead, "The First Year of the War in Missouri," 266.
20. Holcombe, *History of Greene County*, 48; Viles, "Claiborne Fox Jackson," 325; North, *History of Jasper County*, 43.
21. Switzler, et al., *Switzler's Illustrated History of Missouri*, 362; Duyckinck, *National History of the War for the Union*, 318.
22. Crumpler, "Yankee Avenger," 49.
23. U.S. Congress, *Report of the Joint Committee on the Conduct of the War*, 159.
24. U.S. Congress, *Report of the Joint Committee on the Conduct of the War*, 4.

25. Moore, *Missouri*, 40; Snead, *The Fight for Missouri*, 195; Ware, *The Lyon Campaign in Missouri*, 101.
26. Moore, *Missouri*, 39.
27. Anderson, *The Story of a Border City during the Civil War*, 202; Snead, *The Fight for Missouri*, 210.
28. Stevens, *Missouri the Center State*, 278.
29. Crumpler, "Yankee Avenger," 49.
30. Richardson, *The Secret Service, the Field, the Dungeon, the Escape*, 151.
31. Britton, *The Civil War on the Border*, 32.
32. Holcombe, *History of Greene County*, 282; Peckham, *General Nathaniel Lyon and Missouri in 1861*, 216.
33. Peckham, *General Nathaniel Lyon and Missouri in 1861*, 217.
34. Burks, *Thunder on the Right*, 404.
35. Bearss, "Fort Smith Serves General McCulloch," 324.
36. Bearss, "Fort Smith Serves General McCulloch," 330.
37. Duyckinck, *National History of the War for the Union*, 502.
38. Holcombe, *History of Greene County*, 281.
39. Peckham, *General Nathaniel Lyon and Missouri in 1861*, 225.
40. U.S. Congress, *Report of the Joint Committee on the Conduct of the War*, 1863. Montgomery Blair's testimony before the committee, in Washington, February 5, 1862, 154–161.
41. U.S. Congress, *Report of the Joint Committee on the Conduct of the War*, 159.
42. Peckham, *General Nathaniel Lyon and Missouri in 1861*, 252.
43. Howison, "History of the War," 33.

Chapter 10

1. Moore, *Missouri*, 40.
2. Moore, *The Rebellion Record*, 27.
3. Britton, *The Civil War on the Border*, 27.
4. Britton, *The Civil War on the Border*, 27.
5. Lynch, "The Influence of Population Movements on Missouri," 511.
6. Stevens, "Lincoln and Missouri," 116.
7. Edwards, *Shelby and His Men*, 24.
8. Moore, *Missouri*, 40.
9. Britton, *The Civil War on the Border*, 22.
10. Carr, *Missouri, a Bone of Contention*, 180–185.
11. Britton, *The Civil War on the Border*, 30.
12. Britton, *The Civil War on the Border*, 27.
13. Britton, *The Civil War on the Border*, 24–25; Woodson, *History of Clay County, Missouri*.
14. Britton, *The Civil War on the Border*, 27.
15. Du Bois, "The Civil War Journal and Letters," 446–447.
16. Woodson, *History of Clay County, Missouri*, 126; Snead, *The Fight for Missouri*, 209.
17. *History of Cole, Moniteau, Morgan, Benton, etc.*, 28; Payne, "Early Days of War in Missouri," 925–928.
18. Payne, "Early Days of War in Missouri," 926.
19. Britton, *The Civil War on the Border*, 28; Switzler, et al., *Switzler's Illustrated History of Missouri*, 260.
20. Du Bois, "The Civil War Journal and Letters," 446–448.
21. Howison, "History of the War," 333; Woodson, *History of Clay County, Missouri*, 126.
22. "Secession at Lexington, Mo.," *New York Times*, May 5, 1861, 9.
23. Britton, *The Civil War on the Border*, 30.
24. Britton, *The Civil War on the Border*, 31.

Chapter 11

1. Anderson, *The Story of a Border City during the Civil War*, 202.
2. Paris, *History of the Civil War in America*, 168; Moore, *The Rebellion Record*, 101.
3. Paris, *History of the Civil War in America*, 168.
4. Snead, *The Fight for Missouri*, 211.
5. Woodward, *The Life of General Nathaniel Lyon*, 271.
6. Tomes and Smith, *The War with the South*, 313–314; Peckham, *General Nathaniel Lyon and Missouri in 1861*, 254.
7. Barns, *Commonwealth of Missouri*, 362.
8. *The American Annual Cyclopedia*

Notes—Chapter 11

and *Register*, 483; Peckham, *General Nathaniel Lyon and Missouri in 1861*, 254; *Louisville Journal* June 14, 1861; Moore, *The Rebellion Record*, 102.

9. Duke, *Reminiscences of General Basil W. Duke*, 50.

10. Peckham, *General Nathaniel Lyon and Missouri in 1861*, 256.

11. Paris, *History of the Civil War in America*, 168.

12. Crumpler, "Yankee Avenger," 47–51.

13. Stevens, *Missouri the Center State*, 278.

14. Davis, *The Rise and Fall of the Confederate Government*, 2:473.

15. Kirkpatrick, "Missouri in the Early Months of the Civil War," 245.

16. Vandiver, "Reminiscences of General John B. Clark," 232.

17. Stevens, *Missouri the Center State*, 94; Burks, *Thunder on the Right*, 465.

18. Barnes, "Boonville," 602.

19. Vandiver, "Reminiscences of General John B. Clark," 223, 229; Violette, *A History of Missouri*, 224.

20. Vandiver, "Reminiscences of General John B. Clark," 225–228, 234–235.

21. Burks, *Thunder on the Right*, 465.

22. Miller, "General Mosby M. Parsons," 42, 49.

23. Miller, "General Mosby M. Parsons," 33, 36, 41.

24. Snead, *The Fight for Missouri*, 68.

25. Christie, "The Memoirs of Dr. Robert J. Christie," Chapter 6.

26. Miller, "General Mosby M. Parsons," 33–37, 39–41.

27. Peckham, *General Nathaniel Lyon and Missouri in 1861*, 24.

28. Peckham, *General Nathaniel Lyon and Missouri in 1861*, 170; *Missouri State Gazetteer* [1860], 135.

29. Moore, *Missouri*, 42.

30. Stevens, *Missouri the Center State*, 280.

31. Harding, *Service with the Missouri State Guard*.

32. *History of Cole, Moniteau, Morgan, Benton, etc.*, 854; Harding, *Service with the Missouri State Guard*, 7, 12, 14. James Harding and Chester Harding, Jr., were the sons of noted artist Chester Harding. Both brothers went on to serve in the Civil War on the Confederate and Union sides. Biographies of each one often omit mention that they were brothers.

33. Peckham, *General Nathaniel Lyon and Missouri in 1861*, 215.

34. *History of Saline County, Missouri*, 280.

35. *History of Saline County, Missouri*, 273.

36. "Saline Jackson Guards," *History of Saline County, Missouri*, 273.

37. Asbury, *My Experiences in the War 1861–1865*, 5.

38. Holcombe, *History of Greene County*, 284.

39. *History of Saline County, Missouri*, 281; Miller, "General Mosby M. Parsons," 43.

40. Asbury, *My Experiences in the War 1861–1865*, 4.

41. Asbury, *My Experiences in the War 1861–1865*, 3–5. Asbury tells about the transport of powder to Phelps County, Missouri.

42. Fiske, *The Mississippi Valley in the Civil War*, 24; Grover, "Civil War in Missouri," 17; Kirkpatrick, "Missouri in the Early Months of the Civil War," 245; Barns, *Commonwealth of Missouri*, 316.

43. Barns, *Commonwealth of Missouri*, 318; Howison, "History of the War," 333; Woodward, *The Life of General Nathaniel Lyon*, 271.

44. Peckham, *General Nathaniel Lyon and Missouri in 1861*, 175.

45. Barns, *Commonwealth of Missouri*, 317.

46. Stevens, *Missouri the Center State*, 280; McElroy, *The Struggle for Missouri*, 121; Turnbo, "Viewing the Steamboat going up the Missouri River"; Barns, *Commonwealth of Missouri*, 363; Kirkpatrick, "Missouri in the Early Months of the Civil War," 245.

47. Violette, *A History of Missouri*, 355.

48. Barns, *Commonwealth of Missouri*, 363.

49. Stevens, *Missouri the Center State*, 280.

50. Peckham, *General Nathaniel Lyon and Missouri in 1861*, 259; Duyckinck, *National History of the War for the Union*, 320.

51. *New York Herald*, June 20, 1861; Moore, *The Rebellion Record*, 104.

52. Snead, *The Fight for Missouri*, 206–208.

53. Howison, "History of the War," 334.

54. Nicolay and Hay, "Abraham Lincoln: A History, the Advance," 293.

55. *The American Annual Cyclopedia and Register*, 484.
56. Violette, *A History of Missouri*, 355.
57. Lossing, *A History of the Civil War*, 172.
58. Lossing, *A History of the Civil War*, 170.

Chapter 12

1. Peckham, *General Nathaniel Lyon and Missouri in 1861*, 257, 260.
2. Peckham, *General Nathaniel Lyon and Missouri in 1861*, 259.
3. Peckham, *General Nathaniel Lyon and Missouri in 1861*, 260.
4. *The American Annual Cyclopedia and Register*, 483.
5. Woodward, *The Life of General Nathaniel Lyon*, 272.
6. *Missouri State Gazetteer* [1860], 135.
7. Peckham, *General Nathaniel Lyon and Missouri in 1861*, 257; Stevens, *Missouri the Center State*, 280; McElroy, *The Struggle for Missouri*, 121; Barns, *Commonwealth of Missouri*, 361–363; Snead, *The Fight for Missouri*, 211.
8. Switzler, et al., *Switzler's Illustrated History of Missouri*, 362–363.
9. Peckham, *General Nathaniel Lyon and Missouri in 1861*, 257; Leland, "General Lyon," 405–413.
10. Peckham, *General Nathaniel Lyon and Missouri in 1861*, 261.
11. Barns, *Commonwealth of Missouri*, 363.
12. Anderson, *The Story of a Border City during the Civil War*, 202; *Columbia (MO) Statesman*, June 21, 1861, 2, and June 28, 1861, 2.
13. North, *History of Jasper County*, 43; Viles, "Claiborne Fox Jackson," 325.
14. U.S. Congress, *Report of the Joint Committee on the Conduct of the War*, 160.
15. Woodward, *The Life of General Nathaniel Lyon*, 272–274.
16. Richardson, *The Secret Service, the Field, the Dungeon, the Escape*, 152.
17. Richardson, *The Secret Service, the Field, the Dungeon, the Escape*, 152.
18. Stevens, *Missouri the Center State*, 280; Crumpler, "Yankee Avenger," 49.
19. Tomes and Smith, *The War with the South*, 313. Tomes and Smith indicated that troops started leaving St. Louis on June 12. However, the initial battalion left on the train late on the evening of June 11.
20. Stevens, *Missouri the Center State*, 280.
21. Peckham, *General Nathaniel Lyon and Missouri in 1861*, 253–254.
22. Crumpler, "Yankee Avenger," 49; Anderson, *The Story of a Border City during the Civil War*, 202; Peckham, *General Nathaniel Lyon and Missouri in 1861*, 254; Snead, *The Fight for Missouri*, 210.
23. Stevens, *Missouri the Center State*, 280; Peckham, *General Nathaniel Lyon and Missouri in 1861*, 255.
24. Engle, *Yankee Dutchman*, 61; Snead, *The Fight for Missouri*, 211; Livingston, *A History of Jasper County*, 50.
25. Switzler, et al., *Switzler's Illustrated History of Missouri*, 366.
26. Richardson, *The Secret Service, the Field, the Dungeon, the Escape*, 140.
27. Moore, *The Rebellion Record*, 102.
28. Mudd, *With Porter in North Missouri*, 232, 292. Brigadier General John McNeil drew criticism from both Confederate and Union sympathizers alike who regarded his subsequent campaigns in northeast Missouri during the war as excessively brutal and indiscriminate. Officials accused him of the execution of a number of Confederate prisoners in retaliation for the murder of Union soldiers. He played a key part in Union successes north of the Missouri River.
29. Marden, *The Consolidated Encyclopedic Library*, 513; Paris, *History of the Civil War in America*, 273.
30. Grant, *Personal Memoirs of U.S. Grant*, 132.
31. Lademann, "The Battle of Carthage."

Chapter 13

1. Britton, *The Civil War on the Border*, 39.
2. Sweeny, *Journal*, 260n108.
3. Engle. *Yankee Dutchman*, 3.
4. Duyckinck, *National History of the War for the Union*, 502; Engle, *Yankee Dutchman*, 29.
5. Engle, *Yankee Dutchman*, xix, 31–32, 34, 37, 43.
6. Engle, *Yankee Dutchman*, 37, 57.
7. Engle, *Yankee Dutchman*, 59.

8. Knox, *Camp-Fire and Cotton-Field*, 56.
9. *History of Laclede, Camden, Dallas, etc.*, 659.
10. *History of Laclede, Camden, Dallas, etc.*, 660.
11. Knox, *Camp-Fire and Cotton-Field*, 58–59.
12. Richardson, *The Secret Service, the Field, the Dungeon, the Escape*, 152; Knox, *Camp-Fire and Cotton-Field*, 58.
13. Carr, *Missouri, a Bone of Contention*, 233.
14. Carr, *Missouri, a Bone of Contention*, 235.
15. *History of Laclede, Camden, Dallas, etc.*, 661.
16. *History of Laclede, Camden, Dallas, etc.*, 632.
17. *Rolla Express*, June 17, 1861, in *History of Laclede, Camden, Dallas, etc.*, 656.
18. *Rolla Express*, June 17, 1861, in *History of Laclede, Camden, Dallas, etc.*, 656. Missouri Digital Heritage, History of Laclede, Camden, Dallas, Webster, Wright, Texas, Pulaski, Phelps and Dent counties, Missouri, https://mdh.contentdm.oclc.org/digital/collection/mocohist/id/70516.
19. Engle, *Yankee Dutchman*, 62.
20. Crumpler, "Yankee Avenger," 50.
21. Engle, *Yankee Dutchman*, 61; Lademann, "The Battle of Carthage."
22. Lademann, "The Battle of Carthage."
23. Peckham, *General Nathaniel Lyon and Missouri in 1861*, 255.
24. Lademann, "The Battle of Carthage."
25. Lademann, "The Battle of Carthage."
26. U.S. Congress, *Report of the Joint Committee on the Conduct of the War*, 78.
27. Crumpler, "Yankee Avenger," 50.
28. *Rolla Express*, June 17, 1861, in *History of Laclede, Camden, Dallas, etc.*, 656.
29. *History of Laclede, Camden, Dallas, etc.*, 658.
30. Engle, *Yankee Dutchman*, xviii, 26, 56, 61.

Chapter 14

1. Kirkpatrick, "Missouri in the Early Months of the Civil War," 245.
2. Rorvig, "The Significant Skirmish," 127–148.
3. Snead, *The Fight for Missouri*, 206–208.
4. Woodward, *The Life of General Nathaniel Lyon*, 280.
5. Snead, *The Fight for Missouri*, 206–208; Livingston, *A History of Jasper County*, 50.
6. Woodward, *The Life of General Nathaniel Lyon*, 278; Peckham, *General Nathaniel Lyon and Missouri in 1861*, 272.
7. Howison, "History of the War," 333; Woodward, *The Life of General Nathaniel Lyon*, 280. Howison estimated the number of State Guard in Camp Bacon to be 1,800 and not more than 600 armed. Woodward calculated that by Monday, June 17, the day of the engagement, 3,500 troops had assembled at Boonville.
8. Anderson, *Memoirs: Historical and Personal*, 17.
9. *History of Cole, Moniteau, Morgan, Benton, etc.*, 254.
10. Harding, "Old Missouri State Guard," 11.
11. Tomes and Smith, *The War with the South*, 435.
12. Anderson, *Memoirs: Historical and Personal*, 14.
13. Moore, *Missouri*, 43.
14. Stevens, *Missouri the Center State*, 281.
15. Woodward, *The Life of General Nathaniel Lyon*, 279–280.
16. Carr, *Missouri, a Bone of Contention*, 313.
17. Stevens, *Missouri the Center State*, 281.
18. Stevens, *Missouri the Center State*, 281; Barns, *Commonwealth of Missouri*, 363; Peckham, *General Nathaniel Lyon and Missouri in 1861*, 273; Switzler, et al., *Switzler's Illustrated History of Missouri*, 363–364; Howison, "History of the War," 333.
19. Stevens, *Missouri the Center State*, 281; Snead, *The Fight for Missouri*, 209; Kirkpatrick, "Missouri in the Early Months of the Civil War," 244; Rorvig, "The Significant Skirmish," 127–148.
20. Vandiver, "Reminiscences of General John B. Clark," 229.
21. McElroy, *The Struggle for Missouri*, 123.
22. Kirkpatrick, "Missouri in the Early Months of the Civil War," 246.
23. Shoemaker, "Missouri: Heir of

Southern Tradition and Individuality," 440.
24. McElroy, *The Struggle for Missouri*, 123.
25. Leland, "General Lyon," 405–413.
26. Stevens, *Missouri the Center State*, 281; Duyckinck, *National History of the War for the Union*, 322; Adamson, *Rebellion in Missouri*, 125.
27. Barns, *Commonwealth of Missouri*, 365; Switzler, et al., *Switzler's Illustrated History of Missouri*, 363–364; Peckham, *General Nathaniel Lyon and Missouri in 1861*, 269; *The American Annual Cyclopedia and Register*, 483; Woodward, *The Life of General Nathaniel Lyon*, 278.
28. McElroy, *The Struggle for Missouri*, 123; Snead, *The Fight for Missouri*, 211; Adamson, *Rebellion in Missouri*, 125; U.S. Congress, *Report of the Joint Committee on the Conduct of the War*, 160.
29. *The American Annual Cyclopedia and Register*, 483; Tomes and Smith, *The War with the South*, 314; Peckham, *General Nathaniel Lyon and Missouri in 1861*, 269; Snead, *The Fight for Missouri*, 211.
30. McElroy, *The Struggle for Missouri*, 122.
31. *The American Annual Cyclopedia and Register*, 483.
32. Stevens, *Missouri the Center State*, 31; Ward, *The Slaves' War*, 56.
33. Anderson, *The Story of a Border City during the Civil War*, 186–187.
34. *Freemen's Manual*, 39–40, 54.
35. Anderson, *The Story of a Border City during the Civil War*, 181.
36. McElroy, *The Struggle for Missouri*, 122; Barns, *Commonwealth of Missouri*, 365; Adamson, *Rebellion in Missouri*, 125.
37. Adamson, *Rebellion in Missouri*, 123.
38. Adamson, *Rebellion in Missouri*, 125.
39. U.S. Congress, *Report of the Joint Committee on the Conduct of the War*, 154, 161.
40. U.S. Congress, *Report of the Joint Committee on the Conduct of the War*, 154; McElroy, *The Struggle for Missouri*, 133.
41. U.S. Congress, *Report of the Joint Committee on the Conduct of the War*, 161.
42. Plum, "The Southwest Early in the War," 93.
43. Plum, "The Southwest Early in the War," 108.

44. Peckham, *General Nathaniel Lyon and Missouri in 1861*, 267.
45. U.S. Congress, *Report of the Joint Committee on the Conduct of the War*, 184.
46. U.S. Congress, *Report of the Joint Committee on the Conduct of the War*, 78; Peckham, *General Nathaniel Lyon and Missouri in 1861*, 266.
47. McElroy, *The Struggle for Missouri*, 122; Moore, *Missouri*, 42.
48. Turnbo, "Viewing the Steamboat Going up the Missouri River."
49. Tomes and Smith, *The War with the South*, 314.
50. Adamson, *Rebellion in Missouri*, 125.
51. Edwards, *Shelby and His Men*, 25.
52. Switzler, et al., *Switzler's Illustrated History of Missouri*, 363–364.
53. McElroy, *The Struggle for Missouri*, 123; Barns, *Commonwealth of Missouri*, 365.
54. Moore, *Missouri*, 45; Woodward, *The Life of General Nathaniel Lyon*, 280; Snead, *The Fight for Missouri*, 212.
55. McElroy, *The Struggle for Missouri*, 123; Edwards, *Shelby and His Men*, 25; Snead, *The Fight for Missouri*, 213.
56. Rorvig, "The Significant Skirmish," 127–148.
57. McElroy, *The Struggle for Missouri*, 123.
58. Snead, "The First Year of the War in Missouri," 262; Burks, *Thunder on the Right*, 150.
59. *The American Annual Cyclopedia and Register*, 483.
60. Barns, *Commonwealth of Missouri*, 365.
61. McElroy, *The Struggle for Missouri*, 123; Ware, *The Lyon Campaign in Missouri*, 121; Switzler, et al., *Switzler's Illustrated History of Missouri*, 363–364. Estimates of the number of men who went out to meet Lyon's troops varied from 100 to 1,000. Ware found that the "average mind" put them at 500.
62. Snead, *The Fight for Missouri*, 212, 219.
63. Edwards, *Shelby and His Men*, 25.
64. McElroy, *The Struggle for Missouri*, 123.
65. Moore, *Missouri*, 44; Edwards, *Shelby and His Men*, 25; Adamson, *Rebellion in Missouri*, 145.
66. Miller, "General Mosby M. Parsons," 42.

Chapter 15

1. *The American Annual Cyclopedia and Register*, 483; Barns, *Commonwealth of Missouri*, 365; Tomes and Smith, *The War with the South*, 314; Duyckinck, *National History of the War for the Union*, 322; Peckham, *General Nathaniel Lyon and Missouri in 1861*, 269; *The American Annual Cyclopedia and Register*, 483; Adamson, *Rebellion in Missouri*, 125.
2. Switzler, et al., *Switzler's Illustrated History of Missouri*, 363-364; Tomes and Smith, *The War with the South*, 316; Duyckinck, *National History of the War for the Union*, 322.
3. Switzler, et al., *Switzler's Illustrated History of Missouri*, 363-364.
4. *Missouri State Gazetteer* [1860]; Barns, *Commonwealth of Missouri*, 229.
5. Tomes and Smith, *The War with the South*, 314.
6. Duyckinck, *National History of the War for the Union*, 322; Barns, *Commonwealth of Missouri*, 365; Peckham, *General Nathaniel Lyon and Missouri in 1861*, 270.
7. *The American Annual Cyclopedia and Register*, 483; Barns, *Commonwealth of Missouri*, 365; Tomes and Smith, *The War with the South*, 314.
8. Duyckinck, *National History of the War for the Union*, 322.
9. Woodward, *The Life of General Nathaniel Lyon*, 277-278.
10. Adamson, *Rebellion in Missouri*, 126.
11. Peckham, *General Nathaniel Lyon and Missouri in 1861*, 270.
12. Duyckinck, *National History of the War for the Union*, 322; Stevens, *Missouri the Center State*, 281; Britton, *The Civil War on the Border*, 33-34. Duyckinck placed the debarkation point eight miles below Boonville instead of seven.
13. Snead, *The Fight for Missouri*, 212.
14. Stevens, *Missouri the Center State*, 281.
15. Britton, *The Civil War on the Border*, 34.
16. Edwards, *Shelby and His Men*, 25.
17. Rorvig, "The Significant Skirmish," 127-148.
18. Snead, *The Fight for Missouri*, 213.
19. *The American Annual Cyclopedia and Register*, 483; Peckham, *General Nathaniel Lyon and Missouri in 1861*, 270; U.S. Congress, *Report of the Joint Committee on the Conduct of the War*, 79.
20. *The American Annual Cyclopedia and Register*, 483.
21. U.S. Congress, *Report of the Joint Committee on the Conduct of the War*, 79; Britton, *The Civil War on the Border*, 34; Tomes and Smith, *The War with the South*, 316; Peckham, *General Nathaniel Lyon and Missouri in 1861*, 270.
22. Richardson, *The Secret Service, the Field, the Dungeon, the Escape*, 154. Richardson identified the two correspondents as Thomas W. Knox and Lucien J. Barnes.
23. "From Missouri," *New York Tribune*, June 28, 1861.
24. Rorvig, "The Significant Skirmish," 127-148.
25. Britton, *The Civil War on the Border*, 34.
26. Woodward, *The Life of General Nathaniel Lyon*, 277-278; McElroy, *The Struggle for Missouri*, 124; Duyckinck, *National History of the War for the Union*, 320-322; Tomes and Smith, *The War with the South*, 314-316.
27. Tomes and Smith, *The War with the South*, 315-316.
28. Peckham, *General Nathaniel Lyon and Missouri in 1861*, 270.
29. Duyckinck, *National History of the War for the Union*, 322.
30. Barns, *Commonwealth of Missouri*, 363-365.
31. Britton, *The Civil War on the Border*, 35.
32. Tomes and Smith, *The War with the South*, 316.
33. Woodward, *The Life of General Nathaniel Lyon*, 278.
34. Peckham, *General Nathaniel Lyon and Missouri in 1861*, 270.
35. Adamson, *Rebellion in Missouri*, 126-127; Moore, *The Rebellion Record*, 106-107; Ware, *The Lyon Campaign in Missouri*, 123.
36. Tomes and Smith, *The War with the South*, 316.
37. McElroy, *The Struggle for Missouri*, 124.
38. Switzler, et al., *Switzler's Illustrated History of Missouri*, 363-364; Tomes and Smith, *The War with the South*, 316; *The American Annual Cyclopedia and Register*, 483.

39. Anderson, *Memoirs: Historical and Personal*, 17.
40. Tomes and Smith, *The War with the South*, 315–316.
41. Britton, *The Civil War on the Border*, 35.
42. Woodward, *The Life of General Nathaniel Lyon*, 278.
43. Duyckinck, *National History of the War for the Union*, 322; Barns, *Commonwealth of Missouri*, 365; Peckham, *General Nathaniel Lyon and Missouri in 1861*, 270.
44. U.S. Congress, *Report of the Joint Committee on the Conduct of the War*, 79.
45. Ware, *The Lyon Campaign in Missouri*, 123.
46. Britton, *The Civil War on the Border*, 35.
47. Howison, "History of the War," 334.
48. Peckham, *General Nathaniel Lyon and Missouri in 1861*, 273.
49. Livingston, *A History of Jasper County*, 50, 53.
50. Harding, "Old Missouri State Guard," 11; Pollard, *Southern History of the War: The First Year of the War*, 129.
51. Howison, "History of the War," 330.
52. Patrick, "Remembering the Missouri Campaign of 1861," 34.
53. Ware, *The Lyon Campaign in Missouri*, 123.
54. Tomes and Smith, *The War with the South*, 316.
55. Britton, *The Civil War on the Border*, 35.
56. Ware, *The Lyon Campaign in Missouri*, 123; Rorvig, "The Significant Skirmish," 127–148.
57. Woodward, *The Life of General Nathaniel Lyon*, 281.
58. *The American Annual Cyclopedia and Register*, 483.
59. Richardson, *The Secret Service, the Field, the Dungeon, the Escape*, 148.
60. Cullum, *Biographical Register of the Officers and Graduates of the U.S. Military Academy*, 2:11, 22.
61. Barns, *Commonwealth of Missouri*, 365; Peckham, *General Nathaniel Lyon and Missouri in 1861*, 270; Tomes and Smith, *The War with the South*, 315–316.
62. Snead, *The Fight for Missouri*, 213.
63. Peckham, *General Nathaniel Lyon and Missouri in 1861*, 270.
64. Barns, *Commonwealth of Missouri*, 365.
65. Snead, *The Fight for Missouri*, 213; Peckham, *General Nathaniel Lyon and Missouri in 1861*, 274; Tomes and Smith, *The War with the South*, 317; Nicolay and Hay, "Abraham Lincoln: A History, the Border States," 69.
66. Pollard, *Southern History of the War: The First Year of the War*, 129.
67. Peckham, *General Nathaniel Lyon and Missouri in 1861*, 270.
68. Barns, *Commonwealth of Missouri*, 365.
69. Snead, *The Fight for Missouri*, 213; Peckham, *General Nathaniel Lyon and Missouri in 1861*, 271.
70. Barns, *Commonwealth of Missouri*, 365.
71. Duyckinck, *National History of the War for the Union*, 322.
72. Barns, *Commonwealth of Missouri*, 365.
73. Peckham, *General Nathaniel Lyon and Missouri in 1861*, 271; Duyckinck, *National History of the War for the Union*, 322; Switzler, et al., *Switzler's Illustrated History of Missouri*, 363–364.
74. Tomes and Smith, *The War with the South*, 313–318.
75. Peckham, *General Nathaniel Lyon and Missouri in 1861*, 273.
76. Edwards, *Shelby and His Men*, 25.
77. Peckham, *General Nathaniel Lyon and Missouri in 1861*, 271; Tomes and Smith, *The War with the South*, 315; Rorvig, "The Significant Skirmish," 127–148.

Chapter 16

1. Ware, *The Lyon Campaign in Missouri*, 123.
2. Tomes and Smith, *The War with the South*, 316; Woodward, *The Life of General Nathaniel Lyon*, 278; Duyckinck, *National History of the War for the Union*, 322.
3. Peckham, *General Nathaniel Lyon and Missouri in 1861*, 271–273; Duyckinck, *National History of the War for the Union*, 322; U.S. Congress, *Report of the Joint Committee on the Conduct of the War*, 79.
4. Rorvig, "The Significant Skirmish," 127–148.
5. Tomes and Smith, *The War with the South*, 316; Peckham, *General Nathaniel Lyon and Missouri in 1861*, 273.

Notes—Chapter 16

6. Duyckinck, *National History of the War for the Union*, 322.
7. Peckham, *General Nathaniel Lyon and Missouri in 1861*, 271–272; Duyckinck, *National History of the War for the Union*, 321–322.
8. Duyckinck, *National History of the War for the Union*, 322; Tomes and Smith, *The War with the South*, 316–317.
9. Adamson, *Rebellion in Missouri*, 127.
10. Duyckinck, *National History of the War for the Union*, 322; Peckham, *General Nathaniel Lyon and Missouri in 1861*, 272.
11. Duyckinck, *National History of the War for the Union*, 322; Britton, *The Civil War on the Border*, 35.
12. Tomes and Smith, *The War with the South*, 316.
13. Peckham, *General Nathaniel Lyon and Missouri in 1861*, 271; Switzler, et al., *Switzler's Illustrated History of Missouri*, 363–364.
14. McElroy, *The Struggle for Missouri*, 68.
15. Ware, *The Lyon Campaign in Missouri*, 7.
16. Switzler, et al., *Switzler's Illustrated History of Missouri*, 364.
17. *Baltimore (MD) Sun*, June 25, 1861, reprinted in *Carthage (MO) Press*, July 12, 1887.
18. Moore, *Missouri*, 40; Kirkpatrick, "Missouri in the Early Months of the Civil War," 242.
19. Duyckinck, *National History of the War for the Union*, 322.
20. Tomes and Smith, *The War with the South*, 317.
21. McElroy, *The Struggle for Missouri*, 20.
22. Rorvig, "The Significant Skirmish," 127–148.
23. Duyckinck, *National History of the War for the Union*, 323.
24. Woodward, *The Life of General Nathaniel Lyon*, 280.
25. Rorvig, "The Significant Skirmish," 127–148.
26. Duyckinck, *National History of the War for the Union*, 322.
27. Peckham, *General Nathaniel Lyon and Missouri in 1861*, 272
28. Duyckinck, *National History of the War for the Union*, 322; Britton, *The Civil War on the Border*, 35; Tomes and Smith, *The War with the South*, 317.
29. Barns, *Commonwealth of Missouri*, 364-365; Peckham, *General Nathaniel Lyon and Missouri in 1861*, 272; Switzler, et al., *Switzler's Illustrated History of Missouri*, 364; Duyckinck, *National History of the War for the Union*, 322.
30. Rorvig, "The Significant Skirmish," 127–148.
31. Peckham, *General Nathaniel Lyon and Missouri in 1861*, 272.
32. *Missouri State Gazetteer* [1860], 23.
33. Lincoln, *Abraham Lincoln: Complete Works*, 82.
34. Burks, *Thunder on the Right*, 29
35. U.S. Congress, *Report of the Joint Committee on the Conduct of the War*, 79.
36. Peckham, *General Nathaniel Lyon and Missouri in 1861*, 272; Duyckinck, *National History of the War for the Union*, 322.
37. Tomes and Smith, *The War with the South*, 317–318.
38. Duyckinck, *National History of the War for the Union*, 322.
39. U.S. Congress, *Report of the Joint Committee on the Conduct of the War*, 79.
40. Peckham, *General Nathaniel Lyon and Missouri in 1861*, 272; Duyckinck, *National History of the War for the Union*, 322.
41. Britton, *The Civil War on the Border*, 36.
42. Woodward, *The Life of General Nathaniel Lyon*, 284.
43. Leland, "General Lyon," 408.
44. Tomes and Smith, *The War with the South*, 318.
45. Britton, *The Civil War on the Border*, 36.
46. U.S. Congress, *Report of the Joint Committee on the Conduct of the War*, 160. Frank Blair testified before the U.S. Congress: "There were three thousands of them. We killed a great many of them, took a great many with their arms." Blair greatly exaggerated his claims.
47. Rorvig, "The Significant Skirmish," 127–148.
48. Anderson, *Memoirs: Historical and Personal*, 18; Woodward, *The Life of General Nathaniel Lyon*, 281.
49. Kirkpatrick, "Missouri in the Early Months of the Civil War," 246.
50. Anderson, *The Story of a Border City during the Civil War*, 202; Snead, *The Fight for Missouri*, 214; Adamson, *Rebellion in*

Missouri, 127; Peckham, *General Nathaniel Lyon and Missouri in 1861*, 273; Britton, *The Civil War on the Border*, 36; Howison, "History of the War," 334; Pollard, *Southern History of the War: The First Year of the War*, 129; Duyckinck, *National History of the War for the Union*, 323; Barns, *Commonwealth of Missouri*, 365; *The American Annual Cyclopedia and Register*, 483; Pollard, *Southern History of the War: The First Year of the War*, 129; Switzler, et al., *Switzler's Illustrated History of Missouri*, 363–364. Switzler identified the victims by name: Union killed, Jacob Kiburtz Company B Second Regiment and M. N. Coolide Company H First Regiment, 9 wounded, one missing known to have been badly shot; MSG killed: Dr. William Quarles of Boonville and Frank E. Hulen of Pettis, a boy named McCutchen of Boonville died of his wounds shortly after the battle.

51. Howison, "History of the War," 334.
52. *Columbia* (MO) *Statesman*, July 12, 1861, 3–4 and July 19, 1861, 1 and July 26, 1861, 3.
53. *The American Annual Cyclopedia and Register*, 484; Duyckinck, *National History of the War for the Union*, 323–324.
54. *The American Annual Cyclopedia and Register*, 484; Peckham, *General Nathaniel Lyon and Missouri in 1861*, 275.

Chapter 17

1. Barnes, "Boonville," 601.
2. U.S. Congress, *Report of the Joint Committee on the Conduct of the War*, 161. Blair left Boonville on June 18, 1861.
3. Barnes, "Boonville," 606; Moore, *Missouri*, 45. Despite its importance in the outcome of the Civil War, the scene of the battle remained unmarked and unrecorded as late as 1929.
4. Snead, "The First Year of the War in Missouri," 267–268.
5. *Columbia* (MO) *Statesman*, June 21, 1861, 2 and June 28, 1861, 2 and September 20, 1861, 2; Stevens, *Missouri the Center State*, vii. According to the Civil War definition cited by Stevens, a battle was an engagement that killed or wounded 10 or more soldiers. However, this definition does not appear generally to apply.
6. U.S. Congress, *Report of the Joint Committee on the Conduct of the War*, 160; *Liberty* (MO) *Tribune*, June 21, 1861, 3 and June 28, 1861, 1 and July 5, 1861, 2 and July 12, 1861, 1.
7. *Columbia* (MO) *Statesman*, July 19, 1872, 1; *Boonville* (MO) *Weekly Advertiser*, July 24, 1885 and April 30, 1886 and June 15, 1900 and June 21, 1901 and September 12, 1902 and June 23, 1905 and June 21, 1907 and June 25, 1920, 1 and June 20, 1922, 1 and June 13, 1934, 6; *Columbia Missourian*, July 6, 1927, 8. Accounts of the "battle" appeared in the local press well into the twentieth century.
8. *The American Annual Cyclopedia and Register*, 483.
9. Nicolay and Hay, "Abraham Lincoln: A History, the Border States," 69.
10. Snead, "The First Year of the War in Missouri," 268.
11. U.S. Congress, *Report of the Joint Committee on the Conduct of the War*, 160.
12. Peckham, *General Nathaniel Lyon and Missouri in 1861*, 217, 219, 239.
13. Payne, "Fighting in Missouri," 914.
14. *Official Record*, Series I, 3:305; Bridges, "A Confederate Hero," 233–235.
15. "The Death of Hiram Bledsoe," 95.
16. Wilson, "Bledsoe of Missouri," 101–103.
17. Christie, "The Memoirs of Dr. Robert J. Christie," Chapter 7; Carr, *Missouri, a Bone of Contention*, 211.
18. Wilson, "Bledsoe of Missouri," 102.
19. Snead, *The Fight for Missouri*, 217.
20. Howison, "History of the War," 336.
21. Grant, Nathaniel, to Colonel H. K. Craig, May 3, 1861, Records of the Chief of Ordinance, Letters Received (1961), Record Group 156, Washington, DC: National Archives; see also *Sterling Price's Lieutenants*, 191.
22. Patrick, "Remembering the Missouri Campaign of 1861," 21–29, 53n18. The Patrick source is an edited version of the memoirs of Lieutenant William P. Barlow. After the war, Barlow became editor of the Mobile, Alabama, *Register*, and later chief of police in Mobile. He returned to St. Louis in 1877 and worked as a printer until he died on December 27, 1896, at age 58.
23. Ford, "Civil War Reminiscences," 1.
24. Snead, *The Fight for Missouri*, 215.
25. Rorvig, "The Significant Skirmish," 127–148.
26. Pollard, *Southern History of the War: The First Year of the War*, 131.
27. Barnes, "Boonville," 606.

Chapter 18

1. *The American Annual Cyclopedia and Register,* 662; Anderson, *The Story of a Border City during the Civil War,* 204.
2. Tomes and Smith, *The War with the South,* 319; St. Louis County Coroner's Record Book, Missouri History Museum.
3. U.S. Congress, *Report of the Joint Committee on the Conduct of the War,* 161.
4. U.S. Congress, *Report of the Joint Committee on the Conduct of the War,* 184.
5. Nicolay and Hay, "Abraham Lincoln: A History, the Advance," 299.
6. Barns, *Commonwealth of Missouri,* 365; Anderson, *The Story of a Border City during the Civil War,* 203; McElroy, *The Struggle for Missouri,* 125; North, *History of Jasper County,* 43; Woodward, *The Life of General Nathaniel Lyon,* 282–284; Switzler, et al., *Switzler's Illustrated History of Missouri,* 365.
7. *The American Annual Cyclopedia and Register,* 484.
8. Anderson, *The Story of a Border City during the Civil War,* 202; Stevens, *Missouri the Center State,* 281; Anderson, *Memoirs: Historical and Personal,* 21; Adamson, *Rebellion in Missouri,* 129.
9. Howison, "History of the War," 335; Perkins, "Jefferson Davis and General Sterling Price," 399–400.
10. Grover, "Civil War in Missouri." 17–18.
11. Bearss, "Fort Smith Serves General McCulloch," 324.
12. Miller, "General Mosby M. Parsons," 44.
13. Nicolay, *The Outbreak of Rebellion,* 124.
14. Kirkpatrick, "Missouri in the Early Months of the Civil War," 255.
15. Payne, "Early Days of War in Missouri," 927.
16. Barnes, "Boonville," 607.
17. Burks, *Thunder on the Right,* 478.
18. Violette, *A History of Missouri,* 165; Carr, *Missouri, a Bone of Contention,* 215–217.
19. Violette, *A History of Missouri,* 165.
20. Perkins, "Jefferson Davis and General Sterling Price," 399; Cullum, *Biographical Register of the Officers and Graduates of the U.S. Military Academy,* 1:548–571, 2:3–37, 2:72–112, 2:139–180. Class of 1828, out of 33 graduates, Jefferson Davis ranked 23. Class of 1829, out of 46, Robert E. Lee ranked 2. Class of 1838, out of 45, P.G.T. Beauregard ranked 2, Irving McDowell ranked 23. Class of 1841, out of 52, Nathaniel Lyon ranked 11, James Totten ranked 25, Don Carlos Buell ranked 32. Class of 1843, out of 39, Edmund Holloway ranked 19 (accidentally killed by his own men), Ulysses S. Grant ranked 21. Class of 1844, out of 25, Daniel M. Frost ranked 4. Class of 1846, out of 59, George B. McClellan ranked 2, Stonewall Jackson ranked 17, Samuel D. Sturgis ranked 32.
21. Davis, *The Rise and Fall of the Confederate Government,* 1:424.
22. Stevens, *Missouri the Center State,* 281.
23. Edwards, *Shelby and His Men,* 25–26.
24. Pollard, *Southern History of the War: The First Year of the War,* 130–131.
25. Howison, "History of the War," 336.
26. Pollard, *Southern History of the War: The First Year of the War,* 131.
27. Violette, *A History of Missouri,* 357.
28. Anderson, *Memoirs: Historical and Personal,* 20.

Chapter 19

1. *History of Newton, Lawrence, Barry, and McDonald Counties.*
2. Christie, "The Memoirs of Dr. Robert J. Christie," Chapter 6.
3. *History of Cole, Moniteau, Morgan, Benton, etc.,* 418.
4. Richardson, *The Secret Service, the Field, the Dungeon, the Escape,* 138.
5. Cook, "A Border Boy's Recollections of the War," 165.
6. Toombs, "War Memories of a Confederate Boy," 49.
7. Nicolay and Hay, "Abraham Lincoln: A History, the Advance," 295; "The Cole Camp Fight—Reliable Particulars," *New York Tribune,* July 4, 1861.
8. Payne, "Fighting in Missouri," 913.
9. Rorvig, "The Significant Skirmish," 127–148.
10. Ware, *The Lyon Campaign in Missouri,* 97.
11. Christie, "The Memoirs of Dr. Robert J. Christie," Chapter 6.
12. Toombs, "War Memories of a Confederate Boy," 47.

13. Ware, *The Lyon Campaign in Missouri*, 97.
14. Violette, *A History of Missouri*, 357.
15. Anderson, *The Story of a Border City during the Civil War*, 202; Kirkpatrick, "Missouri in the Early Months of the Civil War," 247.
16. Barns, *Commonwealth of Missouri*, 365.
17. Stevens, *Missouri the Center State*, 281.
18. Tomes and Smith, *The War with the South*, 318.
19. McElroy, *The Struggle for Missouri*, 127.
20. Ware, *The Lyon Campaign in Missouri*, 119.
21. *The American Annual Cyclopedia and Register*, 484.
22. U.S. Congress, *Report of the Joint Committee on the Conduct of the War*, 160.
23. U.S. Congress, *Report of the Joint Committee on the Conduct of the War*, 165.
24. Crumpler, "Yankee Avenger," 49.
25. Angus, *Down the Wire Road*, 2, 4.
26. Barnes, "Boonville," 606.
27. Lademann, "The Battle of Carthage."
28. Lademann, "The Battle of Carthage."

Chapter 20

1. Ware, *The Lyon Campaign in Missouri*, 78. Eugene Ware was a soldier in Company E of the First Iowa Infantry, a three-month regiment that was the first main body of Union troops sent to Missouri.
2. Ware, *The Lyon Campaign in Missouri*, 80, 94, 105.
3. Ware, *The Lyon Campaign in Missouri*, 108.
4. Plum, "The Southwest Early in the War," 112.
5. Richardson, *The Secret Service, the Field, the Dungeon, the Escape*, 154, 156.
6. Harding, "Old Missouri State Guard," 14.
7. Burks, *Thunder on the Right*, 400.
8. Richardson, *The Secret Service, the Field, the Dungeon, the Escape*, 153.
9. Ware, *The Lyon Campaign in Missouri*, 119, 126.
10. Bell, "Price's Missouri Campaign," 271.
11. Harvey, "Missouri from 1849–1861," 29.
12. *Liberty* (MO) *Tribune*, June 28, 1861, 2.
13. Plum, "The Southwest Early in the War," 109.
14. Stevens, *Missouri the Center State*, 279. Railroads suffered great damage during the war. Raids occurred against all the Missouri railroads. Confederate General Sterling Price led the most serious raid against the Pacific Railroad. As a result, by the end of the war, the Southwest Branch of the Pacific went bankrupt. The state of Missouri seized it in 1866, renamed it the Southwest Pacific Railroad, and offered it for sale. The Atlantic and Pacific Railroad purchased it as a newly founded company chartered by Congress to build track through Indian Territory to the Pacific Ocean. The Southwest Pacific line gave the A & P access to St. Louis and destinations beyond. The head of the new company was none other than General John C. Frémont, who turned out to be neither an able general nor a railroad builder. After only a year and less than a dozen miles of track, he failed to make a payment on his purchase price, and the state foreclosed. The line changed hands two more times before being sold in 1876 to the St. Louis and San Francisco Railroad, "The Frisco."
15. Nicolay and Hay, "Abraham Lincoln: A History, the Advance," 293.
16. Paris, *History of the Civil War in America*, 321.
17. U.S. Congress, *Report of the Joint Committee on the Conduct of the War*, 3.
18. Plum, "The Southwest Early in the War," 108–109, 112.
19. Pollard, *Southern History of the War: The First Year of the War*, 129; Snead, "The First Year of the War in Missouri," 267; Davis, *The Rise and Fall of the Confederate Government*, 1:424.
20. Barns, *Commonwealth of Missouri*, 365.
21. Stevens, *Missouri the Center State*, 281.
22. *The American Annual Cyclopedia and Register*, 484.
23. *The American Annual Cyclopedia and Register*, 484; Barns, *Commonwealth of Missouri*, 365.
24. Musick, *Stories of Missouri*, 251.
25. Miller, "General Mosby M. Parsons," 43.
26. Christie, "The Memoirs of Dr. Robert J. Christie," Chapter 7.

27. Carr, *Missouri, a Bone of Contention*, 315.
28. Christie, "The Memoirs of Dr. Robert J. Christie," Chapter 7.
29. Duden, *Report on a Journey to the Western States of North America: and a Stay of Several Years Along the Missouri (During the Years 1824, '25, '26, and 1827)*; Goodrich, "Gottfried Duden," 137–138, 144.
30. Goodrich, "Gottfried Duden," 131, 144.
31. Faust, *The German Element in the United States*, 1:441; Engle, *Yankee Dutchman*, 33; Goodrich, "Gottfried Duden," 146.
32. Blum, "The Political and Military Activities of the German Element," 103.
33. Kennedy, *Population of the United States in 1860*, 299.
34. Ryle, *Missouri: Union or Secession*, 9; Du Bois, "The Civil War Journal and Letters," 456.
35. Ware, *The Lyon Campaign in Missouri*, 16.
36. Carr, *Missouri, a Bone of Contention*, 262.
37. Britton, *The Civil War on the Border*, 40; McElroy, *The Struggle for Missouri*, 130; Pollard, *Southern History of the War: The First Year of the War*, 131.
38. "Jackson, C. F., to the citizens of Benton County—Arms for the Union Men in Southwest Missouri," *Glasgow* (MO) *Weekly Times*, June 13, 1861; "Latest by Telegraph-Warsaw, Mo.," *Missouri Republican*, June 1, 1861.
39. Britton, *The Civil War on the Border*, 41.
40. *Liberty* (MO) *Tribune*, June 7, 1861, 2.
41. "The Fight at Cole Camp," *New York Times*, July 7, 1861, 1.
42. Britton, *The Civil War on the Border*, 41.

Chapter 21

1. Britton, *The Civil War on the Border*, 42.
2. Britton, *The Civil War on the Border*, 41.
3. Britton, *The Civil War on the Border*, 42; McElroy, *The Struggle for Missouri*, 131.
4. "Latest by Telegraph-Warsaw, Mo.," *Missouri Republican*, June 1, 1861.
5. Britton, *The Civil War on the Border*, 41–42; *Liberty* (MO) *Tribune*, June 14, 1861, 2 and June 28, 1861, 1.
6. Britton, *The Civil War on the Border*, 42.
7. Britton, *The Civil War on the Border*, 42–43.
8. Union forces later captured Sheriff Keown before the end of the year, and he died in prison.
9. McElroy, *The Struggle for Missouri*, 131.
10. Britton, *The Civil War on the Border*, 43.
11. Davis, *The Rise and Fall of the Confederate Government*, 1:424.
12. Pollard, *Southern History of the War: The First Year of the War*, 131.
13. Pollard, *Southern History of the War: The First Year of the War*, 131.
14. "From Missouri," *New York Tribune*, June 28, 1861.
15. Howison, "History of the War," 335; "War Movements in Missouri," *New York Tribune*, June 23, 1861.
16. Moore, *Missouri*, 46.
17. Lay, *A Sketch of the History of Benton County*, 71; Snead, *The Fight for Missouri*, 216. Lay and Snead give differing accounts of the organization of the Grays and Blues.
18. Howison, "History of the War," 335.
19. Britton, *The Civil War on the Border*, 43.
20. Davis, *The Rise and Fall of the Confederate Government*, 1:424; Pollard, *Southern History of the War: The First Year of the War*, 131; Moore, *Missouri*, 46; "The Cole Camp Fight," *Missouri Democrat*, July 1, 1861.
21. "Biography of Walter S. O'Kane," 1267.
22. *Jefferson City* (MO) *Inquirer*, June 28, 1856, 4 and August 29, 1857, 4.
23. Britton, *The Civil War on the Border*, 43; McElroy, *The Struggle for Missouri*, 131.
24. "The Fight at Cole Camp," *New York Times*, July 7, 1861, 1.
25. Britton, *The Civil War on the Border*, 44; Pollard, *Southern History of the War: The First Year of the War*, 131; Moore, *Missouri*, 46.
26. Britton, *The Civil War on the Border*, 46.
27. "The Fight at Cole Camp," *New York Times*, July 7, 1861, 1.

28. Lay, *A Sketch of the History of Benton County*, 71. Conflicting sources identify Henry Heisterberg as John Heisterberg. According to the 1870 census, John Heisterberg appears to have been Henry's son. Lay also names Harmon Harms instead of Henry Harms, probably the Harmon H. Harms listed in the 1870 census.
29. McElroy, *The Struggle for Missouri*, 131; Snead, *The Fight for Missouri*, 216.
30. Faust, *The German Element in the United States*, 540.
31. Britton, *The Civil War on the Border*, 44.
32. Pollard, *Southern History of the War: The First Year of the War*, 131.
33. Britton, *The Civil War on the Border*, 44.

Chapter 22

1. Howison, "History of the War," 335.
2. Britton, *The Civil War on the Border*, 44.
3. "The Fight at Cole Camp," *New York Times*, July 7, 1861, 1.
4. "The Cole Camp Fight," *Missouri Democrat*, July 1, 1861.
5. "The Fight at Cole Camp," *New York Times*, July 7, 1861, 1.
6. Britton, *The Civil War on the Border*, 44.
7. Britton, *The Civil War on the Border*, 46.
8. Faust, *The German Element in the United States*, 540.
9. Britton, *The Civil War on the Border*, 44–45.
10. McElroy, *The Struggle for Missouri*, 131.
11. Britton, *The Civil War on the Border*, 45.
12. Pollard, *Southern History of the War: The First Year of the War*, 131.
13. "The Fight at Cole Camp," *Missouri Democrat*, June 24, 1861.
14. "Important from Missouri," *New York Tribune*, June 22, 1861; "From Missouri," *New York Tribune*, July 2, 1861; "From Missouri," *New York Tribune*, July 8, 1861.
15. "The Cole Camp Fight," *Missouri Democrat*, July 1, 1861; "Untitled [Boonville-Cole Camp-Jackson]," *Keowee Courier* (Pickens Court House, SC), July 6, 1861; *Daily Dispatch* (Richmond, VA), July 29, 1861.
16. Faust, *The German Element in the United States*, 540; "The Fight at Cole Camp," *New York Times*, July 7, 1861, 1. The *New York Times* listed the names of 22 Home Guards killed in the Cole Camp assault.
17. "The Fight at Cole Camp," *New York Times*, July 7, 1861, 1.
18. Britton, *The Civil War on the Border*, 46; "War Correspondence," *Missouri Democrat*, 2 Jul 1861.
19. Davis, *The Rise and Fall of the Confederate Government*, 1:424.
20. Britton, *The Civil War on the Border*, 46.
21. Pollard, *Southern History of the War: The First Year of the War*, 129.
22. McElroy, *The Struggle for Missouri*, 132; Pollard, *Southern History of the War: The First Year of the War*, 131.
23. Moore, *Missouri*, 46; Davis, *The Rise and Fall of the Confederate Government*, 1:424.
24. Find A Grave, ID 46578454, ID 106667585.
25. Britton, *The Civil War on the Border*, 45–46; Faust, *The German Element in the United States*, 540.
26. Britton, *The Civil War on the Border*, 46; McElroy, *The Struggle for Missouri*, 132; "The Fight at Cole Camp," *New York Times*, July 7, 1861, 1.
27. McElroy, *The Struggle for Missouri*, 132; Davis, *The Rise and Fall of the Confederate Government*, 1:424; Snead, *The Fight for Missouri*, 216; Pollard, *Southern History of the War: The First Year of the War*, 131.
28. McElroy, *The Struggle for Missouri*, 132.
29. "The Fight at Cole Camp," *New York Times*, July 7, 1861, 1; "The Cole Camp Fight," *Missouri Democrat*, July 1, 1861.
30. Britton, *The Civil War on the Border*, 45.
31. Britton, *The Civil War on the Border*, 45.
32. Pollard, *Southern History of the War: The First Year of the War*, 131; "War Correspondence," *Missouri Democrat*, July 1, 1861; "The Cole Camp Fight," *Missouri Democrat*, July 1, 1861.
33. Britton, *The Civil War on the Border*, 46–47.
34. *The American Annual Cyclopedia and Register*, 484.

35. *Boonville* (MO) *Weekly Advertiser*, June 20, 1919, 7.
36. "The Fight at Cole Camp," *New York Times*, July 7, 1861, 1.
37. *History of Cole, Moniteau, Morgan, Benton, etc.*, 493–496; Pollard, *Southern History of the War: The First Year of the War*, 130.
38. Barns, *Commonwealth of Missouri*, 365; Switzler, et al., *Switzler's Illustrated History of Missouri*, 365; Pollard, *Southern History of the War: The First Year of the War*, 130.

Chapter 23

1. Adamson, *Rebellion in Missouri*, 138, 143.
2. Christie, "The Memoirs of Dr. Robert J. Christie," Chapter 6.
3. Nicolay and Hay, "Abraham Lincoln: A History, the Advance," 296.
4. U.S. Congress, *Report of the Joint Committee on the Conduct of the War*, 161.
5. *Official Record*, Operations in Missouri. Series I, 3:382–384.
6. U.S. Congress, *Report of the Joint Committee on the Conduct of the War*, 79.
7. Ware, *The Lyon Campaign in Missouri*, 152.
8. Du Bois, "The Civil War Journal and Letters," 456.
9. Ware, *The Lyon Campaign in Missouri*, 148.
10. Ware, *The Lyon Campaign in Missouri*, 293, 296, 312.
11. Ware, *The Lyon Campaign in Missouri*, 118.
12. Ware, *The Lyon Campaign in Missouri*, 85.
13. Ware, *The Lyon Campaign in Missouri*, 135–136.
14. Ware, *The Lyon Campaign in Missouri*, 103, 137, 153.
15. Ware, *The Lyon Campaign in Missouri*, 112, 142, 155.
16. Ware, *The Lyon Campaign in Missouri*, 105.
17. Ware, *The Lyon Campaign in Missouri*, 28, 106, 114, 134.
18. Britton, *The Civil War on the Border*, 46; Davis, *The Rise and Fall of the Confederate Government*, 1:424; Snead, *The Fight for Missouri*, 216.
19. "John Taylor Hughes," 132–133.
20. Patrick, "Remembering the Missouri Campaign of 1861," 21–60.
21. Richardson, *The Secret Service, the Field, the Dungeon, the Escape*, 148.
22. H. L. Boon correspondence to his father, July 7, 1861; *Glasgow Weekly Times* (MO), July 18, 1861; Wallace, "Gen. E. W. Price," 208.
23. "From Missouri," *New York Tribune*, July 2, 1861.

Chapter 24

1. Lademann, "The Battle of Carthage."
2. McElroy, The Struggle for Missouri, 146.
3. Peckham, *General Nathaniel Lyon and Missouri in 1861*, 199–200; Snead, *The Fight for Missouri*, 188.
4. Snead, *The Fight for Missouri*, 188.
5. *Official Record*, Operations in Missouri. Series I, 3:390.
6. Lyon, *The Last Political Writings of Gen. Nathaniel Lyon*, 200.
7. Du Bois, "The Civil War Journal and Letters," 448.
8. U.S. Congress, *Report of the Joint Committee on the Conduct of the War*, 79–80.
9. Ware, *The Lyon Campaign in Missouri*, 152.
10. U.S. Congress, *Report of the Joint Committee on the Conduct of the War*, 81–82. J. M. Schofield, from Camp Cameron [Boonville], General Orders No. 4, July 2, 1861, summarized Lyon's troop strength: "troops to take up the line of march for the south at 7 o'clock a.m. tomorrow [July 3] Brigadier General and staff 4; Company B Second Infantry 61; Company R Second Artillery 1 officer, 60 men; Recruits U.S. army 1 officer, 134 men; First Regiment Missouri Volunteers 29 officers 866 men; Two companies Second Regiment Missouri Volunteers 6 officers 205 men; Pioneer detachment 1 officer 46 men; Artillery 1 officer 13 men; First Regiment Iowa Volunteers 34 officers 892 men; Total 77 officers 2,277 men; aggregate 2,354; 16 companies 1,375 men and officers left at Boonville."
11. U.S. Congress, *Report of the Joint Committee on the Conduct of the War*, 80, 82.
12. Stevens, *Missouri the Center State*, 283.

13. Nicolay and Hay, "Abraham Lincoln: A History, the Advance," 296.
14. Bearss, "Fort Smith Serves General McCulloch," 327.
15. Holcombe, *History of Greene County*, 284.
16. Pollard, *Southern History of the War: The First Year of the War*, 130–131.
17. Crumpler, "Yankee Avenger," 49.
18. Adamson, *Rebellion in Missouri*, 137.
19. Nicolay and Hay, "Abraham Lincoln: A History, the Advance," 295, 299; U.S. Congress, *Report of the Joint Committee on the Conduct of the War*, 154.
20. Richardson, *The Secret Service, the Field, the Dungeon, the Escape*, 185, 188. General Frémont lost his command in part for issuing written guarantees to the slaves for their freedom from Rebels. The guarantees were in the form of real-estate conveyances, releasing the recipient from all obligations to his master, declaring him forever free from servitude, and with full right and authority to control his own labor. These "Deeds of Manumission," authenticated by the great seal of the Western Department and the signature of its commander, were premature, in the opinion of President Lincoln.
21. Leland, "General Lyon," 408.
22. Plum, "The Southwest Early in the War," 111; Nicolay and Hay, "Abraham Lincoln: A History, the Advance," 296.
23. Ware, *The Lyon Campaign in Missouri*, 142.
24. Woodward, *The Life of General Nathaniel Lyon*, 290.
25. Giffen, "The Strange Story of Major General Franz Sigel," 410.
26. Woodward, *The Life of General Nathaniel Lyon*, 291.
27. Crumpler, "Yankee Avenger," 51.
28. U.S. Congress, *Report of the Joint Committee on the Conduct of the War*, 83.
29. Buegel, "The Civil War Diary of John T. Buegel," 311. A unit of the Third Regiment claimed to have reached Springfield on June 25; however, this seems unlikely.
30. Lademann, "The Battle of Carthage."
31. Du Bois, "The Civil War Journal and Letters," 447.
32. U.S. Congress, *Report of the Joint Committee on the Conduct of the War*, 83.
33. *New York Times*, 11 Jul 1861.
34. Burchett, *Battle of Carthage*; Hinze and Farnham, *The Battle of Carthage*.
35. U.S. Congress, *Report of the Joint Committee on the Conduct of the War*, 82; Stevens, "Lincoln and Missouri," 91. Lincoln created the Southeast District at Cairo. In January 1862, he assigned General Ulysses S. Grant to occupy it. Grant had Fort Defiance constructed to protect the Union supply base and training center for the remainder of the war. It was at Cairo that General Grant began his rise to prominence.
36. Peckham, *General Nathaniel Lyon and Missouri in 1861*, 264–265.
37. U.S. Congress, *Report of the Joint Committee on the Conduct of the War*, 162.
38. U.S. Congress, *Report of the Joint Committee on the Conduct of the War*, 155.
39. U.S. Congress, *Report of the Joint Committee on the Conduct of the War*, 204.

Chapter 25

1. "The Great Battle in Missouri," *New York Times*, August 15, 1861, 4.
2. Wood, *The Siege of Lexington, Missouri*.
3. "The Defeat at Lexington, Mo.," *New York Times*, September 26, 1861, 4.
4. Richardson, *The Secret Service, the Field, the Dungeon, the Escape*, 140.
5. Grierson, *The Valley of Shadows*, 196.
6. Barnes, "Boonville," 605–606.
7. Stevens, *Missouri the Center State*, vii.
8. Richardson, *The Secret Service, the Field, the Dungeon, the Escape*, 151.
9. Erwin, *Guerrilla Hunters in Civil War Missouri*.
10. Cook, "A Border Boy's Recollections of the War," 164–166.
11. Edwards, *Shelby and His Men*.
12. Stevens, *Missouri the Center State*, vii.
13. Stevens, *Missouri the Center State*, viii. The National Park Service puts this number at 27 Union and 15 Confederate.
14. Stevens, *Missouri the Center State*, vii.
15. National Park Service.

Bibliography

Abbott, John S.C. *The History of the Civil War in America*, Vol. 1. New York: Henry Bill, 1863.

Adams, Annie Brown, to Garibaldi Ross, December 15, 1887. In *The Boisterous Sea of Liberty: A Documentary History of America from Discovery through the Civil War*. Edited by David B. Davis and Steven Mintz. New York: Oxford University Press, 1997.

Adamson, Hans C. *Rebellion in Missouri 1861: Nathaniel Lyon and His Army of the West*. New York: Chilton, 1961.

The American Annual Cyclopedia and Register of Important Events of the Year 1861, Vol. 1. New York: D. Appleton, 1864.

Anderson, Ephraim M. *Memoirs: Historical and Personal, Including the Campaigns of the First Missouri Confederate Brigade*. St. Louis: Times, 1868.

Anderson, Galusha. *The Story of a Border City during the Civil War*. Boston: Little, Brown, 1908.

Angus, Fern. *Down the Wire Road in the Missouri Ozarks*. Marionville, MO: Author, 1992.

Asbury, Edgar A. *My Experiences in the War 1861-1865: A Little Autobiography*. Kansas City: Berkowitz, 1894.

Axelrod, Alan. *The Complete Idiot's Guide to the Civil War*, 3rd ed. New York: Penguin, 2011.

Badger, Alexander, to his sister Alice [Alice E. Cayton], Ft. Vancouver, Washington Territory, May 5, 1861. Badger Family Papers, 1852–1950. Missouri History Museum.

Ball, Edward. *Slaves in the Family*, 2nd ed. New York: Farrar, Straus and Giroux, 2014.

Baltimore (MD) *Sun*. June 25, 1861, reprinted in *Carthage* (MO) *Press*, July 12, 1887.

Banasik, Michael E., ed. *Missouri Brothers in Gray: The Reminiscences and Letters of William J. Bull and John P. Bull*. Iowa City: Camp Pope Bookshop, 1998.

Barlow, William P. "Guibor's Battery in 1861." [St. Louis] *Daily Missouri Republican*, August 1, 1885.

Barnes, John B. "Boonville, the First Land Battle of the Civil War." *Infantry Journal* 35 (December 1929): 601–607.

Barns, C.R., ed. *Commonwealth of Missouri; a Centennial Record*. St. Louis: Bryan, Brand, 1877.

Bartels, Carolyn. *The Forgotten Men: Missouri State Guard*. Independence, MO: Two Trails, 1995.

Bearss, Edwin C. "Fort Smith Serves General McCulloch as a Supply Depot." *Arkansas Historical Quarterly* 24 (Winter 1965): 315–347.

Bell, J.P. "Price's Missouri Campaign of 1861." In *Missouri's Sons of the South*, Vol. 2. St. Louis: Missouri Division Sons of Confederate Veterans, 1998.

Bell, John H. "Price's Missouri Campaign, 1861." *Confederate Veteran* 22 (June 1914): 271–272.

Berlin, Ira. "Missouri." In *Freedom: A Documentary History of Emancipation, 1861-1867: The Destruction of Slavery*, Series 1, Vol. 1. New York: Cambridge University Press, 1985.

Bevier, Robert S. *History of the First and Second Missouri Confederate Brigades: 1861-1865. And, From Wakarusa to Appomattox, a Military Anagraph*. St. Louis: Bryan, Brand, 1879.

"Biography of Walter S. O'Kane." *Goodspeed's History of Franklin County*. Chicago: Goodspeed, 1889.

Blackmar, Frank W., ed. *Kansas: A Cyclopedia of State History*, Vols. 1 & 2. Chicago: Standard, 1912.

"Bledsoe's Battery." In *Missouri's Sons of the South*, Vol. 2. St. Louis: Missouri Division Sons of Confederate Veterans, 1998.

Blum, Virgil C. "The Political and Military Activities of the German Element in St. Louis, 1859–1861." *Missouri Historical Review* 42 (January 1948): 103–129.

"The Bombardment of Sumter." *The New York Times*, May 5, 1861, 4.

Boonville (MO) *Weekly Advertiser*. July 24, 1885; April 30, 1886; June 15, 1900; January 21, 1901; September 12, 1902; June 23, 1905; June 21, 1907; June 20, 1919; June 1, 1922; June 20, 1922; June 1, 1934; June 13, 1934.

Bordewich, Fergus M. "John Brown's Day of Reckoning." *Smithsonian* (October 2009): 62–69.

Börnstein, Heinrich. *Memoirs of a Nobody: The Missouri Years of an Austrian Radical, 1849–1866*. Translated and edited by Steven Rowan. St. Louis: Missouri Historical Society, 1997.

Boyce, Joseph. "The Evacuation of Nashville," *Confederate Veteran* 28 (February 1920): 60–62.

Bridges, Hal. "A Confederate Hero: General William Y. Slack." *The Arkansas Historical Quarterly* 10 (Autumn 1951): 233–237.

Britton, Wiley. *The Civil War on the Border*. New York: G.P. Putnam's Sons, 1890.

Broadhead, James O. "St. Louis during the War." Unpublished Manuscript, James O. Broadhead Papers. Missouri Historical Society.

Burks, Walter M. *Thunder on the Right*. Dissertation, Department of History and Government, University of Kansas City, 1962.

"The Camp Jackson Incident." *The Museum Gazette*, May 1999. National Park Service, Jefferson National Expansion Memorial.

Campbell, Robert A. *Campbell's Gazetteer of Missouri*. St. Louis: R.A. Campbell, 1874.

Campbell, Robert A. *The Rebellion Register: A History of the Principal Persons and Places, Important Dates, Documents and Statistics, Military and Political*. Indianapolis: Robert Douglass, 1866.

"Capture of Secessionists at Camp Jackson, Trouble between the Mob and the United States Troops." *New York Times*, May 12, 1861, 1.

Carr, Lucien. *Missouri, a Bone of Contention*. Boston: Houghton Mifflin, 1888.

Castel, Albert. *General Sterling Price and the Civil War in the West*. Baton Rouge: Louisiana State University Press, 1993.

Catton, Bruce. *The Centennial History of the Civil War*. Garden City, New York: Doubleday, 1961.

Catton, Bruce. *The Coming Fury*. Garden City, New York: Doubleday, 1961.

Cayton, Alice E., to her brother [Alexander Badger], St. Louis, May 12, 1861. Badger Family Papers, 1852–1950. Missouri History Museum.

Chappell, Phillip E. "Missouri River Steamboats." *Transactions of the Kansas State Historical Society* 9 (1905–1906): 295–316.

Chauvenet, S.H. "St. Louis in the Early Days of the Civil War and the Capture of Camp Jackson." Unpublished manuscript, no date. Civil War Collection, 1860–1977. Missouri History Museum.

Cheavens, Henry Martyn. "Journal of the Civil War in Missouri: 1861, Henry Martyn Cheavens." Edited by Virginia Easley. *Missouri Historical Review* 56 (October 1961): 12–25.

Cheavens, Henry Martyn. "A Missouri Confederate in the Civil War. The Journal of Henry Martyn Cheavens, 1862–1863." Edited by James E. Moss. *Missouri Historical Review* 57 (October 1962): 16–52.

Cheney, John V., ed. *Inaugural Addresses of the Presidents of the United States: From Taylor to Roosevelt*. Chicago: Reilly & Britton, 1906.

Chittenden, L.E. "The Peace Convention of 1861: Report of the Debates and Proceedings of the Peace Convention Held in Washington, February 1861." *The New York Times*, June 18, 1865, 4.

Christie, Robert J. "The Memoirs of Dr. Robert J. Christie, June 17, 1831–July 27, 1909." Edited by Michael Flanagan, https://flanaganfamily.net/genealo/memoirs.htm#chVI, accessed May 10, 2011.

Clark, Kimball. "The Epic March of Doniphan's Missourians." *Missouri*

Historical Review 80 (January 1986): 134–155.
Cole, Nelson. "No. 2. Report of Captain Nelson Cole, May 16, 1861." In *Official Records*, Series 1, Vol. 3, 10–11. Washington, DC: Government Printing Office, 1881.
"The Cole Camp Fight." *Missouri Democrat*, July 1, 1861.
"Colonel Eberhard Salomon." *The Milwaukee Sentinel*, June 1, 1862.
Columbia (MO) Statesman. May 10, 1861; June 21, 1861; June 28, 1861; July 12, 1861; July 19, 1861; July 26, 1861; September 20, 1861.
Conard, Howard L., ed. *Encyclopedia of the History of Missouri: A Compendium of History and Biography for Ready Reference*, Vols. 3 & 4. New York: Southern History, 1901.
Confederate States of America. "An act recognizing the existence of war between the United States and the Confederate States." 1861. Duke University Libraries.
Connelley, William E. *A Standard History of Kansas and Kansans*, Vol. 1. New York: Lewis, 1918.
Cook, George A. "A Border Boy's Recollections of the War." *The New England Magazine* (New Series) 10 (April 1894): 164–167.
Covington, James W. "The Camp Jackson Affair, 1861." *Missouri Historical Review* 55 (April 1961): 197–212.
Cox, Samuel S. *Union-Disunion-Reunion. Three Decades of Federal Legislation, 1855–1885*. Providence, RI: J.A. & R.A. Reid, 1885.
Crawford, Samuel Wylie. *The Genesis of the Civil War: The Story of Sumter, 1860–1861*. New York: C.L. Webster, 1887.
Crawford, William H. Correspondence to His Parents, n. d. Henry Clay Crawford and William H. Crawford, Letters, 1857–1865 (C0239). State Historical Society of Missouri, Columbia.
Croly, David G.B. *Seymour and Blair, Their Lives and Services with an Appendix Containing a History of Reconstruction*. New York: Richardson, 1868.
Crumpler, Hugh. "Yankee Avenger: Gen. Nathaniel Lyon, Union Commander at the Battle of Wilson's Creek." *Ozarks Watch*, 4 (Spring 1991)/ 5 (Summer 1991): 47–51.

Crute, Joseph H., Jr. *Units of the Confederate States Army*. Midlothian, VA: Derwent Books, 1987.
Cullum, George W. *Biographical Register of the Officers and Graduates of the U.S. Military Academy*, Vol. 1 & 2, rev. ed. New York: J. Miller, 1879.
Curtis, George T. *Constitutional History of the United States from Their Declaration of Independence to the Close of the Civil War*, Vol. 2. New York: Harper & Brothers, 1896.
Daily Dispatch (Richmond, VA). July 29, 1861.
Dark, Harris E., and Phyllis Dark. *Springfield of the Ozarks: An Illustrated History*. Woodland Hills, CA: Windsor, 1981.
Davis, Jefferson. *The Rise and Fall of the Confederate Government*, Vols. 1 & 2. Richmond, VA: Garrett & Massie, 1881.
"The Death of Hiram Bledsoe." *Missouri's Sons of the South*, Vol. 1. St. Louis: Missouri Division Sons of Confederate Veterans, 1998.
"The Defeat at Lexington, Mo." *New York Times*, September 26, 1861, 4.
Denny, James, and John Bradbury. *The Civil War's First Blood: Missouri, 1854–1861*. Boonville, MO: Missouri Life, 2007.
Dick, Franklin A., and Gari Carter. *Troubled State: Civil War Journals of Franklin Archibald Dick*. Kirksville, MO: Truman State University Press, 2008.
Diggs, Lorena. "Hazardous Trip in War Days: Reminiscences of Mrs. P.H. Haggard, 1908." *Confederate Veteran* 39 (1931): 463–465, 475.
"Domestic Intelligence. The Alarm at Charleston." *Harper's Weekly*, 5 (April 20, 1861): 247.
Donald, David H., and Harold Holzer. *Lincoln in the Times: The Life of Abraham Lincoln, as Originally Reported in* The New York Times. New York: St. Martin's, 2005.
Drake, Charles D. *Camp Jackson: Its History and Significance. Oration of Charles D. Drake, Delivered in the City of St. Louis, May 11, 1863*. Saint Louis, MO: Missouri Democrat, 1863.
Du Bois, John Van Duesen. "The Civil War Journal and Letters of Colonel John Van Deusen Du Bois." Edited by Jared C. Lobdell. *Missouri Historical Review* 60 (July 1966): 436–459.

Duden, Gottfried. *Report on a Journey to the Western States of North America: and a Stay of Several Years along the Missouri (During the Years 1824, '25, '26, and 1827).* Edited and Translated by James W. Goodrich and George H. Kellner. Columbia, MO: State Historical Society of Missouri and University of Missouri Press, 2017.

Duke, Basil W. *Reminiscences of General Basil W. Duke.* New York: Doubleday, Page, 1911.

Dunson, A.A. "Notes on the Missouri Germans on Slavery." *Missouri Historical Review* 59 (April 1965): 355–366.

Duyckinck, Evert A. *National History of the War for the Union: Civil, Military and Naval*, Vol. 1. New York: Johnson, Fry, 1862.

Dyer, Frederick H., *A Compendium of the War of the Rebellion*, Vol. 2. Des Moines, IA: Dyer, 1959.

Eakin, Joanne W.C. *The Battle of Rock Creek.* Independence, MO: J.C. Eakin, 1995.

Edwards, John N. *Shelby and His Men; or, the War in the West.* Kansas City: Hudson-Kimberly, 1897.

Emerson, Ralph W. *Miscellanies.* Boston: Houghton Mifflin, 1904.

The Encyclopedia of Americana, Vol. 26. New York: Encyclopedia Americana, 1920.

Engle, Stephen D. *Yankee Dutchman: The Life of Franz Sigel.* Baton Rouge: Louisiana State University Press, 1999.

Erwin, James W. *Guerrilla Hunters in Civil War Missouri.* Charleston, SC: History Press, 2013.

Estes, Claud. *List of field officers, regiments and battalions in the Confederate States army, 1861–1865.* J.W. Burke, 1912.

Ethier, Eric. "Firebrand in a Powder Keg: Nathaniel Lyon in St. Louis." *Civil War Times*, 44 (June 2005): 50–56, 81.

Farrar, Benjamin. "Seizure of U.S. Arsenal at Liberty, Missouri." In *Official Records*, Series 1, Vol. 1. Washington, DC: Government Printing Office, 1881.

Faust, Albert B. *The German Element in the United States with Special Reference to Its Political, Moral, Social, and Educational Influence*, Vol. 1. New York: Houghton Mifflin, 1909.

"The Fight at Cole Camp." *New York Times*, July 7, 1861, 1.

Fiske, John. *The Mississippi Valley in the Civil War.* New York: Houghton Mifflin, 1902.

Ford, Salem H. "Civil War Reminiscences." Collection B194. Missouri Historical Society, St. Louis, 1909.

Frank Leslie's Illustrated Newspaper, Vol. 4 no. 82 (June 27, 1857).

Freemen's Manual, Vol. 1. Columbus, OH: L.L. Rice, 1853.

"From Missouri." *New York Tribune*, June 28 1861; July 2, 1861; July 8, 1861.

Frost, Daniel. "No. 2. Protest to Nathaniel Lyon [Camp Jackson], May 11, 1861." In *Official Record*, Series 1, Vols. 3, 5 & 6. Washington, DC: Government Printing Office, 1881.

Gamble, Hamilton R., and James E. Yeatman to Abraham Lincoln, May 15, 1861 (Conditions in St. Louis). Abraham Lincoln Papers at the Library of Congress.

Gantt, Thomas T., to Brig. Genl. W.S. Harney, May 14, 1861, and Brig. Genl. W.S. Harney to Thomas T. Gantt, May 14, 1861, in Berlin, "Missouri," 413–414.

"General Franz Sigel Dead." *New York Times*, August 22, 1902, 9.

General Index Cards, Compiled Military Service Records. Microfilm M380, Roll 2. Washington, DC: National Archives.

Gerteis, Louis S. *Civil War St. Louis.* Lawrence: University Press of Kansas, 2001.

Giffen, Lawrence E. "The Strange Story of Major General Franz Sigel: Leader and Retreater." *Missouri Historical Review* 84 (July 1990): 404–427.

Glasgow Weekly Times [MO]. July 18, 1861.

Glover, Samuel T., to Abraham Lincoln, Friday, May 24, 1861 (Situation in Missouri). Abraham Lincoln Papers at the Library of Congress.

Goodrich, James W. "Gottfried Duden: A Nineteenth Century Missouri Promoter." *Missouri Historical Review* 75 (January 1981): 131–146.

Gottschalk, Phil. *In Deadly Earnest: The History of the First Missouri Brigade, CSA.* Columbia, MO: Missouri River, 1991.

Grant, Julia D. *The Personal Memoirs of Julia Dent Grant (Mrs. Ulysses S. Grant).* Edited by John Y. Simon. New York: Putnam, 1975.

Grant, Nathaniel. "Seizure of U.S. Arsenal at Liberty, Missouri." In *Official Records*, Series 1, Vol. 1. Washington, DC: Government Printing Office, 1881.

Grant, Nathaniel. Correspondence to Colonel H.K. Craig. 3 May 1861. Record Group 156, Records of the Office of the Chief of Ordinance, Letters Received, 1812–1894 (entry 21). Washington, DC: National Archives.

Grant, Ulysses S. *Personal Memoirs of U.S. Grant*. New York: Charles L. Webster, 1894.

"The Great Battle in Missouri." *New York Times*, August 15, 1861, 4 (Originally *Fort Scott Democrat*, July 7, 1861).

"Great Excitement in St. Louis." *The Constitutional* (Alexandria, LA). May 18, 1861.

Greene, A.C. *900 Miles on the Butterfield Trail*. Denton: University of North Texas Press, 1994.

Greene, Colton. "The Plot to Seize St. Louis." Edited by Bruce S. Allardice. *Civil War Times Illustrated* 35 (May 1998): 17.

Greene, Lorenzo J., Gary R. Kremer, and Antonio F. Holland. *Missouri's Black Heritage*, rev. ed. Columbia: University of Missouri Press, 1993.

Grierson, Francis. *The Valley of Shadows: Recollections of the Lincoln Country 1858–1863*. New York: Houghton Mifflin, 1909.

Grover, George S. "Civil War in Missouri." *Missouri Historical Review* 8 (1913): 1–28.

Guernsey, Alfred H., and Henry M. Alden, eds. *Harper's Pictorial History of the Great Rebellion*, Vol. 1. Chicago: McDonnell Bros., 1866–1868.

Halsey, Francis W. *Great Epochs in American History: Slavery and the Mexican War: 1840–1860*, Vol. 7. New York: Funk & Wagnalls, 1912.

Hammond, William A. *Personal Recollections of General Nathaniel Lyon*. Washington, 1900. War papers (Military Order of the Loyal Legion of the United States. District of Columbia Commandery). No. 33. Huntington Copy: Nicholson collection.

Hammond, William A. "Recollections of Gen. Nathaniel Lyon." *Annals of Iowa*, 4 (Third Series) (July 1900): 415–436.

Harding, Chester. *Adjutant Generals Report of Missouri State Militia for the Year of 1861*. St. Louis: George Knaps, 1862.

Harding, James. "Old Missouri State Guard. General James Harding Gives Personal Reminiscences of Service in Its Ranks." Manuscript. Carthage, MO: Jasper County Records Center, n. d.

Harding, James. *Service with the Missouri State Guard: The Memoir of Brigadier General James Harding*. Edited by James E. McGhee. Springfield, MO: Oak Hills, 2000. Originally printed in the St. Louis *Daily Missouri Republican* as part of a series entitled "Tales of the War," on July 18 and 25, 1885.

Hargett, Janet L. *List of Selected Maps of States and Territories*. Washington, DC: National Archives, 1971.

Harney, William S. "No. 3. General Harney's Letter Transmitting General Frost's Protest, May 18, 1861." In *Official Record*, Series 1, Vols. 3 & 9. Washington, DC: Government Printing Office, 1881.

Harney, William S. *Official Correspondence of Brig. W.S. Harney, U.S. Army, and First Lt. Geo. Ihrie*. Washington, DC: n. p., 1861.

Harvey, Charles M. "Missouri from 1849–1861." *Missouri Historical Review* 2 (October 1907): 23–40.

Haskell, John G. "The Passing of Slavery in Western Missouri." In *Transactions of the Kansas State Historical Society, 1901–1902*, Vol. 7. Edited by George W. Martin. Topeka: Kansas State Historical Society, 1902, 28–39.

Heidler, David Stephen, Jeanne T. Heidler, and David J. Coles, eds. *Encyclopedia of the American Civil War: A Political, Social, and Military History* (5 vols.). New York: W.W. Norton, 2002.

Herklotz, Hildegarde R. "Jayhawkers in Missouri, 1858–1863." *Missouri Historical Review* 17 [First Article] (April 1923): 266–284; 17 [Second Article] (July 1923): 505–513; 18 [Third Article] (October 1923): 64–101.

Herndon, William H., and Jesse William Weik. *Herndon's Lincoln; The True Story of a Great Life; The History and Personal Recollections of Abraham Lincoln*. Chicago: Belford, Clarke, 1889.

"The Heroes of Fort Sumter." *New York Times*, April 19, 1861, 1.

Hinton, Richard J. *John Brown and His Men*. New York: Funk & Wagnalls, 1894.

Hinze, David, and Karen Farnham. *The Battle of Carthage: Border War in*

Southwest Missouri, July 5, 1861, 3rd ed. Gretna, LA: Pelican, 2004.

History of Boone County, Missouri. St. Louis: Western Historical, 1882.

History of Caldwell and Livingston Counties, Missouri. St. Louis: Higginson Book, 1886.

History of Carroll County, Missouri. St. Louis: Missouri Historical Society, 1881.

History of Cole, Moniteau, Morgan, Benton, Miller, Maries, and Osage Counties, Missouri. Chicago: Goodspeed, 1889.

History of Jasper County, Missouri, Including a Condensed History of the State, a Complete History of Carthage and Joplin, etc. Des Moines, IA: Mills, 1883.

History of Laclede, Camden, Dallas, Webster, Wright, Texas, Pulaski, Phelps and Dent Counties, Missouri. Chicago: Goodspeed, 1889.

History of Newton, Lawrence, Barry, and McDonald Counties, Missouri. Chicago: Goodspeed, 1888.

History of Saline County, Missouri. St. Louis: Missouri Historical Society, 1881.

Hodder, Frank H. "The Genesis of the Kansas-Nebraska Act." *Proceedings of the State Historical Society of Wisconsin for 1912* 60 (1913): 69–86.

Holcombe, R.I. *History of Marion County, Missouri* (Reprint of 1884 ed.). Marceline, MO: Walsworth, 1979.

Holcombe, R.I., ed. *History of Greene County, Missouri*. St. Louis: Western Historical, 1883.

Holland, Antonio F. "African Americans in Henry Shaw's St. Louis." In *St. Louis in the Century of Henry Shaw*. Edited by Eric Sandweiss. St. Louis: Missouri Historical Society, 2003.

Houck, Louis. *A History of Missouri* (3 vols.). Chicago: R.R. Donnelley and Sons, 1908.

Howe, Daniel W. *Political History of Secession to the Beginning of the American Civil War*. New York: G.P. Putnam's Sons, 1914.

Howison, Robert R. "History of the War." *Southern Literary Messenger* 37 (June 1863): 321–338.

Hughes, John Taylor, William Elsey Connelley, Dewitt Clinton Allen, and Charles R. Morehead. *Doniphan's Expedition and the Conquest of New Mexico and California* (reprint). Topeka, KS: Authors, 1907.

Hulston, John K. Review of *Rebellion in Missouri: 1861* by Hans C. Adamson. *Civil War History* 7 (September 1961): 337–338.

Hutchinson, Lucy, St. Louis, to brother Robert Randolph Hutchinson, May 22, 1861, Missouri History Museum.

Hyde, William, and Howard L. Conrad. *Encyclopedia of the History of St. Louis: A Compendium of History and Biography for Ready Reference*, Vol. 3, part 2. New York: Southern History, 1899.

"Important from Missouri." *New York Tribune*, June 22, 1861.

"Important from St. Louis." *New York Times*, May 14, 1861, 1.

"Important from St. Louis, Investigation of the Camp Jackson Affair." *New York Times*, May 16, 1861: 1.

Index of service records, Confederate, 1861–1865. Box 107 Reel s735. Jefferson City, MO: Office of Adjutant General.

Ingenthron, Elmo, and Kathleen Van Buskirk. *Borderland Rebellion: A History of the Civil War on the Missouri-Arkansas Border*. Branson, MO: Ozarks Mountaineer, 1980. 42–51.

Irwin, Ray W., ed. "Missouri in Crisis: The Journal of Captain Albert Tracy, 1861." *Missouri Historical Review* 51 (October 1956): 8–21; (January 1957): 151–164.

Iverson, Harold E., *The History of the St. Louis Arsenal, 1826–1861*. Master's Thesis. Washington University, 1963.

Jackson, Claiborne Fox. *Inaugural Address of Governor C.F. Jackson, to the General Assembly of the State of Missouri: January 3, 1861*. Jefferson City, MO: W.G. Cheeney, 1861.

Jackson, Claiborne Fox. "Inaugural Address of Governor Claiborne Fox Jackson, January 2, 1861." *The Messages and Proclamations of the Governors of the State of Missouri*, Vol. 3. Columbia: State Historical Society of Missouri, 1922.

Jackson, Claiborne Fox. "Special Session Message, May 3, 1861." *The Messages and Proclamations of the Governors of the State of Missouri*, Vol. 3. Columbia: State Historical Soc. of Missouri, 1922.

"Jackson, C. F., to the citizens of Benton County—Arms for the Union Men in Southwest Missouri." *Glasgow* (MO) *Weekly Times*, June 13, 1861.

Jefferson City (MO) *Daily Tribune*. August 29, 1893.

Bibliography

Jefferson City (MO) Inquirer. June 28, 1856; August 4, 1857; August 29, 1857.

Jobe, Sybil, ed.. *Centennial History of Newton County, Missouri* (reprint). Neosho, MO: Newton County Historical Society, 1976.

"John Taylor Hughes." In *More Generals in Gray*. Edited by Bruce S. Allardice. Baton Rouge: Louisiana State University Press, 1995, 132–133.

Journal and Proceedings of the Missouri State Convention, Held at Jefferson City and St. Louis, March 1861. St. Louis: George Knapp, 1861.

Kargau, Ernst D. *The German Element in St. Louis: A Translation from German of Ernst D. Kargau's* St. Louis in Former Years. Translated by William G. Bek. Baltimore: Genealogical Publishing, 2000.

Kennedy, D.C. "In St. Louis at the Beginning of the War." In *Missouri's Sons of the South*, Vol. 2. St. Louis: Missouri Division Sons of Confederate Veterans, 1998.

Kennedy, Joseph C.G. *Population of the United States in 1860 Compiled from the Original Returns of the Eighth Census of the United States*, Vol. 1. Washington, DC: Government Printing Office, 1864.

King, W.H. "Early Experiences in Missouri." *Confederate Veteran* 17 (1909): 502–503.

Kirkpatrick, Arthur R. "Missouri in the Early Months of the Civil War." *Missouri Historical Review* 55 (April 1961): 99–108, 235–266.

Knox, Thomas W. *Camp-Fire and Cotton-Field: Southern Adventure in Time of War. Life with the Union Armies, and Residence on a Louisiana Plantation*. New York: Blelock, 1865.

Lademann, Otto C. "The Battle of Carthage, Mo, Friday, July 5, 1861." In *War Papers Read before the Commandery of the State of Wisconsin, Military Order of the Loyal Legion of the United States*, Vol. 4. Milwaukee, WI: Burdick & Allen, 1914.

Lademann, Otto C. "The Capture of 'Camp Jackson,' St. Louis, Mo., Friday, May 10, 1861." In *War Papers Read before the Commandery of the State of Wisconsin, Military Order of the Loyal Legion of the United States*, Vol. 4. Milwaukee, WI: Burdick & Allen, 1914.

Lane, Wheaton J. "Francis Preston Blair, Jr. (1821–1875): Border Statesman." In *The Lives of Eighteen from Princeton* (reprint). Edited by Willard Thorp. Freeport, New York: Books for Libraries Press, 1968.

Larkin, Lew. *Missouri Heritage*. Columbia, MO: American, 1968.

"Latest by Telegraph-Warsaw, Mo." *Missouri Republican*, June 1, 1861.

"Latest News of the Rebellion," *New York Times*, May 11, 1861, 9.

Lay, James Henry. *A Sketch of the History of Benton County*. Hannibal, MO: Winchell & Ebert, 1876.

Leland, Charles G. "General Lyon." *Continental Monthly* 1 (April 1862): 405–413.

Leland, Charles G. "The War between Freedom and Slavery in Missouri." *Continental Monthly* 1 (April 1862): 369–380.

Leser, Frederick. *In Memoriam. Franz Hassendeubel, Colonel 17th Regiment, Miss. Volunteer Infantry. Western Turner Rifles. 1861*. Philadelphia: n. p., 1899.

Liberty (MO) Tribune. June 7, 1861; June 14, 1861; June 21, 1861; June 28, 1861; July 1, 1861; July 5, 1861; July 12, 1861.

Lincoln, Abraham. *Abraham Lincoln: Complete Works, Comprising His Speeches, Letters, State Papers, and Miscellaneous Writings*, Vol. 1. Edited by John G. Nicolay and John Hay. New York: Century, 1907.

Lincoln, Abraham. *The Collected Works of Abraham Lincoln*, Vol. 4. Edited by Roy P. Basler. New Brunswick, NJ: Rutgers University Press, 1953.

Lincoln, Abraham. "Proceedings of Congress. Senate. Afternoon Session. The Message. National Affairs, July 4, 1861." *New York Times*, July 6, 1861, 1.

"Lincoln in Kansas." In *Transactions of the Kansas State Historical Society, 1901–1902*, Vol. 7. Edited by George W. Martin. Topeka: Kansas State Historical Society, 1902.

Lindberg, Kip A. "The Semblance of a Weapon: Arms and Equipment of the Missouri State Guard." In *Sterling Price's Lieutenants: A Guide to the Officers and Organization of the Missouri State Guard, 1861–1865*. Shawnee Mission, KS: Two Trails, 1995.

The Lives of Horatio Seymour and Frank P. Blair, Jr. Philadelphia: T.B. Peterson & Brothers. 1868.

Livingston, Joel T. *A History of Jasper County, Missouri, and Its People*, Vol. 1. Chicago: Lewis, 1912.

Lossing, Benson J. *A History of the Civil War.* New York: War Memorial Association, 1912.

Louisville Journal. June 14, 1861.

Lynch, William O. "The Influence of Population Movements on Missouri before 1861." *Missouri Historical Review* 16 (July 1922): 506–516.

Lyon, Nathaniel. *The Last Political Writings of Gen. Nathaniel Lyon, U.S.A; with a Sketch of His Life and Military Services.* New York: Rudd & Carleton, 1861.

Lyon, William H. "Claiborne Fox Jackson, Missouri Politician, 1860–62." Master's thesis. Chicago: University of Chicago, 1949.

MacDonald, Emmett. Letter to his sister. May 20, 1861. WICR 30997. Wilson's Creek National Battlefield Civil War Museum, Republic, Missouri.

MacDonald, William. *Select Documents Illustrative of the History of the United States, 1776–1861.* New York: Macmillan, 1909.

"Major Anderson, U.S.A., Commanding at Fort Sumter." *Harper's Weekly*, 5 (January 12, 1861): 1, 18.

Marcus, Robert D., and David Burner. *The American Scene: Varieties of American History*, Vol. 1. New York: Appleton-Century-Crofts, 1971.

Marden, Orison S., ed. *The Consolidated Encyclopedic Library*, Vol. 2. New York: Emerson, 1903.

McAfee, A. to the *Weekly*, April 16, 1861. In *History of Monroe and Shelby Counties, Missouri*, Vol. 2. St. Louis: National Historical, 1884, 700–701.

McDonald and Newton Counties Sections of Goodspeed's History of Newton, Lawrence, Barry, and McDonald Counties, Missouri (reprint). Chicago: Goodspeed, 1972.

McElroy, John. *The Struggle for Missouri.* Washington, DC: National Tribune, 1909.

McGhee, James E., ed.. *Service with the Missouri State Guard: The Memoir of Brigadier General James Harding.* Springfield, MO: Oak Hills, 2000.

McGuire, Randy R. *St. Louis Arsenal: Armory of the West.* Mount Pleasant, SC: Arcadia, 2001.

McNamara, J.H. "An Historical Sketch of the Sixth Division, Missouri State Guard, from Its Organization in 1861." A309. Mosby Monroe Parsons Collection. St. Louis: Missouri Historical Society, n.d.

McPherson, James M. *Battle Cry of Freedom: The Civil War Era.* New York: Oxford University Press, 2003.

Mead, Edward H. "That Camp Jackson Episode near St. Louis." In *Missouri's Sons of the South*, Vol. 2. St. Louis: Missouri Division Sons of Confederate Veterans, 1998.

Meigs, William M. *The Life of Thomas Hart Benton.* Philadelphia: J.B. Lippincott, 1904.

Miles, Kathleen W. *Bitter Ground: The Civil War in Missouri's Golden Valley.* Warsaw, MO: Printery, 1971.

Miller, Robert E. "Daniel Marsh Frost, C.S.A." *Missouri Historical Review* 85 (July 1991): 381–401.

Miller, Robert E. "General Mosby M. Parsons: Missouri's Secessionist General." *Missouri Historical Review* 80 (October 1985): 33–57.

Missouri. *Adjutant General's Report of the State Militia for 1861.* Jefferson City, MO: n. p., 1864.

Missouri. Constitutional Convention. *Journal and Proceedings of the Missouri State Convention Held at Jefferson City and St. Louis, March, 1861.* St. Louis: Knapp, 1861.

Missouri. *Missouri's Sons of the South*, Vol. 2. St. Louis: Missouri Division Sons of Confederate Veterans, 1998.

Missouri General Assembly. House of Representatives. *Appendix to the House Journal of the Adjourned Session of the Twenty-Second General Assembly of Missouri.* Jefferson City, MO: J.P. Ament, 1863.

Missouri General Assembly. House of Representatives. *Journal of the House of Representatives, Called Session*, Vol. 21. Jefferson City, MO: J.P. Ament, 1861.

Missouri General Assembly. House of Representatives. *Journal of the House of the State of Missouri at the First Session of the Twenty-First General Assembly.* Jefferson City, MO: W.G. Cheeney, 1861.

Missouri General Assembly. House of Representatives. *Missouri State Convention, 1861–1863; Journal of the House of* the State of Missouri at the Twenty-First Session of the Missouri General Assembly. Jefferson City, MO: W.G. Cheeney, 1861

Missouri General Assembly. Senate. *Journal of the Senate Extra Session of the Rebel Legislature.* Jefferson City, MO: Emory S. Foster, 1865–66.

Missouri General Assembly. Senate. *Journal of the Senate of the State of Missouri at the First Session of the Twenty-First General Assembly.* Jefferson City, MO: W.G. Cheeney, 1861.

"The Missouri State Convention." *New York Times*, March 2, 1861, 1.

Missouri State Convention, 1861–1863 (Special Collections, Record Group 005). Jefferson City, MO: Office of the Secretary of State.

Missouri State Gazetteer and Business Directory. St. Louis, MO: Sutherland & McEvoy, 1860.

Monaghan, Jay. *Civil War on the Western Border 1854–1865.* Boston: Little, Brown, 1955.

Moore, Frank, ed. *The Rebellion Record: A Diary of American Events,* Vol. 1. New York: G.P. Putnam, 1861; see also Vol. 9. New York: D. Van Nostrand, 1866.

Moore, John C. "Missouri." In *Confederate Military History,* Vol. 9. Edited by Clement A. Evans. Atlanta: Confederate, 1899.

Mudd, Joseph A. "What I Saw at Wilson's Creek." *Missouri Historical Review* 7 (January 1913): 89–105.

Mudd, Joseph A. *With Porter in North Missouri: A Chapter in the History of the War Between the States.* Washington, DC: National, 1909.

Musick, John R. *Stories of Missouri.* New York: American Book, 1897.

Neely, Jeremy. *The Border between Them: Violence and Reconciliation on the Kansas-Missouri Line.* Columbia: University of Missouri Press, 2007.

Neumann, Robert, James Joplin, Richard W. Hatcher III, and Mary Markey. *Civil War Campaigns in the Ozarks.* n.p., 1980.

Nevin, David. *The Civil War: The Road to Shiloh—Early Battles in the West.* Alexandria, VA: Time-Life, 1983.

New York Herald. June 20, 1861.

New York Times. May 15, 1861; May 16, 1861; May 27, 1861; July 11, 1861.

"News of the Rebellion: Events in Missouri." *New York Times*, May 25, 1861, 2.

Nicolay, John G. *The Outbreak of Rebellion.* New York: Charles Scribner's Sons, 1882.

Nicolay, John G., and John Hay. *Abraham Lincoln, a History,* Vol. 4. New York: Century, 1909.

Nicolay, John G., and John Hay. "Abraham Lincoln: A History, the Advance." *The Century Illustrated Monthly Magazine* 36 (Jun 1888): 281–392.

Nicolay, John G., and John Hay. "Abraham Lincoln. A History, the Border States." *The Century Illustrated Monthly Magazine* 36 (May 1888): 56–280.

North, F.A., ed. *History of Jasper County, Missouri, Including a Condensed History of the State, a Complete History of Carthage and Joplin, etc.* Des Moines, IA: Mills, 1883.

Oates, Stephen B. *To Purge This Land With Blood: A Biography of John Brown.* New York: Harper & Row, 1970.

"Obituary Mosby Monroe Parsons, Camargo, Nuevo Leon, Mexico, 15 Aug. 1865." *Jefferson City Missouri State Times,* September 29, 1865.

"Obituary of Gen. W.Y. Slack, *Memphis Avalanche,* 8 May 1862." In "Sketch of General W.Y. Slack, of Missouri." *The Land We Love* 6 (March 1869): 357–360.

Official Records. *The War of the Rebellion: A Compilation of the Official Records of the Union and Confederate Armies,* Series 1, Vol. 3. Washington, DC: Government Printing Office, 1881.

Official Register of the Officers and Cadets of the U.S. Military Academy, West Point, New York. Washington, DC: U.S. Government, June 1850.

Owens, Robert. *Hier snackt wi Plattdutsch* [Here We Speak Low German]. Cole Camp, MO: City of Cole Camp, 1989.

Paris, Louis-Philippe-Albert d'Orléans. *History of the Civil War in America,* Vol. 1. Translated by L.F. Tasistro. Edited by Henry Coppée. Philadelphia: Porter & Coates, 1875.

Parrish. William E. *Frank Blair: Lincoln's Conservative.* Columbia: University of Missouri Press, 1998.

Parrish, William E. *Turbulent Partnership: Missouri and the Union, 1861–1865.* Columbia: University of Missouri Press, 1963.

Parsons, Mosby Monroe. Papers, 1847–1869. St. Louis: Missouri Historical Society.
"Partition of Territory in the Old Union." [Richmond, VA] *Daily Dispatch*, August 1, 1861.
Patrick, Jeffrey L. "Remembering the Missouri Campaign of 1861: The Memoirs of Lieutenant William P. Barlow, Guibor's Battery, Missouri State Guard." In *Civil War Regiments: A Journal of the American Civil War* 5 (1997): 21–60.
Paxton, William McClung. *Annals of Platte County, Missouri, from its Exploration down to June 1, 1897.* Kansas City: Hudson-Kimberly, 1897.
Payne, James A. "Early Days of War in Missouri." In *Missouri's Sons of the South*, Vol. 2. St. Louis: Missouri Division Sons of Confederate Veterans, 1998.
Payne, James A. "Fighting in Missouri." In *Missouri's Sons of the South*, Vol. 2. St. Louis: Missouri Division Sons of Confederate Veterans, 1998.
Peckham, James. *General Nathaniel Lyon and Missouri in 1861. A Monograph of the Great Rebellion.* New York: American News, 1866.
Perkins, J.R. "Jefferson Davis and General Sterling Price." In *Missouri's Sons of the South*, Vol. 1. St. Louis: Missouri Division Sons of Confederate Veterans, 1998.
Phillips, Christopher. *Damned Yankee: A Life of General Nathaniel Lyon.* Columbia: University of Missouri Press, 1990.
Phillips, Christopher. "Jackson, Claiborne Fox (1806–1862)." In Lawrence O. Christensen, William E. Foley, and Gary Kremer, eds. *Dictionary of Missouri Biography.* Columbia: University of Missouri Press, 1999.
Phillips, Christopher. *Missouri's Confederate: Claiborne Fox Jackson and the Creation of Southern Identity in the Border West.* Columbia: University of Missouri Press, 2000.
Phillips, Christopher. "The Radical Crusade: Blair, Lyon, and the Advent of the Civil War in Missouri." *Gateway Heritage* 10 (Spring 1990): 22–43.
Phillips, Christopher W. "The Court Martial of Lieutenant Nathaniel Lyon." *Missouri Historical Review* 81 (April 1987): 296–308.
Piston, William Garrett, and Thomas P. Sweeney. "Don't Yield An Inch! The Missouri State Guard." *North & South Magazine* 2 (June 1999):10–26.
Piston, William Garrett, and Thomas P. Sweeney. *Portraits of Conflict: A Photographic History of Missouri in the Civil War.* Fayetteville: University of Arkansas Press, 2009.
Plum, William R. "The Southwest Early in the War." In *The Military Telegraph during the Civil War in the United States*, Vol. 1. Chicago: Jansen, McClurg, 1882.
Pollard, Edward A. *Southern History of the War: The First Year of the War*, 2 ed. New York: Charles. B. Richardson, 1863.
Pompey, Sherman L. *Muster Lists of the Missouri Confederates*, Vol. 4. Independence, CA: Historical & Genealogical, 1965.
Price, Sterling. "General Order No. 8." General Orders, 1861 (C1494). Manuscripts Division. State Historical Society of Missouri, Columbia.
Price, Sterling. Proclamation. "*Standard Extra*, Columbia, Missouri, 1861 (SUNP0886)." State Historical Society of Missouri, Columbia.
Primm, James N. *Lion of the Valley: St. Louis Missouri, 1764–1980*, 3rd ed. St. Louis: Missouri Historical Society, [1983] 1998.
Rader, Perry S. *Rader's Civil Government and History of Missouri.* Jefferson City, MO: Hugh Stephens, 1904.
Rafferty, Milton D. *The Ozarks, Land and Life.* Fayetteville: University of Arkansas Press, 2001.
Ray, Perley O. "The Genesis of the Kansas-Nebraska Act." *Annual Report of the American Historical Association* 1 (1914): 259–280.
Reasoner, Mathew A. "The Old St. Louis Arsenal." Private Manuscript. Missouri Historical Society, 1934.
Reavis, L.U. *The Life and Military Services of Gen. William Selby Harney.* St. Louis: Bryan, Brand, 1878.
Rhodes, James F. *History of the United States from the Compromise of 1850 to the Final Restoration of Home Rule at the South in 1877*, Vol. 3. New York: Harper, 1895.
Richards, Eben, St. Louis, to his wife [Caroline B. Richards], May 13, 1861. D6196, Missouri History Museum.
Richardson, Albert D. *Beyond the Mississippi: From the Great River to the Great Ocean.* Hartford, CT: American, 1867.
Richardson, Albert D. *The Secret Service,*

the Field, the Dungeon, the Escape. Hartford, CT: American, 1865.
Richardson, James D. *A Compilation of the Messages and Papers of the Confederacy, Including the Diplomatic Correspondence, 1861–1865*, Vol. 1. Nashville, TN: United States, 1905.
Robinson, H.E. "Two Missouri Historians." *Missouri Historical Review* 5 (April 1911): 129–137.
Rollins, C.B. "Some Impressions of Frank P. Blair." *Missouri Historical Review* 24 (April 1930): 352–58.
Rombauer, Robert J. *The Union Cause in St. Louis in 1861; an Historical Sketch*. St. Louis: Press of Nixon-Jones, 1909.
Rorvig. Paul. "The Significant Skirmish: The Battle of Boonville, June 17, 1861." *Missouri Historical Review* 86 (January 1992): 127–148.
Rosengarten, Joseph G. *The German Soldier in the Wars of the United States*. Philadelphia: J.B. Lippincott, 1886.
Rowan, Steven, and James N. Primm. *Germans for a Free Missouri: Translations from the St. Louis Radical Press, 1857–1862*. Columbia: University of Missouri Press, 1983.
Ryle, Walter H. *Missouri: Union or Secession*. Nashville, TN: George Peabody College for Teachers, 1931.
St. Louis County Coroner's Record Book 1858–1861, Vol. 4. Missouri History Museum Archives, St. Louis.
St. Louis Republican. July 11, 1861.
"St. Louisan Recalls Days when Slaves Were Sold at Auction at Entrance to the Court House." *St. Louis Star*, January 30, 1922.
Sale, Sara L. "Governor Claiborne Fox Jackson and His Role in the Secession Movement in Missouri, 1861." Master's thesis. Warrensburg: Central Missouri State University, 1979.
"Saline Jackson Guards." *History of Saline County, Missouri*.
Sanborn, Franklin B., ed. *The Life and Letters of John Brown: Liberator of Kansas, and Martyr of Virginia*, 2nd ed. Boston: Roberts Brothers, 1891.
Sandburg, Carl. *Abraham Lincoln: The War Years* (4 vols.). New York: Harcourt, Brace, 1939.
Scharf, J. Thomas, *History of Saint Louis City and County*, Vol. 1. Philadelphia: L.H. Everts, 1883.

Schnake, Friedrich. *Der Ausbruch des Bürgerkrieges in Missouri*, Vols. 11 & 12. Cincinnati, OH: n. p., 1879–1880.
Schnetzer, Wayne, and Carolyn M. *More Forgotten Men: Missouri State Guard*. Independence, MO: Two Trails, 2003.
Schrader, William H. "Reminiscences." n. d. (C1519). Manuscripts Division, State Historical Society of Missouri, Columbia.
Schrantz, Ward L. *Jasper County, Missouri, in the Civil War*. Carthage, MO: Carthage Press, 1923.
"Secession at Lexington, Mo." *New York Times*, May 5, 1861, 9.
Shalhope, Robert E. *Sterling Price; Portrait of a Southerner*. Columbia, MO: University of Missouri Press, 1971.
Sherman, William T. *Memoirs of General William T. Sherman*, Vol. 1, 2nd ed. New York: Appleton, 1886.
Shoemaker, Floyd C. *Missouri and Missourians: Land of Contrasts and People of Achievements*, Vol. 1. Chicago: Lewis, 1943.
Shoemaker, Floyd C. "Missouri: Heir of Southern Tradition and Individuality." *Missouri Historical Review* 36 (July 1942): 435–446.
Shoemaker, Floyd C. "Missouri's Proslavery Fight for Kansas 1854–1855." [Part 1] *Missouri Historical Review* 48 (April 1954): 221–236; [Part 2] 48 (July 1954): 325–340; (Part 3) 49 (October 1954): 41–54.
Shoemaker, Floyd C. *Missouri's Struggle for Statehood 1804–1821*. Jefferson City, MO: Hugh Stephens, 1916.
Shoemaker, Floyd C., ed. *Missouri, Day by Day*, Vols. 1 and 2. Columbia: State Historical Society of Missouri, 1942–1943.
Smith, Edward C. *The Borderland in the Civil War*. New York: Macmillan, 1927.
Smith, William Ernest. *The Blairs during the Civil War and Reconstruction*. Madison: University of Wisconsin, 1924.
Smith, William Ernest. *The Francis Preston Blair Family in Politics* (2 vols). New York: Macmillan, 1933. Reprint. New York: Da Capo Press, 1969.
Snead, Thomas L. *The Fight for Missouri, from the Election of Lincoln to the Death of Lyon*. New York: C. Scribner's Sons, 1886.
Snead, Thomas L. "The First Year of the War in Missouri." In *Battles and*

Leaders of the Civil War, Vol. 1, Centennial War Series, 262–277. Edited by Robert Underwood Johnson and Clarence Clough Buehl. Secaucus, NJ: Castle, 1887.
Snyder, John F. Correspondence to Thomas L. Snead, June 2, 1886. WICR 31022 Cab. 30, Dwr. D, Box 1. Republic, MO: Wilson's Creek National Battlefield Museum.
Stanton, Donald. *The Civil War Reminiscences of General M. Jeff Thompson.* Dayton, OH: Morningside, 1988.
Steele, Philip W., and Steve Cottrell. *Civil War in the Ozarks.* Gretna, LA: Pelican, 2009.
Stephenson, Philip D. *The Civil War Memoir of Philip Daingerfield Stephenson.* Edited by Nathaniel C. Hughes, Jr. Conway: University of Central Arkansas Press, 1995.
Stephenson, Philip D. "My War Autobiography." Vols. 1–8. Mss. 2482, 2657, 1861–1903. Louisiana State University Libraries Special Collections.
Sterling Price's Lieutenants: A Guide to the Officers and Organization of the Missouri State Guard, 1861–1865. Shawnee Mission, KS: Two Trails, 1995.
Stevens, Walter B. *Centennial History of Missouri (The Center State): One Hundred Years in the Union, 1820–1921*, Vol. 1. St. Louis: S.J. Clarke, 1921.
Stevens, Walter B. "Lincoln and Missouri." *Missouri Historical Review*, 10 (January 1916): 63–119.
Stevens, Walter B. *Missouri the Center State: 1821–1915*, Vol. 1. Chicago: S.J. Clarke, 1915.
Stevens, Walter B. *St. Louis, the Fourth City, 1764–1909*, Vols. 1 & 2. St. Louis: S.J. Clarke, 1909.
Sweeny, Thomas W. *Journal of Lt. Thomas W. Sweeny 1849–1853.* Edited by Arthur Woodward. Los Angeles: Westernlore, 1956.
Sweeny, William M. "Brigadier-General Thomas W. Sweeny, U.S.A.—a Biographical Sketch." In *The Journal of the American-Irish Historical Society*, Vol. 2. Edited by Thomas H. Murray. Boston: The Society, 1899.
Switzler, William F., Robert A. Campbell, Alban J. Conant, and George C. Swallow. *Switzler's Illustrated History of Missouri, from 1541 to 1877.* St. Louis: C.R. Barns, 1879.
Tomes, Robert, and Benjamin G. Smith. *The War with the South: A History of the Late Rebellion*, Vol. 1. New York: Virtue & Yorston, 1862–1867.
Toombs, Robert Y. "War Memories of a Confederate Boy." *New England Magazine* 9 (September 1893): 46–50.
Trexler, Harrison A. *Slavery in Missouri, 1804–1865.* Dissertation. Baltimore: Johns Hopkins University, 1914.
Trickett, Dean. "The Civil War in the Indian Territory." *Chronicles of Oklahoma* 17 (September 1939): 315–327.
Trumbull, Lyman, to Abraham Lincoln, May 15, 1861 (Situation in Missouri). Abraham Lincoln Papers at the Library of Congress.
Turnbo, S.C. "Viewing the Steamboat Going up the Missouri River on which Governor Jackson was Aboard in War Times." *The Turnbo Manuscripts.* Springfield-Greene County Library.
The Union Army: States and Regiments, Vol. 4. Madison, WI: Federal Publishing, 1908.
"The Union Forever." *New York Times*, April 21, 1861, 1.
"Untitled [Boonville-Cole Camp-Jackson]." *Keowee Courier* (SC), July 6, 1861.
U.S. Adjutant-General's Office. *Official Army register of the Volunteer force of the United States Army for the years 1861, '62, '63, '64, '65.* Bethesda, MD: University Publications of America, 1994.
U.S. Congress. *Report of the Joint Committee on the Conduct of the War: Department of the West.* Washington, DC: Government Printing Office, 1863.
U.S. Continental Congress. *Journals of the Continental Congress*, Vol. 5. Washington, DC: Government Printing Office, 1906.
U.S. Record and Pension Office. *Missouri Troops in Service during the Civil War [Organization and Status of Missouri Troops. (Union and Confederate) in Service during the Civil War].* Washington, DC: Government Printing Office, 1902.
U.S. Secretary of the Interior. "Table LL—Nativity of foreigners residing in each state and territory." *Statistics of the United States in 1860.* Washington, DC: Government Printing Office, 1866.
"Valuable Arms Captured at Camp Jackson." *New York Times*, May 15, 1861, 1.
Vandiver, W.D. "Reminiscences of General

John B. Clark." *Missouri Historical Review* 20 (January 1926): 223–235.

Viles, Jonas. "Claiborne Fox Jackson." In *The Messages and Proclamations of the Governors of the State of Missouri*, Vol. 3. Columbia: State Historical Society of Missouri, 1922.

Vincent, Thomas M. *In Memoriam, Companion Lieutenant-General John McAllister Schofield*. Washington, DC: Gibson Brothers, 1908.

Violette, Eugene M. *A History of Missouri*. New York: D.C. Heath, 1918.

Vogelgesang, Ernest J. "History of the St. Louis Arsenal, 1861–1877." Master's thesis. Washington University, 1963.

Walker, Mr., to Mr. Cass, December 15, 1857. Robert J. Walker Letter Book, 1883–1848, Robert J. Walker Papers, 1833–1848, DAR.1937.42, Darlington Collection, Special Collections Department, University of Pittsburgh.

Wallace, J.C. "Gen. E.W. Price." In *Missouri's Sons of the South*, Vol. 1. St. Louis: Missouri Division Sons of Confederate Veterans, 1998.

"The War between Freedom and Slavery in Missouri." *The Continental Monthly* 1 (April 1862): 369–380.

"War Correspondence." *Missouri Democrat*, July 2, 1861.

"The War in Missouri." *Harper's Weekly*, Vol. 5, No. 236, July 6, 1861, 431.

"War Movements in Missouri." *New York Tribune*, June 23, 1861.

Ward, Andrew. *The Slaves' War: The Civil War in the Words of Former Slaves*. Boston: Houghton Mifflin, 2008.

Ware, Eugene F. *The Lyon Campaign in Missouri: Being a History of the First Iowa Infantry*. Topeka, KS: Crane, 1907.

Warner, Ezra J. *Generals in Blue: Lives of the Union Commanders*. Baton Rouge: Louisiana State University Press, 1964.

Warner, Ezra J. *Generals in Gray, Lives of the Confederate Commanders*. Baton Rouge: Louisiana State University Press, 1959.

Washburn, Israel. *The Issues: The Dred Scott Decision: The Parties*. Washington, DC: Congressional Republican Committee, 1860.

Webb, William L. *Battles and Biographies of Missourians, or, the Civil War Period of Our State*. Kansas City: Hudson-Kimberly, 1900.

West, Alma M. "The Earlier Political Career of Claiborne Fox Jackson, 1836–1851." Master's thesis. Columbia: University of Missouri, 1941.

Wilkie, Franc B. *Missouri in 1861: The Civil War Letters of Franc B. Wilkie, Newspaper Correspondent*. Edited by Michael E. Banasik. Iowa City, IA: Camp Pope, 2001.

Wilson, James Grant, and John Fiske, eds. "Sigel." In *Appleton's Cyclopedia of American Biography*, Vol. 5. New York: D. Appleton, 1888.

Wilson, Joseph A. "Bledsoe of Missouri." In *Battles and Biographies of Missourians, or, the Civil War Period of Our State*. Edited by William L. Webb. Kansas City: Hudson-Kimberly, 1900.

Wilson, Joseph A. "Bledsoe of Missouri." In *Missouri's Sons of the South*, Vol. 1. St. Louis: Missouri Division Sons of Confederate Veterans, 1998.

Winter, William C. *Civil War in St. Louis: A Guided Tour*. St. Louis: Missouri Historical Society, 1994.

Wood, Larry. *The Siege of Lexington, Missouri: The Battle of the Hemp Bales*. Mount Pleasant, SC: History Press, 2014.

Woodburn, James A. *The Historical Significance of the Missouri Compromise*. Washington, DC: Government Printing Office, 1894 [From the Annual Report of the American Historical Association for 1893].

Woodson, William H. *History of Clay County, Missouri*. Topeka, KS: Historical, 1920.

Woodward, Ashbel. *Life of General Nathaniel Lyon*. Hartford, CT: Case, Lockwood, 1862.

Woodward, Ashbel. Review of *The Life of General Nathaniel Lyon*. *New Englander and Yale Review* 22 (January 1863): 149–153.

Wurthman, Leonard B., Jr. "Frank Blair: Lincoln's Congressional Spokesman." *Missouri Historical Review* 64 (April 1970): 263–88.

Young, William. *Young's History of Lafayette County*, Vol. 1. Indianapolis, IN: B.F. Bowen, 1910.

Zucker, A.E., ed. *The Forty-Eighters, Political Refugees of the German Revolution of 1848*. New York: Columbia University Press, 1950.

Index

Numbers in ***bold italics*** indicate pages with illustrations

A. McDowell 127, 133, 142, 145
Adams, William M. 134
Adams House 136, 139, ***140***, 142
Alexander, Edmund 39
Alton 9
American Zouaves of Missouri *see* Fighting Irish Zouaves
Andrews, George L. 92
antislavery 3, 4, 6, 8, 45, 180
Anzeiger des Westens 104, 105
Apperson, Eliza 203
Arkansas 57, 62, 76, 81–84, 91, 100, 108, 113, 117, 121, 139, 158, 159, 163, 173, 176, 177, 179, 199, 210; defense of 164
Arkansas-Missouri border 210
armed conflict 7, 56, 86
armed neutrality 5, 6, 10, 11, 18, 20, 45, 50, 61, 62, 69, 70, 71, 80, 87, 100, 164
Army of the West 25, 58, 157; *see also* Department of the West
Arnold, Thomas W. 86, 87
Arrow Rock, Missouri 123, 176, 199
Articles of War 20
Asbury, Edgar 98
Ashland, Missouri 170
Atchison, David Rice 99, 177

Backoff, Franz 105
Baden Revolution 112
Ball Town, Missouri 188
barefoot rebel militia 146
Barlow, William P. 93, 204, ***205***, 206, 240n22
Barton, David 146, 159
Bass, Eli 170
Bates, Edward 35, 36, ***37***, 38, 48, 215
Baton Rouge, Louisiana 16
Battle of Carthage 154, 213
Battle of Dry Wood Creek 216
Battle of Vicksburg 219
Battle of Wilson's Creek 154, 214, ***216***
Beauregard, P.G.T. 9, 112
Benton, Thomas Hart 46, 162, 185
Benton County Home Guard 182, 183, 185, 186, 188–196; casualties 193
Bergman, Theodor 193
Big Bethel, Virginia 63
Bird's Point, Missouri 42, 108, 172, 173
Bischoff, Henry 105
Black River 202
Blair, Francis P., Jr. 6–8, 14–16, 19, 24, 30, 35–37, 39, 45, 46, 48, 49, 51–54, ***58***, 59–64, 68–72, 79–81, 83, 86, 91, 92, 102, 103, 114, 127, 128, 133, 134, 136, 147, 152, 162, 165, 199–201, 205, 211
Blair, Francis P., Sr. 48, 162
Blair, Montgomery 6, 24, 30, 36, ***37***, 48, 58, ***59***, 60, 62, 83, 128, 162, 211
Blair family 49, 61
Bland, Peter E. 110
Blandowski, Constantin 61, 114
Bledsoe, Hiram Miller 155, ***156***, 202
Bledsoe's Battery 156, 157
Blue Mills 153
Blues and Grays 57, 86
bogus telegram 19
Bolivar, Missouri 178
Bolton, Dickens, and Company 67
Boonslick 4, 146
Boonville, 1, 20, 76, 93–95, 99–103, 123–127, 129–133, 137, 140, 142, 145, 146, 153, 160, 162, 166, 172–174, 176, 178, 179, 196–201, 209, 210; casualties 148, 240n50; departure ***211***, 212; description 148; fairgrounds 145, 146, 148; fight 130, 134, ***135***, ***137***, 138, 139, 141, ***143***, 152, 154, 165, 172, 177, 178, 185, 204, 205, 240n3; occupation 146–148, 158, 160, 164, 166, 187, 195; prisoners 144; races 143, 144; rains 206–208, 211; retreat 141, 142,

261

144, 145, 147, 158, 178, 179, 185, 186, 195, 199, 202, 211; *see also* Rockkport Road skirmish
Boonville Register 192
border ruffian 35, 100,147, *168*, 177, 218
border states 4, 11, 219, 221*n*13
Börnstein, Henry 92, *104*, 105, 108, 127, 133; proclamation 127
Brand, Horace 141
Breckinridge, John 95
Brill, John 182
Brown, B. Gratz 4, *107*, 108, 109, 121, 141
Brown, John 4, 73, 181
Brown, William 141
Bruegel, John T.: diary 9
Brüh, Carl 193
Buckner, A.H. 23
bushwhackers *see* guerilla warfare
Butterfield Mail 187
Butterfield Stage Line 117

Cairo, Illinois 42, 108, 208, 213, 246*n*35
Cairo and Fulton Railroad 108
call for volunteers 20, 43, 44, 80, 123, 169
Callaway Guard 57, 176, 178
Cameron, Simon 36, 37, 48, 60, 83
Camp Bacon 124, 130, 131, 133, 134, 139, 142–145, 235*n*7; *see also* Camp Vest
Camp Cameron 162, 201
Camp Jackson 1, 7, 9, 10, *11*, 12, 14–17, 19, 21–25, 27, 28, 30–32, 34, 35, 38, 40, 43, 45, 46, 55, 57, 61, 64, 69, 78, 79, 83, 92, 93, 95, 99, 104, 105, 114, 119, 120, 124, 139, 153, 164, 175, 181, 204, 205, 216, 222*n*29; casualties 222*n*38; spectators 10, 29, 136
Camp Lyon 119, 183, 193
Camp Vest 124; *see also* Camp Bacon
Camp Walker, Arkansas 173
Campbell, John Polk 97
Carthage, Missouri 203, 213
casualties 138, 148
Catton, Bruce: on Camp Jackson 35
Cayton, Alice Elizabeth: letter 34
Cedar Creek, Missouri 102
Champion, J. Rock 19
Chase, Salmon *37*, 128
Cheavens, Henry Martyn 169, *170*, 171, 172
Cherokee Nation 20, 82
Chillicothe, Missouri 154, 155
Christie, Robert 167
City of Louisiana 127, 144
Civil War 1–3, 10, 11, 15, 35, 53, 57, 79, 80, 95, 97, 100, 110, 132, 143, 148, 152, 156, 157, 172, 195, 196, 213, 214, 216, 217, 224*n*12, 240*n*5; Missourians in 219
Clark, John B. 23, *93*, 94, 95, 123–125, 130, 145, 165, 176–178, 186, 206

Clinton, Missouri 80, 163, 202, 203, 209
Cole, Hannah 145
Cole, Nelson 40, *41*, 42, 139, 143, 145
Cole Camp 1, 180–183, *184*, 185–189, *191*, 193–196, 198, 202; casualties 192, 193; description 187
Cole Camp Creek 188
Columbia, Missouri 154, 176
comet 209
Conant, Horace A. 68
Confederacy 5, 6, 27, 33, 38, 41, 56, 57, 60, 78, 81, 82, 84, 95, 109, 110, 126, 144, 148, 152, 155, 158, 163–166, 169, 176, 193, 206, 210, 213, 217, 219
Confederate forces 57, 72, 76, 81, 82, 113, 176, 199, 219
Confederate soldiers 15, 63, 81
Confederate States 6, 93, 118, 217
Conner, Minerva 203
Cook, A.H.W. 181–183, 185, 188, 189, 193–195
Cook, George 218
Cordes, Arndt 196
coroner's jury 31
Cowskin Prairie 176
Cravens, Jesse Lamb 203

Davis, Jefferson 6, 9, 17, 27, 42, 66, 73, 93, 163–165, 193; on Boonville 165
Department of the Ohio 128
Department of the West 8, 24, 26, 38, 39, 58–61, 63, 128, 211, 213, 224*n*12
Desoto, Missouri 41, 43
Detjen, Friedrich 193
Dick, F.A. 36, 48, 49
Dickens, Charles 66
Dimick, H.E. 15
divided families 167, 169
Doniphan, Alexander W. 57, 229*n*16
Douglas, Stephen A. 4, 5, 95
Drake, Charles 79
Dred Scott 3, 4, 65
Duden, Gottfried 180
Duke, Basil 19, 51, 95
Dutch *see* Germans

Eastern industrial interests 116
Elsinger, Lieutenant 190
emergency session 79
Emerson, Ralph Waldo 4, 73
Enrolled Missouri Militia 219
Essig, Christian 120
Ewing, Thomas, Jr. 229*n*35

Fairchild, Missouri 207
fairgrounds *135*, 145, 146, 148, 201
Fayette, Missouri 176

Index 263

federal forces 6, 7, 9, 10, 16, 17, 19, 29, 30, 40–44, 49–51, 61–63, 69, 72, 76, 77, 81, 83–86, 88, 90–92, 99, 100, *101*, *103*, 105, 107, 111, 117, 118, 121, 123, 125, 127, 129, 130, 132, 133, 137, 138, 141, 146, 153, 157, 158, 160, 161, 163, 165, 166, 169, 172, 175, 176, 178, 179, 186, 197, 205, 214, 216
federal government 5, 6, 10, 17, 27, 40, 44, 46, 50, 51, 53, 56, 62, 70, 72, 73, 79, 80, 169, 170, 172
Fifth Missouri U.S. Volunteers 16, 40, 91, 107, 119, 199
Fifth Regiment Reserve Corps 28, 127
Fighting Irish Zouaves 110
First Brigade Missouri Volunteers 30, 55
First Iowa U.S. Volunteers 174, 175, 176, 198, 199, *200*, 201, 208, 214, 216
First Kansas Regular Infantry 84
First Regiment of Rifles 57
Florence, Missouri 186
Ford, Salem 157
Forest Hill Plantation 170
Fort Kearney, Kansas 11
Fort Leavenworth, Kansas 11, 81, 84, 85, 87, 89, 125, 128, 174, 212
Fort Scott, Kansas 178, 216
Fort Smith, Arkansas 82, 84, 173, 178
Fort Sumter 8, 109, 112, 117, 120, 152, 203
Fort Wyman, Missouri 121
Fourth Regiment Reserve Corps 107, 109, 121
Frémont, John C. 162, 211, 213, 242*n*14, 246*n*20
Frenchtown 21, 22
Frisco Railroad 116, 177, 242*n*14
Frost, D.M. 10, 16, 17, 23–26; letter to Harney 26
Fugitive Slave Law 53, 54, 127
Fulton, Missouri 57

Gamble, Hamilton R. 35, 214, *215*
Gant, Thomas 53
Gasconade River 76, 77, 91, 105, 117; train wreck 77
General Assembly 1, 5, 11, 17–20, 24, 30, 38, 43, 45, 46, 61, 71, 79, 80, 83, 92, 99, 103, 104, 107, 115–117, 154, 210
German Revolution 7, 112–114, 119, 180, 181
Germans 4, 6, 8, 9, 10, 14–17, 19–21, 23, 27–30, 32–34, 36, 44–46, 49, 50, 52, 56, 60, 81, 83, 95, 102, 104, 105, 109, 110–115, 118–120, 122, 137, 138, 142, 147, 172, 175, 179–183, 185–189, 193, 194, 201, 202; bodyguard 212; Cole Camp 180–182, 184–188, 190–192, 196
Gibbons, John W. 186, 190; attack 191, 192
Glasgow, Missouri 198

Glover, Samuel T. 56, 58; letter 36
Grant, Ulysses S. 109, 110, 120, 246*n*35
Graves, John R. 118, 203
Gray's Creek 99
Great Seal of the State of Missouri 99
Griffin, William 134
Groteheier, Henry 192
guerrilla warfare 121, 167, 196, 217–219
Guibor, Henry *204*, 205, 206, 210
Guibor's Battery 206, 210
gunpowder 17, 19, 77, 95–99, 121, 201

Hain, George 148
Hale, Stephen F. 186
Hallman, H. 109
Hannibal, Abel 183
Hannibal, Missouri 36, 81, 97, 108, 173, 175
Hannibal and St. Joseph Railroad 108, 155, 177, 178
Harbaugh, Charles 88
hard Democrats 4
Harding, Chester 95, 212, 213, 233*n*32
Harding, James 95, 129, 176, 198, 209, 233*n*32
Harmony Springs, Arkansas 81
Harms, Harmon 182, 183, 189, 192, 244*n*28
Harms barn 182, 183, 189, 190, 192
Harney, William S. 8, 12, 23–25, *26*, 30, 32, 33, 36, 38–40, 48–63, 70–72, 81, 83, 104, 110, 123, 128, 181, 211; letter to Lincoln Administration 52; message to Missourians 38
Harney Proclamation 24, *25*, 40, 104
Hassendeubel, Franz 105
Hawn's Mill 86
Heisterberg, Henry 244*n*28
Heisterberg barn 183, 190, 191, 193, 195
Herman, Missouri 160, 172
Hink, Claus 193
Holloway, Edmund Ballard 87, *88*, 89, 90, 125, 153; death 88, 89
Home Guard 9, 20, 24, 28, 32–34, 36, 44, 45, 50, 72, 85, 107–111, 157, 160, 162, 179–183, 185, 186, 189, 193, 210, 219
Home Guard Reserves 107–110
Howison, Robert R. 43
Hughes, John T. 203
Hunter, Clinton 203
Hurst, Edgar V. 203
Hutchinson, Lucy: letter 46

Iatan 92, *101*, 102, 127
Illinois troops 108, 111
Imhauser, Henry 193
Independence, Missouri 4, 8, 57, 86,–90, 108, 123, 125, 153, 158
Indian Territory 82

264 Index

Iowa regiments 81
Irishmen 33, 49, 51, 57
Iron Mountain Railroad 40, 41, 109, 177
Ironton, Missouri 55, 177
Isabella 27

Jackson, Andrew 48
Jackson, Claiborne Fox 1, 4, **5**, 8–12, 14, 17–20, 24, 27, 30, 35, 38, 43–46, 49, 50, 56, 57, 63, 64, 68–74, 76, 77, 79, 80–85, 91–101, 104, 105, 108, 111, 121, 123–131, 134, 140, 141, 144, 145, 147–149, 153–155, 157–159, 163–165, 169–173, 176–178, 181, 184–187, 196–199, 203–206, 208–211, 213–215, 217; blockade 196; column 179, 185, 186–189, 191, 192, 196, 202, 204, 206, 207, 209–213; deposed 217; proclamation 79, 158, 179; retreat 178
Jackson, Missouri: engagement 208
J.C. Swon 55, 92, 101, 102, 211
Jefferson Barracks 91, 108, 173
Jefferson City 1, 2, 16, 17, **18**, 19, 20, 30, 43, 45, 51, 57, 64, 76, 77, 80, 81, 83, 91–100, **101**, 102, **103**, 104, 105, 107, 109, 115, 119, 123, 124, 126, 127, 129, 131, 133, 153, 155, 157, 159, 162, 164, 166, 172–174, 177–179, 186, 196, 198, 199, 209, 211; federal possession **103**; occupation 206, 214

Kallman, Herman 160
Kansas 1, 3, 4, 7, 12, 35, 52, 70, 80–90, 99, 100, 101, 108, 117, 125, 127, 147, 153–155, 157, 159, 163, 168, 173, 177, 178, 199, 202, 204, 205, 209, 214, 216, 217
Kansas City, Missouri 83, 85–90, 108, 153, 157, 159, 177, 202, 209
Kansas-Nebraska Act 3
Kansas Volunteers 80, 108, 173
Kelly, Joseph M. 16, 51, 57, 77, 95, **96**, 97, 99, 131, 144, 145, 176; Kelly's powder 97, 98
Kemper, Frederick 148
Kemper Military School 148
Kentucky 11, 50, 66, 67, 97, 180, 187
Keokuk, Iowa 111, 175, 200, 202
Keown, Bartholomew W. 185, 187, 243n8
Keytesville Station 116, 125
Kranke, Friedrich 193

Lademann, Otto C. **21**
Lamar, Missouri 159, 210
Lamine River 179
Laney, George 218
Lawrence, Kansas 84, 108
Leach, John H. 194
Lebanon, Missouri 55, 212
Lexington 57, 76, 81, 85, 89, 96, 108, 123, 125, 129, 143, 145, 152–159, 163, 165, 166, 172, 175, 176, 178, 179, 198, 199, 202, 203, 206, 210, 214, 216; army 204, 210
Lexington 34
Liberty Arms Depot 8, 11, 57, 85, 124, 156, 202, 206
Liberty Blues 177
Lincoln, Abraham 4–8, 24, 31, 32, 35, 36, 38, 43, 48, 49, 51, 52, 55, 56, 58–60, 62, 63, 66, 78–80, 83, 97, 103, 109, 110, 118, 120, 121, 145, 147, 152, 162, 164, 172, 174, 175, 181, 200, 201, 210, 211, 213, 215, 246n20; cabinet 6, **37**, 58, 128; letter to Blair 49; letter to Harney 52
Lincoln, Mary Todd 146
Lindell Grove 9, 11, 34
Linn Creek, Missouri 97
Little, Lewis Henry 176
Little Blue River 86, 89, 125, 153
Little Dixie 4, 95, 146, 158, 162, 167, 170
Little River engagement 208
Little Rock, Arkansas 81, 92
Little Rock Arsenal 139
Long, John 29
Lothrop, W.L. 32, 91, 134, 136, 145
Louisiana 60, 164, 173
Lynch's Slave Pen 66
Lyon, Nathaniel 1, **7**–12, 14–18, 20–22, 24, 26–31, 35, 36, 38–40, 42, 45, 48–50, 52, 55, 56, 58–64, 66, 68, 69–74, 76, 77, 79–84, 91–95, 99–105, 107–112, 114, 117, 119, 121, 123–134, 136, 138, 139, 141, 142, 144–149, 152, 153, 155, 157, 158, 160, 162, 163, 165, 166, 169, 172, 173, 176, 178, 182, 183, 185, 195, 198–201, 203, 204–206, 208, 210–214, 216; appearance **7**, 69; army 91, 208–214, 245n10; Brigadier General 48, 49, 55, 228n6; call for removal 35; death 214; delay 198, 208–210; departure **211**; edict 209; Harney complaint 30; *New York Times* 30; plan 157, 173, 174, 185, 186, 197, **199**, 208–210; proclamation 63, 162, 163, 187; reinforcements 199; warning 73

Mackey, Alexander 181, 182
Macon, Missouri 81, 175–177
Marion, Missouri 97, 129
Marmaduke, John S. 57, 97, 123, 125, **126**, 129–131, 134, 139–141, 145, 166, 206
Maurice, Thomas D. 139
McBride, James H. **98**, 99, 117, 121
McClannahan, Bud 87, 88
McClellan, George B. 128, 162, 163, 198, 213
McCulloch, Ben **82**, 83, 107, 159, 163, 164, 173, 176, 179, 210, 214

Index

McDonald, Emmet 27
McDonald, J.W.A. 225n24
McDonnell, Patsy 88
McDonough, James 15
McDowell, Joseph N. 15
McIntyre, D.H. 57
McKinney, Francis M. 203
McKinstry, Justus 112, 208, 212
McNeil, John 107, 109, 234n28
Meramec River 117
Mexican War 46, 57, 64, 68, 84, 85, 88, 89, 106, 112, 119, 125, 139, 155, 164, 205
Military Bill 17, 20, 38, 44, 56, 57, 71, 80, 95
military districts 44, 45, 51, 94, 158
Miller, G.W. 97, 99, 147
Miller brothers 195
Mills, Harry R. 97
Minute Men 19, 22, 33, 34, 50, 65, 144, 204
Mississippi River 9, 42, 73, 91, 92, 108, 111, 170, 172, 208
Missouri-Arkansas border 62, 176
Missouri Compromise 3
Missouri Democrat 107, 192
Missouri-Kansas border 3, 80, 85
Missouri River 1, 4, 8, *18*, 76, 80, 86, 91, 92, 99, 100, 102, 103, 123, 125, 129, 132, 137, 146, 153–155, 157–159, 160, 166, 172, 175–177, 179, 198, 209, 210, 216
Missouri State Fair 145
Missouri State Guard 1, 20, 27, 43–46, 50, 56, 57, 61, 62, 69, 70, 76, 78, 80–82, 84–90, 92–94, 96, 97, 98, 99, 103, 111, 113, 117, 123–126, 129, 131, 134, 136–145, 149, 153–158, 163–172, 176, 184–187, 191, 194, 198, *199*, 202–206, 210–214, 216, 219; casualties 149; description 171; divisions 158; flag 144
Missouri volunteers 56, 63, 64, 80, 84, 108, 109
Mitchell, Frank 130
Mitchell, Henry L. 182
Mitchell, Porter 188
Montevallo, Missouri 163, 187, 210
Montgomery, James 108
Moreau Bridge 100
Mormons 86, 94, 126
Mount Vernon, Missouri 212
Mount Zion Church engagement 216
Mueller, Henry 192
Murray, Thomas W. 186

Nebraska 39
Neosho, Missouri 157, 173, 209, 210, 212, 217
Nevada, Missouri 175

New Mexico 46, 64, 165; see also Taos Revolt
New York Times 30, 43, 192, 213, 214, 216
New York Tribune 192
newspapers 12, 14, 15, 42, 53, 79, 115, 147, 149, 152, 164, 175, 177, 192, 194, 195, 208, 214, 240n7
North Missouri Railroad 146, 160, 173

O'Brien, James H. 147
O'Kane, Walter S. 186–191, 194, 196, 204; treachery 189, 194
Old Sacramento Cannon 156
Olive and Pine violence 160, *161*; coroner's jury 162
Olmstead, Henry 109
Osage, Missouri 101
Osage River 77, 79, 83, 97, 129, 159, 173, 178, 187, 196, 206, 207
Osceola, Missouri 207
Osterhaus, Peter 133, 134, 201
Overland Mail Stagecoach 116

Pacific Railroad 19, 77, 94, 99, 105, 107, 116, 123, 173, 177–179, 212, 213, 242n14
Palmyra, Missouri 97, 173
paramilitary 8, 20, 169
Parsons, Mosby 77, *94*, 95, 97, 99, 100, 123, 124, 130, 131, 156, 165, 178, 179, 186, 206
Pearce, N.B. 176
Peyton, R.Y.L. 203
Phelps, John S. 97, 117
Phelps County 117, 118, 121
Pilot Knob, Missouri 177
place names 2
Planter's House hotel 14, 15, 63–68, 74, 76, 80, 81, 84, 103, 105, 172, 205; meeting, 64, 68, 71, 73
Pomme de Terre River 207
Pope, John 213
popular sovereignty 3, 5, 154
Porter, John 142
Potomac River 58
Potosi, Missouri 40–43, 211
Price, Edwin 45, 77, *78*, 79, 206
Price, Sterling 20, 26, 45, 46, 48, 50–52, 56–58, 61–64, 68, *69*, 70–72, 74, 76–82, 84, 91–95, 100, 116, 117, 121–125, 129, 131, 144, 153, 155, 157–159, 163–166, 168–170, 172, 175, 176, 187, 199, 202–205, 208, 210, 214; animosity toward Blair 46; escort 163, 175; march on Lexington 216; Mexican War 165; nepotism 206; plan 159, 163
Price-Harney Agreement 26, 50–52, 56–58, 61–63, 70, 71, 154, 181, 211
Prince, W.E. 85, 87, 89

prisoners 10, 12, 14–16, 19, 22, 23, 26–28, 41, 42, 55, 101, 118, 129, 148, 149, 192–194, 204, 218, 222n29
Pritchard, James A. 203
proslavery 3, 4–6, 23, 53, 147, 153, 158, 168, 177
Public Safety Committee 36

railroads 177, 242n14
Rains, James S. 57, 123, 153, **154**, 155, 157–159, 165, 166, 179, 202, 203, 206
raw recruits 29, 138, 141, 144, 162, 165, 172, 188, 198
Regulars 1, 16, 17, 32, 50, 80, 81, 83, 84, 87, 91, 92, 101, 108, 136, 141, 157; landing at Jefferson City 102
Reiser, Adolph 196
Renick, Missouri 176
Reynolds, Thomas C. 56, 57, 81, 99, 186, 210
Richardson, Henry 102, 103, 133, 142, 143
riots and violence 3, 14–16, 21–24, 26, 28–36, 40, 43, 52, 55, 61, 62, 64, 66, 72, 86, 95, 110, 114, 125, 147, 158, 160, 163, 176, 209; Fifth and Walnut **28**, 29, 30, 31, 34, 40
riverboats 91, 92, 102, 129
Rives, Benjamin Allen 202
Rocheport Road 132–134, 136, 137, 139, 146; *see also* Boonville fight; skirmish
Rock Creek, Missouri 84, 85, 87, 89, 90, 153, 236n61, 239n46
Rock Springs, Missouri 119
Rolla, Missouri 80, 98, 105, 107, 112, 114–127, 157, 160, 172, 173, 177, 197, 199, 209, 212; Union occupation 105
Roup's Point 179
rump legislature 217

Sac River 207
St. Aubert, Missouri 101
St. Charles, Missouri 92, 101
St. James, Missouri 118
St. Joseph, Missouri 11, 52, 55, 81, 85, 86, 146, 173
St. Joseph News 52
St. Louis 1, 3, 4, 7–12, 14–16, 19–23, 25, 27, 28, 30–40, 42–53, 55, 56, 59–61, 63–67, 73, 76, 77, 80, 81, 83–85, 91, 92, 95, 96, 99, 101, 104, 105, 107–112, 114–122, 124, 128, 149, 157, 160–162, 166, 172, 173, 177–180, 197, 198, 203–205, 209; recruitment, 110
St. Louis Arsenal 6–9, 16, 26, 41, 63, 83, 105, 106, 119, 164, 212
St. Louis Blues 96
St. Louis Democrat 41, 42
St. Louis Globe-Democrat 93

St. Louis massacre 10, **11**, 14, 15, 33, 44, 45, 109, 124, 204
St. Louis Republican 4, 14, 37, 42, 60
Salomon, Charles Eberhardt 107, 108, 119, **120**, 121
Salomon, Edward 119
Salomon, Frederick 120
Sanderson, George B. 23
Sarcoxie, Missouri 153
Schofield, John 133
Scott, Winfield 36, 38, 48, 58, 59, 128
secession 1, 2, 4–12, 15, 20, 22, 29, 31, 33, 35, 36, 38, 40–43, 45–47, 49–53, 55–59, 61, 62, 64, 68, 69, 73, 79, 80, 82, 86–89, 91, 95, 97, 101, 106, 110, 114, 117–119, 126, 130, 146, 147, 149, 154, 160, 166, 167, 169, 172, 175–178, 181, 185, 188, 190, 192, 193–195, 198, 206, 208, 210, 211, 214, 217, 219
Second Infantry Company B 91
Second Kansas Volunteer Regiment 84
Second Light Artillery 91
Second Missouri U.S. Volunteers 92, 104
Sedalia, Missouri 177, 178
Sempke, Herman 196
Seventh Missouri U.S. Regiment 198
Seward, William H. **37**, 109, 110
Shelby, Joseph O. 86, 153, 202, 203, 219
Sherman, John 60
Sherman, William T. 30, 60, 110, 229n9
Siege of Vicksburg 110
Sigel, Franz 9, 21, 61, 105, 107, 108, 112, 114, 115, 117–121, 157, 173, 209, 212, 213; appearance 112, **113**, 122
16th Illinois Regiment 101, 155
Slack, William Y. 154, **155**, 157–159, 165, 166, 202
slavery 1, 3, 4, 6, 7, 15, 22, 35, 53, 54, 65–67, 70, 79, 86, 95, 98, 104, 116, 127, 148, 153, 162, 168, 169, 180, 202, 203, 215, 219
Smith, Caleb **37**
Smith, Giles Alexander 110
Smith, Morgan L. 37, 110
Snead, Thomas L. 68, 70, 73, 152, 153
soft Democrats 4
South Carolina 8, 35
South Grand River 203, 206, 209
southern lineage 180
southwest column 99, 105, 107, 127, 160, 173
southwest Missouri 62, 76, 80–82, 97, 100, 105–109, 112–114, 116, 117, 120, 121, 145, 154, 158, 159, 163, 168, 172, 173, 176–178, 187, 191, 195–197, 199, 200, 204, 208, 209, 211–214, 218
Special Order 135 48, 58
Springfield, Missouri 81–83, 97, 99, 107, 116, 117, 119, 121, 122, 157, 173, 178, 209, 210, 212–214, 216

Stanley, David Sloan 87–89
state convention 5, 10, 15, 35, 45, 69, 93, 95, 214, 221*n*9
state militia 1, 9–11, 14, 16–18, 20, 23, 27, 36, 45, 70, 79, 85, 86, 163, 165, 173, 205; surrender 10
steamboats 33, 91, 92, 127, 129, 130, 132, 133, 198
Stevens, Thaddeus 37
Stevens, Walter Barlow 93
Stevenson, John D. 110, 209, 210
Stifel, Charles G. 29, 108
Sturgis, Samuel Davis 84, *85*, 86, 89, 99, 100, 123, 125, 153, 157, 158, 163, 173, 174, 209, 212
Stypes, Charlie 202
suspension of mail 62
Sweeny, Thomas 16, 17, 32, 46, 105, *106*, 112, 114, 121, 208, 209
Syracuse, Missouri 131, 146, 178, 179

Taos Revolt 64
Taylor, Daniel G. 15, 34
Taylor, Zachary 177
telegraph communication 178
Tennessee 11, 97, 180
Texas 82, 98, 99, 108, 117, 155, 163, 173
Third Missouri U.S. Volunteers 9, 61, 105, 107, 108, 113–115, 121, 213; description 119
13th Illinois Infantry Regiment 121
Thompson's Slave Pen 67
Thornton, J.C. 32, 203
Tipton, Missouri 99, 116, 123, 125, 130, 131, 146, 156, 178, 187
tools of war 8, 9, 15–20, 22, 28, 29, 32, 33, 36, 41, 43, 46, 49, 50, 55, 77, 81, 86, 90, 95, 96, 98, 99, 108, 116, 118, 121, *122*, 124, 125, 130, 132, 133, 137–141, 143–146, 156, 157, 160, 165, 166, 171, 173, 176, 179, 182, 183,185, 190, 194, 196, 198, 201, 202, 206, 210
Toombs, Robert Y. 167
Totten, James 32, 91, 92, 102, 127, 134, 136–142, 145, 186, 196, 202
Trans-Mississippi Theater 214, 216
Treat, Samuel 27
Treaty of Guadalupe Hidalgo 64

Turner Society 114, 147
Twain, Mark 36, 91
Tyree, John 187, 188, 192, 194

unionists 1, 15, 17, 37, 40, 42, 43, 46, 49, 51, 53, 55, 68, 85, 96, 99, 148, 163, 167, 170, 180, 182, 218
U.S. Regulars *see* Regulars
Utica, Missouri 101

Victoria, Missouri 42
violence *see* riots
Virginia 4, 11, 52, 58, 97, 128, 162, 188, 198, 217
Voerster, John Diederich 121, 142, 145

Walnut Grove Cemetery 145
War Department 6, 26, 30, 37–39, 44, 49, 50, 52, 55, 56, 59, 60, 63, 81, 128, 155, 162, 174, 180, 181
war material 9, 10; *see also* tools of war
Warrensburg, Missouri 163, 166, 202, 203
Warsaw, Missouri 57, 83, 129, 170, 178, 185–189, 191–194, 196, 198, 202, 204–207, 209, 210
Warsaw Grays 57, 186
Warsaw Southwest Democrat 194
Washington, Missouri 101
Waverly, Missouri 202
Waynesville, Missouri 212
Weightman, Richard Hanson *89*, 153, 165, 166, 203
Welles, Gideon *37*
West Virginia 217
Westminster College 57
Westport, Missouri 86, 87
White, Robert 29, 37
White Cloud 99, 125
Whitehead, George 87
Wide-Awakes 66, 67, 114
Wilcoxson, Hiram 97
Wilkins, Theodore 120
Windsor Guards Cavalry 186; attack 190
Wire Road 173, 212
Wyandotte, Kansas 108
Wyman, Edward 170

www.ingramcontent.com/pod-product-compliance
Lightning Source LLC
Chambersburg PA
CBHW032034300426
44117CB00009B/1055